T0132540

Artificial Intelligence and Smart Agriculture Technology

Artificial Intelligence and Smart Agriculture Technology

Edited by
Utku Kose, V. B. Surya Prasath,
M. Rubaiyat Hossain Mondal,
Prajoy Podder, and Subrato Bharati

CRC Press
Taylor & Francis Group
Boca Raton London New York

CRC Press is an imprint of the
Taylor & Francis Group, an **informa** business

First edition published 2022
by CRC Press
6000 Broken Sound Parkway NW, Suite 300, Boca Raton, FL 33487-2742

and by CRC Press
4 Park Square, Milton Park, Abingdon, Oxon, OX14 4RN

© 2022 Taylor & Francis Group, LLC

CRC Press is an imprint of Taylor & Francis Group, LLC

Library of Congress Cataloging-in-Publication Data
Names: Kose, Utku, 1985– editor. | Prasath, V. B. Surya, editor. |
Mondal, M. Rubaiyat Hossain, editor. | Podder, Prajoy, editor. | Bharati, Subrato, editor.
Title: Artificial intelligence and smart agriculture technology / Utku Kose, V. B. Surya Prasath,
M. Rubaiyat Hossain Mondal, Prajoy Podder, Subrato Bharati.
Description: Boca Raton, FL : Taylor and Francis, 2022. |
Includes bibliographical references and index.
Identifiers: LCCN 2022000641 | ISBN 9781032120799 (hardback) |
ISBN 9781032289069 (paperback) | ISBN 9781003299059 (ebook)
Subjects: LCSH: Alternative agriculture. | Agriculture–Effect of technological innovations on. |
Artificial intelligence. | Agricultural informatics.
Classification: LCC S494.5.D3 A77 2022 | DDC 338.10285–dc23/eng/20220124
LC record available at https://lccn.loc.gov/2022000641

ISBN: 978-1-032-12079-9 (hbk)
ISBN: 978-1-032-28906-9 (pbk)
ISBN: 978-1-003-29905-9 (ebk)

DOI: 10.1201/9781003299059

Typeset in Garamond
by Newgen Publishing UK

Contents

Foreword

Artificial intelligence plays a great role in today's technological advancements. With the rise of computer and communication technologies, it has become more appropriate for computational solutions to take an active part in daily life tasks. As a result, artificial intelligence supported smart tools have become essential components for the 21st century. Actually, before we started to witness its application in smart daily life tools, artificial intelligence-oriented solutions were effective alternatives for solving critical problems in different fields. Thus, many fields such as medicine, finance and education have become interested in using smart tools to deal with active problems. Associated as it is with the well-being of both the earth and human generations, agriculture is among these fields where smart tools have a great role in terms of improving effectiveness and efficiency. Especially because of technology-caused issues over agricultural fields of the earth, it has become more critical to use artificial intelligence for ensuring optimum smart agricultural applications.

Artificial Intelligence and Smart Agriculture Technology is an edited volume that provides a collection of the most recent research efforts into building effective smart tools for agricultural applications. As the lines between technological components from different disciplines are blurred, many research works require multidisciplinary and interdisciplinary collaborations to design alternative solutions when it comes to dealing with actively changing agricultural issues. In especially the last decade, robotic systems and the Internet of Things have become widely followed research flows in agricultural problems. So, today's developments include not only software-oriented touches but also hardware components for running physically equipped solutions.

Moving on from that fact, this book comes with several chapters that inform the reader about the most recent advancements into "physical solutions" for smart agriculture. On the other hand, it is important to ensure strong enough cybersecurity aspects for data-based smart agricultural applications, so I would like to thank the editors for recognising this point and including chapters on the use of popular blockchain and smart tools in agricultural issues. The technological aspects of machine learning and data preprocessing for dealing with specific agricultural issues are critical elements of today's research works. The book also includes specific research works that provide solutions against, for example, agricultural big data analysis and plant disease detection. Thus, as a very recent point of view, the technological side of smart agricultural applications have been successfully captured to provide useful knowledge for interested researchers. In this context, I believe that this volume will be effectively used by researchers, degree students, and even experts from both public and private sectors associated with the field of agriculture. As humankind increasingly faces issues of climate change, this book also gives critical remarks on how to build efficient smart tools for agricultural tasks while preventing negative effects on the climate.

Finally, I would like to thank the dear editors, Dr. Kose, Dr. Prasath, Dr. Mondal, Dr. Podder, and Dr. Bharati, for their critical contribution to the associated literature. There is a great need for new reference books regarding smart tools for present and future world developments, and this book serves as a worthy addition for filling the knowledge gap between artificial intelligence and agriculture. Future generations will need the most current knowledge and the ability to use the most recent technological components, and *Artificial Intelligence and Smart Agriculture Technology* provides all the necessary information for further research works.

I would like to invite all readers to enjoy this book and start working towards a better future with sustainable agricultural infrastructure!

Omer Deperlioglu
Afyon Kocatepe University,
Department of Computer Technologies, Afyon Vocational School,
Afyonkarahisar, Turkey

Preface

When it was first introduced in the literature, artificial intelligence was a technological tool for improving the speed and success rates of critical real-world problems. It was a research field associated with the research works of other major technical fields. However, as a result of changing societies and an increasing need for digital tools to improve daily living standards, artificial intelligence has been rapidly employed in different fields, and a "brave new world" of technologically improved tools has started to be experienced. As a result of this, smart applications are among today's popular research topics. Associated as they are with related research efforts, smart tools are often developed to create smart applications for buildings, environments, campuses, and even cities. In this context, essential touches to specific problem areas are critical for creating the necessary infrastructure for technological solutions. This makes more sense when it is considered for use in areas vital for the future of humanity.

The field of agriculture is one of these vital areas shaping the future of humanity. As all agricultural fields of the earth are important for keeping the sustainability of human-side needs (eating, drinking, living, etc.), technological advancements should always be adapted to dynamically appearing problems. As a critical example, climate crisis and the newly appearing environmental issues have been affecting agriculture for a remarkable time period. As long as technological components are used more in agricultural applications, so there should also be a careful analysis for balanced tools that are not affecting the climate/environment negatively. On the other hand, biologically caused issues such as plant diseases should be solved with smart tools, which are more aware of detailed problem triggers. Furthermore, it has already become a trendy research area to develop self-running smart tools that are robust enough to control agricultural fields and agricultural big data efficiently.

Based on the explanations so far, this edited book was created with the intention of informing an international audience about the latest technological aspects for developing smart agricultural applications. As artificial intelligence takes the main role in this, the majority of the chapters are associated with the role of artificial intelligence and data analytics components for better agricultural applications.

The first two chapters provide alternative, wide reviews of the use of artificial intelligence, robotics, and the Internet of Things as effective solutions to agricultural problems. The third chapter looks at the use of blockchain technology in smart agricultural scenarios. In the fourth chapter, a future view is provided of an Internet of Things-oriented sustainable agriculture. Following that, the fifth chapter provides a governmental evaluation of advanced farming technologies, and the sixth chapter discusses the role of big data in smart agricultural applications. The role of the blockchain is evaluated in terms of an industrial view under the seventh chapter, and the eighth chapter provides a discussion of data mining and data extraction, which is essential for better further analysis by smart tools. The ninth chapter evaluates the use of machine learning in food processing and preservation, which is a critical issue for dealing with issues regarding insufficient food sources. The tenth chapter gives another point for sustainability, and the eleventh chapter focuses on the problem of plant disease prediction, which is among the critical agricultural issues. Similarly, the twelfth chapter considers the use of deep learning for classifying plant diseases. Finally, the book ends with a look at cyber threats to farming automation in the thirteenth chapter and a case study of India for a better, smart, sustainable agriculture in the fourteenth chapter.

All the chapters shape a recent view of the most critical research topics of today's smart agricultural applications. We think that the book provides a valuable view for both technological knowledge and ability that should be known by academicians, scientists, degree students who are the future of science, and industrial practitioners who collaborate with academia.

We are grateful to all the authors for their valuable works. We would also like to thank dear Prof. Deperlioglu for providing his valuable foreword. Any ideas from readers are valued and welcomed.

We wish for a better, sustainable world with accurate technological touches for effective and efficient agricultural outcomes.

Acknowledgements

The editors would like to thank and congratulate everyone who has contributed to the publication of this book. We would like to express our heartfelt gratitude to each of the chapter authors for their contributions, without which this book would not have been possible. Our heartfelt thanks and acknowledgements also go to the subject matter experts who took the time to review the chapters and deliver them on time, thereby improving the quality, prominence, and uniform arrangement of the chapters in the book. Many thanks to the CRC Press Publication team members for their unwavering support and assistance in the publication of this edited book. Finally, we would also like to thank the Institute of Information and Communication Technology of the Bangladesh University of Engineering and Technology, Bangladesh, for providing technical support to some of the editors.

About the Editors

Dr. Utku Kose received a BS degree in 2008 in Computer Education at Gazi University, Turkey, as a faculty valedictorian. He received an MS degree in 2010 from Afyon Kocatepe University, Turkey, in the field of Computers and a DS/PhD degree in 2017 from Selcuk University, Turkey, in the field of Computer Engineering.

Between 2009 and 2011, he worked as a research assistant at Afyon Kocatepe University. He also worked as a lecturer and vocational school vice director at Afyon Kocatepe University between 2011 and 2012; as a lecturer and research centre director in Usak University, Turkey, between 2012 and 2017; and as an assistant professor at Suleyman Demirel University, Turkey, between 2017 and 2019. Currently, he is an associate professor at Suleyman Demirel University.

He has contributed to more than 100 publications, including articles, authored and edited books, proceedings, and reports. He is also on the editorial boards of many scientific journals and serves as one of the editors of the *Biomedical and Robotics Healthcare* book series by CRC Press. His research interests include artificial intelligence, machine ethics, artificial intelligence safety, optimization, chaos theory, distance education, e-learning, computer education, and computer science.

V. B. Surya Prasath graduated from the Indian Institute of Technology Madras, India, in 2009 with a PhD in Mathematics. He is currently an assistant professor in the Biomedical Informatics division at the Cincinnati Children's Hospital Medical Center, and at the departments of Biomedical Informatics, Electrical Engineering and Computer Science at the University of Cincinnati from 2018. He was a postdoctoral fellow at the Department of Mathematics, University of Coimbra, Portugal, from 2010 to 2011. From 2012 to 2015, he was with the Computational Imaging and VisAnalysis (CIVA) Lab at the University of Missouri, USA, as a postdoctoral fellow, and from 2016 to 2017 as an assistant research professor. He had summer fellowships/visits at Kitware

Inc. in New York, USA, The Fields Institute in Toronto, Canada, and IPAM at the University of California Los Angeles (UCLA), USA.

His main research interests include non-linear PDEs, regularization methods, inverse and ill-posed problems, variational and PDE-based image processing, and computer vision with applications in remote sensing and biomedical imaging domains. His current research focuses are in data science and bioimage informatics with machine learning techniques.

M. Rubaiyat Hossain Mondal received BSc and MSc degrees in electrical and electronic engineering from Bangladesh University of Engineering and Technology (BUET), Dhaka, Bangladesh. He obtained a PhD degree in 2014 from the Department of Electrical and Computer Systems Engineering, Monash University, Melbourne, Australia. From 2005 to 2010 and from 2014 to date, he has been working as a faculty member at the Institute of Information and Communication Technology (IICT) in BUET, Bangladesh. He has published a number of papers in journals of IEEE, IET, Elsevier, Springer, Wiley, De Gruyter, PLOS, MDPI, and more. He has published several conference papers and book chapters and edited a book published by De Gruyter in 2021. He has so far successfully supervised 10 students in completing their masters' theses in the field of Information and Communication Technology at BUET, Bangladesh. His research interests include artificial intelligence, image processing, bioinformatics, wireless communications and cryptography.

Prajoy Podder is currently a researcher at the Institute of Information and Communication Technology, Bangladesh University of Engineering and Technology, Dhaka, Bangladesh. He has also worked as a lecturer in the Department of Electrical and Electronic Engineering, Ranada Prasad Shaha University, Narayanganj, Bangladesh.

He received a BSc (Engg) degree in Electronics and Communication Engineering from the Khulna University of Engineering and Technology in Khulna, Bangladesh, in 2014. He recently completed an MSc in Information and Communication Technology from the Bangladesh University of Engineering and Technology.

He has authored or co-authored over 45 journal articles, conference proceedings and book chapters published by IEEE, Elsevier, Springer, Wiley, De Gruyter and others. His research interests include wireless sensor networks, digital image processing, data mining, smart cities, the Internet of Things, machine learning, big data, digital signal processing, wireless communication, and VLSI.

 **Subrato Bharati** received a BS degree in Electrical and Electronic Engineering from Ranada Prasad Shaha University, Bangladesh. He is currently working as a researcher in the Institute of Information and Communication Technology, Bangladesh University of Engineering and Technology, Dhaka, Bangladesh.

He is a regular reviewer of a number of international journals, including from Elsevier, Springer, Wiley, and other reputed publishers. He is an associate editor of the *Journal of the International Academy for Case Studies* and guest editor of a special issue in the *Journal of Internet Technology* (SCI Index Journal). He has been a member of scientific and technical program committees at conferences such as CECNet 2021, ICONCS, ICCRDA 2020, ICICCR 2021, CECIT 2021, and others.

His research interest includes bioinformatics, medical image processing, pattern recognition, deep learning, wireless communications, data analytics, machine learning, neural networks, and feature selection. He has published a number of papers in the journals of Elsevier, Springer, PLOS, IOS Press, and others and has published several IEEE and Springer reputed conference papers. He has also published Springer, Elsevier, De Gruyter, CRC Press, and Wiley book chapters.

Contributors

Adarsh S.
Kerala Blockchain Academy
Kerala University of Digital Sciences,
   Innovation and Technology
Thiruvananthapuram, India

Charles Taiwo Akanbi
Department of Food Science and
   Technology
Obafemi Awolowo University
Ile-Ife, Nigeria

Jide Ebenezer Taiwo Akinsola
Department of Mathematics and
   Computer Science
First Technical University
Ibadan, Nigeria

Anoop V. S.
Kerala Blockchain Academy
Kerala University of Digital Sciences,
   Innovation and Technology
Thiruvananthapuram, India

Asharaf S.
Kerala Blockchain Academy
Kerala University of Digital Sciences,
   Innovation and Technology
Thiruvananthapuram, India

C. T. Ashita
Soka Ikeda College
Chennai, India

Shaeela Ayesha
Department of Computer Science
Government College University
   Faisalabad
Faisalabad, Pakistan

Chittaranjan Baruah
Postgraduate Department of Zoology
Darrang College (affiliated to Gauhati
   University)
Tezpur, India

Subrato Bharati
Bangladesh University of Engineering
   and Technology
Dhaka, Bangladesh

Tapalina Bhattasali
St. Xavier's College (Autonomous)
Kolkata, India

Bhabesh Deka
North Bengal Regional Research and
   Development Centre
Nagrakata, India

C. Gomes
University of the Witwatersrand
Johannesburg, South Africa

Muskan Gupta
School of Computer Science and
  Engineering
Vellore Institute of Technology
Vellore, India

Muhammad Kashif Hanif
Department of Computer Science
Government College University
  Faisalabad
Faisalabad, Pakistan

Md. Mahadi Hasan
Asian University of Bangladesh
Dhaka, Bangladesh

Mohammad Tariq Hasan
School of Business and Economics,
  United International University
Dhaka, Bangladesh

Mohammad Amzad Hossain
School of Business and Economics,
  United International University
Dhaka, Bangladesh

Muhammad Usama Islam
Asian University of Bangladesh
Dhaka, Bangladesh

J. Jayasudha
Sri Ramakrishna College of Arts and
  Science for Women
Coimbatore, India

Oseni Kadiri
Department of Biochemistry,
  Edo State University Uzairue-Iyamho
Auchi, Nigeria

T. Sree Kala
Vels Institute of Science
  Technology and Advanced
  Studies
Chennai, India

Diwakar Kumar
Central University of Gujarat
Gujarat, India

Kusum Lata
Department of Electronics and
  Communication Engineering
The LNM Institute of Information
  Technology
Jaipur, India

M. J. Mathushika
University of Colombo
Colombo, Sri Lanka

Mahadi Hasan Miraz
School of Technology Management
  and Logistics, Universiti Utara
  Malaysia
Kedah, Malaysia

Babatunde Olawoye
Department of Food Science and
  Technology
First Technical University
Ibadan, Nigeria

Oyekemi Popoola
Department of Food Science and
  Technology
First Technical University
Ibadan, Nigeria

Muhammad Jafar Sadeq
Asian University of Bangladesh
Dhaka, Bangladesh

Sandeep Saini
Department of Electronics and
 Communication Engineering
The LNM Institute of Information
 Technology
Jaipur, India

Sanjay H. A.
M. S. Ramaiah Institute of
 Technology
Bengaluru, India

Shumi Sarkar
Department of Business Studies,
 University of Information
 Technology and Sciences
Dhaka, Bangladesh

Xavier Savarimuthu
St. Xavier's College (Autonomous)
Kolkata, India

K. Aditya Shastry
Nitte Meenakshi Institute of
 Technology
Karnataka, India

Farhana Rahman Sumi
Department of Business Studies,
 University of Information
 Technology and Sciences
Dhaka, Bangladesh

Ramzan Talib
Department of Computer Science
Government College University
 Faisalabad
Faisalabad, Pakistan

M. Thilagu
Avinashilingam Institute for Home
 Science and Higher Education
 for Women
Coimbatore, India

B. K. Tripathy
School of Information Technology and
 Engineering
Vellore Institute of Technology
Vellore, India

R. Vinushayini
University of Colombo
Colombo, Sri Lanka

Chapter 1

Smart Farming Using Artificial Intelligence, the Internet of Things, and Robotics: A Comprehensive Review

M. J. Mathushika
University of Colombo, Colombo, Sri Lanka

R. Vinushayini
University of Colombo, Colombo, Sri Lanka

C. Gomes
University of the Witwatersrand, Johannesburg, South Africa

1.1 Introduction

Agriculture continues to remain fundamental to the global economy, with 60% of the world's population relying on it for survival. The Food and Agriculture Organization (FAO) of the United Nations has stated that 5 billion hectares of land, which is 38% of the global land surface, is currently employed in agriculture and related activities. Though this figure seems large, each and every aspect of agricultural activities face

DOI: 10.1201/9781003299059-1

numerous challenges, such as soil testing, efficient planting, controlling weeds, pesticide control, disease treatment, and lack of proper irrigation (Bannerjee et al., 2018). As such, agricultural industries are on the hunt for novel techniques to improve crop yielding and productivity in order to feed the rising population. Smart technologies such as artificial intelligence (AI), the Internet of Things (IoT), and robotics were incorporated into agriculture a few decades ago. They have led to a period of revolution in agriculture and recently have been paid more attention. Although the integration of this trio of smart technologies can maximize farming efficiency, there are some drawbacks that accompany the implementation and commercialization of such automation technologies (Talaviya et al., 2020). This review aims to revise the numerous desirable applications of AI, the IoT, and robotics in various stages of agriculture and present the major challenges and future recommendations for the successful implementation of advanced farming.

1.2 The Role of Artificial Intelligence in Advanced Farming

Artificial intelligence-based technologies support farming by increasing the efficiency of conventional farming and overcoming the challenges and drawbacks faced by traditional farmers. Artificial intelligence (AI) is the process where humans produce artificial machines similar to the human brain but with an ability to deal with larger amounts of data than the human brain. AI directly falls within the computer science field, but it should surpass this boundary to contribute to agriculture (Jha et al., 2019). Various technical devices and instruments have been developed based on AI that have been tested on agricultural fields and optimized. They have been successful in developing various field-steps of agriculture, such as soil testing, weeding, pesticide control, the treating of diseased crops, lack of proper irrigation to match the needs of crops, post-harvest activities such as storage management, optimising storage parameters, etc. Farmers have attained a high output as well as increased quality of output (Talaviya et al., 2020).

On the other hand, AI can be involved in agriculture to mitigate the environmental concern raised due to unfavourable agricultural activities, such as the heavy usage of pesticides, uncontrolled irrigation resulting in loss of water, and water being polluted with fertilizers. The implementation of AI would help in both these ways (Jha et al., 2019). There have been various AI systems proposed and developed by various scientists for various plantations in the past (Bannerjee et al., 2018).

The foremost objective of utilizing AI-based technologies is to reduce the labour force needed to achieve the required yield. Also, questions unanswered by humans are easily attended to by AI-based devices due to their ability to gather large amounts of data from governmental websites up to the real-time field data and analyse them. They can then provide suggestions to problems that would take a lot of time and high-end skills if they were to be made by humans. AI requires training with the biological skills of the farmer and *vice versa*; hence, farmers with the required skills will also need to be trained with these AI technologies (Talaviya et al., 2020).

1.2.1 The Fundamentals of AI Technologies Involved in Agriculture

The foremost step in involving AI in any field is machine learning. The data that needs to be processed should be fed in a machine-readable manner, and the processed solution should be delivered in a human language. As the AI-based machine processes the fed data, it should be able to gather information from the directed databases to meet the problem that has arisen. On occasion, real-time data would be needed for the AI to arrive at a conclusion, where the AI should be competent enough to read the real-time parameters. Weather prediction is an important factor needed to make decisions about the cropping season.

Chatbots are devices that virtually assist farmers with less experience of interaction with technologies by engaging them in conversations. Unmanned aerial vehicles (UAVs) are popular among governmental and institutional officers of farming for detecting any potential harm to the fields, such as the spreading of forest fires, pest invasions, pathogen attacks, and many more by geolocalization (Talaviya et al., 2020).

Neuro-fuzzy logic, fuzzy logic, expert systems, and artificial neural networks (ANNs) are four methods designed to solve problems (Jha et al., 2019). ANNs are the most common method utilized when designing AI-based technologies. An ANN simulates the processes within a human brain in a machine. In the brain, electric signals pass through neurons by axons and synapses. Various algorithms, such as delta-bar-delta, Silva, and Almeida, are used. The difference between conventional computer programmes and these algorithms is that this method allows the machine to perform an inbuilt task (Jha et al., 2019). A hardware-software interface should be built for the user-friendly functioning of the machine by farmers and other stakeholders. "Embedded systems" are machines into which software is fed.

1.2.2 AI in Crop or Seed Selection

High vigour, good germination, and the seedling emergence rate of seeds have always ensured emergence even under varying agricultural conditions and have been the key to optimising yields and ensuring uniformity in production (TeKrony & Egli, 1991). Traditionally, farmers have optimised seed choice based on experience, and any laboratory experiments for seed-choice optimisation are laborious and prone to error. The way that individual seed varieties react to different weather conditions and disease resistance, etc., are understood by AI technical devices by analysing the previous data to a greater extent than could be accessed by a general farmer.

SeedGerm is a phenotyping platform developed from automated seed imaging and phenotypic analysis based on machine learning. The core algorithm of SeedGerm has been developed with features such as background remover, feature extraction and germination detection, and measurements of traits. The hardware design of the SeedGerm system consists of a translucent plastic box and an overhead image sensor. The seed imaging module of SeedGerm ensures high-throughput imaging, which also enables the removal of background. The system also consists of environmental sensors that sense ambient temperature and humidity. SeedGerm is capable of germination scoring and measuring morphological changes, which in turn scores seedling vigour, and hence could analyse the performance of seed batches. These traits could be used by officials in issuing germination certificates (Colmer et al., 2020). A novel method named crop selection method (CSM) was proposed by Kumar et al. (2015).

1.2.3 AI in Crop Management Practices

Sensors and embedded systems have been developed that support the growth conditions in a growth chamber, such as light intensity, humidity, and O_2 and CO_2 levels. They can control crop conditions per prevailing crop growth data in real-time to match optimised parameters (Lakhiar et al., 2018). Trace Genomics is a technological firm that extracts DNA from the soil samples of agricultural lands and quantifies the microbes dwelling within. The data from the soil is analysed with machine-learning technologies. This biological data is combined with the chemical parameters of the soil sample to finally recommend solutions to the farmer, which would be evidence-based on past occurrence data the past. This would help in selecting the best crop to suit the land or *vice versa*.

A continuous and accessible water supply is required for crop cultivation. Due to the scarcity of freshwater, it is highly advised not to exploit more water resources than is necessarily needed by the crop. Hence, AI technologies, which record real-time data regarding soil moisture content and weather conditions, could manipulate the amount of water needed and automate the supply and ceasing of the water (Talaviya et al., 2020). Kumar et al. (2014) listed a few such automated irrigation methods using AI. Mahmood et al. (2016) listed the risks arising due to heavy pesticide usage, which include effects on biodiversity threats, human health, and leaching of excess agrochemicals into waterways, which can cause environmental issues like eutrophication. Facchinetti et al. (2021) designed a small vehicle-like machine called "Rover" to spray pesticide, leading to a reduction of up to 55% in the amount usually sprayed, and improving crop coverage.

1.2.4 AI in Yield Prediction

Prediction models are one of the foremost AI techniques to be readily accepted by farmers, as yield and profit are the major targets of all forms of agriculture. Soil type, soil nutrient content, crop information, and weather conditions are analysed before predicting the yield. Van Klompenburg et al. (2020) has reviewed a large amount of research regarding yield prediction models.

1.2.5 AI in Pest and Weed Management

Partel et al. (2019) describe a method for developing automated machines that could specifically detect weeds and spray them with agrochemicals, which reduces the wastage of weedicide and reduces the exposure of the crop to the agrochemicals. Pasqual and Mansfield, SMARTSOY, and CORAC are examples of pest management systems (Bannerjee et al., 2018).

1.2.6 AI in Storing and Marketing Products

The storage of agricultural products in suited conditions is crucial for maintaining quality before reaching the consumer. Various sensors have been developed in storage chambers for lengthening the post-harvest life of these products. Traditional farmers only understand the conventional markets of their products, but the latest market trends, decisions about the products' price, and information about the consumption pattern of consumers are precisely analysed by market data and can suggest the next round of crops to the farmers (Talaviya et al., 2020).

1.3 The Role of the Internet of Things in Advanced Farming

As we head towards more cultured and urban farming, the necessity and engagement of fresh scientific developments such as IoT-based technology are becoming increasingly vital in diverse farming systems for numerous applications. They help to improve a variety of farming practices in order to increase yield output while preserving or minimizing the impact on the originality of the product.

1.3.1 IoT-Based Soil Sampling

Manufacturers currently present a wide range of sensors and toolkits to support farmers in monitoring the quality of soil and provide solutions to prevent degradation. They enable the intensive care of soil qualities such as water-holding capacity, texture, and absorption rate, which aids in decreasing densification, salinization, acidification, pollution, and erosion by avoiding the overconsumption of fertilizers. The Lab-in-a-Box soil-testing toolkit made by AgroCares is considered to be a comprehensive laboratory in itself due to the extreme services it provides (Ayaz et al., 2019). Any farmer, regardless of lab knowledge, can use it to analyse up to 100 samples per day without having to visit a lab. Remote sensing is currently being utilized to collect regular soil moisture data, which will aid in the analysis of droughts in remote areas. The Soil Moisture and Ocean Salinity (SMOS) satellite, which gives maps detailing the global soil moisture every one to two days, was launched in 2009 for this purpose (Crapolicchio et al., 2010).

In 2014, researchers in Spain employed SMOS L2 to evaluate the soil water deficit index (SWDI) (Pablos et al., 2018). They used a variety of methods to get the soil water parameters with the aim of comparing them to the SWDI calculated from *in situ* data. In addition, the Moderate Resolution Imaging Spectroradiometer (MODIS) sensor is being utilized to scan the different features of soil with the aim of quantifying the danger of land degradation in Sub-Saharan Africa (Zhang et al., 2006). Sensors and vision-based technology aid in determining the distance and depth required for effective seed sowing. To estimate the seed flow rate, many non-contact sensing methods are offered where the sensors are fitted with LEDs that include visible light, infrared, and laser LEDs, along with a radiation reception element. The seed flow rate is calculated using the signal information related to the passing seeds (Ayaz et al., 2019).

1.3.2 IoT-Based Disease and Pest Monitoring

Farmers may drastically decrease their usage of pesticides by accurately recognizing crop pests utilizing IoT-based smart devices, including wireless sensors, drones, and robots. Contemporary IoT-based pest management offers real-time monitoring, disease forecasting, and modelling, making it more fruitful than conventional pest control approaches (Kim et al., 2018). Cutting-edge pest and disease detection techniques depend on image processing, with raw images collected across the farming region using remote sensing satellites or field sensors. Remote sensing imagery typically covers huge areas and provides more effectiveness at a reduced cost. Field sensors, conversely, can support more functions in data collection, such as environmental sampling, plant condition monitoring, and pest threats, in every phase of the crop cycle. IoT-based automatic traps may collect, count, and even describe pest varieties, then upload the data to the cloud for detailed analysis (Ayaz et al., 2019). This IoT-based pest monitoring system is capable of minimizing the total costs while also assisting in the restoration of the natural climate (Oberti et al., 2016).

1.3.3 IoT-Based Fertilization

New IoT-based fertilization technologies aid in the accurate estimation of spatial patterns of fertilizer requirements while requiring minimal labour (Lavanya et al., 2020). The normalized difference vegetation index (NDVI), for instance, which is based entirely on the reflection of visible and near-infrared light from vegetation, examines the status of crop nutrition utilizing satellite images and measures crop health, vegetation vigour, and density (Benincasa et al., 2017). It also helps to analyse soil nutrient levels. Such exact execution can considerably boost fertilizer efficiency while also avoiding environmental side effects. Geo-mapping, GPS accuracy, autonomous vehicles, and variable rate technology (VRT) are now contributing to IoT-based smart fertilization. Besides precision fertilization, other IoT benefits include fertigation (Raut et al., 2017) and chemigation (González-Briones et al., 2018).

1.3.4 IoT-Based Yield Monitoring

A yield monitor developed using IoT-based technologies can be mounted on any associated harvester and connected to the FarmTRX mobile app, which demonstrates real-time harvest data and instantly uploads it to the manufacturers' web-based platform (Ayaz et al., 2019). This app can create high-quality yield maps that the farmer may export to other farm management tools for further analysis. Fruit growth measurement can be really beneficial in the precise evaluation of the quality and production of the yield. Satellite photographs can be a useful tool for monitoring the output of large-scale crops. This method was used to record rice crop production in Myanmar using Sentinel-1A interferometric pictures (Torbick et al., 2017). Colour (RGB) depth photographs are utilized to track the various fruit stages in mango fields (Wang et al., 2017). Similarly, several optical sensors are being used to measure papaya shrinkage, especially during drying conditions (Udomkun et al., 2016).

1.3.5 IoT-Based Irrigation

Embracing upcoming IoT technology is predicted to change the current status of irrigation practices. The application of IoT-based strategies, such as crop water stress index (CWSI) based irrigation management, is projected to lead to a major enhancement in crop efficiency. CWSI computation necessitates the achievement of crop canopy at various times as well as air temperature (Tekelioğlu et al., 2017). A wireless sensor-based monitoring system has been created in which all field sensors are linked to assemble the measured data, which is subsequently delivered to a processing centre where the farm data is analysed using appropriate intelligent software programs. Various other data, such as satellite imaging and meteorological data, are also fed into CWSI models to analyse water needs, and an exclusive irrigation index value is created for each site. Variable rate irrigation (VRI) optimization by CropMetrics, which functions in relation to soil variability or topography and ultimately develops the effectiveness of water usage, is also a good example (LaRue & Fredrick, 2012).

1.3.6 IoT-Based Food Safety and Transportation

Considering the prevailing hunger crisis caused by population growth, there is a significant opportunity to diminish food wastage and enhance food supply by merely adopting a temperature-controlled transportation system. Executing an autonomous system that utilizes wireless sensors to detect and record temperatures electronically, on the other hand, can significantly increase food safety. This approach provides a continuous temperature data stream. Readings can be taken regularly and on time this way, leaving no space for interpretation; in other words, the whole procedure is based solely on facts (Bouzembrak et al., 2019). Furthermore, the recorded data can be kept in the cloud and retrieved from any device connected to the Internet, owing to current technological advancements (Bharati & Mondal, 2021; Podder et al., 2021). Notifications can be delivered in real-time if the temperature exceeds predetermined boundaries, meaning rapid action can be taken to correct the situation. In addition, the IoT provides predictive maintenance by predicting when the monitoring equipment will reach the end of its useful life, allowing it to be substituted before it malfunctions and impacts the quality of products (Popa et al., 2019). Some of the vital technologies utilized and their uses are enumerated in Table 1.1.

Various multipurpose technologies such as cloud computing, communication technologies, etc., are being utilized in IoT-based farming in order to accomplish the

Table 1.1 Vital Technologies and Their Uses in Food Safety and Transportation

Technologies	Uses	References
ComplianceMate	Monitoring food safety and quality with hazard analysis and critical control points (HACCP). Capturing temperatures in rooms and coolers at every minute when it integrates with Touchblock.	(Booth, 2015)
Laird Sentrius	Helping in developing, customizing, and supporting entire cold chain systems. Handling challenging cold chain environments. Ensuring connectivity and consistency. Making implementations easier, less costly, and most effective.	(Ayaz et al., 2019)
CCP Smart Tag (RC4)	Thorough monitoring solution for the food service and food retail industry. Automating the temperature of the environment. Temperature and other data are interpreted and observed on a service provider cloud platform utilizing mobile and web applications.	(Htet Myint, 2020)
TempReporter	Continuous monitoring of temperature. Logs readings automatically.	(Ayaz et al., 2019)

Table 1.2 Common Mobile Apps and Their Diverse Applications in Farming

Mobile apps	Applications
PocketLAI	Irrigation
LandPKS	Soil assessment
AMACA	Machinery/tools
Ecofert	Fertilizer management
AgriMaps	Land management
SnapCard	Spraying applications
SWApp	Irrigation
WeedSmart	Weed management
VillageTree	Pest management
WISE	Irrigation
EVAPO	Irrigation
BioLeaf	Health monitoring
cFertigUAL	Fertigation

Source: Ayaz et al. (2019); Ferguson et al. (2016)

tasks mentioned above. A cloud-based system is adept at handling a broad array of data and formats and can configure these forms for various applications (Tan, 2016). AgJunction has developed an open cloud-based system that collects and distributes data from various precise agriculture controllers, reducing costs and environmental impact (Raj et al., 2021). Additionally, Akisai, Fujitsu's agricultural sector cloud, includes information communication technologies with the intention of elevating the food supply in the next years (Kawakami et al., 2016).

Wi-Fi, LoRaWAN, mobile communication, Zigbee, and Bluetooth are examples of communication technologies that can be used to apply the IoT in advanced farming (Jawad et al., 2017). These technologies allow the automation of the entire agricultural cycle, making agriculture more expedient and effective. Zigbee is extensively utilized for IoT implementation in agriculture among many communication technologies due to its little power consumption, cost-effectiveness and versatility (Farooq et al., 2019). Some of the most commonly used mobile apps and their diverse applications in IoT-based farming are enumerated in Table 1.2.

1.4 The Role of Robotics in Advanced Farming

With technological advancements, robotics applications in digital farming have sparked a surge in interest, transforming typical field activities into innovative technical tasks that are highly beneficial. Various types of robots capable of conducting diverse farming operations, such as planting, field inspection, field data gathering, weed control, precise spraying, and harvesting, have been developed so far, although many are still in the prototype phase.

1.4.1 Robotics in Planting

Planting demands a significant amount of time and effort because the process requires a high level of consistency and precision and typically spans a large agricultural area. For numerous crops, such as corn, wheat, sugarcane, and vegetables, autonomous systems have been established to solve the issues of manual planting (Mahmud et al., 2020; Shi et al., 2019). The Agribot platform was used to create an autonomous seeding robot. An infrared (IR) sensor was employed in this development to verify the integrity of the seed tank, as well as for row identification, and it produced a reasonable outcome in terms of precision in the distance between seeds (Naik et al., 2016). Robots made of galvanized iron in previous research were able to till the soil and sow seeds (Sunitha et al., 2017). Several other robots capable of multitasking, including planting activities, are being used in modern farming (Chandana et al., 2020). As a result, with superior planting quality, the automated process of planting would be much more proficient and suitable for farmers in the near future (Mahmud et al., 2020).

1.4.2 Robotics in Weed Control and Spraying

The most widely used farm duties of field robots are weed control and precise spraying. When compared to blanket spraying, targeted spraying using robots for weed control has given satisfactory outcomes and decreased herbicide consumption to as little as 5–10% (Pinheiro & Gusmo, 2014). Various potential weed robots have been presented and deployed during the past 10 years as the outcome of interdisciplinary cooperation initiatives among several worldwide research groups; however, they are still not fully commercialized. It has been reported that these robots are capable of reducing the use of weed chemicals by 80–90 % (Molina et al., 2011). Some of the robots being used in this sector for various tasks are recorded in Table 1.3.

1.4.3 Robotics in Field Inspection and Data Collection

The use of automation in agricultural inspection required the development of a system that can perform the inspection process without the use of human eyesight. As a result, computer vision is increasingly being utilized to substitute human vision in the examination of plants in agriculture. Computer vision is a cutting-edge image processing technology that has shown promising results and has the potential to replace human eyesight in specific inspection tasks (Ayaz et al., 2019). Autonomous inspection is typically carried out by mounting a camera in a static point on a transportable robot or a drone. The deterrence of diseases and the quality testing of

Table 1.3   Commonly Used Robots and Their Applications for Weed Control and Spraying

Robots	Applications	References
BoniRob	Weed control for row crops. Field mapping.	(Bakken et al., 2019)
AgBot	Autonomous fertilizer application. Weed detection and sorting. Chemical or mechanical weed control.	(Redhead et al., 2015)
Autonome Roboter	Weed control	(Shamshiri et al., 2018)
Tertill	Weed cutting	(Sanchez & Gallandt, 2020)
HortiBot	Transporting and attaching a variety of weed detection and control tools.	(Fountas et al., 2020)
Kongskilde Robotti	Automated and semi-automated mechanical weed control.	(Bogue, 2016)

commodities will become more precise and effective as a result of the self-governing strategy and its execution in the inspection procedure, ensuring future food security. Scouting robots for data collection involves the substantial utilization of advanced sensors for advanced farming (Patmasari et al., 2018). Listed below in Table 1.4 are some of the robots being used for field inspection and data collection with multiple applications.

1.4.4 Robotics in Harvesting

Increased harvesting efficiency and lower labour costs will assure sophisticated food production yield and affordability. As a result, the implementation of autonomous harvesting using robots should be considered an alternate option to solving expenses and labour unavailability. For fruit detection inside the canopy, the earliest experiments used simple monochrome cameras (Gongal et al., 2015). Many current advancements are being incorporated into harvesting robots, including the autonomous recognition of fruits from manifold images or based on the fusion of colour and 3D features (Barnea et al., 2016), multi-template matching algorithms (Bao et al., 2016), symmetry analysis, combined colour distance method and RGB-D data analysis for apples (Garrido-Novell et al., 2012) and sweet-peppers (Lavanya et al., 2020), stereo vision for the detection of apples, and the usage of convolutional neural networks (Zhao et al., 2016) and deep learning algorithms for the recognition of fruits and evasion of hindrance in very condensed foliage (Zujevs et al., 2015).

Table 1.4 Commonly Used Robots and Their Applications in Field Inspection and Data Collection

Robots	Applications	References
TrimBot2020	Automatic bush trimming. Rose pruning.	(Shamshiri et al., 2018)
Wall-Ye	Field mapping. Pruning.	(Fountas et al., 2020)
Ladybird	Surveillance and mapping. Classification and detection of different vegetables.	(Bender et al., 2019)
MARS	Optimizing plant-specific precision agriculture.	(Fountas et al., 2020)
SMP S4	Bird and pest control.	(Shamshiri et al., 2018)
Vine agent	Health monitoring of plants.	(Arguenon et al., 2006)
HV-100 Nursery Bot	Moving of plants and potted trees in greenhouses.	(Shamshiri et al., 2018)
VinBot	Autonomous image acquisition. 3D data collection for yield estimation.	(Shamshiri et al., 2018)
Mantis	Field data collection.	(Stein et al., 2016)
GRAPE	Plant detection. Health monitoring. Manipulation of small objects.	(Roure et al., 2017)

The field examination of a self-governing robot for de-leafing cucumber plants introduced a functional model in a high-wire farming structure (Van Henten et al., 2006). Various studies on robot arm motion planning for agricultural harvesting operations have been done in recent years. A motion scheduling system was successfully implemented with a 51% success rate to synchronize the four arms of a robot for an automated kiwi fruit picking system (Udomkun et al., 2016). Apple tree branches were detected with 94% accuracy using the Contrast Limited Adaptive Histogram Equalization (CLAHE) method in Ayaz et al. (2019). Many research studies are currently in progress for developing simple manipulators and multi-robot systems as well.

1.5 The Challenges and Recommendations of Indulging Technologies in Advanced Farming

A higher quantity of food of high quality is needed in the near future due to the rapid rise in population (Ayaz et al., 2019). Hence, both the yield and quality of agricultural production should be increased by the application of technologies into the field.

Even though 2% of the farming population performs better in terms of quantity and quality as they have access to modern technology, the rest of the population struggles to gain a better yield. This is clear to see because developed countries, such as Australia and most countries in Europe, have already been using new technology and equipment over the past five decades and have reached an exponentially higher yield. Thus, it is clear that modern equipment and technology help in obtaining higher yields, as well as making farms environmentally safe and beneficial (Zha, 2020). In light of this scenario, future agriculture is predicted to develop into a high-tech industry, with networked systems benefiting from artificial intelligence and big data capabilities. From sowing to production forecasts, the resulting systems will converge into a single unit where farm machinery and management will be linked. Agriculture may usher in a new era of superfusion by using sophisticated technology such as agricultural robotics, big data, and cloud-computing artificial intelligence.

The major challenge of introducing technology into advanced farming is the lack of proper knowledge of farmers who practice them in the field. Hence, the major recommendation would be to simultaneously educate farmers about the insights of technological devices and produce a proper information base from individual farming lands in order to optimize the devices in the future. Fear of technological devices and automation technologies replacing the needed labour force had created a reluctance towards these technologies among farmers in agriculture. There is a high chance that utilization of these technologies will be avoided as field management and disease management practices, which were historically performed by experienced farmers, are now given by machines. Hence, it is practically observed that young farmers who have more hands-on experiences with the technologies are readily accepting the technologies into their fields than the old farmers. Hence, they should be slowly admitted and introduced to them (Jha et al., 2019).

The creation of autonomous machines such as tractors is not accepted due to safety considerations. Hence, more precise sensors and controlling technologies should be developed in the future. Also, to employ autonomous agricultural machinery in the field, IoT technologies must be combined to ensure agricultural machinery safety (Kim et al., 2020).

Both cultivation and domestication of species are included in agriculture (Harris et al., 2014). As only cultivation is looked upon by many farmers now, the domestication purpose has been greatly left to scientists and agro-technical officers. Hence, the implementation of AI into the field of domestication would make it easier for farmers to use their knowledge about wild varieties and test them for domestication. AI development and involvement have only been limited to areas of agriculture where profit-gain is the major target; however, the minor fields of agriculture such as horticulture, mixed crop-livestock farming, and arboriculture should also be given enough attention to improvise as well as optimize the services provided by those fields.

IoT devices are employed in open surroundings in most agricultural areas, with the exception of greenhouses, where they are directly exposed to hostile conditions.

Safety devices are required in IoT hardware because environmental variables such as rain, high temperature, humidity, and strong wind may affect their performance (Farooq et al., 2020).

Hacking gathered host properties, farm information, and agricultural data, as well as network and communication interruptions, should be avoided in IoT-based agriculture. Since the IoT employs a distributed network of sensor nodes, a single security protocol is insufficient, and it is necessary to plan for data loss (Paul et al., 2020).

The major challenge for sensor development and agricultural robotic technology is the required spatial and resolution data being unable to be measured as they vary extremely and hence pose difficulties in measuring them. The goal of new analytical methods is to extract new knowledge by combining data and fusing disparate information layers. Network applications must be trustworthy and scalable in order to manage these complex systems.

The main difficulties to be disentangled for the generalization of robotics structures are increasing the speed and accuracy of robots for agricultural applications. The progress in the research related to the field is hindered by the lack of substantial budget allocations and funding. Improving sensing (fruit detection), acting (manipulator movement, fruit attachment, detaching, and collecting), and growing systems (leave pruning and plant reshaping) are some of the features that could be vehemently suggested to improve the efficiency.

It should be noted that the development of a cost-effective and efficient agriculture robot necessitates a multidisciplinary approach involving deep learning and intelligent systems, computer science, dynamic control, crop management, sensors and instrumentation, horticultural engineering, software design, mechatronics, and system integration (Rahmadian & Widyartono, 2020). According to an IDTechEx report, by 2023, more types of robots could be seen in the market with the rolling out of robots used in weeding, vegetable and fruit harvesting, strawberry picking, and apple picking.

AI, IoT, and robotics in agriculture are expected to solve a number of challenges and enable higher quality and productivity. However, there is a need for a technology that integrates and applies these technologies to all aspects of farm management. Therefore, research and development in this particular area should be encouraged, and the governments should be ready to invest in the research sector of agriculture for the well-being of their people.

1.6 Conclusion

Machine learning has enabled deep learning into automated technologies to be directed for use in agriculture. Machines communicate with different databases and produce solutions to timely problems faced by farmers. Adopting smart technologies, AI, the IoT, and robotics for various applications in advanced farming can be highly beneficial to farmers. These technologies have reduced the involvement of labour in the processes, thus reducing the number of human-made mistakes as well as optimizing the processes, which have resulted in high efficiency of production as well as high yield. However, future research and development is needed to overcome the shortcomings associated with these smart technologies in advanced farming.

References

Arguenon, V., Bergues-Lagarde, A., Rosenberger, C., Bro, P., & Smari, W. (2006). Multi-agent based prototyping of agriculture robots. *International Symposium on Collaborative Technologies and Systems (CTS'06)*. https://doi.org/10.1109/cts.2006.57

Ayaz, M., Ammad-Uddin, M., Sharif, Z., Mansour, A., & Aggoune, E. (2019). Internet-of-things (IoT)-based smart agriculture: Toward making the fields talk. *IEEE Access, 7*, 129551–129583. https://doi.org/10.1109/access.2019.2932609

Bakken, M., Moore, R., & From, P. (2019). End-to-end learning for autonomous crop row-following. *IFAC-Papersonline, 52*(30), 102–107. https://doi.org/10.1016/j.ifacol.2019.12.505

Bannerjee, G., Sarkar, U., Das, S, & Ghosh, I. (2018). Artificial intelligence in agriculture: A literature survey. *International Journal of Scientific Research in Computer Science Applications and Management Studies, 7*(3), pp. 1–6.

Bao, G., Cai, S., Qi, L., Xun, Y., Zhang, L., & Yang, Q. (2016). Multi-template matching algorithm for cucumber recognition in natural environment. *Computers and Electronics in Agriculture, 127*, 754–762. https://doi.org/10.1016/j.compag.2016.08.001

Barnea, E., Mairon, R., & Ben-Shahar, O. (2016). Colour-agnostic shape-based 3D fruit detection for crop harvesting robots. *Biosystems Engineering, 146*, 57–70. https://doi.org/10.1016/j.biosystemseng.2016.01.013

Bender, A., Whelan, B., & Sukkarieh, S. (2019). A high-resolution, multimodal data set for agricultural robotics: A ladybird 's-eye view of Brassica. *Journal of Field Robotics, 37*(1), 73–96. https://doi.org/10.1002/rob.21877

Benincasa, P., Antognelli, S., Brunetti, L., Fabbri, C., Natale, A., & Sartoretti, V. (2017). Reliability of NDVI derived by high resolution satellite and UAV compared to in-field methods for the evaluation of early crop n status and grain yield in wheat. *Experimental Agriculture, 54*(4), 604–622. https://doi.org/10.1017/s0014479717000278

Bharati, S., & Mondal, M. R. H. (2021). 12 applications and challenges of AI-driven IoHT for combating pandemics: A review. *Computational Intelligence for Managing Pandemics, 5*, 213.

Bogue, R. (2016). Robots poised to revolutionise agriculture. Industrial Robot: An *International Journal, 43*(5), 450–456. https://doi.org/10.1108/ir-05-2016-0142

Booth, D. (2015). Building capacity: Internet of Things builds capacity for automatic temperature logging. *Journal of Environmental Health, 77*(10), 34–37. Retrieved June 10, 2021, from www.jstor.org/stable/26330268

Bouzembrak, Y., Klüche, M., Gavai, A., & Marvin, H. (2019). Internet of Things in food safety: Literature review and a bibliometric analysis. *Trends in Food Science & Technology, 94*, 54–64. https://doi.org/10.1016/j.tifs.2019.11.002

Chandana, R., Nisha, M., Pavithra, B., Sumana, S., & Nagashree, R. (2020). A multipurpose agricultural robot for automatic ploughing, seeding and plant health monitoring. *International Journal of Engineering Research & Technology, 8*(1).

Colmer, J., O'Neill, C., Wells, R., Bostrom, A., Reynolds, D., & Websdale, D. (2020). SeedGerm: A cost-effective phenotyping platform for automated seed imaging and machine-learning based phenotypic analysis of crop seed germination. *New Phytologist, 228*(2), 778–793. https://doi.org/10.1111/nph.16736

Crapolicchio, R., Ferrazzoli, P., Meloni, M., Pinori, S., & Rahmoune, R. (2010). Soil Moisture and Ocean Salinity (SMOS) mission: System overview and contribution to vicarious calibration monitoring. *European Journal of Remote Sensing*, 37–50. https://doi.org/10.5721/itjrs20104214

Facchinetti, D., Santoro, S., Galli, L. E., Fontana, G., Fedeli, L., Parisi, S., & Pessina, D. (2021). Reduction of pesticide use in fresh-cut salad production through artificial intelligence. *Applied Sciences, 11*(5), 1992. https://doi.org/10.3390/app11051992

Farooq, M. S., Riaz, S., Abid, A., Abid, K., & Naeem, M. A. (2019). A survey on the role of IoT in agriculture for the implementation of smart farming. *IEEE Access*, 7, 156237–156271. https://doi.org/10.1109/ACCESS.2019.2949703

Farooq, M. S., Riaz, S., Abid, A., Umer, T., & Zikria, Y. B. (2020). Role of IoT trechnology in agriculture: A systematic literature review. *Electronics, 9*(2), 319. https://doi.org/10.3390/electronics9020319

Ferguson, J., Chechetto, R., O'Donnell, C., Fritz, B., Hoffmann, W., & Coleman, C. (2016). Assessing a novel smartphone application – SnapCard, compared to five imaging systems to quantify droplet deposition on artificial collectors. *Computers and Electronics in Agriculture, 128*, 193–198. https://doi.org/10.1016/j.compag.2016.08.022

Food and Agriculture Organization of the United Nations. (2021). From: www.fao.org/sustainability/news/detail/en/c/1274219/.

Fountas, S., Mylonas, N., Malounas, I., Rodias, E., Hellmann Santos, C., & Pekkeriet, E. (2020). Agricultural robotics for field operations. *Sensors, 20*(9), 2672. https://doi.org/10.3390/s20092672

Garrido-Novell, C., Pérez-Marin, D., Amigo, J., Fernández-Novales, J., Guerrero, J., & Garrido-Varo, A. (2012). Grading and color evolution of apples using RGB and hyperspectral imaging vision cameras. *Journal of Food Engineering, 113*(2), 281–288. https://doi.org/10.1016/j.jfoodeng.2012.05.038

Gongal, A., Amatya, S., Karkee, M., Zhang, Q., & Lewis, K. (2015). Sensors and systems for fruit detection and localization: A review. *Computers and Electronics in Agriculture, 116*, 8–19. https://doi.org/10.1016/j.compag.2015.05.021

González-Briones, A., Castellanos-Garzón, J., Mezquita Martín, Y., Prieto, J., & Corchado, J. (2018). A framework for knowledge discovery from wireless sensor networks in rural environments: A crop irrigation systems case study. *Wireless Communications and Mobile Computing, 2018*, 1–14. https://doi.org/10.1155/2018/6089280

Harris, D., & Fuller, D. (2014). Agriculture: Definition and overview. *Encyclopedia of Global Archaeology,* 104–113.

Htet Myint, K. (2020). SMS security on Android using RC4 algorithm. *Intelligent System and Computing.* https://doi.org/10.5772/intechopen.90119

IDTechEx Ltd. (2017, March 6). *Agricultural Robots and Drones 2017–2027: Technologies, Markets, Players.* IDTechEx. www.idtechex.com/en/research-report/agricultural-robots-and-drones-2017-2027-technologies-markets-players/525

Jawad, H. M., Nordin, R., Gharghan, S. K., Jawad, A. M., & Ismail, M. (2017). Energy-efficient wireless sensor networks for precision agriculture: A review. *Sensors*, 17(8), 1781. https://doi.org/10.3390/s17081781.

Jha, K., Doshi, A., Patel, P., & Shah, M. (2019). A comprehensive review on automation in agriculture using artificial intelligence. *Artificial Intelligence in Agriculture*, 2, 1–12. https://doi.org/10.1016/j.aiia.2019.05.004

Kawakami, Y., Furuta, T., Nakagawa, H., Kitamura, T., Kurosawa, K., & Kogami, K. (2016). Rice cultivation support system equipped with water-level sensor system. *IFAC-PapersOnLine*, 49(16), 143–148. https://doi.org/10.1016/j.ifacol.2016.10.027

Kim, S., Lee, M., & Shin, C. (2018). IoT-based strawberry disease prediction system for smart farming. *Sensors*, 18(11), 4051. https://doi.org/10.3390/s18114051

Kim, W., Lee, W., & Kim, Y. (2020). A review of the applications of the Internet of Things (IoT) for agricultural automation. *Journal of Biosystems Engineering*, 45(4), 385–400. https://doi.org/10.1007/s42853-020-00078-3

Kumar, R., Singh, M., Kumar, P., & Singh, J. (2015). Crop selection method to maximize crop yield rate using machine learning technique. *2015 International Conference on Smart Technologies and Management for Computing, Communication, Controls, Energy And Materials (ICSTM)*. https://doi.org/10.1109/icstm.2015.7225403

Lakhiar, I., Jianmin, G., Syed, T., Chandio, F., Buttar, N., & Qureshi, W. (2018). Monitoring and control systems in agriculture using intelligent sensor techniques: A Review of the aeroponic system. *Journal of Sensors*, 2018, 1–18. https://doi.org/10.1155/2018/8672769

LaRue, J., & Fredrick, C. (2012). Decision process for the application of variable rate irrigation. *2012 Dallas, Texas, July 29 – August 1, 2012*. https://doi.org/10.13031/2013.42154

Lavanya, G., Rani, C., & Ganeshkumar, P. (2020). An automated low cost IoT based fertilizer intimation system for smart agriculture. *Sustainable Computing: Informatics and Systems*, 28, 100300. https://doi.org/10.1016/j.suscom.2019.01.002

Mahmood, I., Imadi, S., Shazadi, K., Gul, A., & Hakeem, K. (2016). Effects of pesticides on environment. *Plant, Soil and Microbes*, 253–269. https://doi.org/10.1007/978-3-319-27455-3_13

Mahmud, A., Saiful, M., Abidin, Z., Shukri, M., Abiodun, A., & Sahib, H. (2020) Robotics and automation in agriculture: present and future applications. *Applications of Modelling and Simulation*, 4, 130–140.

Molina, I., Morillo, C., García-Meléndez, E., Guadalupe, R., & Roman, M. (2011). Characterizing olive grove canopies by means of ground-based hemispherical photography and spaceborne RADAR data. *Sensors*, 11(8), 7476–7501. https://doi.org/10.3390/s100807476

Naik, N., Shete, V., & Danve, S. (2016). Precision agriculture robot for seeding function. *2016 International Conference on Inventive Computation Technologies (ICICT)*. https://doi.org/10.1109/inventive.2016.7824880

Oberti, R., Marchi, M., Tirelli, P., Calcante, A., Iriti, M., & Tona, E. (2016). Selective spraying of grapevines for disease control using a modular agricultural robot. *Biosystems Engineering*, 146, 203–215. https://doi.org/10.1016/j.biosystemseng.2015.12.004

Pablos, M., González-Zamora, Á, Sánchez, N., & Martínez-Fernández, J. (2018). Assessment of SMADI and SWDI agricultural drought indices using remotely sensed root zone soil moisture. *Proceedings of The International Association Of Hydrological Sciences*, 380, 55–66. https://doi.org/10.5194/piahs-380-55-2018

Partel, V., Charan Kakarla, S., & Ampatzidis, Y. (2019). Development and evaluation of a low-cost and smart technology for precision weed management utilizing artificial intelligence. *Computers and Electronics In Agriculture, 157*, 339–350. https://doi.org/10.1016/j.compag.2018.12.048

Patmasari, R., Wijayanto, I., Deanto, R., Gautama, Y., & Vidyaningtyas, H. (2018). Design and realization of automatic packet reporting system (APRS) for sending telemetry data in nano satellite communication system. *Journal of Measurements, Electronics, Communications, and Systems, 4*(1), 1. https://doi.org/10.25124/jmecs.v4i1.1692

Paul, P., Marroquin, R. S., Aithal, P. S., Sinha, R. R., & Aremu, B. (2020). Agro informatics vis-à-vis Internet of Things (IoT) integration & potentialities—An analysis. *SSRN Electronic Journal*. https://doi.org/10.2139/ssrn.3724421

Pinheiro, F., & Gusmão dos Anjos, W. (2014). Optical sensors applied in agricultural crops. *Optical Sensors – New Developments and Practical Applications*. https://doi.org/10.5772/57145

Podder, P., Mondal, M., Bharati, S., & Paul, P. K. (2021). Review on the security threats of Internet of Things. arXiv:2101.05614

Popa, A., Hnatiuc, M., Paun, M., Geman, O., Hemanth, D., & Dorcea, D. (2019). An intelligent IoT-based food quality monitoring approach using low-cost sensors. *Symmetry, 11*(3), 374. https://doi.org/10.3390/sym11030374

Rahmadian, R., & Widyartono, M. (2020). Autonomous robotic in agriculture: A review. *2020 Third International Conference on Vocational Education and Electrical Engineering (ICVEE)*. https://doi.org/10.1109/icvee50212.2020.9243253

Raj, M., Gupta, S., Chamola, V., Elhence, A., Garg, T., Atiquzzaman, M., & Niyato, D. (2021). A survey on the role of Internet of Things for adopting and promoting Agriculture 4.0. *Journal of Network and Computer Applications, 187*, 103107. https://doi.org/10.1016/j.jnca.2021.103107

Raut, R., Varma, H., Mulla, C., & Pawar, V. (2017). Soil monitoring, fertigation, and irrigation system using IoT for agricultural application. *Intelligent Communication and Computational Technologies*, 67–73. https://doi.org/10.1007/978-981-10-5523-2_7

Redhead, F., Snow, S., Vyas, D., Bawden, O., Russell, R., Perez, T., & Brereton, M. (2015). Bringing the farmer perspective to agricultural robots. *Proceedings Of The 33rd Annual ACM Conference Extended Abstracts on Human Factors in Computing Systems*. https://doi.org/10.1145/2702613.2732894

Roure, F., Moreno, G., Soler, M., Faconti, D., Serrano, D., & Astolfi, P. (2017). GRAPE: Ground Robot for vineyArd Monitoring and ProtEction. *ROBOT 2017: Third Iberian Robotics Conference*, 249–260. https://doi.org/10.1007/978-3-319-70833-1_21

Sanchez, J., & Gallandt, E. (2020). Functionality and efficacy of Franklin Robotics' Tertil™ robotic weeder. *Weed Technology, 35*(1), 166–170. https://doi.org/10.1017/wet.2020.94

Shamshiri, R., Weltzien, C., Hameed, I., Yule, I., Grift, T., Balasundram, S., Pitonakova, L., Ahmad, D., & Chowdhary, G. (2018). Research and development in agricultural robotics: A perspective of digital farming. *International Journal of Agricultural and Biological Engineering, 11*(4), 1–11. https://doi.org/10.25165/j.ijabe.20181104.4278

Shi, Y., Xin (Rex), S., Wang, X., Hu, Z., Newman, D., & Ding, W. (2019). Numerical simulation and field tests of minimum-tillage planter with straw smashing and strip lying based on EDEM software. *Computers and Electronics in Agriculture, 166*, 105021. https://doi.org/10.1016/j.compag.2019.105021

Stein, M., Bargoti, S., & Underwood, J. (2016). Image based mango fruit detection, localisation and yield estimation using multiple view geometry. *Sensors*, *16*(11), 1915. https://doi.org/10.3390/s16111915

Sunitha, K., Suraj, G., Sowrya, C., Sriram, G., Shreyas, D., & Srinivas, T. (2017). Agricultural robot designed for seeding mechanism. *IOP Conference Series: Materials Science and Engineering*, *197*, 012043. https://doi.org/10.1088/1757-899x/197/1/012043

Talaviya, T., Shah, D., Patel, N., Yagnik, H., & Shah, M. (2020). Implementation of artificial intelligence in agriculture for optimisation of irrigation and application of pesticides and herbicides. *Artificial Intelligence in Agriculture*, *4*, 58–73. https://doi.org/10.1016/j.aiia.2020.04.002

Tan, L. (2016). Cloud-based decision support and automation for precision agriculture in orchards. *IFAC-PapersOnLine*, *49*(16), 330–335. https://doi.org/10.1016/j.ifacol.2016.10.061

Tekelioğlu, B., Büyüktaş, D., Baştuğ, R., Karaca, C., Aydinşakir, K., & Dinç, N. (2017). Use of crop water stress index for irrigation scheduling of soybean in Mediterranean conditions. *Journal of Experimental Agriculture International*, *18*(6), 1–8. https://doi.org/10.9734/jeai/2017/37058

TeKrony, D., & Egli, D. (1991). Relationship of seed vigour to crop yield: A review. *Crop Science* 31: 816–822

Torbick, N., Chowdhury, D., Salas, W., & Qi, J. (2017). Monitoring rice agriculture across Myanmar using time series Sentinel-1 assisted by Landsat-8 and PALSAR-2. *Remote Sensing*, *9*(2), 119. https://doi.org/10.3390/rs9020119

Udomkun, P., Nagle, M., Argyropoulos, D., Mahayothee, B., & Müller, J. (2016). Multi-sensor approach to improve optical monitoring of papaya shrinkage during drying. *Journal of Food Engineering*, *189*, 82–89. https://doi.org/10.1016/j.jfoodeng.2016.05.014

Van Henten, E., Van Tuijl, B., Hoogakker, G., Van Der Weerd, M., Hemming, J., Kornet, J., & Bontsema, J. (2006). An autonomous robot for de-leafing cucumber plants grown in a high-wire cultivation system. *Biosystems Engineering*, *94*(3), 317–323. https://doi.org/10.1016/j.biosystemseng.2006.03.005

Van Klompenburg, T., Kassahun, A., & Catal, C. (2020). Crop yield prediction using machine learning: A systematic literature review. *Computers and Electronics in Agriculture*, *177*, 105709. https://doi.org/10.1016/j.compag.2020.105709

Wang, Z., Walsh, K., & Verma, B. (2017). On-tree mango fruit size estimation using RGB-D images. *Sensors*, *17*(12), 2738. https://doi.org/10.3390/s17122738

Zha, J. (2020). Artificial intelligence in agriculture. *Journal of Physics: Conference Series*, *1693*, 012058. https://doi.org/10.1088/1742-6596/1693/1/012058

Zhang, X., Friedl, M., & Schaaf, C. (2006). Global vegetation phenology from moderate resolution imaging spectroradiometer (MODIS): Evaluation of global patterns and comparison with in situ measurements. *Journal of Geophysical Research: Biogeosciences*, *111*(G4). https://doi.org/10.1029/2006jg000217

Zhao, Y., Gong, L., Huang, Y., & Liu, C. (2016). A review of key techniques of vision-based control for harvesting robot. *Computers and Electronics in Agriculture*, *127*, 311–323. https://doi.org/10.1016/j.compag.2016.06.022

Zujevs, A., Osadcuks, V., & Ahrendt, P. (2015). Trends in robotic sensor technologies for fruit harvesting: 2010–2015. *Procedia Computer Science*, *77*, 227–233. https://doi.org/10.1016/j.procs.2015.12.378

Chapter 2

Towards the Technological Adaptation of Advanced Farming through Artificial Intelligence, the Internet of Things, and Robotics: A Comprehensive Overview

Md. Mahadi Hasan
Asian University of Bangladesh, Dhaka, Bangladesh

Muhammad Usama Islam
Asian University of Bangladesh, Dhaka, Bangladesh

Muhammad Jafar Sadeq
Asian University of Bangladesh, Dhaka, Bangladesh

2.1 Introduction

Farming has played a pivotal role since the inception of humankind. The farming revolution has been driven by mechanized hands since the industrial revolution up to the advent of AI, IoT, and robotics technology. Magnificent changes have arisen in problem-solving, situation monitoring, decision-making, market demand analysis, and autopilot machinery, which eventually leads the robotics approach to utilizing hardware, algorithms, software, AI, machine learning, deep learning modelling, and simulation, current knowledge, and experience in the farming sector [1]. Scientists have prophesied that the earth will need 25–70% more food in order to face the food shortage demand by 2050 [2]. AI, IoT, and robotics-based technologies are most likely to succeed at coping with upcoming challenges to handle all situations successfully.

Scientists have iterated that AI is the precursor of the current age [3]. AI has started to play the main role in daily life, thus extending the way of thinking. Artificial intelligence that has been inspired by the human brain and artificial neurons is now able to compute faster than the human brain [4].

Today's IoT is one of the most dependable terms in the technological world [5]. The fast progress in space technology-based science and data communication pertaining to satellite imagery also means the supply of continuous insights pertaining to and on weather data and crop production data to farmers for the purpose of sustainable farming and development [6].

Robotics has opened up new dimensions, new grounds, new operating environments, and new methods through a new level of performance [7]. The implementation of precision farming and actual precision management are some of the possible reactions to this prospect, which depends not only on sensor technology but on what is possible through the accurate utilization of agricultural robots [8].

AI, IoT, and robotics technology will save countless hours of labour, collect crops in actual time, provide more food with fewer resources and reduce human involvement, ensure food security and profit for the economy, decrease the use of chemicals, and minimize environmental pollution.

This chapter provides a comprehensive overview of AI, IoT, and robotics-based advanced farming using different case studies of various AI models, sensors technology, and multitasking robotics. In particular, we briefly discuss the recent implementation, scopes, opportunities, challenges, limitations, and future research directions of AI, IoT, and robotics-based methodology in the farming sector.

The main content of our chapter is as follows:

■ We present an analytical overview of AI, IoT, and robotics-based advanced farming systems.
■ We propose the figure-based conceptual framework of AI, the IoT, and robotics in farming.

■ We outline a comprehensive tabulated overview of problems and solutions addressed through AI, the IoT, and robotics in the agricultural domain.
■ We explore extensively to identify AI, IoT, and robotics-based technological security issues and the associated trust of adoption in the farming sector.
■ We address the challenges in the adoption of technology and put forward a plausible futuristic conversation to move forward with the adoption of technology.

2.2 Technology in Advanced Farming

Farming has foreseen a tremendous emergence in the field of AI, the IoT and robotics. In this section, we have subdivided our focal point of artificial intelligence, the IoT, and robotics to provide a comprehensive overview of the topics to ascertain the various implantation and scopes of these fields through their emergence. Figure 2.1 provides comprehensive conceptual imagery of how technology is implemented in the farming sphere.

Figure 2.1   Conceptual architecture of AI-robotics-IoT integrated farming

2.2.1 AI in Advanced Farming

Pareek and his team [71] have built an artificial neural network (ANN)-based seed distribution model. The presented model consists of a plate seed device, laptop, several types of motors and sensors, Arduino, and LCD monitor used for motor speed control. They applied three input neurons, five hidden neurons, one output neuron-based ANN for cell fill prediction, and particle swarm optimization (PSO) employed for optimum operation purposes.

Chen et al. [72] presented transfer learning-based tomato leaves disease and pest detection methods. The authors used the PlantVillage dataset and their own collected dataset for ResNet-18 training purposes. The transfer learning model achieved 98.06% detection accuracy.

Sarijaloo and his colleagues [73] presented the corn yield performance prediction approach. For training purposes, they used the 2020 Syngenta Crop Challenge dataset. The authors applied traditional machine learning algorithms such as TR (Random Forest), DT (Decision Tree), XGBoost, AB (Adaptive Boosting), GBM, and NN. XGBoost algorithms perform best against other machine learning algorithms.

Wei et al. [74] proposed an intelligent fish feeding system. This consisted of a sensor, motor, feeder, camera, synchronous wheel and belt, drive-linked plate, slide, positioning platform, track, and pond. The authors proved their intelligent feeding system performs better against traditional feeding systems.

Wang and his colleagues [75] presented a sugar prediction approach from sugarcane yield. The authors applied traditional machine learning algorithms such as SVM, RF, LR, DT, NB, and MLP for classification purposes. The multilayer perceptron (MLP) algorithm achieved the best performance over other classification algorithms.

Shadrin and his team [9] proposed a generic low-power embedded method based on AI. They ensured the analysis and prediction of dwarf tomato leaves' growth dynamics monitoring in real time with the aid of recurrent neural networks (RNN).

Furthermore, researchers [10] developed a power-savvy, smart, systematic approach of sensing coupled with AI for seed germination detection. They collected data from 18 containers totalling 2,400 seed images and around 3,000 background images. The proposed system used custom convolutional neural network (CNN) architecture that achieved 97% accuracy at the validation set and 83% average intersection over union at the testing set, which is quite commendable.

Sabanci [11] presented an artificial intelligence-based wheat grain detection system where the author collected 300 images. The proposed method used an ANN and extreme learning machine (ELM) algorithm optimized with the artificial bee colony algorithm that achieved 100% classification accuracy. The ELM achieved a classification accuracy of 90%.

Partel and his colleagues [12] presented an autonomous and artificial intelligent-based herbicide sprayer system. Their sprayer system consists of three video cameras, individual nozzle control, a speed sensor, a pump, a real-time kinematic GPS, relay boards, tubes, pressurized folds, etc. They experimented with YOLOv3 with Darknet53, Faster R-CNN with ResNet50, and Faster R-CNN with ResNet101 for real-time weed detection purposes. Faster R-CNN coupled with ResNet50 provided the best performance in this experiment.

Similar works were done where the authors [13] developed a precision sprayer system with artificial intelligence. They evaluated the sprayer system with artificial plants and real plants.

Seyedzadeh et al. [14] presented an artificial intelligence-based estimate of the discharge of drip tape irrigation systems. The authors simulated their methodology's wide range of temperature (13–53°C) and operating pressure (0–240 kPa) variations. They used six ANN architectures, neuro-fuzzy sub-clustering, neuro-fuzzy C-means clustering, a least-square support-vector machine (SVM) with radial basis function (RBF) kernel, and a least-square SVM with linear kernel for operating pressure and temperature measurement purposes. Overall, the authors noted that the least-square SVM along with RBF kernel, neuro-fuzzy sub-clustering, and ANN with Levenberg-Marquardt achieved the highest performance accuracy.

Kaab and his team [15] proposed an artificial intelligence-based environment for the adverse and positive impacts of sugarcane production measured prediction systems. The authors used ANNs and an adaptive neuro-fuzzy inference system (ANFIS). The ANFIS performed better than the ANNs.

Liu et al. [16] presented deep residual CNN-based invertebrate pest detection methods. The author's dataset included more than 6,000 images. The dataset was constructed as field images, virtual images, random rotations, random crops, random resize, and random-contrast adjustment and was tested on standard pretrained networks.

Tang et al. [17] proposed two AI models, SVM and ANN, for maize evapotranspiration estimation. The authors collected input data from maize fields. The input data consisted of meteorological variables, leaf area index, and plant heights, with continuous measurements of evapotranspiration. The genetic artificial neural network model architecture performed better than the SVM models.

Picon et al. [18] presented three different CNN models for plant disease classification. The authors collected 100,000 real-field crop images taken by cell phones. They also used ResNet50 baseline architecture. The best model achieved 0.98 classification accuracy.

The conceptual architecture of AI in farming is given an overview in Figure 2.2, and a summarized version is visualized in Table 2.1 for understanding the various problems in the agricultural domain being addressed via deep learning and machine learning models.

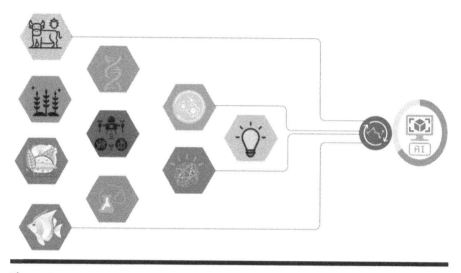

Figure 2.2 Conceptual architecture of AI in farming

Table 2.1 A Comprehensive Overview of the Problems and Solutions Addressed through DL/ML Models in the Farming Domain

Reference	Addressed problem	DL/ML model	Accuracy	Dataset
[19]	Multi-class cassava leaf disease detection	CNN	93%	Kaggle
[20]	Multi-class apple leaf disease detection	Custom CNN, InceptionV3, VGG16	99.6%, 99.4%, 99.5%	PlantVillage
[21]	Multi-class tea leaves disease detection	SVM, DT, RF, C-DCGAN + VGG16	70%, 71.6%, 75% 90%	Dataset curated by authors
[22]	Citrus aurantium diseases detection	Conditional adversarial autoencoders	53.4%	CUB, AWA2, APY
[23]	Multi-class grape leaf disease classification	GAN	92.44%	PlantVillage
[24]	Plant seedlings classification	VGG16	99.48%	Aarhus University, University of Southern Denmark

(Continued)

Table 2.1 A Comprehensive Overview of the Problems and Solutions Addressed through DL/ML Models in the Farming Domain (Continued)

Reference	Addressed problem	DL/ML model	Accuracy	Dataset
[25]	Plant disease detection	AlexNet, AlexNetOWTBn, GoogLeNet, OverFeat, VGG	99.06%, 99.49%, 97.27%, 98.96%, 99.53%	PlantVillage
[26]	Sugar beet leaf spot disease detection	Faster R-CNN	95.48%	Dataset curated by authors
[27]	Multi-class potato disease classification	VGG	83–96%	Dataset curated by authors
[28]	Yellow rust disease detection	Inception-ResNet, Random forest classifier	85%, 77%	Dataset curated by authors
[29]	Plant disease detection	DL	93.67%	PlantVillage

2.2.2 IoT in Advanced Farming

Podder and his team [76] developed an IoT system that decides when irrigation operations begin or end based on weather and farming land conditions. They also provided a farm remote controlling system. This IoT system consisted of various sensors such as moisture, freeze, wind, humidity, pH, etc. The ESP8266 microchip is used for system control, and a Wi-Fi module is used for data transmission.

Khan et al. [77] presented IoT-based farming monitoring methods for bolting reduction in onion farms. The authors divided their system into three levels. At level one, various sensors were used, such as temperature, humidity, and light intensity, to collect environmental parameters. At level two, ThingSpeak software and Wi-Fi was employed for data transmission purposes. At level three, data visualization and monitoring systems were used.

Almalki and his colleagues [78] have proposed IoT and unmanned aerial vehicle-based farming monitoring approaches. They employed various types of sensors such as temperature, rain, humidity, soil moisture, and solar radiation to collect environmental parameters. The drone system comprised a camera, sensor, motors, Raspberry Pi 3 microcontroller unit, propellers, flight controller, battery, and long-range wide-area transmission system. A cloud computing layer was applied to the process for share, visualization, operations, and decision-making purposes.

Addo-Tenkorang and his team [30] presented a low-cost animal monitoring system. The authors included animal health history, location tracking, birth record, and ownership history with their system. The proposed hardware consisted of a 3D printer, micro-tempered solar panels, micro solar inverters, micro recharge-able cells, RFID tags, GPRS, and SIM cards with a roaming function. The soft-ware components included a cloud database system, web services interfaces, mobile gadgets, an operating system, and Google Earth, with proper encryption and security protocols in place.

Al-Khashab et al. [31] developed a water monitoring system. The authors used sensors to calculate water temperature, pH, TDS, turbidity, and conductivity. Sensors were connected to an Arduino Uno. A Wi-Fi module was used for data transmission purposes, and an IoT-based API was used to view sensor data.

Jorda Jr et al. [32] proposed a farm monitoring system to detect the inten-sity emitted by light, moisture measurement of soil, and temperature readings of surroundings. Sensors were used to measure each parameter. These sensors sent data to an Arduino and were then processed by a Raspberry Pi, where they used an MIT App Inventor 2 Android application and an IoT-based gateway to web server monitoring system.

Bodake et al. [33] developed a soil-based fertilizer recommendation system that has a similar output to that of [32].

Khummanee et al. [34] utilized an automated farming system for orchids cul-tivation. The authors used sensors to collect parameters pertaining to the environ-ment, such as temperature, humidity, light, and soil moisture [34].

Righi and his team [35] presented a dairy cattle management system. The authors divided their approach into two parts: MooField and MooServer. The first part acted as a data collection service as well as a service used in the field, whereas the second system was used to store, analyze and generate insight from the data. Their model achieved 94.3% accuracy for prediction purposes.

Chung et al. [36] developed a solar-powered real-time crop growth monitoring system. Temperature, humidity, soil moisture, light, chlorophyll, and CO_2 monitoring sensors were used for input purposes. A Zigbee-based wireless network was utilized for data transmission purposes. The sensing data was applied for the evaluation of environmental conditions, risk measurement and management, and data-driven decision-making.

Ali et al. [37] presented a secure remote user authentication with an agriculture field monitoring system. The sensors collected environmental variables such as tem-perature, humidity, light, soil pH, soil moisture, and CO_2.

Similar monitoring systems were developed by Harun et al. [38], where the authors proposed a Brassica chinensis growth monitoring and indoor climate con-trol system via light-emitting diode. The authors experimented with four different light treatments. They analyzed plant growth based on leaf count, height, dry weight, and chlorophyll.

Koduru et al. [39] presented an IoT-based irrigation approach and real-time monitoring system. The proposed method was divided into two parts. The first part

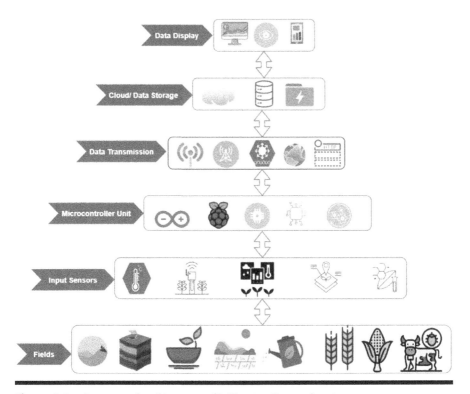

Figure 2.3   Conceptual architecture of IoT in intelligent farming

was the control system, for which they used submersible motors, relay modules such as the 5V10A2 to control the motors, overhead tanks, excess water collection tanks, ultrasonic sensors to control the water level in tanks, and moisture sensors to control the soil moisture. All sensors interacted with a Raspberry Pi 3. For the second part, a farmer's cockpit featured a real-time monitoring application provided by Apple's integration. The weather forecast authors used Yahoo Weather APIs.

An overview of a conceptual architecture of IoT in farming can be seen in Figure 2.3, and a summarized version can be seen in Table 2.2 for understanding the various problems in the agricultural domain that are being addressed via IoT-induced devices.

2.2.3 Robotics in Advanced Farming

Rajalakshmi et al. [79] developed a vision-based robot that performs various farming operations such as seed sowing, spraying, and watering. This robotics system includes a camera, RaspberryPi, Arduino, power supply unit, and pump. For training purposes, the authors used the PlantVillage dataset. The YOLO model was used for weed detection purposes.

Table 2.2 A Comprehensive Table with Problem Overviews and Related IoT Devices for Plausible Solution Approaches in Intelligent Farming

Article	Addressed problem	Input parameter	Data controller	Data transmission	Data display
[40]	Mushroom cultivation monitoring system	Humidity sensor, MQ-135 CO_2 gas sensors	Arduino IDE	Wi-Fi	ThingSpeak
[41]	Potato late blight prevention method	Temperature, humidity, freeze sensors	Cloud	Wi-Fi, Bluetooth, Zigbee, etc	Smartphone, laptop, desktop
[42]	Agriculture monitoring system	Temperature, humidity sensors	Arduino Uno	Wi-Fi, Ethernet Shield	Smartphone, laptop, desktop
[43]	Agriculture monitoring system in rural areas	Temperature, humidity, pressure, luminosity, soil moisture, etc., sensors	Raspberry Pi	Wi-Fi	Web-based interface
[44]	Watering management system	Water level, soil moisture, temperature, humidity, rain intensity sensors	Arduino	Wi-Fi	LCD screen
[45]	Simulated water management	Various simulated sensors	Various simulated engine	Wi-Fi	Application services
[46]	Strawberry disease prediction system	EC1, pH, temperature, humidity, CO_2 sensors	Cloud	Long-range wide area network	Smartphone

[47]	Cow health monitoring system	Accelerometer magnetometer sensors	Raspberry Pi	Wi-Fi	Android application
[48]	Agricultural monitoring system for early plant disease forecast	Air temperature, air humidity, soil temperature, soil volume water content, electrical conductivity, wind speed, wind direction, rain meter, solar radiation, leaf wetness sensors	Arduino ADCs	Cellular network	Web application
[49]	Potato disease prevention system	Humidity, temperature sensors	NodeMCU	Wi Fi, Bluetooth, Zigbee, 3G/ GPRS	Web application

Khadatkar and his team [80] presented an automatic transplanting system. The proposed device consists of a stepper motor, DC motor, 12V power supply battery, feed roller unit, pro-tray belt, two L-shaped rotating fingers, a ground wheel, and an Arduino Uno microcontroller unit. A laptop is used to control the whole system.

Quaglia and his colleagues [50] developed an unmanned ground vehicle (UGV) robotic system to collect crop samples and collaborate with a drone. This system consisted of seven actuators, a robotic arm, sensors, and control devices. Equipped with solar panels, the authors provide two operative modalities: remote monitoring and an on-board analytic tool.

Jawad and his team [51] constructed a wireless power transfer-based efficient drone battery charging system. The drone collects climate conditions information from the agriculture field. They measured drone battery performance based on two strategies: sleep and active. The authors successfully extended 851 minutes of battery life, achieving 96.9% battery power saving. Similar research work into curating an autonomous vehicle and a spraying system was done by Cantelli et al. [52].

Pulido Fentanes et al. [53] developed an autonomous mobile robot system for creating high-quality soil moisture maps. A cosmic ray sensor was applied to count fast neutrons. The authors evaluated their method using soil moisture data. In order to make better quality soil moisture patterns, they applied adaptive measurement intervals and adaptive sampling strategies.

Kim and his colleagues [54] created an autonomously machine-vision-based crop height measurement system. An auto-exposure mode was applied to capture images, and the OpenCV library was used to process images. The system achieved less than 5% error for five different crops.

Kumar and Ashok [55] developed an automated seed sowing robot. The robot consisted of an actuator, sensing device, stepper motors, seed handling unit, microprocessor, servo motors, power transmission, communication, and data controlling processing unit. The author's claimed that seed sowing robots reduce time and human involvement in the agriculture sector.

Thorp and his colleagues [56] created a drone-based daily soil water balance measured model. Pix4D software was used to process images, which were utilized for georeferencing purposes. For visualization and analysis of the data, they used ENVI software.

Mahmud and his team [57] created a spraying robot path planning system. The authors constructed a mobile sprayer robot. They designed a greenhouse environment and a virtual environment where they tried to decipher the shortest path and lowest routing angle. Overall, non-dominated sorting genetic algorithm III achieved better performance.

Distributed multi-quadrotor UAV-based crop monitoring systems have been created by Elmokadem et al. [58]. The author created a virtual environment that used a Gazebo robot simulator framework. The presented system simulated three Iris model quadrotor UAVs.

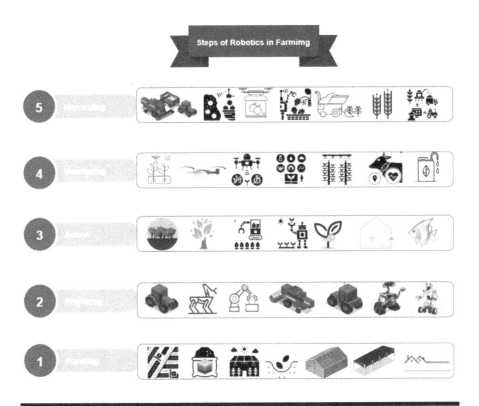

Figure 2.4 **Conceptual framework of robotics in farming**

Similar to Mahmud [57], Srivastava and his colleagues [59] created an optimal route algorithm for UAV-based fertilizers and pesticide spray in the field where a travelling salesman algorithm was applied to find the shortest path.

Raeva et al. [60] created a corn and barley map monitoring system based on UAVs. They used multispectral and thermal sensors. The multiSPEC 4C and senseFly thermoMAP cameras were employed to capture image information from the fields. The UAVs system captured all information from March to August 2016. Pix4mapper was used for image processing purposes.

An overview of the conceptual architecture of robotics in farming can be seen in Figure 2.4, and a summarized version can be seen in Table 2.3 for understanding the various problems in the agricultural domain being addressed via robotic devices.

Table 2.3 A Comprehensive Tabulated Overview of Robotics in Advanced Farming

Article	Addressed problem	Platform	Components	Controlling system
[61]	Fish monitoring system	Fish robotics	ABS plastic, SMA wires, SMA drivers, current, thick polycarbonate backbone, temperature sensors, synthetic skin	PID controller
[62]	Tree trunk detection method	Mobile robot	Ultrasonic sensors, camera, angle sensor, stepper motor, four-wheels, electronic compass, etc.	PI controller
[63]	Automatic spraying system	UGVs robot	Nozzle chamber, Kinect camera, liquid pump and tank, Arduino, Two electromotors, etc	Laptop
[64]	Autonomous navigation algorithm for wolfberry orchards	UGVs robot	Camera, crawler, steering cylinder, steering clutch, gasoline engine, wire rope, air pump, air tank, digital display pressure gauge, oil mist device, etc.	Fuzzy controller
[65]	ROS emulation toolkit	UGVs robotics	GPS, RTK-GNSS, LiDAR, camera, ultrasonic sensors, four-wheel-driving four-wheel-steering electric vehicles, etc.	Computer
[66]	Simulated plants monitoring system	Mobile robot	Sensors, routing algorithm, adaptive search algorithm, etc.	Simulated controlling system

(Continued)

Table 2.3 A Comprehensive Tabulated Overview of Robotics in Advanced Farming (Continued)

Article	Addressed problem	Platform	Components	Controlling system
[67]	Tomato harvesting method	Mobile robot	Camera, ultrasonic sensor, Raspberry Pi, Arduino Mega 2560, servo motors, arm robot, power system, etc.	Computer
[68]	Robot mower track and performance measurement system	Rover	RTK-GNSS, Wi-Fi, Bluetooth, cables, power system, Intel Edison module, Qprel srl etc.	Computer
[69]	Robotics-based modeling and control methods	Mobile robot	Drive wheeled vehicles, Arduino Uno, DC motors, IMU sensor, tracks device, Mobile Tank Robot Kit 10022, etc.	PID, fuzzy logic
[70]	Real-time soil electrical resistivity measurement system	UGVs robot	Four-wheel, four-probes Wenner, DC motors, DGPS, stainless steel, fiber isolation rings, cable, 24-volt battery, inject electric current, software, etc.	Computer

2.3 Challenges in Adoption of Technology

There are obvious challenges and factors that affect the acceptance and adoption of new technologies [81,82]. These challenges can be categorized as the various stakeholders who would be using technology for advanced farming and the perceived issues that will be raised, and security concerns that hinder the adoption of technology in agriculture. There are perceived issues from a human perspective, as well as issues related to research and development that need to be addressed in order to improve the user acceptance of the technology.

The main stakeholders for the new technologies are the farmers who would be using the technology to improve the farming sector. However, there is a big disparity in technical knowledge among farmers all over the world. Although farmers in North

America have successfully adopted technology to create best-case working scenarios, the situation is fully different in Asia and Africa, where technical perspectives are overlooked in general. The main reason for this gap is the lack of resource personnel who would create a knowledge-sharing platform, as well as a lack of interest from farmers to accept the technology as new normal in their life. The main reason for this lack of interest is the lack of overall awareness and knowledge as to how exactly technology may provide tangible developments monetarily, as well as in an eco-friendly way to create a sustainable development architecture for all stakeholders. As for teaching technology at a root level, although various research works are carried out in the research field, the practicality and applicability of these research works are often overlooked. Apart from applicability, there is a substantial gap in fieldwork where trained professionals can go around teaching the importance of technology which is the obstacle for accepting the technology.

There are minor and major security issues related to hacking in cases of AI, IoT, and robotics that needs further attention from researcher communities. The main problem is due to security issues that would lead to disasters in crop harvesting and would lead to food shortages, thus raising an issue of concerned stakeholders being reluctant to adopt the technology. Furthermore, challenges and scopes are continuous processes that need to be addressed with checks and balances and amended to provide sustainable development with tangible outcomes for the whole community.

2.4 Conclusion

This chapter has highlighted various developments in the field of artificial intelligence, the Internet of Things, and robotics, with a short overview of the challenges that may be faced while adopting such technology. It provides a comprehensive review of the aforementioned sectors of technologies that provide an idea of the current status of intelligent farming. Furthermore, the chapter also highlighted the perceived challenges and security concerns that need to be addressed from the standpoint of human-computer interaction design, usability studies, and strengthening security. The authors believe that this chapter will show researchers working in the agriculture domain the current status and future possibilities contributing to the development of intelligent technology-based farming and agriculture research.

References

[1] Ozguven, M. M. (2018). The newest agricultural technologies. *Current Investigations in Agriculture and Current Research*, 5(1), 573–580.
[2] Hunter, M. C., Smith, R. G., Schipanski, M. E., Atwood, L. W., & Mortensen, D. A. (2017). Agriculture in 2050: Recalibrating targets for sustainable intensification. *Bioscience*, 67(4), 386–391.

[3] Jordan, M. I. (2019). Artificial intelligence—The revolution hasn't happened yet. *Harvard Data Science Review, 1*(1).

[4] Reardon, S. (2018). Artificial neurons compute faster than the human brain. *Nature, January 26,* 2018.

[5] Khanna, A., & Kaur, S. (2019). Evolution of Internet of Things (IoT) and its significant impact in the field of precision agriculture. *Computers and electronics in agriculture, 157,* 218–231.

[6] Bhanumathi, V., & Kalaivanan, K. (2019). The role of geospatial technology with IoT for precision agriculture. In *Cloud computing for geospatial big data analytics* (pp. 225–250). Springer, Cham.

[7] Dorigo, M., Theraulaz, G., & Trianni, V. (2020). Reflections on the future of swarm robotics. *Science Robotics, 5*(49).

[8] Shamshiri, R., Weltzien, C., Hameed, I. A., Yule, I. J., Grift, T. E.., Balasundram, S. K., Pitonakova, L., Ahmad, D., & Chowdhary, G. (2018). Research and development in agricultural robotics: A perspective of digital farming. *International Journal of Agriculture and Biological Engineering, 11*(4), 1–14.

[9] Shadrin, D., Menshchikov, A., Somov, A., Bornemann, G., Hauslage, J., & Fedorov, M. (2019). Enabling precision agriculture through embedded sensing with artificial intelligence. *IEEE Transactions on Instrumentation and Measurement, 69*(7), 4103–4113.

[10] Shadrin, D., Menshchikov, A., Ermilov, D., & Somov, A. (2019). Designing future precision agriculture: Detection of seeds germination using artificial intelligence on a low-power embedded system. *IEEE Sensors Journal, 19*(23), 11573–11582.

[11] Sabanci, K. (2020). Detection of sunn pest-damaged wheat grains using artificial bee colony optimization-based artificial intelligence techniques. *Journal of the Science of Food and Agriculture, 100*(2), 817–824.

[12] Partel, V., Kim, J., Costa, L., Pardalos, P. M., & Ampatzidis, Y. (2020). Smart sprayer for precision weed control using artificial intelligence: Comparison of deep learning frameworks. In *ISAIM*.

[13] Partel, V., Kakarla, S. C., & Ampatzidis, Y. (2019). Development and evaluation of a low-cost and smart technology for precision weed management utilizing artificial intelligence. *Computers and Electronics in Agriculture, 157,* 339–350.

[14] Seyedzadeh, A., Maroufpoor, S., Maroufpoor, E., Shiri, J., Bozorg-Haddad, O., & Gavazi, F. (2020). Artificial intelligence approach to estimate discharge of drip tape irrigation based on temperature and pressure. *Agricultural Water Management, 228,* 105905.

[15] Kaab, A., Sharifi, M., Mobli, H., Nabavi-Pelesaraei, A., & Chau, K. W. (2019). Combined life cycle assessment and artificial intelligence for prediction of output energy and environmental impacts of sugarcane production. *Science of the Total Environment, 664,* 1005–1019.

[16] Liu, H., & Chahl, J. S. (2021). Proximal detecting invertebrate pests on crops using a deep residual convolutional neural network trained by virtual images. *Artificial Intelligence in Agriculture, 5,* 13–23.

[17] Tang, D., Feng, Y., Gong, D., Hao, W., & Cui, N. (2018). Evaluation of artificial intelligence models for actual crop evapotranspiration modeling in mulched and non-mulched maize croplands. *Computers and electronics in agriculture, 152,* 375–384.

[18] Picon, A., Seitz, M., Alvarez-Gila, A., Mohnke, P., Ortiz-Barredo, A., & Echazarra, J. (2019). Crop conditional convolutional neural networks for massive multi-crop plant

disease classification over cell phone acquired images taken on real field conditions. *Computers and Electronics in Agriculture, 167*, 105093.

[19] Sambasivam, G., & Opiyo, G. D. (2021). A predictive machine learning application in agriculture: Cassava disease detection and classification with imbalanced dataset using convolutional neural networks. *Egyptian Informatics Journal, 22*(1), 27–34.

[20] Francis, M., & Deisy, C. (2021). Mathematical and visual understanding of a deep learning model towards m-agriculture for disease diagnosis. *Archives of Computational Methods in Engineering, 28*(3), 1129–1145.

[21] Hu, G., Wu, H., Zhang, Y., & Wan, M. (2019). A low shot learning method for tea leaf's disease identification. *Computers and Electronics in Agriculture, 163*, 104852.

[22] Zhong, F., Chen, Z., Zhang, Y., & Xia, F. (2020). Zero-and few-shot learning for diseases recognition of Citrus aurantium L. using conditional adversarial autoencoders. *Computers and Electronics in Agriculture, 179*, 105828.

[23] Zeng, M., Gao, H., & Wan, L. (2021, April). Few-shot grape leaf diseases classification based on generative adversarial network. *Journal of Physics: Conference Series, 1883*, (1), 012093.

[24] Ashqar, B. A., Abu-Nasser, B. S., & Abu-Naser, S. S. (2019). Plant seedlings classification using deep learning. *International Journal of Academic Information Systems Research 3*(1), 7–14.

[25] Ferentinos, K. P. (2018). Deep learning models for plant disease detection and diagnosis. *Computers and Electronics in Agriculture, 145*, 311–318.

[26] Ozguven, M. M., & Adem, K. (2019). Automatic detection and classification of leaf spot disease in sugar beet using deep learning algorithms. *Physica A: Statistical Mechanics and its Applications, 535*, 122537.

[27] Oppenheim, D., Shani, G., Erlich, O., & Tsror, L. (2019). Using deep learning for image-based potato tuber disease detection. *Phytopathology, 109*(6), 1083–1087.

[28] Zhang, X., Han, L., Dong, Y., Shi, Y., Huang, W., Han, L., González-Moreno, P., Ma, H., Ye, H., & Sobeih, T. (2019). A deep learning-based approach for automated yellow rust disease detection from high-resolution hyperspectral UAV images. *Remote Sensing, 11*(13), 1554.

[29] Arsenovic, M., Karanovic, M., Sladojevic, S., Anderla, A., & Stefanovic, D. (2019). Solving current limitations of deep learning based approaches for plant disease detection. *Symmetry, 11*(7), 939.

[30] Addo-Tenkorang, R., Gwangwava, N., Ogunmuyiwa, E. N., & Ude, A. U. (2019). Advanced animal track-&-trace supply-chain conceptual framework: an internet of things approach. *Procedia Manufacturing, 30*, 56–63.

[31] Al-Khashab, Y., Daoud, R., Majeed, M., & Yasen, M. (2019, March). Drinking water monitoring in Mosul City using IoT. In *2019 International Conference on Computing and Information Science and Technology and Their Applications (ICCISTA)* (pp. 1–5). IEEE.

[32] Jorda Jr, R., Alcabasa, C., Buhay, A., Cruz, E. C., Mendoza, J. P., Tolentino, A., Tolentino, L. K. , Fernandez, E. , Thio-ac, A. , Velasco, J., & Arago, N. (2019). Automated smart wick system-based microfarm using Internet of Things. *arXiv preprint arXiv:1911.01279*.

[33] Bodake, K., Ghate, R., Doshi, H., Jadhav, P., & Tarle, B. (2018). Soil based fertilizer recommendation system using Internet of Things. *MVP Journal of Engineering Sciences, 1*(1), 13–19.

[34] Khummanee, S., Wiangsamut, S., Sorntepa, P., & Jaiboon, C. (2018, October). Automated smart farming for orchids with the internet of things and fuzzy logic. In *2018 International Conference on Information Technology (InCIT)* (pp. 1–6). IEEE.

[35] da Rosa Righi, R., Goldschmidt, G., Kunst, R., Deon, C., & da Costa, C. A. (2020). Towards combining data prediction and Internet of Things to manage milk production on dairy cows. *Computers and Electronics in Agriculture, 169*, 105156.

[36] Chung, W. Y., Luo, R. H., Chen, C. L., Heythem, S., Chang, C. F., Po, C. C., & Li, Y. C. (2019, May). Solar powered monitoring system development for smart farming and Internet of Thing applications. In *Meeting Abstracts. Electrochem. Soc., 28*, 1371–1375.

[37] Ali, R., Pal, A. K., Kumari, S., Karuppiah, M., & Conti, M. (2018). A secure user authentication and key-agreement scheme using wireless sensor networks for agriculture monitoring. *Future Generation Computer Systems, 84*, 200–215.

[38] Harun, A. N., Mohamed, N., Ahmad, R., & Ani, N. N. (2019). Improved Internet of Things (IoT) monitoring system for growth optimization of Brassica chinensis. *Computers and Electronics in Agriculture, 164*, 104836.

[39] Koduru, S., Padala, V. P. R., & Padala, P. (2019). Smart irrigation system using cloud and Internet of Things. In *Proceedings of 2nd international conference on communication, computing and networking* (pp. 195–203). Springer, Singapore.

[40] Mahmud, M. A., Buyamin, S., Mokji, M. M., & Abidin, M. Z. (2018). Internet of things based smart environmental monitoring for mushroom cultivation. *Indonesian Journal of Electrical Engineering and Computer Science, 10*(3), 847–852.

[41] Foughali, K., Fathallah, K., & Frihida, A. (2018). Using cloud IoT for disease prevention in precision agriculture. *Procedia computer science, 130*, 575–582.

[42] Mekala, M. S., & Viswanathan, P. (2019). CLAY-MIST: IoT-cloud enabled CMM index for smart agriculture monitoring system. *Measurement, 134*, 236–244.

[43] Ahmed, N., De, D., & Hussain, I. (2018). Internet of Things (IoT) for smart precision agriculture and farming in rural areas. *IEEE Internet of Things Journal, 5*(6), 4890–4899.

[44] Khoa, T. A., Man, M. M., Nguyen, T. Y., Nguyen, V., & Nam, N. H. (2019). Smart agriculture using IoT multi-sensors: a novel watering management system. *Journal of Sensor and Actuator Networks, 8*(3), 45.

[45] Kamienski, C., Soininen, J. P., Taumberger, M., Dantas, R., Toscano, A., Salmon Cinotti, T., Filev Maia, R., & Torre Neto, A. (2019). Smart water management platform: IoT-based precision irrigation for agriculture. *Sensors, 19*(2), 276.

[46] Kim, S., Lee, M., & Shin, C. (2018). IoT-based strawberry disease prediction system for smart farming. *Sensors, 18*(11), 4051.

[47] Unold, O., Nikodem, M., Piasecki, M., Szyc, K., Maciejewski, H., Bawiec, M., Dobrowolski, P., & Zdunek, M. (2020, June). IoT-based cow health monitoring system. In *International Conference on Computational Science* (pp. 344–356). Springer, Cham.

[48] Khattab, A., Habib, S. E., Ismail, H., Zayan, S., Fahmy, Y., & Khairy, M. M. (2019). An IoT-based cognitive monitoring system for early plant disease forecast. *Computers and Electronics in Agriculture, 166*, 105028.

[49] Foughali, K., Fathallah, K., & Frihida, A. (2019). A cloud-IoT based decision support system for potato pest prevention. *Procedia Computer Science, 160*, 616–623.

[50] Quaglia, G., Visconte, C., Scimmi, L. S., Melchiorre, M., Cavallone, P., & Pastorelli, S. (2019, July). Robot arm and control architecture integration on a UGV for precision

agriculture. In *IFToMM World Congress on Mechanism and Machine Science* (pp. 2339–2348). Springer, Cham.

[51] Jawad, A. M., Jawad, H. M., Nordin, R., Gharghan, S. K., Abdullah, N. F., & Abu-Alshaeer, M. J. (2019). Wireless power transfer with magnetic resonator coupling and sleep/active strategy for a drone charging station in smart agriculture. *IEEE Access, 7,* 139839–139851.

[52] Cantelli, L., Bonaccorso, F., Longo, D., Melita, C. D., Schillaci, G., & Muscato, G. (2019). A small versatile electrical robot for autonomous spraying in agriculture. *AgriEngineering, 1*(3), 391–402.

[53] Pulido Fentanes, J., Badiee, A., Duckett, T., Evans, J., Pearson, S., & Cielniak, G. (2020). Kriging-based robotic exploration for soil moisture mapping using a cosmic-ray sensor. *Journal of Field Robotics, 37*(1), 122–136.

[54] Kim, W. S., Lee, D. H., Kim, Y. J., Kim, T., Lee, W. S., & Choi, C. H. (2021). Stereo-vision-based crop height estimation for agricultural robots. *Computers and Electronics in Agriculture, 181,* 105937.

[55] Kumar, P., & Ashok, G. (2021). Design and fabrication of smart seed sowing robot. *Materials Today: Proceedings, 39,* 354–358.

[56] Thorp, K. R., Thompson, A. L., Harders, S. J., French, A. N., & Ward, R. W. (2018). High-throughput phenotyping of crop water use efficiency via multispectral drone imagery and a daily soil water balance model. *Remote Sensing, 10*(11), 1682.

[57] Mahmud, M. S. A., Abidin, M. S. Z., Mohamed, Z., Abd Rahman, M. K. I., & Iida, M. (2019). Multi-objective path planner for an agricultural mobile robot in a virtual greenhouse environment. *Computers and Electronics in Agriculture, 157,* 488–499.

[58] Elmokadem, T. (2019). Distributed coverage control of quadrotor multi-uav systems for precision agriculture. *IFAC-PapersOnLine, 52*(30), 251–256.

[59] Srivastava, K., Pandey, P. C., & Sharma, J. K. (2020). An approach for route optimization in applications of precision agriculture using UAVs. *Drones, 4*(3), 58.

[60] Raeva, P. L., Šedina, J., & Dlesk, A. (2019). Monitoring of crop fields using multi-spectral and thermal imagery from UAV. *European Journal of Remote Sensing, 52*(sup1), 192–201.

[61] Coral, W., Rossi, C., Curet, O. M., & Castro, D. (2018). Design and assessment of a flexible fish robot actuated by shape memory alloys. *Bioinspiration & biomimetics, 13*(5), 056009.

[62] Chen, X., Zhang, B., & Luo, L. (2018). Multi-feature fusion tree trunk detection and orchard mobile robot localization using camera/ultrasonic sensors. *Computers and Electronics in Agriculture, 147,* 91–108.

[63] Hejazipoor, H., Massah, J., Soryani, M., Vakilian, K. A., & Chegini, G. (2021). An intelligent spraying robot based on plant bulk volume. *Computers and Electronics in Agriculture, 180,* 105859.

[64] Ma, Y., Zhang, W., Qureshi, W. S., Gao, C., Zhang, C., & Li, W. (2021). Autonomous navigation for a wolfberry picking robot using visual cues and fuzzy control. *Information Processing in Agriculture, 8*(1), 15–26.

[65] Tsolakis, N., Bechtsis, D., & Bochtis, D. (2019). Agros: A robot operating system based emulation tool for agricultural robotics. *Agronomy, 9*(7), 403.

[66] Dusadeerungsikul, P. O., & Nof, S. Y. (2019). A collaborative control protocol for agricultural robot routing with online adaptation. *Computers & Industrial Engineering, 135,* 456–466.

[67] Oktarina, Y., Dewi, T., Risma, P., & Nawawi, M. (2020, April). Tomato harvesting arm robot manipulator; a pilot project. In *Journal of Physics: Conference Series* (Vol. 1500, No. 1, p. 012003). IOP Publishing.

[68] Martelloni, L., Fontanelli, M., Pieri, S., Frasconi, C., Caturegli, L., Gaetani, M., Grossi, N. , Magni, S. , Pirchio, M. , Raffaelli, M. , Volterrani, M., & Peruzzi, A. (2019). Assessment of the cutting performance of a robot mower using custom built software. *Agronomy*, *9*(5), 230.

[69] Barakat, M. H., Azar, A. T., & Ammar, H. H. (2019, March). Agricultural service mobile robot modeling and control using artificial fuzzy logic and machine vision. In *International Conference on Advanced Machine Learning Technologies and Applications* (pp. 453–465). Springer, Cham.

[70] Ünal, I., Kabaş, Ö., & Sözer, S. (2020). Real-time electrical resistivity measurement and mapping platform of the soils with an autonomous robot for precision farming applications. *Sensors*, *20*(1), 251.

[71] Pareek, C. M., Tewaria, V. K., Machavarama, R. , Nareb, B. (2021). Optimizing the seed-cell filling performance of an inclined plate seed metering device using integrated ANN-PSO approach. *Artificial Intelligence in Agriculture* 5 (2021): 1–12.

[72] Chen, Z., Zhang, X., Chen, S., & Zhong, F. (2021). A sparse deep transfer learning model and its application for smart agriculture. *Wireless Communications and Mobile Computing, 2021.*

[73] Sarijaloo, F. B., Porta, M., Taslimi, B., & Pardalos, P. M. (2021). Yield performance estimation of corn hybrids using machine learning algorithms. *Artificial Intelligence in Agriculture*, 5, 82–89.

[74] Wei, D., Zhang, F., Ye, Z., Zhu, S., Ji, D., Zhao, J., Zhao, F., & Ding, X. (2021). Effects of intelligent feeding method on the growth, immunity and stress of juvenile Micropterus salmoides. *Artificial Intelligence in Agriculture*.

[75] Wang, P., Hafshejani, B. A., & Wang, D. (2021). An improved multilayer perceptron approach for detecting sugarcane yield production in IoT based smart agriculture. *Microprocessors and Microsystems*, *82*, 103822.

[76] Podder, A. K., Al Bukhari, A., Islam, S., Mia, S., Mohammed, M. A., Kumar, N. M., Cengiz, K., & Abdulkareem, K. H. (2021). IoT based smart agrotech system for verification of Urban farming parameters. *Microprocessors and Microsystems*, *82*, 104025.

[77] Khan, Z., Zahid Khan, M., Ali, S., Abbasi, I. A., Ur Rahman, H., Zeb, U., Khattak, H., & Huang, J. (2021). Internet of Things-based smart farming monitoring system for bolting reduction in onion farms. *Scientific Programming, 2021.*

[78] Almalki, F. A., Soufiene, B. O., Alsamhi, S. H., & Sakli, H. (2021). A low-cost platform for environmental smart farming monitoring system based on IoT and UAVs. *Sustainability*, *13*(11), 5908.

[79] Rajalakshmi, T. S., Panikulam, P., Sharad, P. K., & Nair, R. R. (2021, July). Development of a small scale cartesian coordinate farming robot with deep learning based weed detection. In *Journal of Physics: Conference Series* (Vol. 1969, No. 1, p. 012007). IOP Publishing.

[80] Khadatkar, A., Mathur, S. M., Dubey, K., & BhusanaBabu, V. (2021). Development of embedded automatic transplanting system in seedling transplanters for precision agriculture. *Artificial Intelligence in Agriculture*.

[81] Mondal, M. R. H., Bharati, S., & Podder, P. (2021). CO-IRv2: Optimized InceptionResNetV2 for COVID-19 detection from chest CT images. *PLoS One*, *16*(10), e0259179.

[82] Mondal, M. R. H., Bharati, S., & Podder, P. (2021). Diagnosis of COVID-19 using machine learning and deep learning: A review. *Current Medical Imaging*, *17*(12), 1403–1418.

Chapter 3

Artificial Intelligence and the Blockchain in Smart Agriculture: Emergence, Opportunities, and Challenges

Anoop V. S.
Kerala Blockchain Academy, Kerala University of Digital Sciences, Innovation and Technology, Thiruvananthapuram, India

Adarsh S.
Kerala Blockchain Academy, Kerala University of Digital Sciences, Innovation and Technology, Thiruvananthapuram, India

Asharaf S.
Kerala Blockchain Academy, Kerala University of Digital Sciences, Innovation and Technology, Thiruvananthapuram, India

3.1 Introduction

One of the most challenging problems facing the modern world is producing enough food to feed everyone on earth. Agriculture has been one of the domains to be given less attention in the recent past due to several reasons, such as the

DOI: 10.1201/9781003299059-3

undervaluation of the workforce in the sector. According to some statistics, more than 1,000 farmers in India are giving up farming because the youngest in the family is not interested in farming activities. Even though agricultural producers yield 17% more food now than they did just two decades ago, the statistics show that around 900 million people across the world are facing food security issues, including developed countries like the United States of America. This is a serious issue that needs to be addressed in an expedited manner as food production needs to increase by 70% to feed the world by 2050 to satisfy the growing population. Technologies play a crucial role in agriculture, and the demand for technology-enabled farming and agriculture has grown exponentially in the recent past due to the widespread adoption of ICT-enabled systems. The so-called digital smart agriculture comprises technologies such as AI and machine learning, the IoT, and blockchain (Ciruela-Lorenzo et al., 2020) (Adamides, 2020) (Martini et al., 2021). These technologies will help the agriculture sector keep pace and aid stakeholders in solving issues related to poor storage and sanitation systems, low crop yields, and political upheaval, to name a few.

Even though the need for food rises daily with the increased population, the disconnect between the market and the farmer is one of the major reasons farmers receive poor profits. Moreover, there is no appropriate demand-supply analysis, which leads to over- and underproduction. Middlemen manipulated the agro-markets with the black market and hoarding, causing inflation and affecting farmers and consumers badly. Farmer networks across the country are decentralized and distributed and mostly unorganized, lacking yield and profit.

Blockchain technology, known after the celebrated cryptocurrency Bitcoin, is highly acclaimed for its decentralized and distributed infrastructure connecting people across the globe in a peer-to-peer manner without any intermediaries (Nofer et al., 2017) (Zheng et al., 2018). Blockchain technology provides an auditable and tamper-proof distributed ledger, ensuring trust, provenance, and data sanctity. The disruption made by blockchain technology in the financial world can be leveraged in the agriculture sector by forming a completely decentralized and distributed network of farmers trustworthy for consumers without any intermediaries. Tracing produce from farm to fork is a tedious process in the current scenario that can be performed more efficiently by the tamper-resistant data store of the blockchain with a single version of the truth across the globe (Zheng et al., 2018) (Lin et al., 2018). Rather than following more complex digital adoptions, the network itself can provide the backbone infrastructure, ensuring trust, transparency, and traceability, making the process simpler and more efficient.

Artificial intelligence (AI) and blockchain technologies have significant applications in the agricultural sector where current processes can be eliminated or improved. This chapter discusses how the blockchain and AI can enable potential transformations by enabling smart farming principles in agriculture. The major contributions of this chapter can be summarized as follows:

■ It presents prominent and recent literature on using exponential technologies such as the blockchain and AI in the agriculture sector.

■ It discusses a case study on AgroChain, a blockchain-powered transparent marketplace application developed by the Kerala Blockchain Academy.

■ Finally, the future research dimensions of using blockchain and AI technologies for the agriculture sector are discussed.

Section 3.2 discusses some of the recent research advancements using AI and the blockchain for smart agriculture. Section 3.3 outlines some of the areas where technologies such as AI and the blockchain can be used for the betterment of agriculture with a focus on AgroChain, an agricultural traceability solution proposed by the Kerala Blockchain Academy. Section 3.4 describes some of the future research dimensions using the blockchain and AI that can be used in the agriculture sector. Section 3.5 discusses some of the limitations of using AI and the blockchain in agriculture, and Section 3.6 concludes the chapter.

3.2 Literature Review

3.2.1 Overview

There are several approaches and techniques reported in recent literature regarding adopting cutting-edge, new-age technologies such as AI, the IoT, and the blockchain in the agriculture sector that aims to increase productivity, eliminating intermediaries by building resilient supply chain management and thus improving the complex procedures involved between farm and fork. Some of those prominent approaches that discuss the use of AI and the blockchain for the agriculture domain are discussed in this section.

3.2.2 Artificial Intelligence in Agriculture

Farmers face many challenges such as weather forecasting, analyzing climate conditions, and monitoring the health of crops, to name a few. Recently, AI and machine learning have been used extensively in agriculture to tackle many of these challenges. Innovative developments in the field of deep learning have paved the way for developing systems that can take decisions quickly and efficiently for agricultural decision-making processes. AI can help farmers make better decisions on the right time to seed and harvest and on applying required fertilizers at the right time. By analyzing past weather data, machine learning models can predict what climatic conditions will be throughout the year. Analyzing the health status of crops using drones is another area where AI is heavily used, along with predictive analytics capabilities. The AI-based automated monitoring of agriculture using wireless sensor networks has been reported recently (Vijayakumar and Balakrishnan, 2021). This paper presented the potential of AI in agriculture for implementing intelligence from the data collected from wireless sensors. When the authors compared their proposed approach with the state-of-the-art, they could achieve 95% accuracy and claim that the proposed approach can potentially save 92% of water (Vijayakumar and Balakrishnan, 2021).

Jinha Jung et al. discussed the potential of remote sensing and AI for improving the resilience of agricultural production systems (Jung et al., 2021). The authors conducted a systematic review on the use of recent technological advances in remote sensing and AI to improve the resilience of agricultural systems and presented opportunities for the development of tools for the agricultural and human nutritional challenges that may shortly arise (Jung et al., 2021).

To enable sustainable and precision agriculture, nanotechnology and AI can be combined, as discussed by Peng Zhang et al. in their recent work (Zhang et al., 2021). The authors outlined that the convergence of precision agriculture, where farmers respond in real time to changes in crop growth with nanotechnology and AI, offers exciting opportunities for sustainable food production.

A recent work that compares and summarizes various research projects implemented in several European countries was recently reported by Linaza et al. (Linaza et al., 2021). The authors stated that the AI technologies improve decision support at the farm level and allow farmers to apply the optimal number of inputs for each crop, thereby boosting yields and reducing water use and greenhouse gas emissions. This work concluded that there are still a lot of avenues where AI can be used to its full potential in the agricultural sector.

The significant and ever-increasing role of AI, the IoT, and big data was summarized by Misra et al. in a review article (Misra et al., 2020). They discussed the role of these disruptive technologies in several areas in agriculture, such as greenhouse monitoring, intelligent farm machines, drone-based crop imaging, supply chain modernization, social media in the food industry, food quality assessment, and food safety using blockchain-based digital traceability solutions (Misra et al., 2020).

Another recent work that audits various applications of AI in agriculture, such as irrigation, weeding, spraying with the help of sensors, and other means embedded in robots and drones, was reported by Talaviya et al. (Talaviya et al., 2020). This paper surveyed the several significant works of many researchers to identify the current implementations of automation in agriculture and weeding systems through robots and drones (Talaviya et al., 2020).

3.2.3 Blockchain in Agriculture

Blockchain technology, introduced as a tamper-proof data capturing mechanism for the famous cryptocurrency Bitcoin, is considered to be one of the most disruptive technologies since the advent of the Internet. This technology has the potential to change the way businesses function by decentralizing functionalities by eliminating middlemen in business processes. Sectors such as finance, identity management, charity, banking, and insurance now heavily use blockchain platforms for secure data management. Recent years have witnessed blockchain technology being heavily used in the agriculture sector, with many proof-of-concepts being field-tested in problems related to smart farming, agricultural supply chain, and crowdfunding for agriculture, to name a few. Some of those prominent and related works reported in the literature are discussed here. The easy availability of sensors has fuelled the use of IoT devices in agriculture that generates large quantities of data in a short period. This has several applications in areas such as precision farming but at the same time poses several challenges related to quantifying the trustworthiness of the data. Pincheira et al. proposed a method using low-cost IoT devices that act as trustworthy data sources for a blockchain-based water management system used in precision agriculture (Pincheira et al., 2021). This approach outlined the use of digital infrastructure technologies for building a credible and trustworthy ecosystem that incentivizes virtuous behaviours in agricultural practices (Pincheira et al., 2021).

While agricultural production uses the latest advanced machines, pre-harvesting and post-harvesting processes still use traditional methodologies such as tracing, storing, and publishing agricultural data (Pranto et al., 2021). There exists a huge disconnect between actual agricultural production and consumers. As a consequence, farmers are not getting the required funding for production, and many anomalies and delays exist in the payment processes. On the other hand, consumers are not getting updated information on harvesting or the trace or origin of the agricultural products that prevent them from getting high-quality products at affordable prices. Blockchain, IoT devices, and smart contracts can eliminate or reduce the burden if integrated and used properly (Pranto et al., 2021).

An interesting case study that highlighted the use of AgroChain with BigchainDB for building an agricultural product supply chain was reported by Orjuela et al. (Orjuela et al., 2021). To eliminate issues related to trust that occur in centralized systems, this case study proposed the use of a platform using a database based on blockchain technologies. There is a lack of digital marketplaces for trading agricultural goods. Due to this, farmers who work very hard are not getting the required and sufficient payment for their products. Leduc et al. proposed a blockchain-based innovative farming marketplace that supports the trading of agricultural goods between farmers and potentially interested third-party stakeholders (Leduc et al., 2021). While many of the already existing blockchain-based agricultural innovations focus on traceability and tracking, the "FarMarketplace" focuses on trading.

Lei Hang et al. proposed a secure fish farm platform based on blockchain for agriculture data integrity (Hang et al., 2020). The authors used smart contracts to automate the data processing in the fish farm and implement a proof-of-concept using Hyperledger Fabric to showcase the potential applications of the proposed approach.

A detailed review paper that discussed the integration of the blockchain and the IoT in precision agriculture was reported by Torky and Hassanein (Torky and Hassanein, 2020). Their comprehensive survey not only highlighted the importance of integrating the blockchain and the IoT in agriculture but also proposed novel blockchain models that can solve major challenges in the domain.

A bibliometric analysis that maps research trends in blockchain technology in the food and agriculture sector has been reported by Niknejad et al. (Niknejad et al., 2021). Another notable work that models blockchain-enabled traceability in the agriculture supply chain was added to the literature very recently (Kamble et al., 2020). The findings from the study suggest that traceability is the most significant reason for blockchain technology implementation, followed by auditability, immutability, and provenance (Kamble et al., 2020).

On carefully reviewing the related literature on the application of AI and the blockchain in the field of agriculture, the authors could observe that many of the approaches are still in the infancy stage and need more research and development efforts to take that to a mature level. There is active research happening in the use of technologies such as the blockchain, AI, and the IoT for the betterment of the agriculture sector. In the next section, the authors present a case study of AgroChain, a blockchain-powered decentralized, transparent marketplace developed by the Kerala Blockchain Academy. AgroChain was one of the very first blockchain proofs-of-concept in India that discussed the potential of blockchain technology in the agricultural domain.

3.3 Case Study: AgroChain – A Blockchain-Powered Transparent Marketplace

AgroChain is a blockchain-powered transparent agricultural marketplace developed by the Kerala Blockchain Academy (KBA, www.kba.ai) under its "Blockchain for Societal Good" initiative. The platform aims to bring together farmers and consumers under one umbrella and enable a cooperative farming ecosystem by eliminating intermediaries and third parties. In short, AgroChain provides a transparent, tamper-proof, decentralized market ecosystem where farmers and buyers can come together to trade agricultural products effectively. An overall workflow of AgroChain is shown in Figure 3.1.

AgroChain helps create a blockchain-enabled cooperative farming approach that provides a transparent and trusted platform for farmers and investors/customers to cultivate healthy food with better profit. AgroChain aims to implement a zero-debt farming model for kitchen gardens to corporate farms with appropriate market predictions to meet the demand-supply ratio. The biggest challenge in agro-markets is the disconnect between farmers and consumers. This can be solved only through a cooperative platform like AgroChain, where farmers and customers join hands together with experts to cultivate good quality crops for their needs.

Any genuine farmer can register details about their farmland, expertise, previous yield, location, etc., in the AgroChain. The agro-experts and related agencies

AGROCHAIN

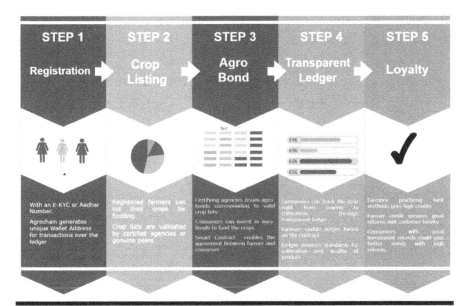

Figure 3.1   The overall workflow of AgroChain

Source: www.iiitmk.ac.in/kba/agrochain/index.html, accessed August 29, 2021

can suggest insights for the farmer regarding suitable crops, expected yield, market predictions, climate details, soil data, etc., with which farmer can finalize the best crop for the farmland that can ensure better yield and maximum profit. Intelligent smart contracts will evaluate the total cost of cultivation, expected yield, and profit at the time of reaping. Based on market predictions, smart contracts can divide the lump sum amount into smaller investment units called agro-bonds.

Agro-bond specifications, once generated, are shared among all the investors/customers for bidding. Investors can view complete details such as the credibility of farmers, farming strategy, expected yield, market prediction, etc., through the transparent agro-ledger. With agro-bonds, farmers have the double benefit of raising initial funds and an assured market, which assures better profit. Farmers have to periodically update the agro-ledger crop details with sufficient information as mentioned in the smart contracts in order to gain credibility. Investors can keep track of the agro-ledger to know the cultivation progress and the market for the produce. AgroChain uses a supervised learning process for evaluating the credibility of farmers as well as investors through the transparent ledger, which reduces the chances of fraud. Smart contracts can provide inputs for machine learning models to learn from demand-supply ratios and make future market predictions, where farmers and investors can

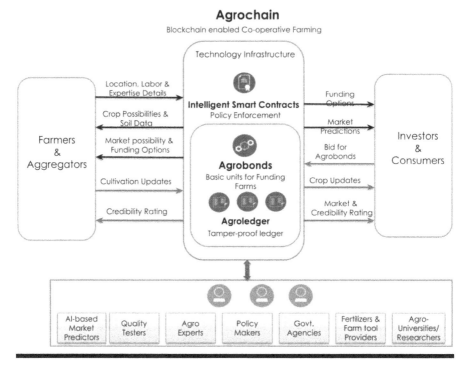

Figure 3.2   AgroChain architecture

leverage the potential of cultivating a crop with high returns in the coming future. A detailed architecture of AgroChain is shown in Figure 3.2.

The key features of AgroChain are:

1. **Agro-bonds**: Financial instruments for trading products over the AgroChain marketplace that are issued as ERC-20 tokens over the public blockchain and can be used to pre-fund farmers for farming and the purchase of products over the marketplace. The token value can be pegged to fiat currency (for regulatory concerns) for easier processing. Token supply limit will be dynamically adjusted based on the production and funding over the platform. The digital tokens can be traded over a simple wallet application included with the AgroChain marketplace. Agro-bonds makes bookkeeping and auditing easier for all the stakeholders.

2. **Smart contracts**: All the farming procedure protocols and financial agreements will be converted into digital smart contracts running over a public blockchain network. Smart contracts are self-executing codes that process business logic and help in user authorization and the security of data access over a blockchain.

3. **Agro-ledger**: Immutable distributed public ledger over the blockchain network, ensuring traceability and transparency of all the transactions.

The major pain points addressed by AgroChain are:

1. AgroChain can maintain the proper demand-supply ratio with market predictions and consumer-farmer cooperation and can avoid crop wastage and price fluctuations and assure a good return for investors and farmers.
2. India's food consumption, currently valued at $370 billion, is expected to reach $1 trillion by 2025. Agro-bonds will pave the way for investors to channel their investments wisely and safely into the agriculture segment to earn better returns.
3. The concept of zero-debt farming will ensure a quick inflow of money into farming and protects farmers from debts and high-interest rates of bank loans and other lending mechanisms. It can eventually reduce cultivation costs and ensure better returns.
4. By joining the AgroChain, agro-allied industries such as the fertilizer and bio-manure industry, mechanized tools, irrigation systems, etc., can ensure uninterrupted services by knowing the stages of cultivation and the needs of farmers from the agro-ledger, which could boost their business. Moreover, farmers can ensure quality services for their farms at better rates.
5. Consumers can escape price fluctuations and receive quality products as every step of cultivation is transparent and satisfies the required standards.
6. Cooperative farming can build customer loyalty, which can increase the value of products as farmers can cultivate according to the needs of consumers.
7. There is no need to have huge farmlands. Even small-scale farmers and kitchen-gardens can sell their products and yield better profits. Rent and electricity charges for cold storage and warehouses will be considerably reduced as the products have buyers readily available.
8. There is guaranteed healthy food for society, as ill practices in farming lead to the poor credit rating of farmers, and they will eventually be out of the network. The investment in food is for generations to survive healthily in this world.
9. Agriculture is an everlasting business domain, and AgroChain promotes safer investment for better profit, better food, and healthy living.

3.4 AI and Blockchain for Smart Agriculture: Future Research Dimensions

It is highly evident that AI and the blockchain play a significant role in the agriculture sector, but this has not yet been explored in its full potential. There are a lot of avenues where AI and the blockchain can be exploited to solve many of the major issues and challenges faced by the agricultural sector. AI can find several applications in agriculture, such as crop yield prediction and forecasting prices for crops. Machine learning algorithms powered by deep learning can analyze large datasets and make predictions on crop yield and the market price for the crops that will help farmers plan and ensure better pricing for their products. Disease diagnosing and taking preventive measures is one of the highly important activities in agriculture. AI-powered image processing techniques can help identify plant diseases with a single image and recommend appropriate remedial measures. Even though some prototypes are being introduced, production-level systems need to be developed and implemented. Predictive analytics, a type of analytics that predicts the outcome using sufficient data points, has sound applications in agricultural data analytics. These predictive analytics can provide meaningful insights to the farmers, such as the right time to sow seeds, apply the fertilizers, and reap the crops. As we know, AI cannot work in isolation. Combining AI with technologies such as the IoT and the blockchain will have more applications if the interoperability and data management aspects are carefully designed. For example, AI combined with the IoT may find an interesting application in crop and soil monitoring. Sensors placed in the soil can detect soil defects and nutrient deficiencies and can alert farmers while recommending the appropriate nutrients that should be supplied with the help of machine learning algorithms. There are several other research and development areas in agriculture such as agriculture robots and drones, intelligent irrigation and spraying techniques, combining precision farming with predictive analytics, pest detection applications using image processing, and using AI in agricultural supply chains, to name a few.

As a credible and tamper-proof data capturing infrastructure, the blockchain finds several potential applications in the agriculture domain. This technological innovation will eliminate third parties and other sorts of intermediaries from the agriculture ecosystem where farmers can transact directly without the need for a trusted third party. In the current centralized scenario, farmers are not getting the deserved price for their commodities due to the unfair play that exists in the ecosystem, and as a result, farmers are forced to leave the agriculture profession. The blockchain offers several advantages and leverages the power of decentralized, immutable, and tamper-proof ledgers that can record transactions, enabling the notion of trust on the platform. Agricultural insurance is one such area where the blockchain may find several use-cases in agriculture. Extreme weather conditions and natural calamities always put agricultural production and food security at risk. This will frequently occur in the future for several reasons, such as global warming and climate change. The normal procedure farmers currently follow is to pay an insurance premium before they start cultivation, and in case of some unfavourable events such as natural calamities, the insurance company pays back the insurance payout. There exists a complex set of procedures in this process, and there are many intermediaries involved. Even after a long period, farmers won't receive the insurance payout due to several factors such as delays from the bank. A blockchain-based solution can solve this issue by directly crediting the amount to the farmers, and the delay with the current system can be solved.

The agricultural supply chain is another area where multiparty involvement heavily occurs. From farm to fork, there are several processes and people that make the entire process complex and time-consuming. Moreover, the agricultural supply chain suffers from many problems, such as food traceability, food safety, and quality. As a result, agricultural producers find it difficult to establish trust with consumers, and the lack of transparency affects the entire process. Here, the blockchain comes into the picture, where data can be recorded on a blockchain platform and verified by end consumers. This will eliminate several other problems, such as the question of food quality and issues with transactions. The current blockchain implementations in the agricultural supply chain are still in their infancy stage and need more research and development to implement them in full swing. The interoperability, transaction speed, and oracles need a considerable amount of attention for building a resilient supply chain. To enable this, producers, consumers, and regulatory bodies should come together with sufficient policy frameworks.

3.5 The Limitations of AI and the Blockchain in Smart Agriculture

There are several advantages in using AI and the blockchain in the agricultural sector, and they offer innovative practices that enable smart agriculture processes. While AI can train machines using large quantities of data that enable them to take intelligent decisions, blockchain technology can bring in the notion of trust by recording the data in a tamper-proof fashion. While these new-age technologies offer several advantages, there are some disadvantages as well. One of the major disadvantages or challenges associated with implementing AI-based solutions is the high cost of implementation. AI solutions may not be affordable for common farmers as they may not be able to buy and use sophisticated hardware or software services. Large farms that are backed by corporates and other organizations can afford them for yielding better productivity. Another concern with the implementation of AI in agriculture is that it may replace several humans in the process as a machine can perform tasks that are labour-intensive for humans. As mentioned, blockchain technology is still in its infancy stage, where a lot of research needs to be done to adopt it for several mainstream applications to reach its full potential. For example, the scalability aspect of the blockchain is crucial for establishing a larger network with several nodes. Also, the transaction speed needs to be increased to near real time and for up-to-the-minute details. But it is important to note that many research and development activities are happening to address these challenges, and the coming years may witness a large-scale adoption of these technologies to eliminate many associated challenges.

3.6 Conclusion

Agriculture is one of the few domains where technological innovations are applied at a slow pace. Very recently, the agriculture domain has witnessed a high momentum in applying technological advancements for eliminating several pain points and inconsistencies that have been prevalent for a long time. Recent literature shows that cutting-edge technologies such as AI, the blockchain, and the IoT can solve many issues faced by various stakeholders in the agriculture ecosystem. With advancements in information and communication technologies, the effectiveness in collecting, storing, processing, and analyzing has been increased multifold. AI systems can use vast amounts of data to analyze patterns and derive conclusions and insights from them. The credibility and sanctity of data is another concern, but with the advent of blockchain technology, the data can be stored in a tamper-proof and immutable ledger. These technologies significantly improve the quality of the processes in agriculture and help build a trusted ecosystem where producers and consumers follow fair practices. This chapter discussed the emergence and applications of AI and the blockchain in promoting a smart agriculture ecosystem where the notion of trust can be taken out from the central authorities and transferred to the platform. It has used AgroChain, which was developed by Kerala Blockchain Academy, as a case study to showcase the efforts in building a trust-free ecosystem in agriculture using the blockchain. Some of the recent trends and future research dimensions using AI and the blockchain in the agriculture sector were also discussed. The authors believe that this chapter will be highly useful for researchers, analysts, and technology practitioners working in the agriculture sector.

References

Adamides, G. (2020). A review of climate-smart agriculture applications in Cyprus. *Atmosphere* 11(9).

Ciruela-Lorenzo, A.M., Del-Aguila-Obra, A. R., Padilla-Meléndez, A., & Plaza-Angulo, J. J. (2020). Digitalization of agri-cooperatives in the smart agriculture context. proposal of a digital diagnosis tool. *Sustainability* 12(4).

Hang, L., Ullah, I., & Kim, D-H. (2020). A secure fish farm platform based on blockchain for agriculture data integrity. *Computers and Electronics in Agriculture* 170:105251.

Jung, J., Maeda, M., Chang, A., Bhandari, M., Ashapure, A., & Landivar-Bowles, J. (2021). The potential of remote sensing and artificial intelligence as tools to improve the resilience of agriculture production systems. *Current Opinion in Biotechnology* 70:15–22.

Kamble, S. S., Gunasekaran, A., & Sharma, R. (2020). Modeling the blockchain enabled traceability in agriculture supply chain. *International Journal of Information Management* 52:101967.

Leduc, G., Kubler, S., & Georges, J-P. (2021). Innovative blockchain-based farming marketplace and smart contract performance evaluation. *Journal of Cleaner Production* 306:127055.

Lin, J., Shen, Z., Zhang, A., & Chai, Y. (2018). Blockchain and IoT Based Food Traceability for Smart Agriculture. *ICCSE'18: Proceedings of the 3rd International Conference on Crowd Science and Engineering.* Pp. 1–6. https://doi.org/10.1145/3265689.3265692

Linaza, M. T., Posada, J., Bund, J., Eisert, P., Quartulli, M., Döllner, J., Pagani, A., Olaizola, I. G., Barriguinha, A., Moysiadis, T., & Lucat, L. (2021). Data-driven artificial intelligence applications for sustainable precision agriculture. *Agronomy* 11(6).

Martini, B. G., Helfer, G. A., Victória Barbosa, J. L., Espinosa Modolo, R. C., da Silva, M. R., de Figueiredo, R. M., Sales Mendes, A., Silva, L. A., & Quietinho Leithardt, V. R. (2021). IndoorPlant: A model for intelligent services in indoor agriculture based on context histories. *Sensors* 21(5).

Misra, N. N., Dixit, Y., Al-Mallahi, A., Singh Bhullar, M., Upadhyay, R., & Martynenko, A. (2020). IoT, big data and artificial intelligence in agriculture and food industry. *IEEE Internet of Things Journal* 1.

Niknejad, N., Ismail, W., Bahari, M., Hendradi, R., & Zaki Salleh, A. (2021). Mapping the research trends on blockchain technology in food and agriculture industry: A bibliometric analysis. *Environmental Technology & Innovation* 21:101272.

Nofer, M., Gomber, P., Hinz, O., & Schiereck, D. (2017). Blockchain. *Business & Information Systems Engineering* 59(3):183–87.

Orjuela, K. G., Gordillo, Gaona-García, P. A., & Montenegro Marin, C. E. (2021). Towards an agriculture solution for product supply chain using blockchain: Case study Agro-Chain with BigchainDB. *Acta Agriculturae Scandinavica, Section B — Soil & Plant Science* 71(1):1–16.

Pincheira, M., Vecchio, M., Giaffreda, R. & Kanhere, S. S. (2021). Cost-effective IoT devices as trustworthy data sources for a blockchain-based water management system in precision agriculture. *Computers and Electronics in Agriculture* 180:105889.

Pranto, T. H., Noman, A. A., Mahmud, A., & Bahalul Haque, A. K. M. (2021). Blockchain and smart contract for IoT enabled smart agriculture. *PeerJ Computer Science* 7:e407.

Talaviya, T., Shah, D., Patel, N., Yagnik, H., & Shah, M. (2020). Implementation of artificial intelligence in agriculture for optimisation of irrigation and application of pesticides and herbicides. *Artificial Intelligence in Agriculture* 4:58–73.

Torky, M., & A. E. Hassanein. (2020). Integrating blockchain and the Internet of Things in precision agriculture: Analysis, opportunities, and challenges. *Computers and Electronics in Agriculture* 178:105476.

Vijayakumar, V., & Balakrishnan, N. (2021). Artificial intelligence-based agriculture automated monitoring systems Using WSN. *Journal of Ambient Intelligence and Humanized Computing* 12(7):8009–16.

Zhang, P., Guo, Z., Ullah, S., Melagraki, G., Afantitis, A., & Lynch, I. (2021). Nanotechnology and artificial intelligence to enable sustainable and precision agriculture. *Nature Plants* 7(7):864–76.

Zheng, Z., Xie, S., Dai, H-N., Chen, X., & Wang, H. (2018). Blockchain challenges and opportunities: A survey. *International Journal of Web and Grid Services* 14:352.

Chapter 4

Artificial Intelligence and Internet of Things Enabled Smart Farming for Sustainable Development: The Future of Agriculture

M. Thilagu
Avinashilingam Institute for Home Science and Higher Education for Women, Coimbatore, India

J. Jayasudha
Sri Ramakrishna College of Arts and Science for Women, Coimbatore, India

4.1 Introduction

Agriculture is an ancient industry that humans have engaged in that has laid the foundation for human civilization. Due to the industrial revolution and the introduction of machinery, demand has reduced gradually due to more yields. Problems such as cost of production, damage to crops, pests, and diseases continue to restrict

DOI: 10.1201/9781003299059-4

the agricultural environment. To solve these issues, we should rely on science and technology. Artificial intelligence (AI) will help satisfy the requirements using smart solutions.

The annual agricultural cycle is made up of several activities related to crop growth and harvest. Loosening the soil, watering, sowing, spraying for fertilizer, and transferring plants are all crucial activities. Figure 4.1 depicts the various stages of farming, such as soil preparation, seed sowing, adding fertilizers, irrigation, weed control, harvesting, and storage.

Soil preparation: This is the first step in farming and involves breaking up large clumps and removing debris from the soil for seed sowing.

Seed sowing: At this stage, the space between two seeds and the depth at which seeds are planted are monitored and cared for. Climatic factors such as temperature, humidity, and rainfall are critical during this stage.

Adding fertilizers: Soil fertility is crucial for growing nutritious and healthy crops. Because fertilizers supply nutrients to agricultural fields that complement the essential elements found naturally in the soil, fertilizers should be

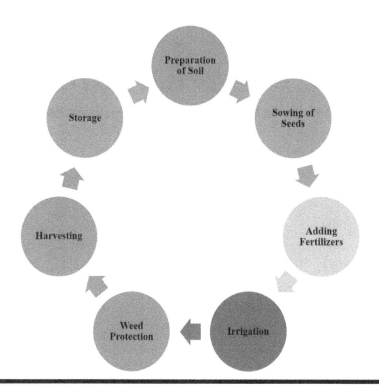

Figure 4.1 Agricultural cycle

used to offer plant nutrients like nitrogen, phosphorus, and potassium. This stage determines the crop's quality.

Irrigation: It is more necessary in farming to keep the soil moist and humid. Crop growth can be hampered by under or overwatering, which, if not done correctly, can result in crop damage.

Weed control: Weeds are surplus plants that grow very close to crops in agricultural fields. Increased weeds reduce productivity, raise production expenses, obstruct harvesting, and degrade crop quality.

Harvesting: This is the process of gathering mature crops from the field. More labourers and money are usually involved. Cleaning, sorting, packing, and refrigeration are all part of the post-harvest process.

Storage: Other than during agricultural seasons, when crops are packed and transported, storage is the post-harvest phase during which products are held safely to ensure food security.

4.1.1 Challenges in Traditional Farming

■ Climate factors, including temperature, rainfall, and humidity, all have a role in the agricultural lifecycle. Farmers are finding it increasingly difficult to make judgments about soil preparation, seeding, and harvesting as a result of increased pollution and deforestation.

■ In order to develop crops, nutrients such as nitrogen (N), phosphorous (P), and potassium (K) are essential for soil. A deficit in these nutrients causes deficiency in the soil, which results in poor crop output.

■ Weed control is very important. Weeds will harm crop growth if not regulated because they will absorb the maximum amount of nutrients from the soil. This causes soil depletion, which has an impact on crop growth.

4.2 Smart Farming

Smart farming is a relatively new concept in modern agriculture, referring to the management of farms utilizing cutting-edge information and communication technology to increase the volume and quality of products produced while lowering the amount of human labour required. Because of the growing importance of smart farming, and issues such as the increasing global population and demand for higher crop yields, there is a need to efficiently use natural resources with the sophistication of information and communication technology (Gorli & Yamini, 2017). Smart farming is far more efficient than traditional farming. Smart farming helps with livestock monitoring, greenhouses, precision farming, and pet tracking, among other things. In the Internet of Things (IoT), sensors are critical for data collection, particularly in agriculture.

4.3 Smart Agriculture for Sustainable Development

The key to improving sustainable agriculture is smart farming. For monitoring farms, IoT drones, sensors, computers, and analytical tools are employed that collect data used to gain insights and promote smart farming. The IoT not only monitors farms but also employs sensors to track humidity, soil moisture, temperature, and light, all of which aid in growth. It enables farmers to keep track of their fields at all times and apply precise inputs. Crops, soil, fields, livestock, and storage facilities are all essential aspects that influence production, and sensor-based systems are employed to monitor them. Precision farming, predictive modelling, and planning are all aided by drones, autonomous robots, and actuators. The following are some of the advantages or benefits of employing sensors in agriculture:

■ It is cheaper and easier, simple to set up and operate, and can be controlled remotely.

■ It is mostly used to meet the demand for higher yields with limited resources of water, fertilizer, and seeds.

■ It is primarily used to measure soil temperature at various levels, humidity, wetness in leaves, rainfall, wind direction, and air pressure, among others.

■ Sensors are used to spray pesticides and fertilizers from agricultural drones.

4.4 AI in Agriculture

AI is one of the emerging technologies in agriculture (Agrawal & Kamboj, 2019). Agriculture has been elevated to a new level with the application of AI-based equipment and tools, and crop production, real-time monitoring, harvesting, processing, and marketing have all improved as a result of this technology (Microsoft AI is using sensors to make farming and healthcare smart, 2019). All agricultural activities are monitored in real-time, the next level of activity is planned based on the information gathered, and necessary measures are taken. Figure 4.2 portrays the applications of AI, such as crop and soil monitoring, disease diagnosis, crop yield prediction, predictive insight, weather forecasting, and agriculture.

4.4.1 AI for Field Condition Management

Farmers are using computer vision and deep-learning algorithms to scan fields and create field maps for in-depth analysis. A positive initiative by Microsoft is the FarmBeats project, which works with farmers to increase productivity and reduce costs.

■ **Soil health** – By monitoring soil health and getting information regarding moisture level, pH level, or nutritional deficiency in the soil. Trace Genomics,

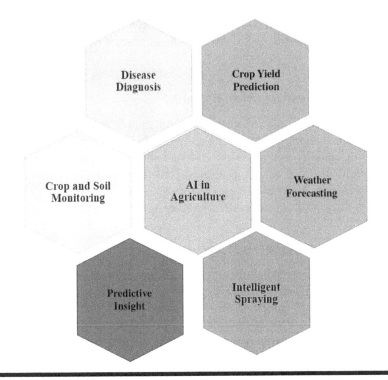

Figure 4.2 **AI in agriculture**

a California-based company, supports analyzing soil, which is done through machine learning, which will be very helpful for growers.

▪ **Water management** – Applications based on AI are used in irrigation systems and to predict dew point temperature.

4.4.2 AI for Crop Management

AI technologies (Fabian Schmidt, 2014) support farmers in getting abundant yields, selecting the best crops and seeds, and resource utilization.

▪ **Monitoring crops**: AI and drone-based monitoring are used nowadays to assess the health and status of crops. Using AI algorithms, SkySquirrel Technologies Inc. provides a detailed health analysis report of vineyards.

▪ **Disease detection**: Diagnosing diseases and pests and checking plant nutrition levels is very important in farming. To diagnose these problems, software called FarmShot can inform growers where fertilizers are needed and in what quantity, as it delivers the images directly to the application of scouting and prescription.

■ **Weed control**: AI models are used to detect and discriminate against harmful weed growth on the farm and guide farmers to take necessary action against it.

4.4.3 AI for Livestock Management

AI also helps farmers monitor the health of farm animals, which enables us to find out early sickness and injuries, making an infected animal isolated from the herd. With robotic milking machines and AI-based sensing systems, it is possible to assess the milk quality of cows. Cainthus is an AI technology-based dairy company that monitors cattle behaviour using a cow facial recognition system. It helps with increased production and reduces stress levels on the cows.

4.4.4 AI for Precision Agriculture

Precision agriculture is making use of AI to reinforce agriculture. With the help of AI, farmers can get guidance about the right sowing time, nutrient management time, crop rotation and harvesting time, and so on.

■ **Handling labour shortage**: Only very few are interested in farming, and insufficient labour dealing with farm-oriented work is very complicated. Now, AI-powered machines are implemented on farms to sort out this issue, such as by assisting farmers and reducing costs.
■ **Agriculture chatbots**: Chatbots are used for providing advice and suggestions for solving farm-related problems, which helps farmers to make clear decisions.

4.4.5 AI for Weather Forecasting

Weather-based information helps farmers plan their farming activities better. Farmers can utilize AI-based models to forecast weather trends and increase agricultural precision. Colorado-based company aWhere is using AI models and satellite feeds to forecast weather and analyze crop sustainability.

4.4.6 AI for Better Decision-Making

AI can gather data on soil health, generate fertilizer recommendations, track weather, and monitor crop readiness. This information can aid farmers in making better decisions throughout the crop-growing process. Farmers can collect and handle significantly more data using AI than they could without it and at a much faster rate. Farmers may utilise AI and predictive analytics to solve problems such as market demand analysis, pricing projections, and determining the ideal time to sow and harvest.

4.4.7 AI for Cost Savings

AI-assisted precision agriculture assists farmers in producing more crops using fewer resources. Precision farming helps farmers increase yields while lowering costs by combining knowledge on the best soil management practices, variable rate technologies, and data management techniques. As a result, herbicide use is reduced, harvest quality is improved, earnings are increased, and significant cost savings are realized.

4.5 Machine Learning in Agriculture

Machine learning, a branch of AI, when paired with large data and high-performance computing technology, opens up new possibilities and ideas for agricultural operations. With the help of computer vision, it determines the yield by bringing together the earliest phases of soil preparation, seed planting, and water supply assessment.

4.5.1 Management of Species

1. **Species breeding**
   Species breeding is a time-consuming process that impacts the efficiency of water and fertilizer consumption, as well as climatic change, disease resistance, and nutrient content for greater flavour. It assesses the performance of crops in different climates using historical field data by putting new traits into species using deep learning algorithms. As a result, new models are created with deep learning that anticipate genes that contribute to a plant's favourable attributes.
2. **Species recognition**
   Machine learning is used to evaluate the colour and shape of leaves, as well as leaf vein architecture, to learn about leaf properties and offer more accurate and faster results.

4.5.2 Management of Field Conditions

1. **Soil management**
   Soil is a highly changeable natural resource in agriculture. By evaluating this data, insights are provided into climate change, which has an impact on yield. Machine learning algorithms examine the evaporation process, soil moisture, and temperature to better understand ecosystem dynamics and the influence of agriculture.
2. **Water management**
   Water management is one of the most significant farming operations since it affects climatological, hydrological, and agronomic balance. Many of the machine learning-based applications developed thus far are related to

predicting daily or periodical evapotranspiration, enabling more efficacious irrigation systems and temperature forecasting, which recognizes weather events and evaporation.

4.5.3 Crop Management

1. **Yield prediction**

   Crop supply and demand, crop management, and yield mapping and estimating are all defined by yield prediction (Pantazi et al., 2018), which is one of the most significant and popular fields in precision farming. The multidimensional analysis of crops can be done utilizing computer vision and real-time data, such as economic factors and weather conditions, to anticipate yield for farmers and the general public.

2. **Crop quality**

   Humans analyze crops based on experience, while machines generate important knowledge from prior data and make connections to disclose new qualities, allowing for effective identification and classification of crop features, hence increasing product pricing and reducing waste.

3. **Disease detection**

   Under pest and disease control, uniform spraying of pesticides over the field in open-air and greenhouse conditions is a common method. As a result, large quantities of insecticides are necessary, resulting in huge financial and environmental costs. In precision agriculture management with machine learning, agrochemical information is tailored in terms of time, geographical area, and impacted plants.

4. **Weed detection**

   Weeds are one of the most serious challenges to agricultural productivity, and identifying and distinguishing between crops is extremely challenging. By combining computer vision and machine learning techniques, we can increase discrimination and detection at a low cost and with no negative consequences for the environment.

4.5.4 Livestock Management

1. **Livestock production**

   Machine learning can accurately forecast and estimate farming factors, improving the economic efficiency of livestock such as cattle and eggs. With the help of weight-predicting technologies, farmers can adjust diets and conditions ahead of slaughter day.

2. **Animal welfare**

   To help us categorize animals, we assess chewing signals, and movement, standing, moving, eating, and drinking patterns. These help us forecast sickness, weight increase, and production in animals.

3. **Farmer's little helper**

    A crucial component in the agricultural process is planning. Various solutions should be examined after some discussion before making a final selection to analyze the growth in farming products. Specialized chatbots are now being developed to speak with farmers and offer them helpful comments and ideas. They are thought to be intelligent workers since they provide farmers with solutions to difficult problems.

4.5.5 Models Behind

In the crop management process, machine learning models are utilized to analyze farming conditions and animal management. The most common supervised models discussed in the literature review are support-vector machines, random forests, artificial neural networks and deep learning.

Support-vector machines (SVMs) are binary classifiers that use a linear hyperplane to divide data instances into two groups. SVMs are also utilized in agricultural yield and quality prediction algorithms, such as classification, regression, and clustering.

The random forest (RF) is a sophisticated machine-learning classifier that can be utilized in land remote sensing. This RF classifier is used for land resource monitoring, evaluation, and management. It is also used to forecast crop yields in large fields. The RF classifier depends on the parameters chosen, but it always has an impact on classification accuracy.

Artificial neural networks (ANNs) are a simplified model of biological neural network with complex capabilities such as pattern formation, cognition, learning, and decision-making that mimic human brain capability. These models are utilized in weed detection, disease diagnosis, and crop management and assist regression and classification. As a result, the recent development of ANNs with dep learning has broadened the area of ANN applications in many fields, including agriculture.

4.6 How Data Analytics Is Transforming Agriculture

Data analytics help corporate operations by combining information and technology to collect data from several business entities. It can provide real-time data on marketing, product demand, sales, and financials. As a result, adopting analytics in the agricultural field will increase productivity while reducing manual labour.

4.6.1 Predictive Analytics

Big data analytics predicts future outcomes based on past or historic data with the help of three analysis techniques called the "Big 3": analysis, decision trees, and neural networks. Some other models, such as ensemble models and random forests, are also used. Predictive analytics is used to solve complex business problems (Vijayabaskar, 2017), such as crop prediction, yield prediction, and consumer buying habits.

4.6.2 Recommendation System

Based on behavioural data and functional patterns, the recommendation system generates suggestions as an output. It is a type of intelligent application system that guides users through decision-making. In the agriculture industry, recommendation engines examine weather and soil conditions and recommend crops depending on their investigations. The purchase behaviour of agri-items is analyzed using methods such as association rules with Apriori, collaborative filtering, content-based, and hybrid methods.

4.6.3 Data Mining

In agriculture, the application of data mining is extremely significant. Many data mining techniques (Kaur et al.,2014) are utilized in farming, particularly pattern mining, which finds patterns in vast datasets. In farm management and precision agriculture, for example, K-means and GPS-based technologies can be used to analyze different soils and cluster diverse sorts of soil types.

4.7 Agriculture's Data Analytics Benefits

1. **Increasing innovation and productivity**
   More visibility into operations and possibilities to enhance resources and production are provided by soil sensors, GPS-equipped tractors, and weather tracking. Real-time data provides the necessary information for determining where and how to plant.
2. **Greater understanding of environmental challenges**
   Farmers may utilize data analytics to monitor the health of their crops in real time, produce predictive analytics for future yields, and make resource management decisions based on historical patterns.
3. **Reducing waste and improving profits**
   To keep a prosperous agribusiness, one must continue to innovate and develop new ways to solve problems. Agri firms can now address sales-related questions from a single platform thanks to data analytics.
4. **Improving supply chain management**
   Both communication and collaboration efforts are needed to improve the current agriculture value chain. Precision agriculture (Pham & Stack, 2018) technologies help farmers track their crops more easily along the supply chain. Furthermore, with the help of this tool, each farmer may transmit essential

information about product offerings and services to retailers, distributors, and other critical stakeholders.

4.8 The Challenges of AI in Agriculture

Despite the fact that AI technologies and achievements have been applied in agriculture, it is still in its infancy compared to other disciplines. The majority of farmers and agricultural equipment manufacturers have not gone into great detail about modern technologies and AI. The following are some of the reasons:

- Data acquisition in agriculture is not an easier task compared to other industries.
- Applying, testing, validating, and popularizing AI technologies are tough.
- There is a lack of knowledge about agriculture as well as AI technologies.
- Farmers may face severe problems as a result of privacy and security issues such as cyber assaults and data breaches. Unfortunately, many farmers are at risk from these dangers.
- Because AI cannot exist without the usage of other technologies such as big data, sensors, and software, it should be utilized in concert with them.

With the ceaseless development of AI technology, its large-scale application in the agricultural field will eventually be realized soon. AI can aid society by enhancing human lives and supplying high-quality food items while also providing significant economic benefits. As a result, AI has the potential to uplift the future of agriculture.

4.9 The IoT and Sensors in Agriculture

The IoT refers to a collection of devices such as hardware, sensors, software, and electrical gadgets that are connected to a network via the Internet in order to gather and share data (Doshi et al.,2019). Data can be collected and shared between digital machines and biological beings, whether human or animal. The concept of connecting things was first proposed in the 1970s, but Kevin Ashton invented the term Internet of Things (IoT) in 1999. The IoT makes our lives smarter, not only in home automation but also in industries with automating processes, precision farming, livestock monitoring, healthcare, and so on.

4.9.1 The Need for the IoT

Before the evolution of the IoT in various areas, Internet connectivity began to uplift the markets. Even now, high-speed Internet connectivity is important for interconnecting IoT devices. Everything was done manually prior to IoT adoption, including scheduling tasks, allocating employees, reminders, and predictions. The major advantages of using the IoT in business are as follows:

- It saves time and money.
- It generates more revenue.
- It provides better decisions.
- It monitors overall business processes.

4.9.2 Applications of the IoT

The IoT is a technology that has gradually gained attention and is now quietly shaping our future by connecting several communicating embedded devices that make precise decisions to make work easier. The applications of the IoT are multiple and are making their footprint in various areas such as smart homes, smart cities, wearables, self-driving cars, smart farming, healthcare, smart supply chains, and smart grids.

4.9.3 The Role of Sensors in the IoT

Sensors are crucial in the development of IoT solutions. Sensors are devices that detect external data and replace it with a signal that both humans and machines can understand. Sensors are currently used in a range of industries, including the healthcare, industrial, logistics, transportation, agriculture, disaster relief, and tourism planning industries. All of these areas use sensors to collect timely data, which gives us proper decisions and high security. Without sensors, we cannot collect data to create an IoT environment. The IoT offers several benefits. Some are industry-specific, and some are of personal use, such as smart home equipment.

4.9.4 Sensors in Smart Farming

Depending upon the usage, various types of sensors (Boursianis et al., 2020) are utilized in smart farming. Agriculture sensors are utilized in smart farming to provide information (Ayaz et al., 2019) that helps farmers monitor and enhance their crops by adapting to environmental changes. The following sensors are utilized in drones, robotics, and weather stations in agriculture.

- **Acoustic sensor**: These sensors are required for farm management and pay attention to soil management, fruit harvesting, weeding, the monitoring and identification of pests, the classification of seed kinds, and pest monitoring. They work by detecting changes in noise levels.
- **Optical sensor**: These sensors use light to determine the amount of organic matter and minerals in the soil. They analyze the density and characteristics of

the soil using light. Optical sensors based on fluorescence are used to identify mature fruits and classify crops. These sensors measure the ability of the soil to reflect light across the electromagnetic spectrum. They are used to characterize grove canopies, such as olives and related crops, when combined with microwave scattering.

■ **Ultrasonic ranging sensor**: Sensors in this category are a good choice because of their inexpensive cost, ability to function in a range of applications, and simplicity of use and adaptability. Tank monitoring, spray distance measuring, crop canopy monitoring, and weed detection are all frequent applications.

■ **Telematics sensor**: These sensors are used to interlink devices in agriculture to collect data and operate machinery from remote areas. They also provide the option to record the data obtained previously for automatic operations.

■ **Argos sensor**: Sensors in this category are used to collect geographic data to study crops, yield forecasts, identify pests, etc. (Fabian Schmidt, 2014). Several sensors are available for remote sensing; the Argos sensor is a notable one.

■ **Soft water level-based (SWLB) sensor**: SWLB sensors are used to assess the hydrological behaviour of farms to check the flow and level of water. This includes measuring the prediction, flow of the stream, and presence of water.

■ **Field-programmable gate array (FPGA)-based Sensor**: Due to their flexibility of reconfiguration, FPGA-based sensors have lately been employed in agriculture for real-time plant transpiration, irrigation, and humidity. These sensors are costly and consume more power. FPGA-based sensors provide the greatest solutions by addressing these difficulties.

■ **Temperature sensor**: These sensors are used to measure the temperature of the environment either in analogue or digital mode. They are not only used in agriculture but also in automobiles and air-conditioning systems.

■ **Soil-moisture sensor**: These are used to determine the moisture content of the soil (Bhatnagar et al., 2020). Soil moisture sensors help farmers find the perfect moisture content in the environment (Soil Moisture Sensor: Innovation for Precision Farming, 2020).

■ **Airflow sensors**: These are used to assess soil air permeability and moisture percentages and to identify soil structure to differentiate between different types of soil. To identify soil structure, pressure is required to force a predetermined amount of air into the solid ground at a prescribed depth.

■ **Electrochemical sensors**: These are mainly used to determine the quantities of nutrients in the soil. The regular method of soil analysis is very expensive when compared to these sensors. They can also detect macro and micronutrients, as well as salt and pH levels in the soil.

4.9.5 Architectural Design

IoT architecture consists of various interconnected IoT system components that ensure sensor-generated device data is gathered, saved, and processed, as well as device actuators that carry out orders supplied via a user application. To monitor the crops, temperature and humidity sensors, as well as soil moisture sensors, are connected to a microcontroller. A Wi-Fi module connects all of the sensor devices to the Internet. The Wi-Fi connection is used to send sensor data to the end-user and store it in the cloud for later use. Successfully sensed data is processed and saved in a database for future use and delivered to an ATmega328 Arduino microcontroller. The collected data can be viewed on an LCD monitor. A web area is built, and the data acquired by the sensors is updated regularly over Wi-Fi. A GSM module connected to the microcontroller transmits messages to the authorized person regarding farm conditions.

4.9.6 ATmega328 Arduino Microcontroller

The ATmega328P is a high-performance, low-power, 8-bit resolution AVR RISC microprocessor. It is widely used on Arduino boards with 32K of program memory. The controller's Advanced RISC architecture speeds up program execution and can resist high temperatures. The device works with a voltage range of 1.8 to 5.5 volts. The architectural design of an IoT device with sensors, power supply, cloud, GSM module, Wi-Fi module, message alert, and LCD display is shown in Figure 4.3.

4.9.7 GSM Module

A GSM module is essentially a GSM modem attached to a PCB with various types of outputs, including RS-232. The SIM900A is a small and dependable wireless module that integrates a comprehensive dual-band GSM/GPRS solution into an SMT module that may be used in a variety of applications with low power

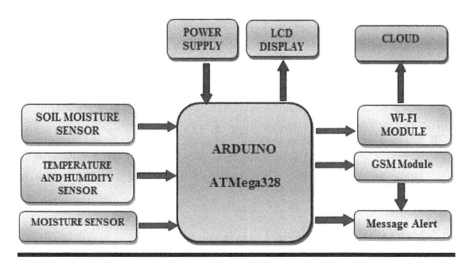

Figure 4.3 **Architectural design of IoT device with sensors**

consumption. The SIM900A provides GSM/GPRS 900/1800MHz capability for voice, SMS, data, and fax. It is especially thin and compact at 24 mm x 24 mm x 3 mm.

4.9.8 Supporting Technologies for Smart Farming

Precision farming is successful only when communication is done periodically between participating objects (Mat et al., 2018). So, before planning a smart farm, we should select networks with high speed for better data connectivity. To achieve reliable communication, network operators are very important in the agriculture sector. Depending on the requirements, various communication models and technologies are used. A few are discussed here:

4.9.8.1 Zigbee

Zigbee is a wireless protocol developed for low-cost communication networks. It can hold around 65,000 nodes with different topologies: star, mesh, and tree. During farm monitoring, the sensor nodes transfer data to various interlinked objects with the help of Zigbee to the server. Drip irrigation and fertilization are two important applications that use the concept of Zigbee to check soil moisture content and fertilization and send the status via SMS to the farmer. Zigbee typically has a greater range than Bluetooth.

4.9.8.2 Bluetooth

Bluetooth is a wireless communication standard used in communication between devices of shorter distances. Bluetooth Low Energy (BLE) consumes less power, is cheaper and easy to use, and is commonly known as Bluetooth Smart. A moisture and temperature sensor with BLE has been introduced for monitoring agricultural environments and weather conditions and checking light and ambience via smartphone. Wi-Fi is also used when LAN communications are employed in smart agriculture.

4.9.8.3 Smartphones

Mobile phones are one of the major technologies used today in rural areas to communicate with each other. Due to price drops, the smartphone industry has reached great heights. Cellular networks are stepping up in developing countries and provide an opportunity to reach remote areas with dispersed farms. Several pieces of equipment, including GSMs, gyroscopes, barometers, inertial sensors, and microphones, are controlled by smartphone via mobile applications, allowing farmers to monitor their farms 24 hours a day, seven days a week.

4.9.8.4 Cloud Computing

Smart agriculture is data-driven and produces massive volumes of data regularly (Rajeswari et al., 2017). We need improved technology and tools to manage such data so that it can be processed efficiently and at a reasonable cost. Farmers can use cloud-based services to store and retrieve data as it becomes more vital. Moving to cloud-based services is undoubtedly advantageous because it provides knowledge-based repositories with a wealth of information on farming techniques. Cloud-based decision support systems can handle a wide range of data types and can customize them for specific purposes.

4.9.9 How is Data Collected from Sensors?

A smart agriculture system is installed on a farm with three sensors, namely a temperature sensor, a moisture sensor, and a humidity sensor, which takes readings at regular intervals and send messages about the farm's condition to the farmer. The data collected from these sensors can be inspected using various machine learning algorithms, and the outcomes will assist farmers in understanding facts on weather and soil monitoring and management. For example, a decision tree algorithm with information gain applied to the sensor dataset would provide knowledge on the significance of the features on which the prediction or classification is made.

4.10 Drones in Agriculture

A drone is a kind of unmanned autonomous vehicle (UAV) or unmanned aircraft system (UAS). It is a flying robot that can be controlled remotely to fly autonomously using software, GPS, and sensors. In recent years, drones have been used in the military for anti-target practice, intelligence gathering, and finding weapons warehouses. Due to the continuous growth of the world population and limited resources, the agriculture industry should be given more precedence, especially for food production and soil exploitation. Drone usage in agriculture seems essential when compared to all other industries for assessing the health state and yield of a crop.

Drones are small and lightweight vehicles that use navigation systems and recording devices such as cameras and other sensors that allow the drones to monitor crop conditions and chemical spraying. Image capturing helps the farmer detect plant health, maximize productivity, quality, yield, weeds, and soil conditions. This data is interpreted with algorithms to provide useful information such as leaf area, anomaly detection, treatment efficacy, and yield prediction, the height and density of the plants, sections of the field or orchard that are water-stressed and need to be watered, and constantly assessing the state of the soil, which leads to a higher yield.

4.10.1 Drone Components

A drone is composed of electronic speed controllers, GPS, battery, antenna, camera, ultrasonic and collision-avoiding sensors, altimeter, accelerometer, and so on (Ipate et al., 2015). Mostly, GPS on a drone identifies the precise location, sensors are used to identify colours and collect infrared and ultrasonic wavelengths, recognize heat-signatures, and identify minerals, and agri-based sensors are used to monitor crop health, water quality, and soil composition (Stehr, 2015). Some drones are used for obstacle detection in various directions, like the front, back, below, above, and both sides.

4.10.1.1 Types of Drones

Drones are popular tiny flying devices controlled by a remote (Mogili & Deepak, 2018). They are categorized as.

- **Single rotor**: A single-rotor drone is a model with only one rotor, like a helicopter in design and structure. Single-rotor drones are much more efficient because of their higher flying times when compared to multi-rotor drones, which are much more expensive and require special training to fly properly.
- **Multi-rotor**: Multi-rotor drones look like a helicopter with many rotors. These extra rotors are useful for maintaining balance when compared with single-rotor drones. One drawback to the multi-rotor drone is that it is unable to carry an overload, as it loses its balance. Multi-rotor drones are classified as tricopter, quadcopter, hexacopter, and octocopter. The multi-rotor drone has its drawbacks, such as a flying time of 30 minutes and limited speed. It is not suitable for large-scale projects. One of the most useful tools for crop management in the field, rotary drones can hover over difficult regions and are easy to fly across the field. Since battery life is an issue as power drains quickly due to multi-rotors, flying time is less during heavy winds.
- **Fixed-wing**: Fixed-wing drones have wings, like regular aeroplanes, so that they can stay afloat with minimal energy. Due to their enhanced flying time and fuel efficiency, these drones are best suited for longer-range missions such as mapping and surveillance. However, fixed-wing drones are more expensive than multi-rotors.
- **Hybrid**: Hybrid drones combine the advantages of fixed-wing and rotor-based aircraft. As a result of the advent of new generation sensors, hybrid vehicles have found new life and direction. Vertical lift is utilized to elevate the drone into the air using an accelerometer and gyro.

Drones are used in agriculture to increase efficiency by collecting real-time data and managing crops. Various IoT principles can be applied to agriculture drones to enhance the agriculture industry as the IoT becomes increasingly commercialized.

Drones are simple to operate and can be used by farmers to collect high-resolution photos and perform mapping and analysis. They are one of the most frequently used agricultural strategies for analyzing and forecasting the proper production and use of resources.

4.10.1.2 UAVs in Smart Agriculture

Unmanned aerial vehicles (UAVs) are becoming more popular in smart agriculture for meeting the increasing demands on agriculture due to the high population (Daponte et al., 2019). Drones with sensors and cameras implemented with IoT and machine learning concepts will help us to achieve efficiency and precision agriculture. Since 1980, UAVs have been used to address the challenges and traditional procedures in agricultural technology.

Uses for Agricultural Drones

- **Irrigation monitoring**: Drones equipped with hyperspectral, thermal, or multispectral sensors detect sections of land that are excessively dry or in need of agricultural improvement. Drone monitoring helps increase water efficiency and disclose potential pooling/leaks in irrigation (Phakare & Dharwadkar, 2021) by offering irrigation monitoring yield calculations (Tsouros et al., 2019) of the vegetation index to help realize the health of crops and emitted heat/energy. In many farm jobs, drones have taken the place of humans. Simply put, everything will be mechanized soon.
- **Crop health monitoring and surveillance:** Tracking the health of the plants and spotting pests early on is critical. Near-infrared spectroscopy (NIRS) light in leaves is used by agriculture drones to locate sick plants. Crop health may be tracked and flaws discovered using multispectral imaging, which can help save crops. It assesses only the necessary fertilizer based on data collected by drones, saving the farmer money on fertilizer.
- **Field soil analysis**: This tool aids farmers in determining the specifics of soil conditions. Seed planting patterns, accurate field soil analyses, irrigation, and nitrogen-level management can all benefit from multispectral sensors. Farmers can use 3D precise photogrammetric mapping to examine their soil conditions properly.
- **Planting**: This is a new type of job that can be performed by drones. Drone-planting systems lower expenses by nearly 85% while simultaneously improving consistency and efficiency.
- **Agricultural spraying:** Periodically, crops will be given chemicals called fertilizers, and these can cause harm to humans due to direct contact. This can be avoided, and the work can be carried out easier by using drones with RGB and multispectral sensors that can identify problematic areas. This is more efficient when compared to the work done by humans.

■ **Livestock tracking:** Drone surveys not only assists farmers in keeping track of their crops but also in monitoring their herds/cattle. They can help locate a missing animal in the herd, detect injured animals, and detect illnesses early. This allows the poacher to separate the animal from the rest of the herd, preventing illness from spreading to the entire herd.

Drones typically contain a navigation system, GPS, several sensors, high-resolution cameras, programmable controllers, and autonomous drone tools. Farmers can use satellite photos as a starting point for farm management. UAVs can obtain more precise data for precision agriculture than satellites with current technology. Agritech software is used to process the data and create useful information.

4.10.1.3 Steps for Capturing Data from an Agriculture Drone

1. **Examining the area**: This identifies the area that will be examined. The first stage is to define a border, followed by an analysis of the region, and finally, to transfer the technical GPS data into the drone's navigation system.
2. **Using autonomous drones**: Because UAVs are self-contained, flight patterns are entered into their pre-existing data collection systems.
3. **Data uploading**: Once all of the essential data has been captured using sensors such as a multispectral or RGB sensor, it is processed using a variety of software for further analysis and interpretation.
4. **Output**: After collecting the data, it is structured in such a way that farmers can easily understand it, bringing them closer to precision farming. Popular methods for displaying large amounts of data include 3D mapping and photogrammetry.

4.10.2 Benefits of Drone Technology

New technology is introduced daily that reduces the restrictions for the usage of drones (Bharati & Mondal, 2021). The use of drones in the context of agriculture offers many advantages over other businesses that use drones.

1. **Enhanced productivity**: Crop health, soil health, and environmental factors can all be monitored often and effectively to boost production. Complete irrigation planning can help the farmer increase yield.
2. **Effective and adaptive techniques**: Because drones are always monitoring the field, farmers may get regular information on their crops and find ways to address disputes by changing their farming practices. This means they can quickly adjust to changing weather conditions and only deploy resources as needed, avoiding waste.

3. **Increased farmer safety**: Farmers can use drones to spray nutrients on sick crops, higher crops, and in congested areas like powwows.
4. **Less resource wastage**: Agri-drones allow for the most efficient use of all resources, including fertilizer, water, seeds, and pesticides. When compared to people, this employs the most efficient resources.
5. **Accuracy rate**: Drone analysis has always aided farmers in calculating precise land size, crop classification, and soil mapping.
6. **Insurance claims**: Farmers utilize the data collected by drones to file crop insurance claims in the event of damage. Drones are used in the agricultural insurance market to collect reliable data. It is very useful for monetary repayment to farmers if the damages that occurred are captured.

Agricultural drone technology is without a doubt India's agrarian future. Smart farming's challenges and future opportunities have the potential to change traditional farming processes in innumerable ways. Although the technology is more difficult to grasp, once learned, it will produce results in no time.

4.11 Challenges and Future Opportunities in Farming

Smart farming/agriculture has the potential to play a vital role in fulfilling the world's rising population's incremental food demands. However, the industry is confronted with a number of major difficulties.

■ **Interoperability between various standards**: Many of the readily available tools and technologies do not adhere to the same technological standards or platforms, resulting in a lack of consistency in end-user analysis. In many circumstances, the construction of additional gateways is required for data translation and transmission across standards.
■ **Learning curve**: In a number of scenarios, establishing the correct IoT architecture and sensor network might be a difficult undertaking.
■ **Access in rural places**: In many remote rural communities around the world, especially in developing countries, strong, stable Internet connectivity is absent. Until network performance and bandwidth speeds are considerably improved, digital farming will be impossible to implement.
■ **Making sense of huge data**: On a modern networked agricultural farm, there are literally millions of data points. However, because it is practically impossible to monitor and manage each and every data point, digital agriculture is gradually becoming big data-driven – but the technology is only helpful if users use the data given.
■ **Non-awareness of the numerous farm production functions**: If users are not informed of the various agricultural production functions, they must be able to define the correct production function. There is always the potential for incorrect input application (for example, providing too much nitrogen

fertilizer), resulting in crop damage unless the farmer is aware of this shifting production function.

▪ **New business entrance barriers**: Farmers may face challenges when migrating data streams from an older platform to a newer one, and there is a risk of data loss. The resources and platforms of a big agro-IoT operator may not be compatible with existing equipment or systems.

▪ **Scalability and setup issues**: A farmer should be given IoT technologies that are fully scalable (access points, gateways, etc.). In other words, both a large commercial farm and a small garden/cropland should be able to use the same technology and reap the same benefits. For agriculture to become completely self-sufficient, self-configurable technology is essential.

▪ **Risks of energy depletion**: The requirement for powerful data centres and gateways/hubs to operate smart sensors and other devices may result in excessive energy consumption, necessitating additional resources to replenish that energy. Energy consumption is influenced by the development of new agricultural IoT equipment.

▪ **Challenges of indoor farming**: Technology support for indoor farming requires further attention. The absence of daily climatic changes and regular seasons must be considered while creating smart indoor agricultural systems. Indoor plant farmers must be able to rely on technology to create optimal growing conditions (light, temperature, and water availability).

▪ **Failures in technology and their consequences**: If smart irrigation sensors go down, for example, plants are likely to be under or overwatered. Food safety may be jeopardised if the technological resources in the storage areas fail. Even a few minutes of delay due to a power outage can be disastrous, particularly if no backup plan is in place.

▪ **E-waste is becoming more prevalent**: A new concern has emerged in the shape of electronic garbage (E-wastes). In a nutshell, frequent hardware upgrades are rendering older equipment obsolete, and dumping them is creating landfills in many areas.

▪ **Physical labour loss**: A considerable portion of the agricultural labour force will lose their job as the IoT spreads and processes become more automated. Precision agriculture has unquestionable benefits, but the widespread replacement of manual workers may bring public dissatisfaction.

▪ **The security issue**: Malware and data theft are a problem in almost all types of connected systems, and the situation is exacerbated by many farmers' preference for somewhat less expensive devices and resources that lack the necessary safety assurances. To make agricultural IoT more accessible to customers, more security and provisioning standards are required.

▪ **Benefits that aren't immediately apparent**: Before investing in a "new technology" such as for smart farming, users understandably want to know what type of return they may expect. Many people still see modern agricultural technology as risky and uncertain, and they are unwilling to employ it. When individuals have a greater grasp of agritech and receive sufficient training, such fears should fade away.

To address these difficulties, governments, investors, and agricultural technology innovators will need to work together. According to the report, *Agriculture 4.0: The Future Of Farming Technology*, due to technological developments, water and chemical substances will no longer be applied consistently across entire fields. Instead, producers will focus on a small number of areas and use the bare minimum of resources. As a result of advancements in agriculture, farms and agricultural activities will have to be run significantly differently. Drones, robots, sensors, and GPS technologies will all be used in agriculture in the future. Farms will be more cost-effective, gainful, safe, and environmentally friendly with the application of precision agriculture, sophisticated machinery, and robotic systems.

4.12 Conclusion

Agriculture is one of the most ancient and significant activities that has difficulty in making a profit. Semi-automated devices have reduced the work of farmers in a variety of jobs, including ploughing, harvesting, fertilizer spraying, and so on. All of these semi-automated machines are powered by human labour. With advancements in AI, machine learning, information and communications technology, and the IoT, farmers can anticipate agricultural output, crop management, crop quality management, disease detection, weed identification, soil management, and water management. Machine learning algorithms analyze data collected in the field and develop predictions in order to make the best possible decisions. To summarize, the application of developing technologies will successfully turn traditional agriculture into smart farming with additional benefits, including food security, cost reduction, increased production, and more sustainable practices.

References

Agrawal, K., & Kamboj, N. (2019). Smart agriculture using IOT: A futuristic approach. *International Journal of Information Dissemination and Technology, 9*(4), 186–190.

Ayaz, M., Ammad-Uddin, M., Sharif, Z., Mansour, A., & Aggoune, E. H. M. (2019). Internet-of- Things (IoT)-based smart agriculture: Toward making the fields talk. *IEEE Access, 7*, 129551–129583.

Bhatnagar, V., Singh, G., Kumar, G., & Gupta, R. (2020). Internet of Things in smart agriculture: Applications and open challenges. Project: *Usage of IoT for Agriculture in modern era.*

Bharati, S., & Mondal, M. R. H. (2021). 12 applications and challenges of AI-driven IoHT for combating pandemics: A review. *Computational Intelligence for Managing Pandemics, 5*, 213.

Boursianis, A. D., Papadopoulou, M. S., Diamantoulakis, P., Liopa-Tsakalidi, A., Barouchas, P., Salahas, G., & Goudos, S. K. (2020). Internet of things (IoT) and agricultural unmanned aerial vehicles (UAVs) in smart farming: A comprehensive review. *Internet of Things*, 100187.

Daponte, P., De Vito, L., Glielmo, L., Iannelli, L., Liuzza, D., Picariello, F., & Silano, G. (2019, May). A review on the use of drones for precision agriculture. In *IOPConference Series: Earth and Environmental Science* (Vol. 275, No. 1, p. 012022). IOP Publishing.

Doshi, J., Patel, T., & Kumar Bharti, S. (2019). Smart farming using IoT, a solution for optimally monitoring farming conditions. *Procedia Computer Science, 160*, 746–751.

Earth Observing System. (2020). *Soil Moisture Sensor: Innovation for Precision Farming*. Retrieved from https://eos.com/blog/ soil-moisture-sensor

Fabian Schmidt. (2014). Agricultural sensors: Improving crop farming to help us feed the world. Retrieved from www.dw.com/en/agricultural-sensors-improving-crop-farming-to-help-us-feed-the-world/a-17733350

Gorli, R., & Yamini, G. (2017). Future of smart farming with Internet of Things. *Journal of Information Technology and Its Applications, 2*(1).

IANS. (2019) Microsoft AI is using sensors to make farming and healthcare smart. Retrieved from www.thenewsminute.com/article/microsoft-india-using-ai-sensors-make-farming-and-healthcare-smart-95390.

Ipate, G., Voicu, G., & Dinu, I. (2015). Research on the use of drones in precision agriculture. *University Politehnica of Bucharest Bulletin Series, 77*(4), 1–12.

Kaur, M., Gulati, H., & Kundra, H. (2014). Data mining in agriculture on crop price prediction: Techniques and applications. *International Journal of Computer Applications, 99*(12), 1–3.

Mat, I., Kassim, M. R. M., Harun, A. N., & Yusoff, I. M. (2018, November). Smart agriculture using internet of things. In *2018 IEEE conference on open systems (ICOS)* (pp.54–59). IEEE.

Mogili, U. R., & Deepak, B. B. V. L. (2018). Review on application of drone systems in precision agriculture. *Procedia computer science, 133*, 502–509.

Pakhare, A., & Dharwadkar, N. V. (2021). Literature review on agricultural Internet of Things. In *Proceedings of International Conference on Big Data, Machine Learning and their Applications* (pp. 25–37). Springer, Singapore.

Pantazi, X. E., Moshou, D., Alexandridis, T., Whetton, R. L., & Mouazen, A. M. (2016). Wheat yield prediction using machine learning and advanced sensing techniques. *Computers and electronics in agriculture, 121*, 57–65.

Pham, X., & Stack, M. (2018). How data analytics is transforming agriculture. *Business horizons, 61*(1), 125–133.

Rajeswari, S., Suthendran, K., & Rajakumar, K. (2017, June). A smart agricultural model by integrating IoT, mobile and cloud-based big data analytics. In *2017 International Conference on Intelligent Computing and Control (I2C2)* (pp. 1–5). IEEE.

Stehr, N. J. (2015). Drones: The newest technology for precision agriculture. *NaturalSciences Education, 44*(1), 89–91.

Tsouros, D. C., Triantafyllou, A., Bibi, S., & Sarigannidis, P. G. (2019, May). Data acquisition and analysis methods in UAV-based applications for precision agriculture. In *2019*

15th International Conference on Distributed Computing in Sensor Systems (DCOSS) (pp. 377–384).

Vijayabaskar, P. S., Sreemathi, R., & Keertanaa, E. (2017, March). Crop prediction using predictive analytics. In *2017 International Conference on Computation of Power, Energy Information and Communication (ICCPEIC)* (pp. 370–373). IEEE.

Chapter 5

A Science, Technology, and Society Approach to Studying the Cumin Revolution in Western India

Diwakar Kumar
Central University of Gujarat, Gujarat, India

5.1 Introduction

At 196,024 square kilometres, Gujarat is located on India's western coast. Approximately 6% of India's total geographic area and about 5% of its population are accounted for in this piece of land (APRU, 1998). Only around one-third of the Indian coastline is in Gujarat. South, central, and north Gujarat, and Saurashtra-Kachchh make up the state's basic geographic structure. A sizable portion of Gujarat, primarily in the state's central and northern regions, is mostly flat plains. Mountainous terrain can be found on the outskirts of the eastern part of the state, where it shares a border with Maharashtra, Madhya Pradesh, and Rajasthan (Centre for Development Research, 1998). For obvious reasons, the Gulf of Khambhat contains parts that are below mean sea level (MSL). Additionally, the soil type varies across the state of Gujarat. In south Gujarat, alluvial soil of medium depth is most common. Saurashtra has soils ranging from medium black to coastal alluvial, while the central part of Gujarat has medium black soil that is indicative of that area (Director of Census Operation, 1992a). A tropical monsoon climate prevails in Gujarat. Whenever the southwest rainfall dominates, approximately 90–95% of total annual precipitation occurs. While the amount of rainfall in the Kachchh district is around 340 mm, the amount in the southern hills of Dangs and Bulsar varies between 800 and 900 mm. Overall, an average of 800 mm of rain falls on the main parts. 52% of Gujarat can be utilized in agriculture. 85% of wasteland located in Kachchh accounts for more than 23% of Gujarat land area. About 17% of the area is covered by water bodies, while about 10% is covered by dense forest. 19% of the wasteland is affected by salt, and 11% is barren and rocky (Director of Census Operations, 1992b).

About 1.1 million people are employed in the agriculture, forestry, and fishing-related processing industries. The family businesses employing these people have fewer than two employees each. It is unfortunate that the share of agricultural production in the state's gross domestic product has fallen from over 30% 10 years ago to just over 21% today (Directorate of Economics and Statistics, Gujarat, Economic Development Through Maps, 1995). The figure in India is lower at 26% – however, even in rural areas, farming is still a mainstay. Even a small farming family needs an income that comes from seasonal migration or from remittances in order to survive. It is difficult to take the share of agriculture in total labour absorption figures seriously as opposed to on the ground realities. Literal literacy is at 61%, with an exceptionally lower figure of 36% in the planned programme area that comprises a substantial part of the target population (Directorate of Economics and Statistics, 1998).

The area where crops are grown makes up 41% of the total cropped area. This is a list of the grains grown: pearl millet, sorghum, paddy, maize, wheat, and different types of pulses. Cultivated land under oilseeds such as groundnut, castor, and sugarcane make up 18% of the total cropped area. Land under cotton cultivation comprises 14% of the total cropped area. The other 1% are crops such as tobacco and sugarcane. Non-foodgrain crops in Gujarat's agricultural produce are expressed by these figures. Cotton and groundnut are the two primary cash crops (Director of Economics and Statistics, 1999).

The Gujarat state, Gujarat mainland, Saurashtra region, and Kachchh can be grouped together in terms of groundwater resources. All water-bearing units have experienced a decrease in water levels on the Gujarat mainland. Alluvial sub-aquifer levels have dropped due to excessive pumping. The water level shrunk by about 40 to 60 meters between 1982 and 1991. The overpumping of subaquifers is clearly visible. In Saurashtra, the landscape is similar, where the water table dropped between 0 and 4 meters between 1982 and 1991 (DES, 2000). This ratio was extremely variable (as much as several tens of meters). For the same reason, overuse of groundwater reserves is again documented in numerous locations, particularly in the area around the city of Surat in the southern part of the state of Gujarat. Rising extraction by private firms for domestic, farming, and business purposes, as well as extraction that the government sponsors for cities to supply clean water, are among the primary reasons for falling water levels in several regions of the country. Salinity is a major source of soil degradation caused by groundwater resources, seawater intrusion, and the use of deeper saline aquifers for irrigation. Most of the soil in coastal areas is saline (Institute of Rural Management, 1999).

Water scarcity has recently gotten a lot of attention due to substantial debate over the true value of water. Another major reason for waste, misallocation, and environmental deterioration is that it is not valued appropriately (CVG, 1997). It is generally agreed that water has a number of critical socio-economic and environmental functions, and because of this, it is an important public good. Even among those in agreement, there is limited agreement on the manner in which it should be treated in different contexts, including sector allocation, pricing, and efficiency of use (CGWB, 1998). Water has a value equal to the price at which the people who use it are willing to pay for its use. Given that water markets are often unavailable for many purposes, and even when they are available are frequently imperfect, it is difficult to estimate the value of water accurately. The economic value of a resource is the additional economic output that could be realized through its use (Dubash, 2000). In the context of scarcity of physical resources, the total amount of renewable water available per capita in north Gujarat is only 427 m3/year.

Aquifers are the primary source of water for a variety of uses all year. Because the fragile water ecology in the region is not suitable for water-intensive economic activities, such activities are not encouraged in this area. But 448 m3 of water is used annually, and the remainder (89.5%) is used in agriculture, including dairy farming (Gass et al., 1996). One of the most important sources of income in rural Gujarat is farming. In regions with water shortages due to lack of power supply and limited irrigation water, it takes precedence. While cash crop cultivation still accounts for a secondary source of income, crop production plays a major role in the economy of south and central Gujarat, which is teeming with water (Bhatia, 1992).

Gujarat's groundwater pressure has greatly increased since the arrival of green revolution innovations and water-intensive crops. As groundwater levels have decreased, a lack of accessible groundwater has downtrodden resource-poor, small, and marginal farmers. In places where the well has dried up, people have to buy expensive water from water-rich well owners who often charge extortionate prices for water (Graham et al., 1996). Drip irrigation could reduce irrigation water use by 43% in north Gujarat. Therefore, in order to take care of water-stressed regions, it is critical to spread water-saving technology at least in alfalfa in the north of Gujarat, but also elsewhere (Singh et al., 2004).

It is pretty impressive that weather insurance is different from traditional yield insurance, which is market-based and financially sustainable. It has the potential to change the lives of rural agrarian households by helping to combat the production risk that often limits household productivity. The benefits enumerated in the analysis include a premium structure that is more favourable for commercial and horticulture crops and quick payouts that provide greater benefits to vulnerable groups of farmers. After a couple of years of implementation on a wider scale, a full-scale analysis of the scheme would show more concrete results. To start, though, there are substantial concerns that must be addressed regarding weather index products.

The inadequate number of weather stations on the network and in various locations must be curbed as quickly as possible (IRMA & UNICEF, 2001). Starting out with huge startup costs seems to necessitate a previously inactive role for the government in expanding the network of tamper-proof weather stations. With this being said, government-owned weather stations will enhance the level of data transparency and security for the insured. The product should be suitably designed to protect against catastrophic losses for a weather-based crop insurance scheme to arise as an operational risk alleviation tool (World Bank, 2007).

Making a major educational push to introduce weather index insurance has become essential in rural areas of Patan. Farmers are unaware of the intricacies of their insurance claims, and current claim structures are highly technical and complex, so most insured farmers know nothing about the coverages and variability in weather conditions that would lead to claims. A further complication is that private insurers may be selling similar-value products with identical premium rates but varying payout triggers (M. D., 2002). The insured will have no idea that the payouts may be wildly different for the same crop in the same area. Inability to recognize the unique qualities of the product may prevent farmers from purchasing it (Kumar et al., 2004). In addition, in-depth research should be conducted (continuously) regarding the accompanying coarsen risks for several crops grown in the countryside to provide insurance providers with relevant technical information. At present, the pressing challenge is to resolve the various challenges described above so that a powerful risk mitigation tool for farmers can be developed (Nair, 2010).

5.2 Methodology

This study investigated primary and secondary data over several months. The study was broken down into various phases, starting with field testing the study design and collecting primary data from various stakeholders. Secondary data collection was primarily interacting with concerned actors. After looking into the ways climate change affects farmer community lives, there was in-depth online secondary research focusing on how climate change is constructed and deconstructed on various levels.

Direct interaction with the key stakeholders was used to collect primary data. Secondary research was used to determine the main stakeholders. Focus group discussion was used to collect data at the community level, while personal interviews were employed at the institutional level. A questionnaire was administered by some of the formal and informal institutions and organizations.

5.3 Cumin Cultivation in Salt and Water Stress Areas of Patan

There have been numerous analyses that examine the significance of irrigation in Indian agriculture, and they all agree: irrigation has been a critical factor in agricultural growth and production. Although irrigated lands account for one-third of India's total cropland, their production far exceeds that of rain-fed farming (Kumar, 2018). Irrigation is an important input in a monsoon-based system with unlikely precipitation and large areas with precipitation far below 1,000 millimetres per year. With appropriate watering mechanisms, high-yielding varieties, fertilizers, and other inputs, increased productive potential for the land, along with a major impact on the resulting production, is possible (Vyas, 2006). In the case of agriculture and rural development, there has been an inverse relationship between irrigation expansion and both the growth and development of rural areas. Agricultural expansion, shifting cropping patterns, higher yields, and increased reliability are the major influences of India's irrigation.

Increasing irrigation facilities alone has helped to increase foodgrain production by about 52%, and improving management, agricultural practice and high-yield varieties accounted for around 48%, as per the report of the National Commission for Integrated Water Resources Development Plan (NCIWRDP) (Bandyopadhyay et al., 2002). The availability of irrigation water increases the productivity of croplands while also making them less susceptible to droughts. Production of highly mechanized foods gradually increases and simultaneously raises the nutritional and health levels of people who consume those processed foods. Irrigated agriculture, through which two-thirds or more of agricultural production is delivered, has had a major impact on job production in rural areas. According to the government, approximately 8.7 million person-years of incremental employment have been generated as a result of the irrigation potential created during the Eighth Plan. The employment and income impact of irrigation development has a significant multiplier effect because it creates inter-sectoral and interregional linkages through production growth and income flows.

The rise in the water table in semi-arid and arid areas causes the salts present in the soil profile and groundwater to be mobilized and released into the environment. Initial salt leaching occurs and the soil in the root zone becomes salt-free, resulting in an increase in agricultural production. Water table elevation causes hydraulic gradients to be disturbed, resulting in saline groundwater being transported into non-saline areas and streams, causing salinity issues to be encountered in streams. The groundwater table rises to within two to three meters of the soil surface when it reaches this level, and it contributes significantly to the evaporation from the soil surface as well as the uptake of water by plants. This upward flux of water results in a gradual concentration of salts in the shallow depths of the soil profile as a result of the upward flux of water. When soil salinity is present in the early years, crop yields

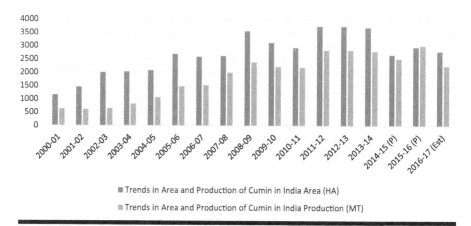

Figure 5.1 **Trends in area and production of cumin in Gujarat**

Source: Kumar (2017)

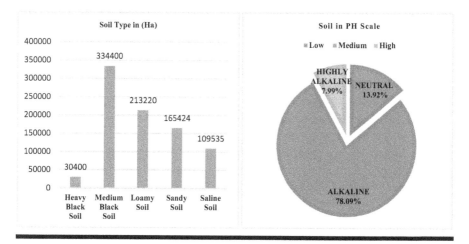

Figure 5.2 **Patan soil type and soil on PH scale**

are reduced; however, as the severity of the problem increases, lands are abandoned because excess salts render the soil completely unproductive. Problems with soil salinity arise when the soil and hydrological conditions are conducive to the accumulation of soluble salts in the root zone of plants.

An adequate supply of salt is required for the formation of saline soils. Salts present in the soil and groundwater, salts applied through irrigation, salts in the soil transported with alluvium, and salts accumulated as a result of the weathering of the soil are all common sources of salt. When it comes to humid climates, where the salts are continuously leached out by excessive rainwater, these soils are not commonly found in large quantities. Saline soils, on the other hand, are quite common in semi-arid and arid regions, where there is insufficient precipitation to allow the salts originally present in the soil profile to leach out of the soil profile. Salts are commonly found in the soils of arid and semi-arid regions, with the amount varying depending on the water-transmitting characteristics of the soil and the climatic conditions, particularly rainfall (Kumar, 2019). Because of increased run-off in black soil areas, which have a higher clay content primarily composed of montmorillonite, effective rainfall is significantly less than actual rainfall in these areas. There is no way to leach the salts that have accumulated because of weathering.

5.3.1 Desert Development Programmes and Cumin Cultivation in Patan

Physiography, unreliable agro-climatic conditions, and dissimilar sociocultural geographies all contributed to the state of backwardness in the desert regions of the country (Joshi, 2000). Geo-climatic conditions forced residents of these regions to endure hardships, which necessitated the implementation of the desert development project as a centrally sponsored scheme in 1977–1978 (Ministry of Agriculture, 2000). The goal of the project was to use land restoration and desert preservation strategies to control desertification in the arid regions, as well as increase agricultural production. The Desert Development Programme evaluation study was instigated by the Planning Commission after hearing it from the Programme Evaluation Organization (NBARD, Potential Linked Credit Plan 2000–01, 2000a).

Gujarat is one of India's most industrialized states, ranking third in terms of GDP per capita (Ministry of Rural Development, 1999). Agriculture accounts for a lower percentage of the gross domestic product compared to other parts of India.

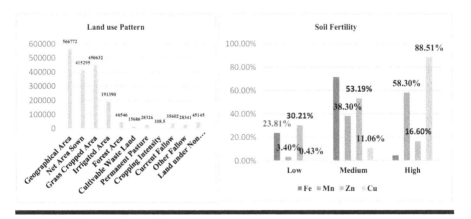

Figure 5.3   Patan land use pattern and fertility status
Source: KVK (2021)

Additionally, approximately 66% of the populace resides in the countryside, the majority of whom are employed in agriculture. Extending across central and nor-thern Gujarat, physical and agro-climatic conditions vary greatly (NBARD, 2000b). About nine months of the year see over 90% of the precipitation fall. Major obstacles to intensive agricultural production include erratic rains and frequent droughts. With between 340 millimetres in the district of Kachchh and 650 millimetres in the southern hills, the amount of rainfall varies greatly. Limited water resources, coupled with decreasing groundwater reserves, severely limit irrigation options. In addition, soil erosion is a major constraint on agricultural productivity. Only about 10% of Gujarat's total land area is covered by forests. Foodgrains make up 41% of all crops that are cultivated. Cotton and groundnut are the major cash crops (NBARD, 2000c). Agriculture is almost exclusively rain-fed, and even with irriga-tion, crop needs are seldom met. Agricultural landholdings are on the whole small and scattered, while farm machinery is still in its infancy.

Outside of agriculture, economic activities are restricted in the hamlets. Sales of livestock and excess production, such as dairy products, can be difficult, if not impossible. A small number of villagers are engaged in occupations that require specialized training. Women who are engaged in handicraft activities are finding success. Migration can be observed in all of the village's neighbourhoods. People are looking for work in other rural or urban areas (Kumar & Biswal, 2014). Due to a lack of job opportunities near or in their villages, many villagers move between cropping seasons. Remittances have a substantial impact on the local economies (NBARD, 2000d).

An additional 1,200 watershed development projects have been executed across various programs in Gujarat by the Rural Development Department since 1995 in response to the problematic natural resource depletion. Above all, 70% of these are operated by non-governmental organizations. The guidelines for a comprehen-sive list of all government-sponsored watershed development projects in Gujarat include a lot of common information that determines project implementation, pro-gramme content, and other components. Much of the overall approach to tackling the problem of resource scarcity centres on sustainability, participation, empower-ment, and decentralization (Shah, 2000a).

NGOs have a strong presence in Gujarat. For many years, they have been involved in the development of watersheds. They take part in government policy dialogues and are a leading voice for implementing watershed development strat-egies (NBARD, 1998). A number of NGOs have developed implementation strategies that are tailored to their unique situation or background, while regional solutions are implemented by further NGOs, implementing solutions established on the issues related to coastal salinity. The National Bank for Agriculture and Rural Development (NABARD) established a Watershed Development Fund in 1999 in order to coordinate watershed development efforts throughout the country. It aims to strengthen watershed development initiatives that encourage more involvement

Table 5.1 Integrated Watershed Management Projects

Name of project/year	Villages covered	Area treated under project (Ha)	Project cost (lakh)
IWMP-IV	Madhutra	2700	405
2009-10	Vauva	3000	405
IWMP-III	Santhali	1000	150
2009-10	Javantri	700	105
	Memdavad	2000	300
	Chalvada	1400	210
	Kamalpur	600	90
IWMP-1	Dhokavada	2600	390
2009-10	Barara	1200	180
	Jakhotra	1800	270
Total	10	17000	2505

Source: IWMP (2009)

from their participants. A significant percentage of Scheduled Castes/Scheduled Tribes (SC/ST) population, a high level of rain-fed agriculture, and a high potential for watershed development are the selection criteria for watersheds. NABARD's regional watershed management cell, which began operations in August 1999, has already begun to carry out projects during the preliminary stages. The programme needs to grow, which means that the number and make-up of staff will also have to increase (Groetschel et al., 2000).

5.4 Climate Change and Its Affect on Cumin Cultivation

A rise in global temperatures has produced its own unique mark on the globe, including India, where people have been alarmed for the past few years. Due to the impact of climate change, numerous agricultural and horticultural crops are experiencing the same plight. The flower of spice crops, fruit, and seed development is based on numerous factors such as the weather, photoperiod, sunlight hours, wind, and others (Murugan et al., 2012). When it gets too hot, a crop starts shedding its seeds. When it gets dry, the pollination and flowering of a crop may decrease, and plant growth may be negatively affected by arid conditions and violent winds. A fall in temperature during the early stage crop causes bolting. Pests such as aphids and diseases like powdery mildew can be attracted to spice crops, such as coriander, fenugreek, and cumin, which are typically found to have high rainfall and humidity levels

(Rosenzweig et al., 2001). Due to the impact of the environment, the seed manufacture and storage life of spice crops are influenced as well. Major research work has already been initiated by combining classical and modern breeding techniques to find new ideotypes for drought tolerance. A lot of different aspects of crop management have been completely remodelled, including things like water conservation, irrigation, organic management, mulching, and situation-specific cropping systems (Lobell & Field, 2007).

Crop production is dependent on climate factors such as solar radiation, temperature, and precipitation. Crop growth is also highly affected by disease, pests, and soil nutrient availability (McMichael, 2001). Thus, higher temperatures, altered precipitation and transpiration patterns, and increased exposure to extreme temperatures and precipitation events will affect plant development, growth, yield, and ultimately the production of crop species (Ewart et al., 2005).

Changes in mean climatic conditions are likely to impact agricultural crop yields. Increased warmth and significantly changed growing seasons has reshaped patterns of precipitation, mainly in rain-dependent regions. Warming has likely enhanced crop yields in some locations, reduced them in others, and had no effect in locations where yields were stable to begin with. Depending on how the region is classified, semi-arid and rain-fed regions would be most susceptible to crop failures resulting from increased soil drying and warming. Based on information compiled by Monteith (1981), two primary climatic causes of variation in yield include temperature and rainfall. Each of these two causes has a significantly larger impact than variation in the amount of light that is applied to crops (Murugan et al., 2007). New investigations on these crops recently have received new energy by fears that the global food supply and the quality of food might be affected on large and small scales by climate and weather changes in the future. As a result, changes in mean temperature and rainfall will become more common in the future (Long et al., 2005).

A 0.5°C increase in mean maximum temperature and a 0.5°C decrease in mean minimum temperature have been noted in Kachchh district over the past 100 years. The district averages 373 mm of rainfall annually, with 11 years of severe drought and 12 years of excessive rainfall. During the past two decades, over 10 tornadoes

Table 5.2   Changes in Climatic Pattern in Gujarat State

	Mean temperature (C°/year)	Mean maximum temperature (C°/Year)	Mean maximum temperature (C°/year)	Mean maximum temperature (C°/year)
Annual	+0.01	+0.01	+0.02	+1.41
Winter	+0.02	+0.01	+0.033	No trend
Summer	+0.01	+0.01	+0.02	-0.03
Monsoon	+0.01	+0.01	+0.1	+1.27

Source: GEER (2017)

associated with heavy rainfall have been reported every two decades (GEER, 2017), whereas prior to the early 1990s, only five tornadoes occurred every two decades. The India Meteorological Department conducted an analysis of its observational records, which go back to the year 1951, from 282 surface meteorological stations and 1,451 rainfall stations. For these surface meteorological stations, 27 rain gauges, as well as 18 others, are located in Gujarat. The results show how warming and rainfall changes vary across space and time. This has the potential to cause severe water shortages in the country that rely on rain-fed agriculture and water. Below, trends seen in Gujarat (1951–2010) are listed on a yearly and seasonal basis (GEER, 2017).

The district's agriculture is dependent on rainfall, and so is the size of the agricultural sector. Due to changes in temperature and rainfall, projections indicate that cumin production in the Patan district is expected to be impacted. The traditional crop area was reduced from 77% to 13%, and this shift was attributable to growth in alternative crops such as oilseeds, fodder, vegetables, and spices. The results of recent surveys on social and economic conditions show that there is an increase in insect and pest damage in horticulture crops. Changes in the climate, as well as changes in other related factors, have been identified as potential causes (GEER, 2017).

5.5 Socio-Economic Status of Patan Farmers

The landholding pattern, which states that the average landholding size in the district is 2.51 hectares, can be found in the statistics. More than 2 hectares (77.27%) of the total land is owned by 64,826 cultivators. The remaining 89,559 small and marginal farmers (58.04%) belong to the remaining cultivators. Plantation crops,

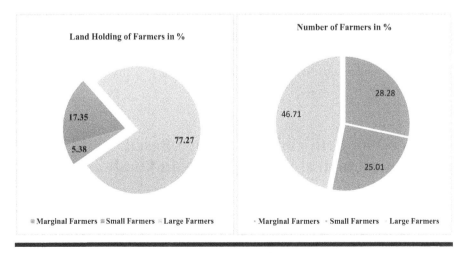

Figure 5.4   Number of farmers and their land holding status

Source: KVK (2021)

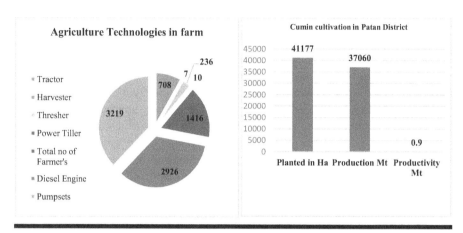

Figure 5.5 **Technologies used by farmers and cumin production in Mt**
Source: KVK (2021)

medicinal and aromatic plants, fruits, vegetables, and spices all contribute significantly to the economy. Planting agriculture and horticulture crops can help improve people's livelihoods while also helping to generate new jobs and increase people's income by making a market out of the products they produce (KVK, 2021).

A tremendous market opportunity has been created for farmers by increasing demand for horticultural products from domestic and international customers. Farmer families in rain-fed areas also benefit from the sector as it facilitates the growth of horticulture. Farm income is diversified by growing and selling crops, fruits, and vegetables on one's farm. Drip irrigation, such as the micro-irrigation concept, saves water while also ensuring the sustainability of the soil. Fruits such as ber, aonla, citrus, and so on, as well as vegetables such as carrot, cauliflower, and cabbage, and high-value spice crops such as cumin, dill-seed, and chilli, can be grown in the district, where the local government receives technical and financial assistance from both the National Horticulture Board and the state government (KVK, 2021).

5.6 Need for Artificial Intelligence-Based Meteorological Developments in Rural Farming Practices

Weather prediction and climate change are dependent on simulations of the atmosphere and other components of the Earth's climate system, including the ocean and ice sheets (IPCC, 2013). Human-caused climate change has been the subject of an enormous amount of scientific research over the past decades. Artificial intelligence

(AI) advancements, particularly in the subfield of machine learning and neural networks, have ignited enthusiasm for artificial weather prediction and climate modelling, as well as numerical modelling, both on their own and in conjunction (Peter et al., 2015). There are a range of concerns related to AI in different areas, and not all of these problems fit into a single definition of AI. There are a number of definitions of computation, but this one is particularly relevant here because it is used to refer to the study of the computations that allow us to perceive, reason, and act (Srivastava et al., 2014).

Many AI projects focus on tasks that computers are unable to perform but that humans are excellent at. When it comes to forecasting weather and climate, this method is not technically correct. To date, we have not been able to resolve these issues sufficiently using computers, but even less so with humans (Ionel, 2009). In other words, forecasting atmospheric dynamics two weeks ahead has proven to be impossible with current technology.

However, as long as "human beings can do something" is defined more broadly, the problem setting is appropriate (Zhang, 2019). Humans have been able to identify and implement some of the physical laws they've discovered and were then able to code those laws into mathematical models. Doing as well – or better – than the models created by humans may be the overall goal of AI in the context of weather and climate forecasting.

Machine learning is one of the subsets of AI. Over the past decade, this field has seen a substantial rise in demand (Leutbecher & Palmer, 2008). The main reason for recent progress in AI is this exponential increase in demand. It is also the most interesting and directly applicable part of AI for the problem setting of weather and climate forecasting. To put it in extremely simple terms, machine learning is the practice of "learning" from data. "Learning" can be defined in various ways (Richardson, 2000). For example, learning can involve understanding data structure, creating forecasts, or many other things. Some people may divide machine learning into categories according to the approach used. These categories include supervised learning and unsupervised learning. Supervised learning is a form of machine learning that uses connections between input and output pairs to help learners improve their predictions includes time series forecasting, which connects two or more measurements over time, but also more abstract problems, such as image recognition (the connection between an image and the label of an image). Unsupervised learning is distinguished by the fact that the output to be predicted (the result) is already known when the learning process is complete (Williams, 2017).

"The scientist describes what is; the engineer creates what never was."
Theodore von Kármán

Research on the effectiveness of weather forecasting is located at the border between science and engineering (Kursinski et al., 1997). The goal of science is to gain new knowledge and understanding, regardless of whether it is useful or not. Engineering, on the other hand, attempts to solve a problem with desired accuracy using limited resources. One could summarise it like this: science is more interested in finding out why something works, whereas engineering is more interested in ensuring that something works (C3S ERA5, 2019). Research on machine learning presents a significant challenge for a researcher because of the current state of knowledge. Understanding why something works or fails is difficult with many data-driven methods (Compo, 2011). This can be done in one of two ways: returning to the

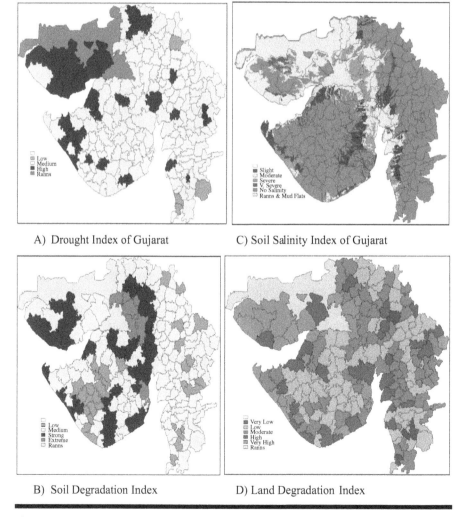

A) Drought Index of Gujarat   C) Soil Salinity Index of Gujarat

B) Soil Degradation Index   D) Land Degradation Index

Figure 5.6   Drought and Salinity Index of Gujarat

Source: GEER (2017)

earlier methodology and developing new questions based on data-driven forecasting methods as a "measure" to obtain a deeper understanding of the underlying dataset or system; or finding a different angle from which to approach the problem and asking new questions that use data-driven forecasting methods as a "measure" (Poli, 2016). So, even engineering-based research, such as discovering good prediction methods empirically, can be used for scientific knowledge discovery (Scher, 2020).

The above map of Gujarat depicts its vulnerability towards a long history of frequent droughts and a need for such advanced technologies aided with AI to smartly deliver the frequent climate change effects and needed concerns over such predictions. Due to frequent past droughts and nearness to the seashore, the salinity index remains noticeable. Salinity in the soil has proven to lower the productivity of cumin in the Patan district, and at the same time, the soil degradation index and land degradation index needs concern from the government of Gujarat and the government of India for a better policy briefing for such regions as the Patan district in Gujarat.

5.7 Conclusion and Future Perspective

As with all processes of change, the pace of climate change is gradual. This pacifies the population. Increasingly, our lives are being impacted by climate change from how we live, what we eat, what we wear, and where we travel. Changes in frequency, intensity, duration of precipitation, and temperature and humidity all have an impact on climate change. Changes in temperature and precipitation will have a significant impact on agriculture in India. It is necessary to look into the issues related to climate change with rigour. The Patan district, which is a semi-arid region, requires attention from the government and policymakers. Nevertheless, Patan cumin production has dropped for a while because of continuous droughts and subsequent floods. It was the government of Gujarat and the government of India that came together to solve farmers' issues to raise the socio-economic status of farmers living in such remote places. In response, many government and non-government institutions were set up to monitor the changes and deliver information on those changes to local farmers. In this regard, the meteorological department came up with their prediction, and Krishi Vigyan Kendras were the disseminators of knowledge and an intermediary to make farmers understand the technicalities of the meteorological department and crop their plants accordingly. It is the advancement of technology that has amalgamated with AI ion which a high degree of empirical testing shows us an architecture that is able to "learn" and predict the state one to 14 days ahead with a high level of skill (Krasnopolsky et al., 2005). The effectiveness of a machine-learning method for a particular problem is revealed by how well it transfers to data that was not used to train the method (McGovern, 2017). Dynamic systems form the context in which this question must be answered. To accomplish this, we divide the system's phase space into regions and evaluate whether the neural network is capable of producing reliable forecasts in regions that were deliberately excluded from training data (Rasp & Lerch, 2018). This is an additional step that we take in addition to the forecast quality, along with investigating whether a long run of consecutive neural network forecasts can go off in an unexplored region on its own.

5.8 Limitations of the Study

This study was carried out in the Patan district, and therefore its conditions, such as climatic conditions and geography, are entirely different from other parts of India. While interviewing the respondents, it may happen that some amount of data has not been expressed by the respondents. Gujarat is a male-dominant society, and during the survey, female respondents were often used to provide insights as the males were not available in villages. To collect data from such a complex situation limits the study to these villages only.

References

Agro-Climatic Regional Planning Unit. (1998). Agro-climatic regional planning, recent developments. Ahmedabad: Recent developments, *APRU Working Paper No 10*.

Bandyopadhyay, J., Mallik, B., Mandal, M., & Perveen, S. (2002). Dams and development: Report on a policy dialogue. *Economic and Political Weekly*, 37(40), 4108–4112. http://www.jstor.org/stable/4412689

Bhatia, B. (1992). Lush fields and parched throats: Political economy of groundwater in Gujarat. *Economic and Political Weekly, XXVII*, 51–52.

C3S ERA5. (2019). *Fifth Generation of ECMWF Atmospheric Reanalyses of the Global Climate*. Retrieved from Copernicus Climate Change Service Data Store (CDS): https://cds.climate.copernicus.eu.

Centre for Development Research. (1998). *An Assessment of European-aided Watershed Development Projects in India from the Prospective of Poverty Reduction and the Poor*. Centre for Development Research. Copenhagen: Centre for Development Research.

CGWB. (1998). *Groundwater Problems of Mehsana District*. West Central region Ahmedabad: Central Ground Water Board.

Compo, G. (2011). The twentieth century reanalysis project. *Quarterly Journal of the Royal Metrological Society*, 1–28.

CVG. (1997). *Valuing Groundwater Economic Concepts and Approaches*. Committee on Valuing Groundwater and Committee on Geoscience, Environment and Resources, Water Science and Technology Board. National Research Council.

DES. (2000). *Socio-Economic Review, Gujarat State 1999-2000*. Gandhinagar: Government of Gujarat.

Director of Census Operation. (1992a). *District Census Handbook*. New Delhi, Gujarat, District Panch Mahal: Census of India, Series-7.

Director of Census Operations. (1992b). *District Census Handbook.* New Delhi, Gujarat, District Panch Mahal: Director of Census Operations, Series-7.

Director of Economics and Stastics. (1999). *Statistical Outline of Gujarat 1998.* Gandhinagar: Government of Gujarat.

Directorate of Economics and Statistics. (1995). *Gujarat, Economic Development Through Maps.* Gandhinagar: Government of Gujarat.

Directorate of Economics and Statistics. (1998). *Statistical Outline of Gujarat.* Gandhinagar: Government of Gujarat.

Dubash, N. K. (2000). Ecological and socially embedded exchange: Gujarat model of water markets. *Economic and Political Weekly,* 1376–85.

Ewart, F., Rounsevell, M., Reginster, I., Metzger, M., & Leemans, R. (2005). Future scenarios of European agriculture land use: Estimating changes in crop productivity. *Agric. Ecosyst. Environ.*(doi:10.1016/j.agee.2004.12.003), 101–116.

Gass, G. M., Kumar, D., & McDonald, D. (1996). *Groundwater Degradation and its Socioeconomic and Health Impacts: Practical and Policy Option for Migration.* VIKSAT Natural Resource Institute Collaborative Research Project.

GEER, F. (2017). *Climate Change Adaptation for Natural Resource Dependent Communities in Kachchh, Gujarat: Strengthening Resilience through Water & Livelihood Security and Ecosystem Restoration.* Gandhinagar: National Adaptation Fund on Climate Change.

Graham, G., Kumar, D., & David, M. D. (1996). *Groundwater Degradation and its Socio-economic and Health Impacts: Practical and Policy Operations for Migration.* VIKSAT-Natural Resource Institute Collaborative Research Project.

Groetschel, A., Neuhof, M. I., Rathmann, I., Rupp, H., Santilana, X., Soger, A., & Werner, J. (2000). *Watershed Development in Gujarat: A problem Oriented Survey for the Indo-German Watershed Development Programme.* Ahmedabad/Berlin: Humboldt Universitat Zu Berlin & Centre for Advanced Training in Rural Development.

Institute of Rural Management. (1999). *Report on Agriculture Problems and Prospects in Gujarat.* Anand: IRMA.

Ionel, M. N. (2009). Data assimilation for numerical weather prediction: A review. In K. Seon, & X. Liang, *Data Assimilation for Atmospheric, Oceanic and Hydrologic Applications.* Springer.

IPCC. (2013). *Climate Change 2013: The Physical Science Basis.*

IRMA, & UNICEF. (2001). *White Paper on Water in Gujarat.* Narmada Water Resources and Water Supply. Institute of Rural Management Anand.

IWMP. (2009). *Integrated Watershed Management Program.* Office of Deputy Conservator of Forest, Patan: Government of Gujarat.

Joshi, S. (2000). Agriculture in Gujarat. *Progress and Potential.*

Krasnopolsky, V. M., Rabinovitz, M. S., & Chalikov, D. V. (2005). New approach to calculation of atmospheric model physics: Accurate and fast neural network emulation of longwave radiation in a climate model. *Monthly Weather Review,* 1370–1383.

Kumar, D. (2018). Development of agricultural bioinformatics in India: Issues and challenges. *Asian Biotechnology and Development Review, 20*(3), 3–18.

Kumar, D. (2019). Exploring Innovations in policy for agriculture bioinformatics and cultivation of scientific and sustainable skills in India. *International Journal of Innovative Knowledge Concepts, 7*(3), 2454 2415.

Kumar, D. M., Singhal, L., & Rath, P. (2004). Value of groundwater case studies in Banaskatha. *Economic and Political Weekly, 39*(31), 3498–3503.

Kumar, D., & Biswal, D. (2014). Socio-Economic Factors of Migration in Jharkhand: An Exploratory Analysis. *6th International Seminar on Human Resource.* Ranchi: Institute for Social Development & research.

Kumar, V. (2017, 06 13). *Cumin: Supply Chain Constraints and Prospects.* Department of Economic Analysis and Research. Mumbai: NBARD. Retrieved from APEDA AgriExchange, Indian Production of Cumin (HSCODE-1103): http://apeda.in/agriexchange/India%20Production/India_Productions.aspx?hscode=1103

Kursinski, E., Hajj, G., Schofield, J., Linfield, R., & Hardy, K. (1997). Observing earth atmosphere with radio occultation measurements using the global positioning system. *Journal of Geophysical Research: Atmosphere,* 23429–23465.

KVK. (2021, 06 21). *Welcome to Krishi Vigyan Kendra Patan.* Retrieved from National Agricultural Research System (NARS): https://kvk.icar.gov.in/aboutkvk.aspx

Leutbecher, M., & Palmer, T. (2008). Essential forecasting. *Journal for Computational Physics,* 3515–3539.

Lobell, D., & Field, C. (2007). Global scale climate crop yield relationships and the impacts of recent warming. *Environ. Res. Lett.,* doi:10:1088/1748–9326/2/1/014002.

Long, S., Ainsworth, E., Leakey, A., & Morgan, P. (2005). Global food security: Treatment of major food crops with elevated carbon dioxide or ozone under large scale fully open air conditions suggests recent model may have overestimated future yields. *Phil. Trans. R Society B, 360*(doi:10.1098/rstb.2005.1749), 2011–2020.

M. D. (2002). *Reconciling Water Use and Environment: Water Resources Management in Gujarat.* Vadodara: Gujarat Ecology Commission.

McGovern, A. (2017). Using artificial intelligence to improve real-time decision making for high impact weather. *Bulletin of the American Meteorological Society,* 2073–2090.

McMichael, A. (2001). Impact of climatic and other environmental changes on food production and population health in the comming decades. *Proc. Nut. Soc.* (60), 195–201.

Ministry of Agriculture. (2000). *Common Approach for Watershed Development.* New Delhi: Department of Agriculture Cooperation.

Ministry of Rural Development. (1999). *Swarnjayanti Gram Swarozgar Yojana Guidelines.* New Delhi: Government of India.

Monteith, J. (1981). Presidential Address to the Royal Meteorological Society. *doi:10.1256/smsqj.45401*(107), pp. 749–774.

Murugan, M., Backiyarani, S., Joseph Rajkumar, A., Hiremath, M., & Shetty, P. (2007). Yields of small cardamom (Elettaria cardamom M) variety PVI as influenced by levels of nutrients and neem cake under rainfed condition in southern western Ghats India. *Caspian Journal Environmental Science, 5*(2), 19–25.

Murugan, M., Shetty, P. K., Ravi, R., Anandhi, A., & Rajkumar, A. J. (2012). Climate change and crop yields in the Indian cardamom hills, 1978–2007 CE. *Climate Change*(110), 737–753.

Nair, R. (2010, August). Weather based crop insurance in India: Towards a sustainable crop insurance regime? *Economic and Political Weekly, 45*(34), 73–81.

NBARD. (1998). *Programme Report for Gujarat: Proposed Watershed Development Programme Through NGOs.* Mumbai: NABARD.

NBARD. (2000a). *Potential Linked Credit Plan 2000-01.* Ahmedabad: NABARD.

NBARD. (2000b). *Potential Linked Credit Plan 2000-01.* Ahmedabad: NABARD.

NBARD. (2000c). *Annual Credit Plan 2000-01.* Ahmedabad: NABARD.

NBARD. (2000d). *State Rural Credit Seminar 2000-01 & Agrivision 2010*. Ahmedabad: Gujarat State Focus Paper.

Peter, B., Alan, T., & Gilbert, B. (2015). The Quiet revolution of numerical weather prediction. *Nature*(525), 47–55.

Poli, P. (2016). ERA-20C: An atmospheric reanalysis of the twentieth century. *Journal of Climate*, 4083–4097.

Rasp, S., & Lerch, S. (2018). Neural networks for postprocessing ensemble weather forecasts. *Monthly Weather Review*, 3885–3900.

Richardson, D. (2000). Skill and relative economic value of the ECMWF ensemble prediction system. *Quarterly Journal of the Royal Meteorological Society, 126*(563), 649–667.

Rosenzweig, C., Iglisias, A., Yang, X., Epstein, P., & Chivian, C. (2001). Climate change and extreme weather events implications for food production, plant disease and pests. *Glo Change Hum Health, 2*(2), 90–104.

Scher, S. (2020). *Artificial Intelligence in Weather and Climate Prediction Learning Atmospheric Dynamics*. Department of Meteorology. Stockholm University.

Shah, A. (2000a). Watershed Plus. *A Report of a Workshop in Watershed Developments*. Ahmedabad: Watershed.

Singh, O., Sharma, A., Singh, R., & Shah, T. (2004). Virtual water trade in dairy economy: Irrigation water productivity in Gujarat. *Economic and Political Weekly, 39*(31), 3492–3497.

Srivastava, N., Hinton, G., Krizhevsky, A., Sutskever, I., & Salakhutdinoy, R. (2014). Dropout: A simple way to prevent neural networks from overfitting. *Journal of Machine Learning Research, 15*(56), 1929–1958.

Vyas, J. N. (2006). The sustainability of irrigated agriculture in India. *World Affairs: The Journal of International Issues*, 64–84.

Williams, P. D. (2017). A census of atmospheric variability from seconds to decades. *Geophysical Research Letter, 44*(21), 201–211.

World Bank. (2007). *India – National Agricultural Insurance Scheme: Market Based Solutions for Better Risk Sharing*. World Bank.

Zhang, F. (2019). What is the predictability limits of midlatitude weather? *Journal for Atmospheric Sciences, 76*(4), 1077–1091.

Chapter 6

The Role of Big Data in Agriculture

C. T. Ashita
Soka Ikeda College, Chennai, India

T. Sree Kala
Vels Institute of Science Technology and Advanced Studies, Chennai, India

6.1 Introduction

Big data is a large collection of organised and unstructured data that can be mined for information and analysed to create prediction algorithms for better decision-making. Apart from government departments, other segments such as telecommunications, marketing, education, healthcare, and different industrial sectors functionally use big data applications (Domarad, 2017). Agriculture is an area where it is gaining pertinence as a technology since there has been the apparent utilization of livestock monitoring devices, soil sensors, and other sensor equipment (Figure 6.1). The ultimate goal is to assist farmers, agriculturists, and scientists in implementing good agricultural techniques. Here we will see how big data plays a major role in different aspects of agriculture and farming.

6.2 Recent Study and Survey on Global Urbanization

As per a new study directed by the United Nations, the worldwide populace will reach 9.8 billion by 2050, an increment of 2.2 billion from now. This means that

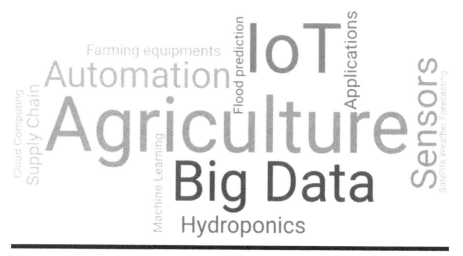

Figure 6.1　**Agriculture technology**

in order to feed the expanding population, we will need to increase crop production dramatically. Unfortunately, the rapid increase in urbanization and detrimental effects of climate change have resulted in the loss of a significant portion of farmland (Patten, 2016).

Today, there is a pressing need to provide more nutrition to the developing world's population, despite a scarcity of farming land. We will investigate how big data and agritech (or farming innovation) can assist with this issue in this chapter.

6.3　What Role Does Big Data Play in Agriculture?

Policymakers and industry leaders are turning to technological factors such as the Internet of Things (IoT), big data, big data analytics and cloud computing to support the agricultural community in dealing with the increasing rise in food demand and managing climate change (Figure 6.2).

The first phase of the technological process of data collection is aided by IoT devices. Sensors installed on tractors and trucks, as well as in fields, soil, and plants, help capture real-time data from the ground. Experts then incorporate much of the information gathered with other data accessible in the cloud, such as climate information, to determine patterns. These patterns can help identify and control various issues that can affect the operation of a farm. They can also inform predictive algorithms that can detect issues before they occur.

6.3.1　The Top Four Big Data Applications at the Farm

The possibilities for big data applications are vast, and we've barely scratched the surface. Tracking tangible goods, collecting real-time data, and forecasting circumstances

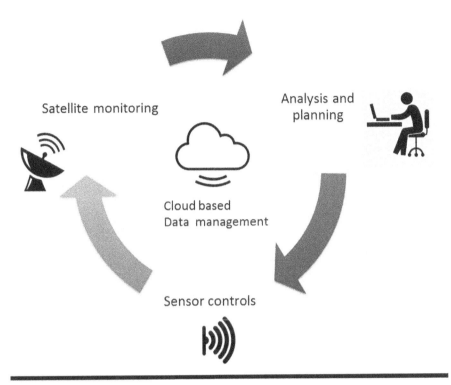

Figure 6.2 **Smart agriculture**

can all be game-changers in farming. Here we shall examine a few instances where big data can provide benefit.

1. **Providing food for an ever-growing population**

   Governments are seeking to address this as one of the biggest challenges, and increasing the production of current farmlands is one approach. Farmers may use big data to get specific information on rainfall patterns, fertilizer requirements, water cycles, and other topics. This enables them to make educated decisions about which crops to plant and when to harvest for maximum profit. In the end, precise decisions boost farm production.

2. **Using pesticides in an ethical manner**

   Pesticide administration has for some time been a troublesome issue because of its negative ecological impact. Farmers can better manage this with the help of big data, which can tell them which pesticides to apply, when to use them, and how much to use. Farmers can follow regulatory requirements and avoid chemical abuse in food production by monitoring it on a regular basis. Furthermore, selective use of pesticides to eliminate weeds and insects leads to higher profitability.

3. **Optimizing farm machinery**
   Sensors have been integrated into farming equipment by companies like John Deere, and big data applications have been deployed to enable fleet managers to manage their fleet better. This kind of monitoring can be lifesaving for big farms, as it informs users of tractor availability, fuel refill notifications, and servicing due dates. In essence, this improves farm equipment usage while also ensuring its long-term health.
4. **Taking care of supply chain difficulties**
   Every year, a third of the food produced for human use is lost or squandered, according to McKinsey. This is a startling reality, given the industry's ongoing battle to close the supply-demand gap. Food supply cycles from producer to market must be shortened to address this. By tracking and improving delivery truck routes, big data can assist in achieving supply chain efficiencies.

6.3.2 Challenges Presented by Implementing Big Data Solutions in Agriculture

- In farm management information systems, the creation of high-quality data is a major difficulty, and huge real-time data offers little to help.
- Strict enforcement of data-ownership, privacy, and security laws stifles innovation.
- Due to the massive amount of unstructured and heterogeneous data, domain experts and qualified data scientists are required.
- A successful business model necessitates the long-term integration of data from several sources, which is often a difficult undertaking.
- Business models must provide for a proportional split of the profits among the stakeholders.
- Impoverished low-cost solutions for farmers in developing nations are a difficulty.

6.4 Big Data in Precision Agriculture

Agriculture is a field and a process that is highly reliant on the weather of a certain location at a specific moment. A farmer's success will thus be determined by how well he or she forecasts the weather and plans all of his or her agricultural tasks to coincide with what the weather dictates. As a result of the interaction between weather and agriculture, precise weather predictions are required in order for farmers to make informed decisions that will not result in losses (Precision Agriculture, n.d.).

As a result of the necessity to accurately predict the weather, weather forecasting departments have grown in popularity in practically every country on the planet. These departments are in charge of informing farmers about the projected rainfall in a given location, the temperature that will prevail in that location, the humidity levels, and a variety of other weather-related issues. Farmers can make the best agricultural decisions thanks to the analysis and application of information provided by forecasting departments (Sharma, 2020; Talend, 2020).

Agriculture and farming will require quick and reliable weather information in the future to ensure continuing success in the agricultural industry.

6.4.1 Farmer's Suitability for and Use of Meteorological Data

6.4.1.1 Creating Irrigation Schedules for the Farm

A farmer can construct an irrigation plan that factors in water availability at a given time on a farm as well as water that the farm is projected to get when it rains in the future using meteorological information about rainfall expected in a specific area. This allows a farmer to plant and water his plants using the farm's existing water until the rains arrive. When the rains start, the farmer should then gather the rainwater so that he or she has enough water to irrigate the crops. This irrigation schedule is designed to ensure that no water is wasted at any point during the watering process.

6.4.1.2 Amount of Renewable Energy That the Farm Will Receive

A farmer can utilize weather forecasting to know and plan for the renewable energy that his or her land will be exposed to. Forecasting will allow a farmer to determine how much solar, wind, and anaerobic energy a farm will receive, as well as how this renewable energy will be used on the farm.

Solar and wind energy can be harvested by a farmer by erecting solar panels and wind turbines, respectively. Harvesting and storing this energy will allow the farmer to put it to good use while avoiding any damage that the wind and solar would have caused.

6.4.1.3 Assists in the Safe Handling of the Farm

A farmer can improve farm safety and efficiency by studying forecast information. A farmer can take required action in the animals' and birds' shade based on temperature and humidity information, ensuring that the animals and birds are not exposed to excessive temperatures and humidity. When it is predicted that the weather will be cold, a farmer should take steps to guarantee that the animals will be warm enough when the cold arrives.

Humidity information also allows a farmer to arrange for the best levels of storage for both feeds and harvested crops. Forecast information also enables a farmer to be prepared for really harsh weather situations such as frost, storms, and drought, ensuring that the farm is not harmed when these extreme weather conditions occur.

6.4.2 Weather Forecasting Through Satellite

Meteorology will transition from traditional weather forecasting techniques to satellite weather forecasting in order to provide reliable and precise information that will aid future farming. Because of its worldwide coverage, high resolution, and accuracy, satellite weather forecasting will be favoured.

Another advantage of satellite forecasting is its capacity to predict the weather for a longer length of time. This is in contrast to other traditional forecasting systems, which have very limited time spans and provide farmers with insufficient time to prepare. As a result, farmers will rely more on satellite forecasting in the future due to its multiple benefits.

6.4.3 Forecasting Schedules Created Just for You

The majority of current weather forecast information sometimes contradicts itself and only anticipates the weather for a short period of time, leaving the farmer with very little time to plan. Farmers have been known to make judgments based on erroneous information, which has resulted in some costly mistakes.

Farmers and farming agencies are increasingly taking on board their own meteorological specialists in an attempt to eliminate the inaccuracy of weather forecast information in print and audio-visual media. These meteorologists are in charge of providing farmers and agricultural authorities with custom weather forecasts. Following receipt of the information, these specialists are responsible for advising the agricultural organisation and farmers on the best course of action to take based on the available data.

This strategy of hiring professionals to create custom weather forecasts is more expensive than using inexpensive weather forecast information from the media, but it is more useful to farmers in the long run.

6.4.4 Weather Factors That Have an Impact on Farm Planning and Operations

- The hours when the sun is shining brightly.
- The highest and lowest temperatures.
- The wind's speed, direction, and strength.
- Extreme weather events, such as thunderstorms, hail, fog, heat waves, cyclones, tornadoes, and a variety of others.
- Dew and precipitation.
- Radiation from the sun.

6.5 Forecasting Floods

Floods are one of the most common and costly natural catastrophes in terms of human damage and economic loss around the world. Weather forecasts have improved in accuracy and precision, allowing for more accurate localised precipitation totals, storm duration estimations, and even storm movement predictions. Localized flood predictions, on the other hand, are falling behind.

We know that flooding will happen again, therefore improving predicting models and obtaining up-to-date, high-quality, and readily available data are essential.

6.5.1 Flood Monitoring and Forecasting Are Difficult Tasks

Floods are notoriously hard to forecast. These are the major concerns.

- **Historical Data Is Scarce**
  To determine the dangers and likelihood of flooding for downstream rivers and floodplains, we need historical data. Unfortunately, historical data is only available for the past 100 years or so and only for specific streams and rivers. We are aware of significant historical or geologic events from the past. They are, however, merely educated estimates, and we do not utilise them to predict future events.

- **Data and Models with a Lot of Complexity**
  Obtaining and modelling complicated combinations of hydrological, meteorological, and topographic variables, as well as their interconnections, is an additional problem. To ensure maximum lead time for flood predictions and alerts, many of them require real-time availability.

  The reaction of the drainage basin to rainfall, snowmelt, and any other water inputs is critical for accurate models and predictions. This is determined by current hydrologic conditions, weather, and geography. Any modification to the drainage basin, whether man-made or natural, has an impact on how it responds to flooding.

- **Environments of Cities**
  Cities are densely populated, feature many buildings and roads, and are often found near huge bodies of water. They change and evolve all the time. This is an ideal combination for flooding events such as flash floods and storm surges.

  During strong rainstorms, the water is quickly directed into city drains and river channels by less absorbent surfaces such as roads and buildings. The speed and volume of excess run-off can cause quick flooding by overloading municipal drains and waterways.

  Flooding is difficult to predict due to the lack of a lag time between precipitation and flooding, and it can occur without warning.

■ **Flood Modelling and Forecasting with New Approaches**
When it comes to flood modelling and forecasting, there are a number of obstacles to overcome. This is due to the extensive network of existing monitoring stations, as well as the numerous datasets that are combined to feed multiple complex algorithms. Change takes a long time to implement since the ripple effects affect many teams, and it typically necessitates buy-in and coordination from multiple departments or organisations.

Although progress in these complicated systems appears to be gradual, agencies, scholars, and businesses are developing novel solutions. Listed below are a few examples.

■ **Internet of Things (IoT)**
In our connected society, the IoT is the next logical step in flood monitoring. Sensors are becoming more affordable, dependable, and capable of serving real-time data.

Flood Network, based in the United Kingdom, is an IoT platform that allows consumers to buy their own sensors and connect them to an existing network of flood monitoring equipment. Every 15 minutes, sensors record water levels and deliver alerts when the water levels are too high. In order to improve responsiveness, Flood Network collaborates with local organisations and exchanges data with modellers and forecasts. It has gained a lot of traction in the United Kingdom, and many more cities are joining the movement.

The US government is also investing in the IoT. They want to build, construct, and test a network of low-cost flood inundation sensors in collaboration with corporate partners. The sensors are part of a scalable wireless mesh network that measures and reports rising water and flood conditions to operations centres, first responders, and citizens in real time.

■ **Big Data and Machine Learning**
Floods and weather are inextricably linked, so more accurate and precise weather forecasts allow for improved flood forecasts. A big element of this is big data. Satellites, radars, ships, weather models, and a variety of other sources generate tens of gigabytes of data per day for weather organisations like the US National Oceanic and Atmospheric Administration (NOAA). Big data technology has vastly improved storm movement, strength, and duration forecasting, and lead time.

Companies are also attempting to profit from increasingly accurate weather forecasts. Right now, hyperlocal forecasting is all the rage.

Users can get up-to-the-minute forecasts with great visuals of temperature, clouds, and precipitation with hyperlocal weather apps such as Dark

Sky. Weather-dependent businesses such as construction and aviation are being targeted by start-ups like ClimaCell, which promises military-grade forecasts.

The Weather Company, which is owned by IBM, has made a significant investment in Deep Thunder weather technology. Deep Thunder makes projections for areas as small as 0.1 square kilometres using advanced physics. In addition, they construct weather effect models using machine learning and cognitive approaches. These are designed to assist businesses in predicting how weather affects consumer purchasing behaviour, insurance claim validity, and even the number of repair crews required following large storms.

Hyperlocal weather forecasts are a significant step towards more accurate flood forecasting. Many governments and agencies can still identify possible flash flooding and issue warnings ahead of time. We should expect significant advances in flood modelling and forecasting at finer sizes as these technologies evolve.

■ **Crowdsourcing**

Crowdsourcing has proven to be effective in a variety of applications, including traffic reporting, marketing, and even providing finance for new goods. Scientists and governments have recognized the potential of this out-of-the-box data collection method and are using it to record floods.

Because flooding in urban areas is difficult to anticipate, models and forecasts rarely provide accurate or timely information at the street level. Obtaining real-time information from the people on the ground is crucial for flood emergency management.

The information can also be used after a flood to help with damage assessments and to improve flood models that already exist. For example, residents can contribute information to a publicly accessible web map using MIT's RiskMap. Users can message a chatbot through a variety of social media channels. They are given a one-time URL through which they can submit information such as location, water depth, photo, and description.

In early 2017, RiskMap put its method to the test during a big flood in Indonesia. In just 24 hours, almost 300,000 people accessed the public website during the experiment. The map was also included in the Uber app to assist drivers in avoiding floodwaters.

iSeeFlood is another example of crowdsourcing. It offers an iOS and Android app that collects flood observations in order to assist emergency management and improve existing flood models. To improve the content on the public web map, the app adds social media data. It determines if tweets are relevant to live flooding occurrences using machine learning and natural language processing algorithms, then parses the text for location information or flood characteristics.

6.6 What Role Do Automation and Big Data Play in Feeding the World?

Whether you believe it or not, food production is undergoing a silent revolution that will soon transform the entire process of growing, producing, and distributing food around the world, as well as in local cities and towns. This is referred to as food production system automation. Scientists used to call this hydroponics, and the term still has a lot of clout when it comes to defining what's going on in Japan and China, the United Kingdom and the European Union, and the United States. As technology advances, it will also make mobile learning and big data analytics increasingly possible.

6.6.1 The Benefits of Hydroponic Food Production

There are a variety of reasons why the automation of food production via hydroponics is altering the farming environment. The benefits of producing food using hydroponic techniques are several, including reduced land use and increased food production, reuse and recycling of water, and reduced transportation costs, which lends itself to a growing and urbanised population around the world.

6.6.2 What Role Do Big Data and Automation Play in Hydroponics?

Fujitsu has developed a cloud platform called Akisai in Japan. This system analyses large amounts of data collected from various sensors located throughout greenhouses. Fans for ventilation and heating units can be turned on remotely or automatically using this information to produce veggies. Furthermore, the cloud service's collection of big data is resulting in improved food quality.

In the United States, Freight Farms, a company that makes high-volume crop production shipping freight units, is combining hydroponics and big data by gathering information from farmers in their network and uploading the finest growing settings from their customers.

Essentially, they are constructing a tailored e-learning development programme for their users to learn the finest strategies for growing their crops through their data collection. It is quite evident that every farmer who becomes a freight farmer is exponentially better than someone who started recently because they are building it upon more than 40 or 50 people who have been doing it now for a few years. Rather than conducting research and development, it is better that they actually work with the network of farmers get to see the emerging results.

In China, a new company named Alesca has taken old and disused shipping containers and turned them into amazingly automated hydroponic tiny farms (Figure 6.3). The mini farms require only two hours or less of human labour per week

Figure 6.3 **Hydroponic farming**

to maintain, while the rest of the maintenance is handled by computer software and robotics. The idea behind shipping containers is that they may create microclimates that are ideal for each type of vegetable plant being grown. Furthermore, on a per square meter basis, these small farms outperform any comparable farming approach.

They achieve this by creating the right habitat for each species of plant using cutting-edge automation, appropriate LED lighting, and the latest software components. The plants are monitored by sensors that provide information to remote operators on their health, growth, and whether or not the nutrients provided and the general environment need to be adjusted to obtain the best growth conditions.

Alesca believes that local concept zero-mile food is the wave of the future for highly and intensely produced local food for today's and tomorrow's densely inhabited dense urban metropolises.

6.6.3 The Challenges of Automated Food Production

The expense of such hydroponically generated food has long been one of the most significant impediments to this sort of automated food production's success. Because of the high electrical demands and costs associated with feeding, cooling, heating, and lighting systems, scaling up production has hitherto been difficult. In the past, the great amount of personal labour that the system required kept this form of food production from being either economical or scalable.

However, thanks to new software and increased automation of hydroponic farms, this is all changing to the point where soil-less farming techniques can at least achieve a sufficient industrial and commercial scale to help feed the globe.

6.7 Conclusion

We are stepping into a new age of technology where simple agriculture and farming practices have been influenced by scientific data to make food production more efficient in highly sterile farming conditions. With the application of big data, techniques such as hydroponics, selective weather conditions, soil testing, and choosing the right insecticide have helped increase the productivity of foodgrains to the staggering demands. The future of modern farming and agriculture depends on big data and supporting technology to sustain mankind and its food demand.

References

Domarad, N. (2017, September 28). How big data is changing flood monitoring and forecasting. *DataStand*. www.thedatastand.com/flood-forecast-big-data/

Patten, B. (2016, February 10). *How automation and big data are helping to feed the world*. *Datafloq*. https://datafloq.com/read/how-automation-big-data-are-helping-feed-world/1844

Precision Agriculture. (n.d.). Big data in precision agriculture. *Precision Agriculture*. Retrieved July 4, 2021, from https://precisionagricultu.re/big-data-in-precision-agriculture/

Sharma, R. (2020, April 28). Big data applications in agriculture: Role, importance & challenges. *upGrad*. www.upgrad.com/blog/big-data-applications-in-agriculture/

Talend. (2020). Big data and agriculture: A complete guide. *talend*. www.talend.com/resources/big-data-agriculture/

Chapter 7

Blockchain-Based Agri Manufacture Industry

Mahadi Hasan Miraz
School of Technology Management and Logistics, Universiti Utara Malaysia, Kedah, Malaysia

Mohammad Tariq Hasan
School of Business and Economics, United International University, Dhaka, Bangladesh

Farhana Rahman Sumi
Department of Business Studies, University of Information Technology and Sciences, Dhaka, Bangladesh

Shumi Sarkar
Department of Business Studies, University of Information Technology and Sciences, Dhaka, Bangladesh

Mohammad Amzad Hossain
School of Business and Economics, United International University, Dhaka, Bangladesh

Subrato Bharati
Bangladesh University of Engineering and Technology, Dhaka, Bangladesh

DOI: 10.1201/9781003299059-7

7.1 Introduction

Intelligent manufacturing and subjects relevant to the future of manufacturing have been covered in depth (Al Faruqi, 2019; Aslam et al., 2020). This study provides a means for successfully implementing the future of manufacture (Miraz, 2020a; Miraz, 2020b). This includes the hybrid system, technological maturation, production processes, situation on the market, availability for environment technical scalability, and industry-academia cooperation (Banjanović-Mehmedović & Mehmedović, 2020; Bousdekis et al., 2020). In addition, the integration of artificial intelligence (AI) into modern industrial manufacturing is very important. AI, which consists of many physical robots, provides a coordinating method for many robots (Chen, 2017; Clark et al., 2020). Interactions among robots interacting with the environment as a desired collective action are expected to be responsible for this. This is also known as robotic cellular systems (Collins, 2020; Connolly-Barker et al., 2020).

7.2 Background

Manufacturing contributes significantly to the national economy (Davidson, 2020; Davies et al., 2017). The effects of advanced manufacturing on the economy, culture, and the country's economic portfolios must be taken into account by policymakers and the public (Demir et al., 2019; Derigent et al., 2020). Raising public awareness and winning the support of politicians is not always easy (Egger & Masood, 2020; Fantini et al., 2020). One huge problem is that most people are unfamiliar with what manufacturing looks like (Miraz, Hasan, et al., 2020; Miraz, Hye, Alkurtehe, et al., 2020), and most people still think of the factories and mills of the past (Miraz, Hye, Wahab, et al., 2020). The first significant challenge to redefining future developments is to impact the economy, society, and policymakers (Ge et al., 2020; Guo, Zhong, Lin, et al., 2020).

Additive manufacturing has become more widely accepted as a "direct manufacturing" process due to increased materials, properties, performance, and quality (Hye et al., 2020; Miraz et al., 2019). The manufacture of additives should not be considered a simple production process. It offers further productivity improvements and changes how products are manufactured and delivered (Jeyanthi, 2018). The jet engine fuel nozzle is an example of a well-documented and valuable contribution to additive development by way of component consolidation. The fuel tube incorporates most components of the ancient design into a single model but weighs 25% lower. It is also more efficient as it uses an additive manufacturing process (Krugh & Mears, 2018; Lee et al., 2019).

Concerning the business model, manufactured service is becoming a critical driver of value production. In these instances, output initiates and allows technology to create value (Lee et al., 2015). Most manufacturers recognize that manufacturing and service overlap because the environment has shifted from product delivery to continued customer interaction (Lee et al., 2018; Li et al., 2017). Advanced system processing and prompt action are the new paradigms of innovative and cost-effective services (Li et al., 2020; Lins & Oliveira, 2020). There are more effective mixed business models for manufacturing services (Ma et al., 2020; Maresova et al., 2018). For example, Rolls-Royce uses an entirely different device to track performance and identify problems, which gives another choice to consumers when they purchase a generator. As a result, the company has turned the product into a service (Nahavandi, 2019; O'Donovan et al., 2018). As an additional example, Babolat has developed tennis rackets with sensors to generate data that allows the company to provide coaching services (Pacaux-Lemoine et al., 2017; Paschek et al., 2019).

7.3 Expand Manufacturing

In the past three decades, some have anticipated that all plants will be filled with robots within 10 years, leading to the heavy usage of robotics in factories and no human workers (Saldivar et al., 2015). The job of the human operator will also be eliminated in factories decades later and will continue in the foreseeable future (Miraz, Hasan, et al., 2020; Miraz, Hye, Alkurtehe, et al., 2020). A network of hybrid systems for humans and machines is embedded in manufacturing additives, subtractions, and cyber-physical structures, on a micro- and macro scale in digital and analogue processes (Zhou et al., 2015). The production of additives will not replace human beings entirely, nor will the manufacturing of subtractions (Zhou et al., 2019). Instead, they will work together to assign duties equally. It is important to research individual structures (Zhou et al., 2018). Of similar or greater significance are additive and subtractive production and the interaction between composites and metals. This is also essential for the effective and proper operation of hybrid systems (Zhong et al., 2017; Zhou et al., 2020).

The three primary manufacturing groups are shaping, machining (subtractive), and additive manufacturing (Zhang et al., 2020; Zheng et al., 2020). A national chart shows the relationship between process cost and output volume. Shaping is ideal for large sizes to achieve low unit costs by the amortization of many initial capital expenditures in equipment and machinery (Wang et al., 2020; Whittle, 2019). The load size for the machining of additives may be moderate (Villalba-Díez et al., 2020; Villalonga et al., 2020). It is significant to note that breakthroughs in subtractive and additive products have led to a shift to direct manufacturing (Sun et al., 2020; Tao et al., 2019). This increases the cost-effectiveness of production additives (Skobelev & Borovik, 2017; Smith, 2020). Similar technical and economic analyses for manual and intelligent integrity should be carried out (Shi et al., 2020). Therefore, the objectives are:

1. To develop secure production management.
2. To evaluate the proposed agri-blockchain model.

7.4 Agri-Blockchain

Innovation analysts undertook lengthy and rigorous research to evaluate the extent to which agri-blockchain technology may assist the agricultural industry (Demestichas et al., 2020). They examined over 130 blockchain businesses operating in the field. This research included invention, features, and more in-depth exploration of each part.

7.4.1 Blockhain-Based Food Chain

Determining the source of food products is crucial for keeping customers loyal and believing in a company's integrity (Fleming et al., 2019). Blockchain technology can essentially guarantee that any type of fruit or vegetable sold in a local farmers' market is safe to buy, like the ones grown in-region from local farms (Potts, 2019). Contemporary food supply chains, such as those used by food stores, have no practical way of ensuring that all the goods are kept and handled as required by a single supplier. Thus, because retail has already started tracing food product origins using the blockchain, larger food service operators are likely to follow suit.

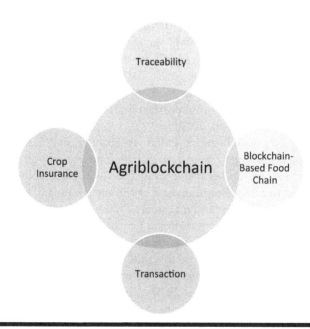

Figure 7.1   **Agri-Blockchain transformation**

The difficulty of discovering food sources is also greatly decreased with this strategy (Demestichas et al., 2020). For example, the mangoes at Walmart were traced, which shows how important it is to know where your items come from. Conversely, suppose a product does not meet a retailer's requirements. In that case, it is imperative to reduce the time required to trace the origins of a product, which enables merchants to separate the defective goods promptly and, therefore, minimize the threat to humans (Miraz, 2020a; Miraz et al., 2019; Miraz, Hye, Alkurtehe, et al., 2020; Miraz, Hye, Wahab, et al., 2020).

7.4.2 Transactions

The blockchain can aid farmers in various unique ways, including streamlining transaction processes and levelling the playing field for smaller farms in developing countries (Albayati et al., 2020; Beck et al., 2016; Bharati, 2021). According to the United Nations, billions of dollars of food is wasted every year worldwide (Hanson et al., 2015). This occurs for many reasons, but in part, it is because those who produce food in undeveloped countries have comprehensive market contact, which means they cannot sell all the food they make.

The agriculture sector is a crowded market, so competition for clients is fierce (Kamilaris et al., 2019). A start-up company has developed a unique execution procedure, and the hope is that by implementing it they can get a foothold in the industry (Xiong et al., 2020). The feature of their product is that it enables easy access to participants and operations (Li et al., 2020). In addition to all of the above, another vast benefit the blockchain offers to agricultural producers is the capacity to price their products more effectively and efficiently (Verma, 2021). As a result, they are able to manage their output to fit the demand for their products (Vangala et al., 2020).

7.4.3 Crop Insurance

Farmers are provided with custom smart contracts to provide crop insurance and get compensation when a loss occurs (Xiong et al., 2020). Generally, it is an arduous and burdensome process on both the grower's and company's sides (Yadav & Singh, 2019). Predictable weather anomalies lead to inaccurate estimates and delayed reporting of losses (Iyer et al., 2021). In addition, there is an opportunity for fraud, which introduces operational chaos (Heires, 2016). A damage claim can be activated if specific meteorological conditions are met, shortening the claims process for farmers and insurers (Kim & Laskowski, 2018).

7.4.4 Traceability

The growing contemporary style of agrifood is always lower than expected (Chen et al., 2020). The agri-blockchain opens up a new process of food cultivation from farm to house, confirming the legitimacy of that entire process (Kamble et al., 2020). In addition, product harvesting information gives harvest statistics and information on who harvested the product (Kamilaris et al., 2021). This also provides a quick and easy method for consumers to find out about their products, such as the farm in which some grass-fed beef was reared, in a matter of seconds (Hang et al., 2020). The unalterable nature of blockchain information means that it offers verifiable information with absolute certainty and makes it practically impossible to counterfeit (Lin et al., 2018).

7.5 Shifts in Manufacturing

Within 50 years, the Fourth Industrial Revolution – Industry 4.0 – will begin and may be overdue. Several parameters characterize the state of the process in every step of development.

Simple, functional automation, standardizations in mass production, and automation expanded thanks to the Second Industrial Revolution (Industry 2.0) (Al Faruqi, 2019; Clark et al., 2020). A wide range of checks and quality criteria were applied for the unification process. Fundamental pick-and-place and component feeders, which use vibrations as a transport system, are generally used for complex, hardwired automation (Banjanović-Mehmedović & Mehmedović, 2020; Davies et al., 2017; Guo, Zhong, Lin, et al., 2020). The objective was to increase the utilization of hard-coded automation (Hodgkins, 2020). Since systems were often designed with extensive process labour, efficient use of processes was a major difficulty (Hozdić & Butala, 2020; Jian-zhong, 2014; Kamilaris et al., 2021).

These advances were included in the Third Industrial Revolution (Industry 3.0), which encouraged further automation, digitalization, and networking (Li et al., 2017; Li, Wang, Liu, et al., 2020; Lin et al., 2018). This approach has delivered a considerably higher automation rate, productivity and process diversity. Advanced robots and programs, which have never been reproduced, are inside their own class. Adaptable automation should take account of a product variable such as a size fluctuation or several products that vary similarly. While these technologies have several capabilities, including process monitoring, control, and management sensors, machines of specialized instruments and tools, such as numerical control equipment, 3D printers, and robots, are also incorporated in the Third Industrial Revolution (Pacaux-Lemoine et al., 2017; Paschek et al., 2019).

These are the various technologies that have enabled Industry 4.0 and are Industry 4.0 and Industry 3.0's last distinct elements (Sachsenmeier, 2016). The use of each other's subnetworks allows computers to be connected to internal subnetworks in real-time (Saldivar et al., 2015; Shan et al., 2020). Sensors, data exchange, and networking give unequalled strength for manufacturing and industrial enterprises (Smith, 2020; Tao et al., 2019; Xiong et al., 2020). However, these companies must likewise address safety concerns.

Table 7.1   Industry 4.0 Technologies Described in the Literature

No.	Technology	Technology definition
1	IIoT (Industrial Internet of Things)	It is possible to manage complex systems in real time by interacting with humans, computers, artefacts, and information and communications technology systems.
2	CPS (Cyber-Physical Systems)	Developing worldwide business networks in order to bring the physical and digital worlds together.
3	Big data collection and analysis	To make informed decisions, data must be extracted from enormous amounts of data.
4	Cloud services for products	In order to expand their usefulness and related services, cloud computing is being used in goods to collect information from vast amounts of data.
5	Additive manufacturing	As an example, when it comes to chip removal, 3D printing outperforms conventional machines such as lathes or frying machines.
6	Simulations/analysis of virtual models	Computer-aided design (CAD) is a virtual model analysis technique that uses finite element analysis, in which simulations simulate the attributes of applied simulations dynamics.
7	Integrated engineering systems	Information technology support systems are being used in product development and production to facilitate knowledge exchange.
8	Augmented reality	A computer graphics technique that involves superimposing simulated signals on top of a genuine image of the outside environment.
9	Flexible manufacturing lines	For example, RFID or the construction of processes can be used to automate digitally with sensors and data. Manufacturing systems that can be reconfigured (RMS).
10	Cybersecurity	Cyberattacks on Internet-connected devices, such as data information, hardware, and software, are protected from being carried out.

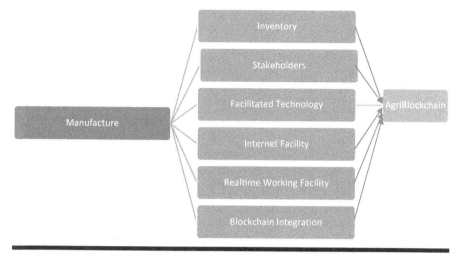

Figure 7.2 Research framework for Blockchain-based agri-management

7.6 Research Framework

This section reveals the framework of this research. This framework demonstrates the integration of manufacture for agri-blockchain transformation.

7.7 Development of Agri-Blockchain

As mentioned, the blockchain is already having a significant impact on the way business is done. This includes minimizing the danger of fraudulent activities, increasing transaction speeds, helping farmers manage and analyze crops, and much more.

1. **Agri-blockchain**: A blockchain business whose focus is on facilitating peer-to-peer agriculture transactions and processing while cutting out the middlemen.
2. **Agritech**: A commodity management solution based on the blockchain and interconnected with global grains markets. The platform helps process complex agricultural transactions employing smart contracts.
3. **Agriculture distributed ledger**: A social entrepreneurship project is designed to help farmers trace the source of their food, gain more accessible access to funding, and store their transactions data.
4. **BlockBase**: An online marketplace for smaller farms and landlords to directly access and rent individual micro-farms throughout the world, without the complication or expense of a large organization.

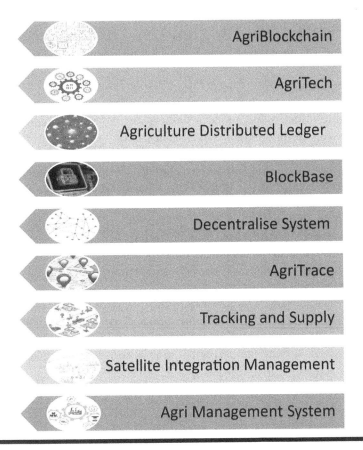

AgriBlockchain

AgriTech

Agriculture Distributed Ledger

BlockBase

Decentralise System

AgriTrace

Tracking and Supply

Satellite Integration Management

Agri Management System

Figure 7.3   **Blockchain-based agri-manufacturing**

5. **Decentralize system**: A firm that provides insurance for farmers via its decentralized insurance applications, which uses the blockchain.
6. **AgriTrace**: A firm that is creating a transparent digital food supply chain to harness quality food data to establish a blockchain of food, tracing the food's journey.
7. **Tracking and supply**: Uses identification tools for animals, transporters, fresh food packages, and fresh food packaging to trace products throughout the supply chain.
8. **Satellite integration management**: Provides crop insurance to guard against the loss of produce using satellites to monitor rainfall and have a system that pays out automatically when the forecast is correct.
9. **Blockchain-based agri-management system**: Finally, construct an integrated blockchain-based agri-management system.

7.8 Research Process

In this section, the researcher demonstrates the description of the research process:

1. **Theoretical Study**

   A study of theory in which the theoretical study is carried out through literature to determine problems and gaps in the field of study. As a result, most of the information was obtained from reading printed and online resources. Furthermore, current challenges surrounding Industry 4.0 and its associated limits were discovered through the services of industry experts. Once the information is gathered, the existing manufacturing sector will be analyzed, and implemented aspects will be adopted in the production industry (Industry 4.0).

2. **Development of Advanced Manufacturing**

   In this stage, the development of an Industry 4.0 is carried out once the parameters are identified for the manufacturing industry. This consists of three phases:

   The results of Phase 2 developed the integrated strategy. In this research, Phase 3 is the vital phase. There are various steps in this phase. These include:

   In this stage, the investigator employed a tool for modelling, such as Buzz (Pinciroli & Beltrame, 2016a), a basic swarm system language (Wang &

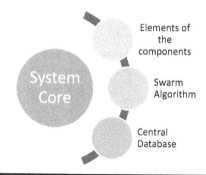

Figure 7.4   Development of advanced manufacturing

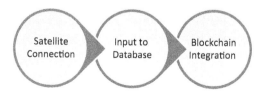

Figure 7.5   Integration phase

Vergne, 2017). Conceptually, Buzz supports this compositional approach, giving both the robot and the swarm the key features required to describe swarm activity accurately (Guo, Zhong, Lin, et al., 2020). Robotic instruction handling procedures for individual robots use primitive single-robot guidance and management of neighbourhood data (Cole et al., 2019). Dynamically managed and shared robot knowledge among all swarm members is possible using swarm-based primitives (Beni, 2004). Self-organization is built into the foundational architecture of the Buzz runtime platform because it relies on entirely decentralized operations (Chakraborti et al., 2019). When speaking of new primitives, such as heterogeneous robot swarms, it may be broadened to incorporate new primitives and, therefore, heterogeneous robot swarms may be utilized on different platforms, including the robot operating system. The interface displays how long it will take to accomplish the task (Pinciroli & Beltrame, 2016b). Real-world swarm algorithms are used to demonstrate Buzz's capabilities. (Şahin, 2004). Finally, the runtime platform is evaluated to test scalability and power.

3. **Developed Model**

   Several strategies are applied to examine and analyze the proposed integrated model: case study and expert review.

   At the selected organization, an expert review to build an agri-blockchain management system is implemented, and the planned integration is validated.

   In order to ensure the accuracy of the research finding, expert reviews from the industry were done to evaluate the suggested model, which helps build qualitative data analysis for the implementation of Industry 4.0. Experts chose based on their knowledge and experience in the manufacturing industry regarding Industry 4.0. The incorporation of new feedback from experts helps to strengthen and enhance the suggested integrated model for the sector. The results of the developed model and case study were contrasted with the industrial experts. A highly performant workstation was constructed to evaluate experts' feedback to get the most benefit from this step. The expert found that the new agri-blockchain system's robustness is highly efficient in the agriculture industry.

7.9 Research Hypotheses

The proposed integrated model demonstrates Industry 4.0 implementation in the agri-blockchain industry.

7.9.1 To the Body of Knowledge

The main goal of the research is to contribute to new information or expertise for production enhancement in Industry 4.0. Thus, it enhances industrial production while at the same time providing an easy process for supply chain management. In addition, the relationship between manufacturing and consumers is ideal; they have harmonious interaction in the domestic and international sectors.

7.9.2 To the Potential Clients

This company has earned a favourable reputation by meeting the needs of a diverse range of clientele worldwide. Moreover, clients can discover easy access to industrial production access points.

7.9.3 To the Stakeholders

The manufacturing industry is about to enter a new age with the emergence of Industry 4.0. An emphasis is placed on manufacturing firms, as well as residents and the countryside, in Industry 5.0. It will affect corporate strategy, and that will give employees a better living experience through Industry 4.0.

7.9.4 Novel Theories/New Findings/Knowledge

Industry 4.0 is implemented in the manufacturing industry in this model due to the new industrial approach. Once this is allowed, producers will edit the model's data, resulting in many different possibilities. For example, the industry might use the data to decide on a more efficient industrial production method for the future. It will also give a boost to the promotion of new products. To ensure that the most efficient use of corporate resources is achieved, the model's variables must be altered. This methodology came about because companies began to appreciate the importance of managing their supply chain operations. Therefore, the result of this research has produced several contributions to the body of knowledge in manufacturing sector domains, both fully automated and virtual production.

7.10 Conclusion

The new decentralized technology of the blockchain in various farm sectors is a system that can re-engineer and redesign several existing procedures, including the settlement of transactions, tracking the provenance of food, and the management of customer demands. Due to the tremendous advancement of modern technology, staying informed of the most recent advances is an absolute must to remain ahead of competitors and manufacturers.

References

Al Faruqi, U. (2019). Future Service in Industry 5.0. *Jurnal Sistem Cerdas, 2*(1), 67–79.

Albayati, H., Kim, K., & Rho, J. J. (2020). Acceptance of financial transactions using blockchain technology and cryptocurrency: A customer perspective approach. *Technology in Society*, 1–20.

Aslam, F., Aimin, W., Li, M., & Ur Rehman, K. (2020). Innovation in the era of IoT and Industry 5.0: Absolute innovation management (AIM) framework. *Information, 11*(2), 124.

Banjanović-Mehmedović, L., & Mehmedović, F. (2020). Intelligent manufacturing systems driven by artificial intelligence in Industry 4.0. In *Handbook of Research on Integrating Industry 4.0 in Business and Manufacturing* (pp. 31–52): IGI Global.

Beck, R., Stenum Czepluch, J., Lollike, N., & Malone, S. (2016). Blockchain–the gateway to trust-free cryptographic transactions.

Beni, G. (2004). *From swarm intelligence to swarm robotics.* Paper presented at the International Workshop on Swarm Robotics.

Bharati, S. (2021). Business intelligence and industry 5.0. *Journal of the International Academy for Case Studies, 27*, 1–3.

Bousdekis, A., Apostolou, D., & Mentzas, G. (2020). A human cyber physical system framework for operator 4.0–artificial intelligence symbiosis. *Manufacturing letters, 25*, 10–15.

Chakraborti, T., Kulkarni, A., Sreedharan, S., Smith, D. E., & Kambhampati, S. (2019). *Explicability? Legibility? Predictability? Transparency? Privacy? Security? The emerging landscape of interpretable agent behavior.* Paper presented at the Proceedings of the international conference on automated planning and scheduling.

Chen, Y. (2017). Integrated and intelligent manufacturing: Perspectives and enablers. *Engineering, 3*(5), 588–595.

Chen, Y., Li, Y., & Li, C. (2020). Electronic agriculture, blockchain and digital agricultural democratization: Origin, theory and application. *Journal of Cleaner Production, 268*, 122071.

Clark, A., Zhuravleva, N. A., Siekelova, A., & Michalikova, K. F. (2020). Industrial artificial intelligence, business process optimization, and big data-driven decision-making processes in cyber-physical system-based smart factories. *Journal of Self-Governance and Management Economics, 8*(2), 28–34.

Cole, R., Stevenson, M., & Aitken, J. (2019). Blockchain technology: Implications for operations and supply chain management. *Supply Chain Management: An International Journal, 24*(4), 469–483.

Collins, K. (2020). Cyber-physical production networks, real-time big data analytics, and cognitive automation in sustainable smart manufacturing. *Journal of Self-Governance and Management Economics, 8*(2), 21–27.

Connolly-Barker, M., Gregova, E., Dengov, V. V., & Podhorska, I. (2020). Internet of Things sensing networks, deep learningenabled smart process planning, and big data-driven innovation in cyber-physical system-based manufacturing. *Economics, Management and Financial Markets, 15*(2), 23–29.

Davidson, R. (2020). Cyber-physical production networks, artificial intelligence-based decision-making algorithms, and big data-driven innovation in Industry 4.0-based manufacturing systems. *Economics, Management, and Financial Markets, 15*(3), 16–22.

Davies, R., Coole, T., & Smith, A. (2017). Review of socio-technical considerations to ensure successful implementation of Industry 4.0. *Procedia Manufacturing, 11*, 1288–1295.

Demestichas, K., Peppes, N., Alexakis, T., & Adamopoulou, E. (2020). Blockchain in agriculture traceability systems: A review. *Applied Sciences, 10*(12), 4113.

Demir, K. A., Döven, G., & Sezen, B. (2019). Industry 5.0 and human-robot co-working. *Procedia Computer Science, 158*, 688–695.

Derigent, W., Cardin, O., & Trentesaux, D. (2020). Industry 4.0: Contributions of holonic manufacturing control architectures and future challenges. *Journal of Intelligent Manufacturing*, 1–22.

Egger, J., & Masood, T. (2020). Augmented reality in support of intelligent manufacturing–A systematic literature review. *Computers & Industrial Engineering, 140*, 106195.

Fantini, P., Pinzone, M., & Taisch, M. (2020). Placing the operator at the centre of Industry 4.0 design: Modelling and assessing human activities within cyber-physical systems. *Computers & Industrial Engineering, 139*, 105058.

Fleming, A., Stitzlein, C., Jakku, E., & Fielke, S. (2019). Missed opportunity? Framing actions around co-benefits for carbon mitigation in Australian agriculture. *Land Use Policy, 85*, 230–238.

Ge, J., Wang, F., Sun, H., Fu, L., & Sun, M. (2020). Research on the maturity of big data management capability of intelligent manufacturing enterprise. *Systems Research and Behavioral Science, 37*(4), 646–662.

Guo, D., Zhong, R. Y., Lin, P., Lyu, Z., Rong, Y., & Huang, G. Q. (2020). Digital twin-enabled graduation intelligent manufacturing system for fixed-position assembly islands. *Robotics and Computer-Integrated Manufacturing, 63*, 101917.

Guo, D., Zhong, R. Y., Ling, S., Rong, Y., & Huang, G. Q. (2020). A roadmap for Assembly 4.0: Self-configuration of fixed-position assembly islands under graduation intelligent manufacturing system. *International Journal of Production Research*, 1–16.

Hang, L., Ullah, I., & Kim, D.-H. (2020). A secure fish farm platform based on blockchain for agriculture data integrity. *Computers and Electronics in Agriculture, 170*, 105251.

Hanson, C., Lipinski, B., Friedrich, J., & O'Connor, C. (2015). What's food loss and waste got to do with climate change? A lot, actually. *World Resources Institute*.

Heires, K. (2016). The risks and rewards of blockchain technology. *Risk Management, 63*(2), 4–7.

Hodgkins, S. (2020). Cyber-physical production networks: Artificial intelligence data-driven Internet of Things systems, smart manufacturing technologies, and real-time process monitoring. *Journal of Self-Governance and Management Economics, 8*(1), 114–120.

Hozdić, E., & Butala, P. (2020). Concept of socio-cyber-physical work systems for Industry 4.0. *Tehnički vjesnik, 27*(2), 399–410.

Hye, A. K. M., Miraz, M. H., Sharif, K. I., & Hasan, M. G. (2020). Factors affecting on e-logistic: Mediating role of ICT & technology integration in retail supply chain in Malaysia. *Test Engineering & Management, 82*, 3234–3243.

Iyer, V., Shah, K., Rane, S., & Shankarmani, R. (2021). *Decentralised Peer-to-Peer Crop Insurance*. Paper presented at the Proceedings of the 3rd ACM International Symposium on Blockchain and Secure Critical Infrastructure.

Jeyanthi, P. M. (2018). Industry 4. O: The combination of the Internet of Things (IoT) and the Internet of People (IoP). *Journal of Contemporary Research in Management, 13*(4).

Jian-zhong, F. (2014). Development status and trend of intelligent manufacturing equipment. *Journal of Mechanical & Electrical Engineering, 31*(8).

Kamble, S. S., Gunasekaran, A., & Sharma, R. (2020). Modeling the blockchain enabled traceability in agriculture supply chain. *International Journal of Information Management, 52*, 101967.

Kamilaris, A., Cole, I. R., & Prenafeta-Boldú, F. X. (2021). Blockchain in agriculture. In *Food Technology Disruptions* (pp. 247–284): Elsevier.

Kamilaris, A., Fonts, A., & Prenafeta-Boldú, F. X. (2019). The rise of blockchain technology in agriculture and food supply chains. *Trends in Food Science & Technology, 91*, 640–652.

Kim, H. M., & Laskowski, M. (2018). Agriculture on the blockchain: Sustainable solutions for food, farmers, and financing. *Supply Chain Revolution, Barrow Books*.

Krugh, M., & Mears, L. (2018). A complementary cyber-human systems framework for Industry 4.0 cyber-physical systems. *Manufacturing letters, 15*, 89–92.

Lee, J., Azamfar, M., & Singh, J. (2019). A blockchain enabled cyber-physical system architecture for Industry 4.0 manufacturing systems. *Manufacturing letters, 20*, 34–39.

Lee, J., Bagheri, B., & Kao, H.-A. (2015). A cyber-physical systems architecture for Industry 4.0-based manufacturing systems. *Manufacturing letters, 3*, 18–23.

Lee, J., Davari, H., Singh, J., & Pandhare, V. (2018). Industrial Artificial Intelligence for Industry 4.0-based manufacturing systems. *Manufacturing letters, 18*, 20–23.

Li, B.-h., Hou, B.-c., Yu, W.-t., Lu, X.-b., & Yang, C.-w. (2017). Applications of artificial intelligence in intelligent manufacturing: A review. *Frontiers of Information Technology & Electronic Engineering, 18*(1), 86–96.

Li, X., Wang, B., Liu, C., Freiheit, T., & Epureanu, B. I. (2020). Intelligent manufacturing systems in COVID-19 pandemic and beyond: Framework and impact assessment. *Chinese Journal of Mechanical Engineering, 33*(1), 1–5.

Li, X., Wang, D., & Li, M. (2020). Convenience analysis of sustainable e-agriculture based on blockchain technology. *Journal of Cleaner Production, 271*, 122503.

Lin, J., Shen, Z., Zhang, A., & Chai, Y. (2018). *Blockchain and IoT based food traceability for smart agriculture.* Paper presented at the Proceedings of the 3rd International Conference on Crowd Science and Engineering.

Lins, T., & Oliveira, R. A. R. (2020). Cyber-physical production systems retrofitting in context of Industry 4.0. *Computers & Industrial Engineering, 139*, 106193.

Ma, S., Zhang, Y., Liu, Y., Yang, H., Lv, J., & Ren, S. (2020). Data-driven sustainable intelligent manufacturing based on demand response for energy-intensive industries. *Journal of Cleaner Production, 274*, 123155.

Maresova, P., Soukal, I., Svobodova, L., Hedvicakova, M., Javanmardi, E., Selamat, A., & Krejcar, O. (2018). Consequences of Industry 4.0 in business and economics. *Economies, 6*(3), 46.

Miraz, M. (2020a). Blockchain in automotive supply chain. *International Supply Chain Technology Journal, 6*(6), 1–12. doi:10.20545/isctj.v06.i06.02

Miraz, M. H. (2020b). Factors affecting e-logistics in Malaysia: The mediating role of trust. *Journal of Advanced Research in Dynamical and Control Systems, 12*(3), 111–120. doi:10.5373/jardcs/v12sp3/20201244

Miraz, M. H., Hasan, M. G., & Sharif, K. I. (2019). Blockchain technology implementation in Malaysian retail market. *Jour of Adv Research in Dynamical & Control Systems, 11*(5), 991–994.

Miraz, M. H., Hasan, M. T., Sumi, F. R., Sarkar, S., & Majumder, M. I. (2020). The innovation of blockchain transparency& traceability in logistic food chain. *International Journal of Mechanical and Production Engineering Research and Development (IJMPERD) 10*(3), 9155–9170.

Miraz, M. H., Hye, A. K. M., Alkurtehe, K. A. M., Habib, M. M., Ahmed, M. S., Molla, M. S., & Hasan, M. T. (2020). The effect of blockchain in transportation Malaysia. *International Supply Chain Technology Journal, 6*(1), 1–10. doi:10.20545/isctj.v06.i01.02

Miraz, M. H., Hye, A. K. M., Wahab, M. K., Alkurtehe, K. A. M., Majumder, M. I., Habib, M. M., & Alsabahi, M. A. (2020). Blockchain securities to construct inclusive, digital economy globally. *International Supply Chain Technology Journal, 6*(1), 1–11. doi:10.20545/isctj.v06.i01.03

Miraz, M. H., Kabir, A., Habib, M. M., & Alam, M. M. (2019). *Blockchain technology in Transport Industries in Malaysia.* Paper presented at the 2nd International Conference on Business and Management.

Nahavandi, S. (2019). Industry 5.0—A human-centric solution. *Sustainability, 11*(16), 4371.

O'Donovan, P., Gallagher, C., Bruton, K., & O'Sullivan, D. T. (2018). A fog computing industrial cyber-physical system for embedded low-latency machine learning Industry 4.0 applications. *Manufacturing letters, 15*, 139–142.

Pacaux-Lemoine, M.-P., Trentesaux, D., Rey, G. Z., & Millot, P. (2017). Designing intelligent manufacturing systems through human-machine cooperation principles: A human-centered approach. *Computers & Industrial Engineering, 111*, 581–595.

Paschek, D., Mocan, A., & Draghici, A. (2019). *Industry 5.0-The Expected Impact of Next Industrial Revolution.* Paper presented at the Thriving on Future Education, Industry, Business, and Society, Proceedings of the MakeLearn and TIIM International Conference, Piran, Slovenia.

Pinciroli, C., & Beltrame, G. (2016a). Buzz: A programming language for robot swarms. *IEEE Software, 33*(4), 97–100.

Pinciroli, C., & Beltrame, G. (2016b). Buzz: An extensible programming language for heterogeneous swarm robotics. Paper presented at the 2016 IEEE/RSJ International Conference on Intelligent Robots and Systems (IROS).

Potts, J. (2019). Blockchain in agriculture. *Available at SSRN 3397786.*

Preuveneers, D., & Ilie-Zudor, E. (2017). The intelligent industry of the future: A survey on emerging trends, research challenges and opportunities in Industry 4.0. *Journal of Ambient Intelligence and Smart Environments, 9*(3), 287–298.

Sachsenmeier, P. (2016). Industry 5.0—The relevance and implications of bionics and synthetic biology. *Engineering, 2*(2), 225–229.

Şahin, E. (2004). *Swarm Robotics: From Sources of Inspiration to Domains of Application.* Paper presented at the International workshop on swarm robotics.

Saldivar, A. A. F., Li, Y., Chen, W.-n., Zhan, Z.-h., Zhang, J., & Chen, L. Y. (2015). *Industry 4.0 with Cyber-Physical Integration: A design and Manufacture Perspective.* Paper presented at the 2015 21st international conference on automation and computing (ICAC).

Shan, S., Wen, X., Wei, Y., Wang, Z., & Chen, Y. (2020). Intelligent manufacturing in industry 4.0: A case study of Sany heavy industry. *Systems Research and Behavioral Science, 37*(4), 679–690.

Shi, Z., Xie, Y., Xue, W., Chen, Y., Fu, L., & Xu, X. (2020). Smart factory in Industry 4.0. *Systems Research and Behavioral Science, 37*(4), 607–617.

Skobelev, P., & Borovik, S. Y. (2017). On the way from Industry 4.0 to Industry 5.0: From digital manufacturing to digital society. *Industry 4.0, 2*(6), 307–311.

Smith, A. (2020). Cognitive decision-making algorithms, real-time sensor networks, and Internet of Things smart devices in cyber-physical manufacturing systems. *Economics, Management, and Financial Markets, 15*(3), 30–36.

Sun, Y., Li, L., Shi, H., & Chong, D. (2020). The transformation and upgrade of China's manufacturing industry in Industry 4.0 era. *Systems Research and Behavioral Science, 37*(4), 734–740.

Tao, F., Qi, Q., Wang, L., & Nee, A. (2019). Digital twins and cyber-physical systems toward smart manufacturing and industry 4.0: Correlation and comparison. *Engineering, 5*(4), 653–661.

Vangala, A., Das, A. K., Kumar, N., & Alazab, M. (2020). Smart secure sensing for IoT-based agriculture: Blockchain perspective. *IEEE Sensors Journal.*

Verma, M. (2021). Smart contract model for trust based agriculture using blockchain technology. *International journal of research and analytical reviews, 8*(2), 354–355.

Villalba-Díez, J., Molina, M., Ordieres-Meré, J., Sun, S., Schmidt, D., & Wellbrock, W. (2020). Geometric deep lean learning: Deep learning in Industry 4.0 cyber-physical complex networks. *Sensors, 20*(3), 763.

Villalonga, A., Beruvides, G., Castaño, F., & Haber, R. (2020). Cloud-based industrial cyber-physical system for data-driven reasoning. A review and use case on an Industry 4.0 pilot line. *Statistics, 34*, 35.

Wang, B., Hu, S. J., Sun, L., & Freiheit, T. (2020). Intelligent welding system technologies: State-of-the-art review and perspectives. *Journal of Manufacturing Systems, 56*, 373–391.

Wang, S., & Vergne, J. P. (2017). Buzz factor or innovation potential: What explains cryptocurrencies' returns? *PLoS One, 12*(1), 1–16. doi:10.1371/journal.pone.0169556

Whittle, T. (2019). Interaction networks in the production and operations environment: Internet of Things, cyber-physical systems, and smart factories. *Journal of Self-Governance and Management Economics, 7*(2), 13–18.

Xiong, H., Dalhaus, T., Wang, P., & Huang, J. (2020). Blockchain technology for agriculture: applications and rationale. *Frontiers in Blockchain, 3*, 7.

Yadav, V. S., & Singh, A. (2019). *Use of blockchain to solve select issues of Indian farmers.* Paper presented at the AIP Conference Proceedings.

Zhang, H., Yan, Q., & Wen, Z. (2020). Information modeling for cyber-physical production system based on digital twin and AutomationML. *The International Journal of Advanced Manufacturing Technology*, 1–19.

Zheng, P., Xu, X., & Chen, C.-H. (2020). A data-driven cyber-physical approach for personalised smart, connected product co-development in a cloud-based environment. *Journal of Intelligent Manufacturing, 31*(1), 3–18.

Zhong, R. Y., Xu, X., Klotz, E., & Newman, S. T. (2017). Intelligent manufacturing in the context of Industry 4.0: a review. *Engineering, 3*(5), 616–630.

Zhou, G., Zhang, C., Li, Z., Ding, K., & Wang, C. (2020). Knowledge-driven digital twin manufacturing cell towards intelligent manufacturing. *International Journal of Production Research, 58*(4), 1034–1051.

Zhou, J., Li, P., Zhou, Y., Wang, B., Zang, J., & Meng, L. (2018). Toward new-generation intelligent manufacturing. *Engineering, 4*(1), 11–20.

Zhou, J., Zhou, Y., Wang, B., & Zang, J. (2019). Human–cyber–physical systems (HCPSs) in the context of new-generation intelligent manufacturing. *Engineering, 5*(4), 624–636.

Zhou, K., Liu, T., & Zhou, L. (2015). *Industry 4.0: Towards Future Industrial Opportunities and Challenges.* Paper presented at the 2015 12th International conference on fuzzy systems and knowledge discovery (FSKD).

Chapter 8

Agricultural Data Mining and Information Extraction

K. Aditya Shastry
Nitte Meenakshi Institute of Technology, Karnataka, India

Sanjay H. A.
M. S. Ramaiah Institute of Technology, Bengaluru, India

8.1 Introduction: Agriculture and Data Mining

Farming remains an essential domain in most nations. It is the main supplier of nutrition for the inhabitants of the globe. It is a highly conventional process that has been subjected to numerous transformations over time for effectively generating more nutrition (Tian et al. 2019; Wang et al. 2019).

Nevertheless, this domain is now confronted with serious challenges. The expected global population will increase to more than 9 and 10 billion between 2040 and 2090, respectively (The World Bank, 2021). In the coming two decades, the global production of food must increase by at least 50% to match this growing population. This means strengthening the farming sector, which can greatly influence the ecosystem, and reducing land degradation due to storms and river corrosion, and the contamination of the atmosphere because of chemicals, etc. To lessen these adverse impacts, a quick and sustainable transformation of the farming production process is needed by the appropriate allotment of farming resources with the smart application of farming practices. It is vital to make all the farming systems robust

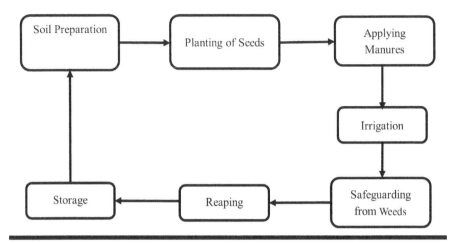

Figure 8.1 **Farming process**

Source: Pravar (2020)

to changes in the weather (Issad et al., 2019). Figure 8.1 indicates the farming procedure (Zhang, 2018).

The farming process can be partitioned into various segments, as demonstrated in Figure 8.1 (Pravar J N, 2020):

- **Soil preparation**: This forms the preliminary phase in agriculture in which cultivators prepare the soil for planting the seeds. It comprises splitting huge clusters of soil by eliminating garbage such as rocks, twigs, etc. It also involves combining manures and plant material, relying on the crop category to enable effective crop growth.
- **Planting of seeds**: This involves determining the proper gap between two seeds, the depth for sowing the seeds, etc. During this process, weather conditions such as temperature, moisture, and rainfall play a significant part.
- **Applying manures**: Manures consist of ingredients such as potassium (K), nitrogen (N), and phosphorous (P), which are beneficial for proper crop growth. This phase positively impacts the growth of crops as it acts as a supplement to the soil nutrients.
- **Irrigation**: This phase assists in preserving soil moisture and sustaining humidity. Excessive or insufficient usage of water may hinder crop development, leading to damaged crops.
- **Safeguarding from weeds**: Weeds are undesirable elements that sprout adjacent to crops or at farm borders. They tend to decrease harvests, thus leading to excessive losses and reduced yield quality.
- **Reaping**: This is the technique of collecting mature crops from pastures and needs a lot of workers. It comprises managing activities related to "post-harvest", such as clean-up, arranging, wrapping, and conserving.

■ **Storing**: This comprises preserving the food that is generated from farming safely and securely so that it is not spoilt. The packaging and shipping of crops is also included in this stage.

Issues encountered by agriculturalists while using conventional cultivation techniques are summarized below:

■ The farming lifecycle is significantly impacted by climatical elements such as moisture, temperature, and rainfall. Ever-rising disforestation and smog adversely impact the climate, leading to unpredictable weather conditions for cultivators to grow their crops.
■ Each harvest involves certain soil nutrients: N, P, and K form the three vital soil nutrients. A shortage of these nutrients will generate lower yields and bad crops.
■ Controlling weeds is very much necessary since it negatively influences crop growth.

These obstacles may be overcome using data mining (DM) technologies. DM represents the extraction of intelligence or knowledge from large datasets. In farming ecosystems, DM has risen along with other technologies to generate fresh prospects. Usually, DM techniques require a "knowledge discovery process" to discover useful information from large datasets (training data). The data in DM comprises a set of instances. Typically, a specific instance is characterized by a set of features (attributes or variables). They can be nominal, binary, ordinal (i.e., ordering is important), or numeric. The "trained" DM technique is tested on unseen data called "test data" using suitable performance metrics based on statistics and mathematics. Figure 8.2 presents a DM approach (Liakos et al., 2018).

The tasks of DM are usually categorized into diverse types such as classification, regression, clustering, association analysis, and anomaly detection. Two popular approaches adapted by learning models are supervised and unsupervised learning. In

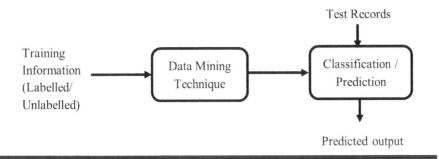

Figure 8.2   Data mining approach

Source: Liakos et al. (2018)

supervised learning, known target attributes are provided to the DM algorithm for training purposes. The trained model is then applied to test data that has no target features. In contrast, unsupervised learning deals with determining any patterns that may be hidden. However, there are no target labels or features present in the data. Thus, no difference exists between training and test data.

Lately, DM has been playing a key part in farming. DM in farming can deliver accurate forecasts related to harvests and climate, usage of manures, and insecticides. It can determine seed quality and crop production.

This chapter comprises six sections. The second section describes the different DM techniques that are being employed in agriculture. Unique case studies on agricultural DM are discussed in section 8.3. Section 8.4 gives an outline of the research challenges in agricultural DM that may be explored. A synopsis of the chapter is given at the end.

8.2 Data Mining Techniques in Farming

With the advent of digital machinery, tools, networks, sensors, etc., the world has become dependent on information. Owing to the growing volume and complexity of data, analysts are facing the arduous task of analyzing huge datasets. This has steered the advancement of effective DM methods (Issad et al., 2019). This section provides an overview of the popular DM techniques being utilized in farming.

8.2.1 Classification

The "supervised" technique classifies the given training data into class labels (Mondal et al., 2021). Here, every data component is mapped to some known classes. In the farming domain, categorization has widespread applications, especially in the categorization of infections associated with crops. Commonly used classification methods in farming include: decision tree (DT), support vector machine (SVM), artificial neural network (ANN), Bayesian network (BN), k-nearest neighbour (KNN), and deep learning (DL).

In Bayesian networks, a group of traits and the dependence connections among them are modelled. They are based on likelihood and are modelled graphically. A BN employs probabilities to determine the classes.

Decision trees are categorization techniques that construct trees (Belson, 1959). A DT gradually arranges the information in reduced identical subgroups. Simultaneously, a linked tree graph is constructed. Every internal node of the tree composition characterizes a distinct assessment on a chosen attribute, while every branch signifies the consequence of this assessment. Leaf nodes signify the outcome or forecast obtained after the route from "root" to "leaf" is followed. This path is usually denoted by a rule for categorization.

The support-vector machine was first designed by Cherkassky et al. (2004) and Podder et al. (2021). An SVM generates a "hyperplane" for linearly categorizing data records. They can be extended to non-linearly separable data by utilizing the "kernel trick", which transforms information from a lower to a higher dimensional space. They can also be extended to multiclass classification problems using the concept of multiple hyperplanes. They are also being adapted for regression and clustering tasks. They can handle overfitting, making them valuable in a broad variety of applications (Suykens and Vandewalle, 2013; Chang and Lin, 2013).

An artificial neural network is a supervised technique that is normally utilized for regression and classification applications. The learning techniques frequently utilized in ANNs comprise "radial basis function" networks (Broomhead & Lowe, 1988), "perceptron" procedures (Rosenblatt, 1958), "backpropagation" (Linnaimnaa, 1976), and "resilient backpropagation" (Riedmiller & Braun, 1993). Likewise, a great number of ANN-based training techniques were developed.

A "deep ANN" is generally known as deep learning (LeCun, 2015; Goodfellow et al., 2016). They represent a novel area of DM, which allows the computational methods to be comprised of numerous layers to interpret complicated information utilizing several abstractions. One of the key benefits of DL is that in certain situations, the feature extraction stage is done by the technique. These models have considerably enhanced the state-of-the-art techniques in diverse areas and businesses involving farming. Deep ANNs are ANNs with several hidden layers among the input and output layers and can be supervised, partly supervised, or unsupervised.

Ensemble learning (EL) techniques focus on enhancing the accuracy of predictive models by integrating a combination of base learners. This leads to the generation of hybrid solutions from individual solutions from base learners that are effective. The accuracy of the final solution increases if the diverse base classifiers are combined. DTs are normally employed as the base learners in EL techniques such as "random forest" (Breiman, 2001), in which many boosting and bagging techniques are proposed.

A random forest (RF) is appropriate for categorizing large information. It signifies a compilation of trees that are structured in nature. Majority voting is used in an RF for classifying the test records.

Instance-based models signify techniques for discovering patterns by assessing unseen records. These techniques become more complex as data grows. The highly popular learning procedures belonging to this group are the k-nearest neighbour (Fix & Hodges, 1951), "locally weighted learning" (Atkenson et al., 1997), and "learning vector quantization" (Kohonen, 1988). The KNN categorizes unseen input information corresponding to the "K" labelled records nearest to the test records, in which the "K" value is specified (Bharati et al., 2018). Consequently, the highly elected category amongst the closest "K neighbours" from the labelled records is allocated to the unseen input information.

8.2.2 Clustering

In an "unsupervised" technique, class labels are not present. The clustering process involves splitting the records into clusters using the data. The records that fall into the same group/cluster should possess higher similarities than the records that belong to different clusters. This method is employed when there is a lack of predefined classes in the datasets (Witten et al., 2016). The types of clustering methods are discussed below.

In partitioning techniques, numerous groups are created from the information. "K-means" represents a frequently applied method that seeks to segment information into "K" clusters. This is employed in the farming domain for accomplishing numerous jobs, such as segmentation of images for identifying illnesses. Hierarchical techniques construct a hierarchy of clusters known as a "dendrogram". "Agglomerative" or "divisive" techniques (Sahoo et al., 2016) are types of hierarchical methods.

Density-based approaches cluster entities as per certain functions. Grid-based techniques quantise the information into a limited quantity of units to generate a grid formation upon which the entire clustering processes are completed. Model-based approaches indicate the usage of fixed assortment prototypes to perform grouping (Nagar, 2015).

8.2.3 Association Analysis

Association analysis is employed to find important interactions among entities that belong to large amounts of data. It involves the identification of associations or patterns between features of a dataset by recognizing the frequent items appearing together. The popularly used "association rule mining" methods are "Apriori", "AprioriTid", "Dic", "Eclat", and "FP-Growth".

8.2.4 Prediction

Prediction comprises exploring information patterns that lead to realistic forecasts. Another name for this is "predictive analytics". Widely utilized methods include "time series" and "regression". A time series is specified as a progression of records that are organized with respect to time. They are utilized to uncover concealed information from raw data. This involves the analysis of statistical information with respect to time.

Regression represents a supervised learning technique that intends to deliver the forecast of a target feature from known input features. The well-established techniques consist of linear, logistic (Cox, 1958), and stepwise regression (Efroymson, 1960). Furthermore, advanced regression techniques have been built.

These forecasting techniques are frequently applied in agriculture for predicting crop yields, diseases, pests, and soil moisture.

8.2.5 *Data Mining with Other Methods*

This section provides details of other techniques frequently used with DM. These methods are used in several domains dealing with large and complex datasets (Olson and Delen, 2008). They can be normally integrated with other DM methods. They can be employed directly or used to enhance the effectiveness of other approaches. Fuzzy logic (FL), genetic algorithm (GA), and principal component analysis (PCA) techniques are discussed here that can be effectively integrated with DM methods. "Fuzzy" interpretation is a means to depict the vagueness linked with hypotheses, and GAs assist in determining effective hypotheses in a specified form.

Fuzzy logic makes it feasible to handle ambiguity in an extremely insightful and natural manner. It represents a meticulous statistical concept customized to handle subjective or uncertain events. It offers a numerical formalism for modelling social competencies. Consequently, incorrect ecological trends that pose trouble while being modelled using conventional reasoning can be interpreted in an effective way. "Fuzzy systems" fit into the category of knowledge-based methods in which analysis is done based on "fuzzy sets". FL plays a major role in DM since many of the concepts learned in DM are fuzzy. Several techniques presume that the datasets are accurate for analysis. Nevertheless, in many practical situations, they are inaccurate. There exists a certain extent of ambiguity. Accuracy, effectiveness, and comprehensiveness should be achieved in DM techniques. For handling complicated systems, a growing need exists to build systems that are interpretable and simple. For resolving the ambiguity that exists between fuzziness and accuracy, fuzzy set theory plays a major part in developing robust, intelligible, and less complicated systems by the validation and usage of vague values in a DM method.

Genetic algorithms represent stochastic optimisation techniques built on the notions of biological choices and evolutionary methods that were designed by Holland (Holland, 1992). They are particularly effective in resolving hard optimisation challenges and are frequently thought of as a component of a DM technique. The technique begins with a population, and a new population is created later using crossover and mutation operators. The choice of solutions permits the generation of novel enhanced results by utilizing their "fitness". GAs fit into a group of likelihood techniques. However, they are extremely diverse when compared to other methods since they integrate components of immediate and random distribution. Potential outcomes are stronger in comparison to the prevailing search techniques since they retain a populace of probable results, whilst remaining techniques consider just one point during searching. A GA is employed in DM to increase the performance of techniques such as DT.

Principal component analysis forms a dimensionality reduction technique. It signifies an algebraic technique for transforming probable associated features to a group of linearly unrelated traits. PCA is valuable once there is information about a sufficient amount of features comprising certain duplicity. The latter implies that certain traits are correlated to each other. Due to this duplicity, it can be utilized to lessen the detected features into a lesser quantity of principal components. This technique is robust to noisy information.

8.3 Case Studies in Agricultural Data Mining

This segment discusses the different applications of DM in farming in the form of case studies.

8.3.1 Yield Prediction

Accurate crop yield prediction (CYP) forms a vital component in farming since it can increase profits for stakeholders. This forms a prediction task and can be effectively handled as a DM technique. Hence, a lot of research has been done in this case.

Chlingaryan et al. (2018) analysed the works in CYP and the assessment of nitrogen in precision farming. In Varman et al. (2017), diverse devices comprising temperature and moisture sensors and additional fixed information were utilized to recommend the appropriate harvest and implement smart irrigation by forecasting temperatures of air and soil along with moisture. The work proposed several machine learning techniques such as "feedforward neural networks", etc. The authors observed that the "long short-term memory" model performed better than others.

The time series prediction technique was demonstrated in Balakrishnan and Muthukumarasamy (2016). The two prevailing methods utilized were: SVM and naive Bayes (NB), along with AdaSVM and AdaNB for time series forecast. The findings demonstrate a reasonable accuracy for the recommended methods with respect to correctness and categorization error.

For boosting the harvest of crops, Kumar et al. (2017) devised a method for sugar cane administration centred on a variety of devices to precisely examine factors such as temperature, moisture, and dampness required for healthful crop development. To recommend several metrics that are valuable for improving harvest, dual methods KNN clustering and SVM were utilized. In Rajeswari et al. (2017), a smart technique was recommended. The technique presents an assessment for the superior harvest series, the subsequent crop to mature for effective produce, and the overall harvest in the region considered for experimentation. By way of actual land testing, the grower would be capable of achieving the modern manure conditions for harvest cultivation to accomplish enhanced harvest produce plus a decrease in the price of fertilizers. To determine valuable knowledge from the raw information, the C5.0 categorization technique and association rule DM methods were utilized.

Blagojević et al. (2016) utilized an ANN for forecasting peach produce. The inputs considered were shoot size, berry mass, shoot width, the quantity of manure, and the start of the produce. The outcomes of the harvest forecast were demonstrated by a network application. Plotting of harvest categories is crucial in diverse farming products. It provides data that could be useful, particularly for harvest assessment.

To focus on-field production and hence harvest produce, cultivators can additionally execute yearly or seasonal crop rotation strategies. Certainly, a decent choice of crops leads to better yields. The farming policies can be decided by utilizing diverse soil information and the needs for crops. In this regard, numerous methods are being employed to deliver all the material required to develop effective crop sequencing schemes without compromising the health of soil and productivity. Table 8.1 summarizes these papers.

Table 8.1   Data Mining Applications in Yield Forecast and Weather Change Effects on Production

Referred paper and its objective	DM methods	Data used for experiments	Preprocessing of information
Forecasting the harvest of five crops (Balakrishna and Muthusamy, 2016)	SVM, NB, AdaSVM, AdaNB	Weather information and past production data of crops	Irrelevant attributes were disregarded
Forecast of wheat ripened oxidation	SVM	Weather and infection data	-
Estimation of air temperature, soil temperature, and moisture (Varman et al. (2017))	ANN (FF ANN, LSTM, GRU)	Temperature and moisture information along with additional fixed information	The number of records was reduced by sampling
The evaluation of ecological factors affecting performance and the association among them (Sellam and Poovammal (2016))	Regression method	Ecological factors (region under farming, yearly rain, and nutrition cost indicator)	-
Forecast of soil humidity (Matei et al., 2017)	KNN, SVM, Logistic Regression, ANN, DT, RF, etc.	Climate station information	

(Continued)

Table 8.1   Data Mining Applications in Yield Forecast and Weather Change Effects on Production   (Continued)

Referred paper and its objective	DM methods	Data used for experiments	Preprocessing of information
Wheat yield forecast (Cai et al., 2019)	RF, SVM, ANN, LASSO	Atmosphere and satellite information, wheat harvest information, harvesting region	–
Demonstrating the long duration impacts of various soil administration methods on harvests produce, storage of soil natural carbon and conservatory vapours discharges (Cillis et al., 2018)	Regression model	Historic climate information, harvest charts and additional land information.	–
Discovery and detection of illnesses and infections and scrutinizing of nutritious development factors (Kumar et al. 2017)	KNN, SVM	Pictures and radar information (temperature, dampness, and moisture)	Greyscale pictures
Forecasting the produce of the harvest and the determination of the finest harvest series (Rajeswari et al., 2017)	DT and Association Rule DM	Historic harvest series and data on soil nutrients	Removal of noisy records.
Peach harvest forecast (Blagojević et al., 2016)	ANN	Shoot size, berry mass, shoot texture, the quantity of manure, and starting of the produce	–

8.3.2 Identification of Diseases

The identification and control of diseases and pests is of vital concern in farming. Spraying pesticides on crops and their associated area is the commonly employed technique for handling this. Though this technique is successful, it incurs a huge economic burden and damages the environment. The harmful consequences of these pesticides on the environment include the pollution of rivers, damage to ecosystems and wildlife, excess deposits in crops, etc. DM and machine learning form an integrated component of precision farming in which agricultural compounds are handled effectively.

In Chung et al. (2016), the scientists developed a technique for the identification and examination of the Bakanae infection concerning rice saplings. In particular, the purpose of the research was the precise identification of the pathogen Fusarium fujikuroi for two rice cultivars. This automatic identification of affected crops boosted grain harvest and consumed less time compared to the manual process.

Wheat is one of the most economically grown crops around the globe. The following studies demonstrate the classification of wheat crops as unhealthy or healthy.

During Moshou et al. (2014), a scheme for automatic distinction among water-stressed Septoria tritici infested and healthful frost wheat coverings was demonstrated. The technique utilized a least-squares (LS) SVM technique with visual multisensory blending. The researchers in Moshou et al. (2004) devised an approach to discriminate between yellow rust infested or healthful wheat, using ANN techniques and spectral reflectance traits. The precise discovery of either infested or healthful crops facilitates the exact application of insecticides on the ground. In Moshou et al. (2005), a practical identification product based on a self-organizing map (SOM) neural network to distinguish between yellow rust infested and healthy wheat was developed. The purpose of the work was the early detection of yellow rust before it infected the plants. Lastly, the researcher Ferentinos (2018) demonstrated a convolutional neural network (CNN)-centred technique to detect the infection centred on leaf pictures with adequate precision to categorize among healthful and unhealthy leaves in a variety of crops. Table 8.2 outlines the aforementioned works in the case of disease identification.

8.3.3 Identification of Weeds/Wildflowers

The identification of wildflowers and their proper management are vital issues in farming. Several agriculturists reveal that weeds form one of the most crucial menaces to the production of crops. The correct identification of wildflowers is important to organic farming as they remain difficult to identify and differentiate from crops. In this regard, DM models in combination with sensors can pave the way for the accurate identification and differentiation of weeds with less expense and without adversely impacting the environment. DM for wildflower identification

Table 8.2 Applications of Data Mining in Infection Recognition

Referred article and its goal	*DM techniques*	*Attributes*	*Outcomes*
Identification and distinction among healthful Silybum marianum crops and those affected by the fungus Microbotyum silybum (Pantazi et al., 2017)	ANN/XY Fusion	Pictures with foliage varieties utilizing a handheld detectable and NIR mass spectrometer	Achieved 90%+ accuracy
Categorization of organisms and automated identification of thrips authors (Ebrahimi et al., 2017)	SVM	Area indicator: fraction of key thickness to minimal thickness; and colour indicators: tone, wetness, and intensity	Attained mean percentage error less than 3%
Identification of Bakanae infection, Fusarium fujikuroi, in rice saplings (Chung et al., 2016)	SVM	Morphologic and colour characteristics from healthful, and those infested from Bakanae. infection, rice saplings	Obtained 85% plus accuracy
Identification of N stressed, yellow oxidation infested and healthful wintertime wheat coverings (Pantazi et al., 2017)	SOM	Hyperspectral reflectivity imagery pictures	Accomplished 95%+ accuracies
Automatic distinction among water strained Septoria tritici infested and healthful winter wheat coverings (Moshou et al., 2014)	SVM / LS-SVM	Ethereal reflectivity and fluorescence attributes	95%+ accuracy attained
Identification of yellow rust infested and healthful wheat (Moshou et al., 2004)	ANN / MLP	Spectral reflectance traits	97%+ accuracy achieved

(Continued)

Table 8.2   Applications of Data Mining in Infection Recognition   (Continued)

Referred article and its goal	DM techniques	Attributes	Outcomes
Identification of yellow oxidation infested and healthful winter wheat underground conditions (Moshou et al., 2005)	ANN / SOM	Information synthesis of hyper-ethereal reflection and multispectral fluorescence imagery	97%+ accuracy obtained
Identification and analysis of crop infections (Ferentinos, 2018)	DNN / CNN	Leaf images of healthful and infected crops	98%+ accuracy attained

can facilitate the innovation of devices and machines to remove weeds, which decreases the demand for weedkillers. Here, certain works for identifying weeds are presented.

In Pantazi et al. (2012), the writers introduced a novel technique founded on ANN and imagery to detect Silybum marianum, a wild plant that is difficult to destroy and triggers crop damage. In Pantazi et al. (2012), the researchers designed a novel approach centred on DM methods and hyperspectral imagery for the identification of crop and weed varieties. The central objective remained the precise identification and differentiation of the varieties for financial and ecological reasons. In Binch & Fox (2017), the scientists devised a technique for the identification of weeds centred on support vector networks (SVN) in pasture harvesting.

Table 8.3 reviews the aforementioned articles with regards to the detection of weeds.

8.3.4 Crop Quality

This segment discusses the works for the detection of attributes linked through the quality of crops. The correct discovery and categorization of harvest quality traits can boost the cost of products and decrease the garbage. In Zhang & Yang (2017), the researchers demonstrated a technique for the identification and categorization of botanic and non-botanic external substances implanted within yarn covering while reaping. The purpose of the research was to enhance the quality whilst reducing the harm to fibre. Another research, Hu et al. (2017), dealt with the production of pears, and in particular, a technique was demonstrated for the detection and distinction of pears. The method employed DM techniques with hyperspectral reflectivity imagery. Table 8.4 highlights the aforementioned works.

Table 8.3 Applications of Data Mining in the Detection of Wildflowers

Referred paper and its objective	DM techniques	Attributes	Outcomes
Identification and mapping of the weed Silybum marianum (Pantazi et al., 2017)	CP ANN	Ethereal groups of red, green, and NIR and smoothness level	97%+ accuracy observed
Identification of crop Zea mays and weed varieties (Pantazi et al., 2017)	ANN/ SOM	Ethereal traits from hyperspectral imagery	Near 100% accuracy was achieved
Coverage on performance of categorization techniques for pasture vs. weed identification (Binch & Fox, 2017)	SVN	Camera imagery of pasture and numerous kinds of weeds	93%+ accuracies achieved

Table 8.4 Applications of Data Mining in Deciding the Quality of Crops

Referred article and its objective	DM techniques	Attributes	Outcomes
Identification and categorization of botanic and non-botanic external substance implanted in yarn covering (Zhang & Yang, 2017)	SVM	Small wave electromagnetic hyperspectral diffusion imagery showing yarn along with botanic and non-botanic varieties of externalsubstance	More than 90% accuracy was achieved
Detection and distinction of Korla aromatic pears into deciduous-calyx or persistent-calyx types (Hu et al., 2017)	SVM	Hyperspectral reflectivity imagery	More than 91% accuracy was achieved
Forecast and categorization of the geographic source for rice samples (Maione et al., 2016)	Ensemble Learning/ RF	20 organic substances discovered in the makeup of rice samples with inductively paired plasma form spectroscopy	More than 92% accuracy was achieved

Table 8.5 Applications of Data Mining in Species Identification

Referred article and its objective	DM techniques	Attributes	Outcomes
Detection and categorization of three pulse varieties (Grinblat et al., 2016)	DL / CNN	Lode foliage imagery of white, red, and soybeans	Achieved more than 90% accuracy

8.3.5 Gathering of Species

The major objective is the automated detection and categorization of plant varieties to prevent human errors, as well as to lessen the categorization period. A technique for the detection and categorization of three pulse varieties via foliage lode shapes was demonstrated in Grinblat et al. (2016). Lode geomorphology contains precise data concerning foliage characteristics. It is a perfect instrument for plant recognition with respect to colour and form. Table 8.5 reviews the above research for species recognition.

8.3.6 Soil Management

This segment provides the applications of DM for forecasting and determining farming soil features. Soil is a diverse geological source with complex activities and procedures. Soil features permit scientists to interpret the changing aspects of environments and their impacts on farming. The precise assessment of land requirements may lead to superior soil administration. Soil temperature on its own performs a vital part for the precise assessment of the weather change impacts of an area and its ecological settings. It is a major atmospheric factor influencing the cooperative activities regarding earth and the environment. Furthermore, soil moisture has an essential part of crop harvest irregularity. Nevertheless, soil measurements normally consume more time and are costly. Hence, a minimal amount and a reliable outcome for the correct assessment of soil could be attained using computational assessment centred on DM methods.

In Nahvi et al. (2016), the scientists devised a novel technique built on an extreme learning machines (ELM) approach for assessing day-to-day climate information. The goal remained the precise assessment of ground temperature for farming administration. Table 8.6 reviews the aforementioned articles with regard to soil management.

Table 8.6 Applications of Data Mining in Soil Management

Referred article and its objective	DM techniques	Attributes	Outcomes
Assessment of soil aeration in farming development (Coopersmith et al., 2014)	ANN, KNN	Precipitation and probable ET information	Accuracy between 91% and 94%
Forecasting the soil conditions (Morellos et al., 2016)	SVM/LS SVM and Regression /Cubist	100+ soil records from topsoil level of an arable area	Error below 0.09% achieved
Technique to assess day-to-day soil temperature at six diverse depths in two diverse weather environmental areas of Iran: Bandar Abbas and Kerman (Nahvi et al., 2016)	SaE-ELM	Day wise meteorological conditions such as highest, lowest, and mean air temperature; global planetary heat; and ecological tension	R^2 of around 98% was achieved
Assessment of soil moisture (Johann et al., 2016)	ANN	Information of forces working on a carve and velocity	R^2 of around 80% attained

8.4 Discussion

From the examined articles, it can be observed that prior to the application of DM methods, certain preprocessing measures need to be performed. For image data, the majority of the works used image preprocessing measures prior to obtaining the attributes. These extracted attributes were then fed to the method. The preprocessing techniques comprised reshaping the images, etc. The articles on deep learning employed preprocessing techniques such as reduction of image size, greyscale pictures, scaling information, PCA and whitening techniques, etc. Remote sensing pictures captured from elevated heights by satellites/drones were preprocessed utilizing orthorectification, vision fitting and mosaicking, atmospheric adjustment, radiometric and symmetrical modification, cutting, and cleaning. In the case of other types of data, certain works did not consider the preprocessing phase of their accumulated information, specifically those that utilized sensors. Additional works dealt with missing information using the Expectation-Maximization method, quality of information (choice of information, decrease of records, removal of invalids, noisy information, disregarding less important attributes).

The present survey revealed the efficiency of DM to handle practical issues in farming. The following are some of the observations from this paper:

- The majority of the traditional DM-based methods recommended for harvest management were restricted to particular crops as opposed to DL-based techniques, which were employed for several crops to identify numerous illnesses. Furthermore, the majority of the illness detection and categorization products were applied to a particular tissue of the plant (foliage or fruit).
- For image processing-centred procedures, the outcomes of DM methods were extremely reliant on the picture quality that frequently involved more processing. Furthermore, pictures considered for learning may not reveal the actual circumstances of the illness. To conquer these constraints, it was essential to integrate the vision analysis with actual sensing information in the DM procedure for farming. The proper handling of numerous diverse resources of data is vital for making dependable decisions.
- Several reviewed articles dealt with straightforward contextual pictures. However, in actuality, this may not be the case. Hence, the strategy and advancement of methods that take into account the background complexity of the picture is required.
- Various DM methods were examined and contrasted by taking into account the analysis of farming information. Therefore, as per our research, it was observed that DL methods delivered decent outcomes with respect to accuracy in the discovery as well as categorization of illnesses.
- Based on the impact of feature configurations on DM precision, it was essential to construct and build techniques to achieve optimum feature configurations, particularly for evolutionary and DL techniques. Pretraining could enhance the techniques, as demonstrated in Brahimi et al. (2017). Visions of discovered traits may have a crucial part, particularly in interpreting the working of the method that permits the scientists to build designs.
- Mobile technology provides cultivators with the prospect to actively take part in the gathering and handling of ground information in real-time utilizing portable gadgets. Hence, it is vital to build prototypes that consume less time and memory, and offer a decent precision to be incorporated in portable gadgets. Distributed DM approaches can be effective in this case.
- In farming, information is very critical. Data forms a useful means for reaching appropriate choices at the proper period and in the correct position. DM methods operate on diverse categories of information (pictures, sensors information, etc.) containing historic information and current information. The information utilized in the examined articles comes from diverse resources such as PlantVillage, remote sensing information, information gathered through administration, climate location information, and so on.
- DM methods remain extensively utilized in numerous farming jobs. There is no specific technique of DM to resolve difficulties in farming. Furthermore,

the precision of DM techniques varies depending on the attributes and the volume of the dataset. To achieve maximum accuracy, it is critical to create hybrid prototypes that would enhance assessment, forecast, and judgment.

■ In precision farming, numerous sensors and various machines such as drones and rovers produce non-conventional information such as pictures and streams delivering several device-generated information. Due to the difficulty of the features to be supervised and administered in a farming atmosphere, besides the trouble in gathering measurements of certain significant features due to probable sensor damages, integrating DM through current enhanced methods of artificial intelligence may provide significant support to enhance correctness and unambiguousness, along with resolving issues in the farming domain.

■ The concept of "real time" in farming is crucial. Obtaining good quality data in real time presents a terrific possibility for increasing effectiveness and efficiency. In a real-time approach, the limitation is that the job needs to be completed inside the predefined time limit. Certain articles claim to design schemes that encounter the requirements of the agriculturalist in real time built on diverse tools comprising sensor machinery and information broadcast strategies. Nevertheless, information processing utilizing DM methods adopts the conventional method of processing information after the initial information is shifted to the processing centre. To construct practical applications, it is essential to have a great number of combinations and a farming data compilation product that delivers an all-in-one facility for information acquisition and administering.

8.5 Research Challenges of Data Mining in Farming

Employing DM to enhance farming production involves several issues in accumulating, administering, and manipulating information. One of the biggest challenges of smart farming is how to ensure information safety and confidentiality. Another vital issue in farming knowledge products is that information accessibility and quality are frequently bad and must be improved prior to usage. This challenge is more complicated when a vast amount of information is involved in real time. Scalability, along with the assimilation of spatial and semantic information in DM, also presents a challenging issue.

8.5.1 Confidentiality

In farming products, the accumulated information comprises personal data regarding the cultivators such as his or her identity, geographic site, financial data, business information, etc. Several agriculturists whose information is available across digital platforms will not realize how their information is being used. In fact, cultivators may not realize that their private data is being gathered and wonder for what is the information being used? DM permits firms to collect and investigate huge volumes of data concerning agriculturalists, possibly enough to generate character or emotional summaries of the farmers. There is even the likelihood that this data may be applied against the cultivator or merely disclosed to others, which can generate a harmful impact on his or her actions. Agriculturalists should be assured that their information will be examined to create useful ideas without revealing the information to their competitors. Knowledge obtained from information utilizing DM is an exceptionally useful source that could create a danger to the confidentiality of cultivators.

8.5.2 Quality and Accuracy of Information

In precision farming, data is vital where large content needs to be gathered and converted into knowledge. Since this form of raw data is massive, conventional analytic devices cannot analyse it effectively. The application of DM in this domain considerably aids the agriculturist to effectively administer his or her harvests by delivering an efficient assessment leading to beneficial decisions.

Acquiring reliable and useful information from a DM method requires that the quality of data be good. Data in farming is typically collected from diverse resources with completely diverse databank designs and models, rendering it unclean, complicated, with a bunch of absent records and distinct programming specifications for similar areas. The information accumulated via these techniques comprises several issues such as missing information, programming mistakes, etc. Handling this kind of information is not simple and requires considerable work for cleaning and preprocessing prior to being employed in the DM method.

The information requirement for prototypes poses many hurdles and questions such as ambiguity and shortage of information and hence needs processing and conversion to guarantee quality and reliability. Enhancing the interoperability of information offers fresh prospects for all kinds of evaluation and advancement of innovative systems.

8.5.3 Significance of Spatial Information

The objective of smart farming administration is to execute and assess site-specific harvest handling to reduce ecological harm and boost revenue. This study points out that traditional DM methods are normally aimed at relational files, and spatial data from physically dispersed locations are frequently not used. Innovative DM systems designed for spatial files are needed in smart farming to consider interactions in the information, such as spatial and terrestrial autocorrelation.

8.5.4 Inclusion of Farming Field Experience in Data Mining

Farming is an interdisciplinary domain comprising environment and ecological disciplines, farming finances, soils, plant reproducing, etc. In precision farming, the information required for a DM task might arise from diverse sources. This information, which comes from the sensor and elevated throughput data, in particular, poses novel issues such as: in what way should the information generated be defined so that its significance is correctly explained, it is protected throughout time, and it is workable mechanically through semantic interoperability instead of specialist? Integrating field expertise remains a demanding issue in DM. So, semantic DM can be imagined as a solution to the combination of farming domain expertise into DM and continues as a crucial area of research.

8.5.5 Scalability of Data Mining Techniques

Because of advancements in precision farming, vast volumes of information are being produced via the enhanced usage of tools. In specific, remote devices continually generate heterogeneous information. Possessing vast volumes of information is beneficial since they might undoubtedly reveal actual associations existing between them. Nevertheless, for taking practical decisions in farming where agriculturalists should make numerous choices each time, an issue arises: can DM techniques cope with the quantity of information gathered within a sufficient period? Hence, the DM techniques controlling these large datasets must be scalable by utilizing unique exploration approaches to manage exponential exploration challenges. A critical problem for scalability in farming DM is the design of parallel and distributed techniques.

8.6 Conclusion and Future Scope

The farming segment is presently facing an inflow of data, mainly due to GPS and scientific improvements in sensors and information collection. Farming enterprises currently produce not only crops but additionally generate large volumes of data. Vast volumes of information regarding soil and crop features facilitating greater functioning effectiveness are frequently encompassed in these records. Hence, suitable methods must be employed to discover knowledge. DM methods try to discover those information patterns, which are both useful and noteworthy for administering the crops.

In this chapter, a survey on the usage of DM methods in farming was demonstrated and reviewed. These methods are utilized to resolve numerous farming challenges occurring in harvest monitoring techniques, such as infection and pest supervision and harvest projection. The advantages of DM methods over conventional techniques make DM essential for the assessment of farming information.

The reader of this chapter will be able to learn about the types of farming applications that presently use DM techniques, the features of the information that are being utilized in diverse situations, the shared resources of information, along with the common approaches and methods used for information analysis. Open research challenges were discovered, along with obstacles for a larger acceptance of the DM. Numerous methodologies for resolving these difficulties and overcoming these obstacles have been examined.

The potential of DM in precision farming is appealing. Consequently, it could start a fresh area for farming research and development. This requires suitable procedures and methods to handle intelligent farming jobs in a reliable and effective manner. Nevertheless, its usage is not straightforward. It is confronted with exceptionally tough questions, such as confidentiality, information quality, spatial and semantic information combination, and scalability problems.

By using DM with sensor information, agricultural systems are progressing into actual AI structures, delivering valuable suggestions and intuitions for taking significant decisions and choices with the definitive possibility of production expansion. In the upcoming years, it is anticipated that the use of DM approaches could be prevalent, permitting the prospect of unified and relevant devices. Currently, all the methods are related to specific techniques and are not sufficiently linked with choice-making procedures, as witnessed in other domains. The combination of computerized information recording, information evaluation, DM operation, and choice-making could offer valuable outcomes leading to knowledge-based farming for boosting production levels and improving the quality of bio-products.

References

Atkeson, C. G., Moore, A. W., & Schaal, S. (1997). Locally weighted learning. *Artif. Intell.*, 11, 11–73. https://doi.org/10.1023/A:1006559212014

Balakrishnan, N., & Muthukumarasamy, G. (2016). Crop production-ensemble machine learning model for prediction. *Int. J. Comput. Sci. Softw. Eng.* 5, 148.

Belson, W. A. (1959). Matching and prediction on the principle of biological classification. Appl. Stat, 8, 65–75. https://doi.org/10.2307/2985543

Bharati, S., Podder, P., Mondal, R., Mahmood, A., & Raihan-Al-Masud, M. (2018, December). Comparative performance analysis of different classification algorithm for the purpose of prediction of lung cancer. In International Conference on Intelligent Systems Design and Applications (pp. 447–457). Springer, Cham

Binch, A., & Fox, C. W. (2017). Controlled comparison of machine vision algorithms for Rumex and Urtica detection in grassland. *Comput. Electron. Agric.*, 140, 123–138. https://doi.org/10.1016/j.compag.2017.05.018

Blagojević, M., Blagojević, M., & Ličina, V. (2016). Web-based intelligent system for predicting apricot yields using artificial neural networks. *Sci. Hortic. (Amst.)*, 213, 125–131. https://doi.org/10.1016/j.scienta.2016.10.032

Brahimi, M., Boukhalfa, K., & Moussaoui, A. (2017). Deep learning for tomato diseases: Classification and symptoms visualization. Appl. *Artif. Intell.* 31, 299–315. https://doi.org/10.1080/08839514.2017.1315516

Breiman, L. (2001). Random forests. *Mach. Learn.*, 45, 5–32. https://doi.org/10.1023/A:1010933404324

Broomhead, D. S., & Lowe, D. (1988). Multivariable functional interpolation and adaptive networks. *Complex Syst*, 2, 321–355.

Cai, Y., Guan, K., Lobell, D., Potgieter, A. B., Wang, S., Peng, J., Xu, T., Asseng, S., Zhang, Y., You, L., & Peng, B. (2019). Integrating satellite and climate data to predict wheat yield in Australia using machine learning approaches. *Agric. For. Meteorol.*, 274, 144–159. https://doi.org/10.1016/j.agrformet.2019.03.010

Chang, C., Lin, C (2013). LIBSVM: A Library for support vector machines. *ACM Trans. Intell. Syst. Technol.* 2013, 2, 1–39. https://doi.org/10.1145/1961189.1961199

Cherkassky, V., & Ma, Y. (2004). Practical selection of SVM parameters and noise estimation for SVM regression. *Neural networks*, 17(1), 113–126.

Chlingaryan, A., Sukkarieh, S., & Whelan, B. (2018). Machine learning approaches for crop yield prediction and nitrogen status estimation in precision agriculture: a review. *Comput. Electron. Agric.*, 151, 61–69. https://doi.org/10.1016/j.compag.2018.05.012

Chung, C. L., Huang, K. J., Chen, S. Y., Lai, M. H., Chen, Y. C., & Kuo, Y. F. (2016). Detecting Bakanae disease in rice seedlings by machine vision. *Comput. Electron. Agric.* 121, 404–411. https://doi.org/10.1016/j.compag.2016.01.008

Cillis, D., Maestrini, B., Pezzuolo, A., Marinello, F., & Sartori, L. (2018). Modeling soil organic carbon and carbon dioxide emissions in different tillage systems supported by precision agriculture technologies under current climatic conditions. *Soil Tillage Res.*, 183, 51–59. https://doi.org/10.1016/j.still.2018.06.001

Coopersmith, E. J., Minsker, B. S., Wenzel, C. E., & Gilmore, B. J. (2014). Machine learning assessments of soil drying for agricultural planning. *Comput. Electron. Agric.*, 104, 93–104. https://doi.org/10.1016/j.compag.2014.04.004

Cox, D. R. (1958). The regression analysis of binary sequences. *J. R. Stat. Soc.* Ser. B, 20, 215–242. https://doi.org/10.1111/j.2517-6161.1958.tb00292.x

Cristianini N., Ricci E. (2008) Support vector machines. In: Kao MY. (eds) *Encyclopaedia of Algorithms*. Springer, Boston, MA. https://doi.org/10.1007/978-0-387-30162-4_415

Ebrahimi, M. A., Khoshtaghaza, M. H., Minaei, S., & Jamshidi, B. (2017). Vision-based pest detection based on SVM classification method. *Comput. Electron. Agric.*, 137, 52–58. https://doi.org/10.1016/j.compag.2017.03.016

Efroymson, M. A. (1960). Multiple regression analysis. *Math. Methods Digit. Comput.*, 1, 191–203.

Ferentinos, K. P. (2018). Deep learning models for plant disease detection and diagnosis. *Comput. Electron. Agric.*, 145, 311–318. https://doi.org/10.1016/j.compag.2018.01.009

Fix, E., & Hodges, J. L. (1951). Discriminatory analysis–nonparametric discrimination consistency properties. *Int. Stat. Rev.*, 57, 238–247.

Goodfellow, I., Bengio, Y., & Courville, A. (2016). Deep Learning. MIT Press: Cambridge, MA, USA, 216–261

Grinblat, G. L., Uzal, L. C., Larese, M. G., & Granitto, P. M. (2016). Deep learning for plant identification using vein morphological patterns. *Comput. Electron. Agric.*, 127, 418–424. https://doi.org/10.1016/j.compag.2016.07.003

Issad, H. A., Aoudjit, R., & Rodrigues, J. J. P. C. (2019). A comprehensive review of data mining techniques in smart agriculture. *Engineering in Agriculture, Environment and Food*, 12(4), 511–525. https://doi.org/10.1016/j.eaef.2019.11.003

Holland, J. H. (1992). Adaptation in Natural and Artificial Systems: an Introductory Analysis with Applications to Biology, Control, and Artificial Intelligence. The MIT Press.

Hu, H., Pan, L., Sun, K., Tu, S., Sun, Y., Wei, Y., Tu, K (2017). Differentiation of deciduous-calyx and persistent-calyx pears using hyperspectral reflectance imaging and multivariate analysis. *Comput. Electron. Agric.*, 137, 150–156. https://doi.org/10.1016/j.compag.2017.04.002

Johann, A. L., de Araújo, A. G., Delalibera, H. C., & Hirakawa, A. R. (2016). Soil moisture modeling based on stochastic behaviour of forces on a no-till chisel opener. *Comput. Electron. Agric.*, 121, 420–428.

Kohonen, T. (1988). Learning vector quantization. *Neural Netw.*, 1(1), 303. https://doi.org/10.1016/0893-6080(88)90334-6

Kumar, S., Mishra, S., Khanna, P., & Pragya (2017). Precision sugarcane monitoring using SVM classifier. *Procedia Comput. Sci.* 122, 881–887. https://doi.org/10.1016/j.procs.2017.11.450

LeCun, Y., Bengio, Y., & Hinton, G. (2015). Deep learning. *Nature*, 521, 436–444. https://doi.org/10.1038/nature14539

Liakos, K., Busato, P., Moshou, D., Pearson, S., & Bochtis, D. (2018). Machine Learning in agriculture: A review. *Sensors*, 18(8), 2674. MDPI AG. http://dx.doi.org/10.3390/s18082674

Linnainmaa, S. (1976). Taylor expansion of the accumulated rounding error. *BIT*, 16, 146–160. https://doi.org/10.1007/BF01931367

Maione, C., Batista, B. L., Campiglia, A. D., Barbosa, F., & Barbosa, R. M. (2016). Classification of geographic origin of rice by data mining and inductively coupled plasma mass spectrometry. *Comput. Electron. Agric.*, 121, 101–107. https://doi.org/10.1016/j.compag.2015.11.009

Matei, O., Rusu, T., Petrovan, A., and Mihuț, G. (2017). A data mining system for real time soil moisture prediction. *Procedia Eng.* 181, 837–844. https://doi.org/10.1016/j.proeng.2017.02.475

Mondal, M. R. H., Bharati, S., & Podder, P. (2021). CO-IRv2: Optimized InceptionResNetV2 for COVID-19 detection from chest CT images. *PLoS One*, 16(10), e0259179.

Morellos, A., Pantazi, X.-E., Moshou, D., Alexandridis, T., Whetton, R., Tziotzios, G., Wiebensohn, J., Bill, R., & Mouazen, A. M. (2016). Machine learning based prediction of soil total nitrogen, organic carbon and moisture content by using VIS-NIR spectroscopy. *Biosyst. Eng.*, 152, 104–116. https://doi.org/10.1016/j.biosystemseng.2016.04.018

Moshou, D., Bravo, C., Oberti, R., West, J., Bodria, L., McCartney, A., & Ramon, H. (2005). Plant disease detection based on data fusion of hyper-spectral and multi-spectral fluorescence imaging using Kohonen maps. *Real-Time Imaging*, 11(2), 75–83. https://doi.org/10.1016/j.rti.2005.03.003

Moshou, D., Bravo, C., West, J., Wahlen, S., McCartney, A., & Ramon, H. (2004). Automatic detection of "yellow rust" in wheat using reflectance measurements and neural networks. *Comput. Electron. Agric.*, 44, 173–188. https://doi.org/10.1016/j.compag.2004.04.003

Moshou, D., Pantazi, X.-E., Kateris, D., & Gravalos, I. (2014). Water stress detection based on optical multisensory fusion with a least squares support vector machine classifier. *Biosyst. Eng.*, 117, 15–22. https://doi.org/10.1016/j.biosystemseng.2013.07.008

Nagar, K. (2015). Data mining clustering methods: A review. *Int. J. Adv. Res. Comput. Sci. Softw. Eng.*, 5, 575–579.

Nahvi, B., Habibi, J., Mohammadi, K., Shamshirband, S., & Al Razgan, O. S. (2016). Using self-adaptive evolutionary algorithm to improve the performance of an extreme learning machine for estimating soil temperature. *Comput. Electron. Agric.*, 124, 150–160. https://doi.org/10.1016/j.compag.2016.03.025

Pantazi, X. E., Tamouridou, A. A., Alexandridis, T. K., Lagopodi, A. L., Kontouris, G., & Moshou, D. (2017). Detection of Silybum marianum infection with Microbotryum silybum using VNIR field spectroscopy. *Comput. Electron. Agric.*, 137, 130–137. https://doi.org/10.1016/j.compag.2017.03.017

Podder, P., Khamparia, A., Mondal, M. R. H., Rahman, M. A., & Bharati, S. (2021). Forecasting the Spread of COVID-19 and ICU Requirements. *International Journal of Online and Biomedical Engineering (iJOE)*, 17(05), pp. 81–99. https://doi.org/10.3991/ijoe.v17i05.20009

Pravar J. N. (2020, November 4). Artificial Intelligence in Agriculture: Using Modern Day AI to Solve Traditional Farming Problems. *Analytics Vidhya*. www.analyticsvidhya.com/blog/2020/11/artificial-intelligence-in-agriculture-using-modern-day-ai-to-solve-traditional-farming-problems/

Rajeswari, S., Suthendran, K., & Rajakumar, K. (2017). A smart agricultural model by integrating IoT, mobile and cloud-based big data analytics. *In: International Conference on Intelligent Computing and Control (I2C2)*, 1–5. DOI: 10.1109/I2C2.2017.8321902.

Riedmiller, M., & Braun, H. (1993). A direct adaptive method for faster backpropagation learning: The RPROP algorithm. *Proceedings of the IEEE International Conference on Neural Networks, USA*, 1, 586–591. DOI: 10.1109/ICNN.1993.298623.

Rosenblatt, F. (1958). The perceptron: A probabilistic model for information storage and organization in the brain. *Psychol. Rev*, 65(6), 386–408. https://doi.org/10.1037/h0042519

Sahoo, S., Dhar, A., & Kar, A. (2016). Environmental vulnerability assessment using Grey Analytic Hierarchy Process based model. *Environmental Impact Assessment Review*, 56, 145-154.

Sellam, V., & Poovammal, E. (2016). Prediction of crop yield using regression analysis. *Indian J. Sci. Technol.* 9 (38), 1–5. doi:10.17485/ijst/2016/v9i38/91714.

Suykens, J. A. K., Vandewalle J. (1999). Least Squares Support Vector Machine Classifiers. *Neural Process. Lett.*, 9, 293–300. https://doi.org/10.1023/A:1018628609742

The World Bank Data. (2021) [WWW Document]. https://data.worldbank.org/indicator/SP.POP.TOTL

Tian, F., Wu, B., Zeng, H., Zhang, X., & Xu, J. (2019). Efficient identification of corn cultivation area with multitemporal synthetic aperture radar and optical images in the google earth engine cloud platform. *Remote Sens.*, 11(6), 629. https://doi.org/10.3390/rs11060629

Varman, S. A. M., Baskaran, A. R., Aravindh, S., & Prabhu, E. (2017). Deep learning and IoT for smart agriculture using WSN. *In: IEEE International Conference on*

Computational Intelligence and Computing Research (ICCIC), pp. 1–6. doi: 10.1109/ ICCIC.2017.8524140.

Wang, S., Azzari, G., & Lobell, D. B. (2019). Crop type mapping without field-level labels: random forest transfer and unsupervised clustering techniques. *Remote Sens. Environ.* 222, 303–317. https://doi.org/10.1016/j.rse.2018.12.026

Witten, I., Frank, E., Hall, M., & Pal, C. (2016). Data mining: Practical machine learning tools and techniques, Fourth. ed. Morgan Kaufmann. https://doi.org/10.1016/ C2009-0-19715-5

Zhang, M., Lin, H., Wang, G., Sun, H., & Fu, J. (2018). Mapping paddy rice using a convolutional neural network (CNN) with Landsat 8 datasets in the Dongting lake area, China. *Remote Sens.,* 10(11), 1840. https://doi.org/10.3390/rs10111840

Zhang, M., Li, C., & Yang, F. (2017). Classification of foreign matter embedded inside cotton lint using short wave infrared (SWIR) hyperspectral transmittance imaging. *Comput. Electron. Agric.,* 139, 75–90. https://doi.org/10.1016/j.compag.2017.05.005

Chapter 9

Machine Learning and Its Application in Food Processing and Preservation

Babatunde Olawoye
Department of Food Science and Technology, First Technical University, Ibadan, Nigeria

Oyekemi Popoola
Department of Food Science and Technology, First Technical University, Ibadan, Nigeria

Oseni Kadiri
Department of Biochemistry, Edo State University, Uzairue-Iyamho, Auchi, Nigeria

Jide Ebenezer Taiwo Akinsola
Department of Mathematics and Computer Science, First Technical University, Ibadan, Nigeria

Charles Taiwo Akanbi
Department of Food Science and Technology, Obafemi Awolowo University, Ile-Ife, Nigeria

DOI: 10.1201/9781003299059-9

9.1 Introduction

One critical aspect of agricultural produce (plant and animal) is that it deteriorates quickly shortly after being harvested in the case of plant produce or after being slaughtered when it comes to animals. One way to minimize or eliminate the deterioration of agricultural produce is through processing and preservation (Olawoye et al., 2020a). The processing and preservation of food or farm produce involves the application of scientific and engineering principles that modify the produce and hence extend its shelf life, as well as meeting the nutritional demand of consumers. With a continuous increase in world population, the demand for processed food and agricultural products will increase by double or triple in the next decade. Along with this trend, there has been a tremendous shift in the processing and preservation of food owing to industrial evolution, which has brought about the use of advanced machines for the processing and preservation of agricultural produce (Deng et al., 2021).

Due to inconsistency in humans operating these advanced machines, as well as a large volume of data relating to the food properties generated from the machines, there has been increasing pressure for migration into the development of automated food processes, as well as the development of intelligence techniques capable of analyzing higher data volume, which contains redundant and irrelevant information (Olawoye et al., 2020b). On the other hand, the huge demand for processed food has resulted in some problems, such as food adulteration, contaminated food, food toxicants, and food with short shelf storage. As a result, there is a need for an intelligent food processing system aimed at solving problems emanating from food processing and preservation that will, in turn, improve food productivity and security (Guardado Yordi et al., 2019).

Machine learning in combination with high-performance computers could mine and extract high-dimensional information in data, thereby providing solutions for intelligent food processing and preservation, and hence introducing food productivity into a new era. Unlike other modelling tools, machine learning has the tendency of being learned without rigorous knowledge of computer programming and holds the key to intelligent decision systems (Makrogiannis et al., 2013). Various machine learning techniques in conjunction with other non-machine learning tools have been developed and used for analyzing large quantities of data, such as for the extraction of information, independent component analysis, principal component analysis, speed up robust features, modelling, partial least squares (PLS), decision trees, artificial neural networks, naive Bayes, random forest, k-nearest neighbour, support-vector machine, etc. (Martinez-Garcia et al., 2016).

Machine learning techniques and algorithms as tools for modelling, predicting, and optimizing the various process have attracted much attention and have found application in many fields such as aquaculture (Zhao et al., 2021), medicine and healthcare (do Nascimento et al., 2021), mining and petroleum (Otchere et al., 2021), weather and stocks forecasting (Ekpezu et al., 2021), robotics (Collins et al.,

2021), agricultural production (Olawoye et al., 2020c), speech recognition (Prasanth et al., 2021), and so on. This is due to its ability to learn a process without prior knowledge of the processing operations or variables and to obtain better performance with high and accurate precision when dealing with big data (large volumes of data). The present advancements in food processing and preservation have called for the application of machine learning in food (Saha & Manickavasagan, 2021). Therefore, this chapter aims to provide information on machine learning applications in food processing and preservation and also to provide guidance for industries, researchers and workers in the field.

9.2 Introduction to Machine Learning

Arthur Samuel came up with the name machine learning (ML) to illustrate the manner in which a computing device may gain the capacity for engaging in a checkers game in a fashion that is defined as the process of learning "whether it is carried out by humans or animals" (Samuel, 1959). This definition later became more general to mean the field of study that provides the capacity for computers to learn without explicit programming. The practice of explicit programming enabled astronomers as well as geodesists from the early 18th century to offer the cheapest means to describe planetary orbits using data to aid mariners to sail the ocean (Stigler, 1986). The ML discipline is a specialist area relating to artificial intelligence (AI) meant for enabling computer systems to automate data on how to do a desired task (Ali et al., 2016). Predictive analytics methods for ML are currently being used in several domains (Akinsola et al., 2019). ML is applicable in several sectors of healthcare, research, engineering, business, and finance. It is a fundamental technology that uses huge data and data mining technology for decision-making, forecasting, or prediction. The disruptive technology occasioned by AI being propelled by ML has affected many areas of human endeavour (Hinmikaiye et al., 2021) through which the development of automation, as well as intelligent systems in food processing and preservation, is essential. Lately, ML has found application in food processing and preservation, but this has not commanded so much attention.

9.3 Machine Learning Techniques and Algorithms

ML can be classified into four categories: learning problems, statistical inference, hybrid learning problems, and learning techniques (Brownlee, 2019). Each of these broad categories is sub-divided as follows:

a. **Learning problems**: unsupervised learning, reinforcement learning, and supervised learning.

b. **Statistical inference**: transductive learning, deductive inference, and inductive learning.
c. **Hybrid learning problems**: multi-instance learning, self-supervised learning, and semi-supervised learning.
d. **Learning techniques**: multi-task learning, online learning, ensemble learning, active learning, and transfer learning.

Along with reinforcement learning, deep learning, and evolutionary learning, the most popular methods for ML techniques include supervised learning, semi-supervised learning, and unsupervised learning.

Supervised learning (SL) trains the identified system using input and output data to anticipate future outputs. Based on data input and output, the predictive model is built (Brownlee, 2020). Examples of supervised learning models from two separate categories are classification and regression. SL is mostly used to predict and classify numerical values, for instance, regression and associated class prediction, respectively.

The objective of the unsupervised learning (UL) approach is to identify inherent structures of data in addition to hidden data formations. For making conclusions, a corpus that is made up of data input in the absence of identified results can be employed. Clustering can be both a form along with UL, that is, the most prevalent. UL is employed in the context of data aggregation to identify unknown patterns. It is used primarily in a market systematic investigation, image sensing, cardiovascular disease prediction (treatment), in addition to other ailments. k-medoids, as well as Fuzzy C-models, are all algorithms necessarily used in executing clustering; self-organization representations, k-means, hidden Markov models, Gaussian mixing models, subtractive clustering, and hierarchical clustering are all methods for implementing clustering.

Both UL and SL are linked to semi-supervised learning (SSL). SSL is concerned with unlabelled training data (that is, a small amount of unlabelled data) and methods including learning problems as a part of or a class of machine learning. SSL can also be referred to as preparative learning or transductive learning (Zhu & Goldberg, 2009). SSL approaches comprise transduction SVM, co-trained, self-trained, and models with generatively modifiable mixture, in addition to expectation-maximization (EM) visual-based techniques (Zhu, 2008).

Reinforcement learning (RL) technology is an ML approach that addresses how software agents should maximize the concept of a combined reward in an environment. Improvement is about taking suitable measures to maximize rewards in a certain circumstance. Different devices and software seek the best possible behaviour or approach to a specific scenario. For example, for advanced industrial technology, RL is commonly employed in PC gaming and robotics.

Deep learning (DL) is a component of ML that makes use of algorithms for explicit tasks instead of data representations. DL is useful regarding the domain of natural language processing (NLP), board game programs, computer vision, voice ID, machine translation, audio identification, medication planning, social network filtration, bioinformatics, medical picture analysis, and product inspections. ML pertains to a semi-supervised form of learning or supervised learning type when being applied in DL.

DL structures such as deep neural networks were designed to provide equal outcomes in certain circumstances of excellently distinguishable attributes compared to human experts in addition to recurring neural networks. DL networks are not only new but have astonishing features when handling images for classification. A computer model in a deep type of learning is directly used for classification purposes to learn from images, textual material or sound. DL designs can achieve cutting-edge precision, specificity, and perhaps superior performance in comparison to humans. These techniques are trained via the usage of an all-encompassing array of labelled data in addition to multilayered neural network designs.

Evolutionary learning (EL) is a subset of evolutionary computation, a population-based specialized algorithm for metaheuristic optimisation. An evolutionary algorithm (EA) uses the biological procedures of modification, replication, the combination of genes, and selection (Vikhar, 2016).

9.4 Machine Learning Algorithms

9.4.1 Naive Bayes

The classifiers of Bayes are probabilistic classifiers based on Thomas Bayes' basic probabilistic law, shown in equation 1 as Bayes' theorem.

$$P(B \mid A) = \frac{P(B \mid A) \times P(A)}{P(B)} \tag{1}$$

The link between A and B is shown by equation 1, which is conditional probability and probability.

The naive Bayes (NB) algorithm is a non-complicated, autonomous algorithm that suggests that a feature of an algorithm is not reciprocally likely. Comparatively sophisticated Bayesian network algorithms assess ambiguity, allowing for more complex information from the data being analyzed.

The Bayesian network codes probabilistic relationships with directed acyclic networks for a combination of interest nodes in undeterminable terms. The NB network is relatively simple and is a direct acyclic network of nodes with just one parent having many nodes with strong independence between child nodes inside their parents (the node not identified).

9.4.2 Support-Vector Machine

Neural networks are intimately connected to support-vector machine (SVM) algorithms in the classical multilayer perceptron. SVMs revolve around the general idea of a deviation between two data types on either side of the hyperplanes (Ali & Smith, 2006).

The maximization of the limit of the predicted generalization error, and hence the maximal distance feasible between the hyperplanes, has been demonstrated, and cases on both sides reduced the upper limit. SVM classification allows data from many classes after creating vectors to divide the best hyperplanes into a space for features or parameters. According to Kecman (2005), the hyperplane positioned in the highest range at the nearest locations of data is ideally characterized.

9.4.3 Neural Network

Artificial neural networks (ANNs) utilize an element that classifies network weights without consideration for creating an uncompromising problem of non-convex minimization, as with traditional training of neural networks (Ayodele, 2010; Bharati et al., 2021). An ANN is a classification problem-solving learning algorithm. There are numerous parallel, dynamic, and interlinked neuron network systems in an ANN model. A neuron is used to create results utilizing inputs via a specific mathematical processor (Ko et al., 2010).

9.4.4 k-Nearest Neighbour

k-nearest neighbour (KNN) is referred to as a lazy classifier. It is a learner based on instances. It is an algorithm that uses nearest neighbour in determining labelled points. The way to categorize a particular dataset with a fixed apriorist is easy and unambiguous K-means clusters of algorithms (suppose k clusters). K-means algorithms are employed when labelled data is not accessible (Smola and Vishwanathan, 2008). KNN uses a specific technique of transforming approximate thumb rules into a very accurate predictive rule. Due to algorithms with weak learning capabilities, general principles can, if nothing else, be marginally dependable in relation to random with an accuracy of around 55%. However, an improved algorithm can probably create one classifier with 99% accuracy (Manikandan and Sivakumar, 2018) with enough data.

9.4.5 Decision Tree

A decision tree (DT) has capabilities for fixing missing values, decision-tree pruning, continuous attributes values collection, rules of derivatives, and so on. Korting (n.d.) opined that in many situations, the DT technique utilizes the responsiveness of the characteristics/vector in many cases. Classes for the new cases can be found according to learning instances. This method produces the output that predicts the target variable. The arrangement of crucial data as it concerns tree classification technique can be understood easily (Nadali et al., 2011).

9.5 Machine Learning Application to Food Processing and Preservation

ML, an AI component, plays an important part in the creation of value for food processing and preservation, birthing operational processes for a new business model in the agrifood industry (Di Vaio et al., 2020). Different food industry stakeholders have applied ML algorithms in the supply chain to rethink and redesign the whole business model for sustainability and food security. According to Kovalenko (2020), applying AI and ML solutions has offered food production businesses various benefits and chances to save money, mechanize, enhance processes, and reduce human error (Di Vaio et al., 2020). AI helps to improve the logistics and predictive analysis of supply chain management and to enhance transparency to reduce food perishability drastically.

According to Marvin et al. (2017), recent improvements in food safety regarding data science have led to a debate over huge amounts of data being generated daily (Marvin et al., 2017), a phrase typically unconnected to food security. AI requires a smart/intelligent user interface (IUI) based on the principles of ML (Akinsola et al., 2021). ML is the potential technique for data-intensive food security analysis to solve the analytical problems caused by the drift of data (Deng et al., 2021). An excess of data has been harnessed to several food-related problems. For example, pre-harvest, terrain and weather data for predicting pathogen pollution on farms has been examined (Strawn et al., 2013), while retail auditing, keeping of records as well as paperless have allowed 1.4 million internal cooking temperature monthly chickens measurements to ensure food security (Yiannas, 2015). Highlighted below are various ML applications in food processing and preservation.

9.5.1 Grading and Sorting of Fruits Using Artificial Intelligence

These days, the use of technology in food establishments has become a vital component of the production of food and process delivery. Food processors now produce food aided by robotics as well as the processing of data. Technology, to a significant extent, could enhance packaging and improve shelf life in addition to food safety. There is also improvement in food quality with reduced production costs with the use of drones, robotics, 3D printings, and machines (SDP, 2021). In ML, AI is being applied for the assessment of food quality. In the past, processors had to employ several workers to carry out tedious and regular procedures associated with the selection of food. Presently, the manual sorting of an enormous quantity of foods based on shape as well as size has been substituted with AI. For example, AI has been easily used to identify which plant is appropriate for potato chips and which is preferable for use in making French fries. The sorting of vegetables having improper color is also being performed using this same technique, reducing the possibility of vegetables being rejected by consumers. Food designs and manufacturers such as TOMRA have developed peelers and sorters with enhanced processing ability and accessibility, which helps proliferate food quality and safety. This is accomplished by utilizing technologies that have a base of operations on a core sensor in addition to a camera that helps to identify the food based on shape (diameter, width, length), color, and distinguishing biological features. The camera possesses an adaptable spectrum that is suitable for grading, sorting, and peeling food optically. The sorting of foods using automated systems certainly lowers the costs of labour, enhances process speeds, and increases yield quality. Each stage of the food chain supply is monitored using AI, ensuring inventory and price control forecast, as well as tracing the direction of goods right from the farm to end users, hence making certain there is transparency. The role of classification and decision-making is important in ML with regard to fruit classification and the process of grading (Naik & Patel, 2017).

9.5.2 Grading and Sorting of Fruits Using Machine Learning

Appearance is an important quality attribute of fruits that influences not only their market worth, selection, and consumers' choice, but to a large degree, their quality internally. Texture, shape, color, visual flaws, and size are usually examined to determine fruits' outside quality. The classification and grading of fruit are crucial and tedious tasks because retailers need to be aware of the several categories of fruits to enable them to decide their prices (Pérez et al., 2017). Manually controlling the external quality of fruits takes a lot of time and needs a large workforce. Therefore, for automatic control of the external quality of foods and products from agriculture, systems visioned by computers have had widespread usage in food industries over the years and have turned out to be scientifically and powerfully capable for works that are demanding (Naik & Patel, 2017). Several ML algorithms such as SVM, convolutional neural network (CNN), PCA, ANN, and KNN, among others, have been used for the sorting and grading of several types of fruits. The frequency of use of the above algorithms is dependent on their speed, economic importance, accurate inspection, measurement, and computing tasks. Obtaining information like fruit and vegetable examination, estimation of yield, area of the leaf, grading, and classification of plants is usually done using these algorithms.

Artificial neural networks and simple and multiple linear regression were used for estimating mango fruit size, maximum thickness, length, and maximum width, with an achievement of 96.7% success rate accuracy (Schulze et al., 2015). Multiple linear regression was used to determine the maximum diameter, projected area, length, and equatorial section of kiwi fruit with an achievement of 98.3% accuracy (Fu et al., 2016). Mango was classified using a Fourier-descriptor for the extraction of shape features, in addition to an SVM with an almost 100% result classification (Sa'ad et al., 2015). A PCA, feedforward neural network, and biogeography-based optimization were used for classifying 18 classes of fruits with an accuracy of 89.11% (Zhang et al., 2016). Apple fruit was also classified using NB with an accuracy of 91% (Miriti, 2016). Girshick et al. (2014) used PCA coupled with a neural network for the classification of date fruit with respect to their shape and texture. Texture and color attributes, in addition to neural networks, were used to classify orange fruit defects with an accuracy of 88%. Classification of fruit with texture and color features was performed by Jana & Parekh (2016) with an ANN with an accuracy of 83–98%. A description of color and geometric features was carried out by Liming & Yanchao (2010) for grading strawberries, with an accuracy of 88.80%. A multilayer perception neural network was presented by Moallem et al. (2017) for detecting apple defects, with 89.20% and 92.50% accuracy for defected and healthy apples, respectively. An optimized presentation for the classification and segmentation of diseased apples was carried out by Khan et al. (2019), and features were selected by a genetic algorithm with a 97.79% rate of recognition. KNN was used as a classifier by Seng & Mirisaee (2009) for the classification of fruit based on roundness of shape, mean color, perimeter, and area.

9.5.3 Grading and Sorting of Fruits Using Support-Vector Machine

SVM is one of the potent algorithms used for several types of linear and non-linear classification of data. Defects in mangoes (degree of mango browning) was detected automatically using a least-squares SVM (Zheng and Lu, 2012), while tomatoes were reduced dimensionally and classified using PCA coupled with SVM, with an achievement of 92% accuracy (Semary et al., 2015). SVM, in addition to PCA with a backpropagation neural network, were employed for estimating quality attributes and classifying strawberries based on maturity status (Liu et al., 2014), with an accuracy of 100% achieved by SVM for classification of ripeness stage.

9.5.4 Fruit Grading and Sorting Using Artificial Neural Network

The ANN has become widely known for performing a significant function in intensifying the most recent technology. Resulting from the rise in industrial automatic systems and Internet connectivity, it now requires little skill and effort to gather data and oversee the process of sterilization, extrusion, and the drying of foods. With the uprising revolution of industries, the ANN has found rewarding application in food processing establishments, accomplishing effective roles such as in food sorting, grading, quality, safety checks (Nayak et al., 2020), and for better knowledge of various attributes in the food sector. ANNs perform a significant function in the processing of several foods ranging from fruits to vegetables, various cereal grains, wine, meat, soft drinks, olive oil, fish, and fruit juices. Estimation of fruit quality is an important prerequisite as a result of understanding consumers' complex perceptions in large areas. Fruits such as coffee fruit, grapes, dates, strawberries, mulberries, bananas, and pomegranates, among others, have been processed using neural networks. Identification of diseased fruit was made using k-means clustering, which was used for texture, color, image segmentation, and structure characteristics, in addition to an ANN (Awate et al., 2015). Tomato fruits are sorted using texture, color, and shape characteristics. With an accuracy of 84.4%, a probabilistic neural network as a classifier was used to detect a defect (Arjenaki et al., 2013). Feedforward and radial basis probabilistic neural networks have also been used for fruit classification.

9.5.5 Coffee Fruit Using Artificial Neural Network

There has been a day-to-day decline in coffee fruit production as a result of a shortage in labour and immigration issues, making the manual operations of coffee processing a voluminous task. A technique for identifying coffee fruit using neural networks and visual prostheses was developed by Fuentes et al. (2020), allowing coffee manufacturers to reduce the rate and increase the quantity of their final product. Coffee fruit has been classified by these authors as ripe or unripe by the potential of the newly developed technique for improved quality.

9.5.6 Dragon Fruit Using Artificial Neural Network

The technique of sorting and grading dragon fruits with the use of an ANN is made up of three arrangements of layers that include an input layer, hidden layer, and output layer with weights and bias functions linked to neurons. The bias functions and the number of hidden layers are determined by the algorithm of the ANN used.

9.5.7 Dates Using Artificial Neural Network

ANNs are seldomly used for dates processing. Dates have been categorized using probabilistic neural networks, a new technique propounded by Fadel (2007). The separation of dates using color attributes was also observed by this author. Five varieties of the fruit were considered for the proposed technique, as well as the consideration of 15 types of date fruit images. An enhanced classification of reliability has been identified using this technique.

9.5.8 Oil Palm Fruits Using Hyperspectral and Machine Learning

Precise grading based on the ripeness stages of fresh oil palm fruits before processing is a crucial issue encountered by exporters and producers of oil palm. The general market appeal and market value of the produced palm oil is a function of the ripeness or maturity (Junkwon et al., 2009). One of the problems encountered during the production of oil is fresh oil palm fruit grading regarding its maturity. Traditional methods used by workers involve a little cut of the fruits to check the color of the mesocarp and count the number of fruits loose per bunch (Shaarani et al., 2010). Hyperspectral imaging is a method that has been applied extensively to evaluate the interior quality characteristics of fruits. The characteristics include flesh, acidity, skin color, sugar content, starch index, and firmness (Lorente et al., 2012). A hyperspectral device in addition to ML was used by Bensaeed et al. (2014) to grade oil palm fruit based on ripeness. Scanning of fresh bunches of fruits using a hyperspectral device was done, noting their reflectance at varying wavelengths. Fresh oil palm fruits totalling 469 were classified as underripe, ripe, and overripe, with the measuring of the characteristics of fruits in the near-infrared and visible wavelength (400–1000 nm) regions. An ANN was used to classify the regions of different wavelengths through the processing pixel-wise. The established ANN design effectively classified the fruits into underripe, ripe, and overripe attributes.

9.5.9 Papaya Fruits Using Machine Learning

The prediction of ripening of papaya fruit using random forest (RF) based on image processing techniques was carried out by Pereira et al. (2018) with an achievement of 94.7% accuracy. Three categories of papaya fruits were graded by Behera et al. (2020) using ML approaches with regards to their stage of maturity (mature, partially mature, and immature). Three feature sets and three classifiers (KNN, SVM, and NB) were used.

9.5.10 Orange Classification and Grading Using Machine Learning

The identification of deformities and flaws on the surface of orange fruits was carried out by Behera et al. (2020) using SVM (regression) and k-means clustering with an achievement of 90% accuracy, while the severity of disease was computed using fuzzy logic. A segmentation of the sample of images prepared was first done with k-means clustering for separation of the foreground, background, and parts of defected oranges that represent the regions of interest. An SVM was then used to extract and train 13 texture features from the regions of interest. Test sample feature and trained sample feature were classified accordingly through an SVM. How severe the disease is has formed the basis for the second measurement.

9.5.11 Machine Learning for Automatically Detecting and Grading Multiple Fruits

Several algorithms have been developed and tested for the categorization and correct grading of fruit texture, shape features, color extraction, and edge. Four different fruit types were discriminated against and analysed based on maturity (Bhargava & Bansal, 2020). Four different classifiers, including sparse representative classifier, SVM, ANN, and KNN, were employed for the quality classification of the fruits (apples, banana, avocado, and oranges). KNN, sparse representative classifier, ANN and SVM had a maximum accuracy of 80%, 85.51%, 91.03%, and 98.48%, respectively, while the defected maximum accuracy of 77.24%, 95.72%, 82.75%, and 88.27%, respectively, were achieved. SVM was seen to be more effective in evaluating the quality.

9.6 Drying of Fruit and Vegetables

The application of ML-based algorithms in the drying of food is an interesting and novel approach in drying technology. Microstructural characterization, process optimization, material properties determination, and mathematical modelling are some of the major areas of food drying research. Expressing this research information through ML algorithms is essential to advancing research in food drying technology.

Some existing mathematical models for the drying of various food products are categorized into first, second, and third generational models. The most effective has been reported to be fourth-generation models, which are physics-based and multi-scale (Welsh et al., 2018; Rahman et al., 2018). Optimal drying conditions, reduced energy consumption, and product quality improvement are some of the major goals of modelling strategies. Though the development of this model can be computationally expensive and time-consuming, it can, however, be implemented for the understanding of lower processing time and computational cost for food and horticulture drying. In an ML-based model, an ANN has been developed for the real-time prediction of drying rates, calculation, and drying processes. There has been attempted research toward developing food drying models using ML algorithms (Jumah & Mujumdar, 2005)

Islam et al. (2003) demonstrated the ability of an ANN in predicting the entire drying rates curves of potato slices during convective drying under different drying conditions. In a related study by Hernandez-Perez et al. (2004), mango and cassava drying kinetics was predicted using a heat and mass transfer model developed from an ANN. The product shrinkage was considered as a function of its moisture content. The empirical relationship was used in the calculation of shrinkage.

$$\delta = \delta_0 \Delta \delta_f + 1 - \Delta x x_0 \qquad (9.1)$$

The moisture content on a dry basis at time t, and the moisture at time zero are represented by X and X_0, δ_0 represents the initial thickness of the slab, δ_0 is the initial thickness while δ_f is the fraction of the initial slab thickness at the end of drying.

Using microwave-assisted fluidized bed drying, an ML-based network was developed to predict the drying kinetics of corn in a study by Li, Chen & Liang et al. (2019). The influence of training algorithms and transfer functions were studied using 170 neurons. The tainrp and transig transfer functions accurately predict the drying system of the shelled corn (Li, Chen & Liang et al., 2019).

An ML network was developed for the prediction of the drying kinetics of pistachio nuts in a study by Omid et al. (2009). It was shown that the best prediction of pistachio nut moisture content was obtained when the first and second hidden layers were eight and five, respectively.

A recent study shows the ability of AI control coupled with the low-field nuclear magnetic resonance relaxometry (LF-NMR) technique in detecting the endpoint of carrots drying. Several other researchers have used ML-based modelling for the prediction of drying kinetics in sugar beet pulp (Merino et al., 2017), seedy grapes (Çakmak & Yıldız, 2011), potatoes (Islam et al., 2003), grains (Li & Chen, 2019), and apples (Aghbashlo et al. (2011).

9.7 Detection of Quality of Oil

Today, the detection of adulteration in the safety of food, and to a great extent in edible oils, has become a significant issue, with researchers devising suitable techniques to detect their adulteration.

9.7.1 Detection of Quality of Olive Oil

Oils made from olive, in addition to virgin olive oil, are more costly than other types of vegetable oil. As a result, adulterants (oils such as coconut oil, sunflower oil, maize oil, and hazelnut oil) that are of poor quality and reduced price are usually added (Mildner-Szkudlarz & Jeleń, 2008). Hence, continuous care is necessary to curtail the activities of adulterating olive oil products and to protect consumers and the industry in general. PCA coupled with various ML algorithms such as KNN, DT, NB, linear discriminant analysis (LDA), SVM and ANN has been applied in detecting adulterants in olive oil, with their performances being compared based on their exactness (Ordukaya & Karlik, 2017). PCA using a specific application based on an array of sensors has been studied by Taurino et al. (2002) to identify the contamination of different olive oils. Two new processes were identified and classified to control the quality of 12 kinds of olive oil with the use of an electronic nose in addition to an ML algorithm.

9.7.2 Detection of Extra Virgin Olive Oil Quality

Extra virgin olive oil is usually called "liquid gold" for the reason that it possesses a distinctive aroma and flavour, as well as health benefits (Meenu et al., 2019). As a result of its complicated and time-consuming production process, it is highly profit-oriented, hence it is regularly made impure with additional oils. Oils such as low-quality canola oil, sunflower oil, palm oil, and hazelnut oil are usually added as adulterants, which may be detrimental to the health of consumers. Hazelnut is normally added to adulterate extra virgin olive oil because their fatty acid compositions have a striking resemblance (Wong et al., 2019), hence making it uneasy to verify the existence of low concentrations of hazelnut oil in extra virgin olive oil. Extra virgin olive oil adulteration was studied by Hou et al. (2020) utilizing LF-NMR coupled with ML algorithms that include SVM, LDA, KNN, CNN and DT. The results efficiently differentiated unadulterated extra virgin olive oil from contaminated oil from high oleic sunflower and hazelnut. An 89.29% accuracy, 81.25% precision, and 81.25% recall was reported that yielded the opportunity for a swift two min identification of unadulterated extra virgin olive oil with the one that was contaminated with oil from high oleic sunflower and hazelnut with a volume ratio in a range of between 10–100%. It was concluded that LF-NMR coupled with CNN is an achievable rapid method for extra virgin olive oil authentication. LF-NMR in combination with PCA discriminant analysis and regression analysis has also been used to analyze the adulteration of sesame oil with soybean oil, peanut oil adulterated with rapeseed oil, soybean oil, or palm oil, as well as qualified oils adulterated with oil that has been previously used for frying (Zhang et al., 2013), respectively.

9.7.3 Detection of Quality of Edible Oils

A particular type of oil's fatty acid profile can be imitated through different types of oil mixture, resulting in deceptive adulteration of oil as well as incorrect labelling of edible oils endangering the safety of food and causing health hazards. An ML approach was used by Lim et al. (2020) to reveal the pattern of fatty acids for 10 dissimilar types of plant oils and their variability on the inside. This method allows for the capacity to control the quality of the product and dictate the favourable cost of oils and therefore allows for awareness of detailed labelling by consumers. Consumer concern for oils obtained from sea buckhorn, walnut, sesame, hemp, pumpkin, and walnut by cold pressing has increased as a result of their great nutritive and health importance. Due to the high commercial and industrial value of the above oils, some unjust producers and retailers have used this opportunity to make an illicit profit by substituting the basic materials of these oils with low-quality ones such as sunflower oil. Berghian-Grosan & Magdas (2020) also invented and efficiently tested a novel approach for validating the authenticity of edible oils established on rapid Raman spectra processing using ML algorithms. The application of PCA to Raman data is one of the highly accomplished methods applied to confirm the authenticity of edible oils as well as detecting the adulteration of olive oil (Zhang et al., 2011). The detection of adulteration in addition to the initial magnitude of adulteration was accomplished with this approach. A fast and exact adulteration detection of oil samples in addition to the degree of adulteration is the principal benefit of this approach.

9.7.4 Detection of Quality of Peanut, Soybean, and Sesame Oils

Cluster analysis and PCA have been demonstrated as effective tools for discrimination and finding a resemblance of oil samples (Mildner-Szkudlarz & Jeleń, 2008). A type of approach was developed to differentiate expensive vegetable oils from cheaper low-quality ones like soybean oils. The volatile flavour compounds of peanut, soybean, and sesame oils free of pollutants were differentiated with peanut and sesame oils that were mixed with impurities from soybean oil using gas chromatography time-of-flight mass spectrometry combined with PCA and cluster analysis (Zhao et al., 2013).

9.7.5 Detection of Quality of Sesame Oil

Sesame oil is a widely known fragrant oil that is welcomed to a great degree across the world, hence its consumption on the increase. It is usually employed for enhancing flavour in addition to its good taste and appealing odour. It also contains several nutritional compounds such as tocopherols, inorganic elements, sesamin, sesamol, fatty acids, and sesamolin, which have useful biological activities (Soltani et al., 2021). Adulteration is usually associated with high priced edible oils such as sesame oil. Low-quality oils like rapeseed oil are usually added as an adulterant to a great degree to sesame oil, hence there is a great need to create a rapid, pragmatic, and low-cost method for discovering and quantifying the contamination of sesame oil. The authenticity of sesame oil was detected by Soltani et al. (2021) using PCA models, while the quantity of pure and adulterated oils was envisaged using an ANN and an SVM.

9.7.6 Detection of Sesame Oil Quality with Sunflower Oil, Hazel Oil, and Canola Oil

The bioactive properties, odour, flavour, and taste of sesame oil make it an oil of great value. This results in consumers agreeing to purchase it at a very high price because of increasing knowledge of the benefits of consuming healthful and good quality food. Sesame oil is, however, subjected to risks of adulteration with cheaper vegetable oils, negatively affecting the health of consumers. Undiluted sesame oil was differentiated and classified from adulterated vegetable oils using cluster analysis of Fourier transform infrared spectroscopy spectra in addition to a PLS approach which was used to obtain a calibration curve to find out the correlation between the real concentration of adulterant (Ozulku et al., 2017).

9.8 Food Recognition and Classification

The diverse nature of food and its intrinsic characteristics have posed a great challenge to food processors and researchers in detecting and distinguishing foods. However, these challenges can be overcome through the use of machine vision, which has the advantage of being a non-destructive, long-term, and low-cost approach to food recognition. Foods, fruits, and vegetable identification based on ML provide an important means for intelligent food pattern recognition (Deng et al., 2021). Also, during food classification, accurate identification of food or crop species is necessary for effective crop breeding, food processing, and nutritional composition. Research has tried to classify fruit and vegetable-based processing operation, geographical location and origin, as well as species using spectrophotometric data; however, with the advent of ML, food classification and pattern recognition have become more accurate and rapid (Chen et al., 2021). Food pattern recognition using ML techniques uses the information regarding the class membership of the food samples in a particular group or category for the classification of a new unknown food sample into one of the known classes based on its pattern of measurement. An ML procedure for food pattern recognition is based on the following steps: training selection, testing dataset calibration consisting of objects of known class membership from which variables are measured; selection of variables in which houses the information for the aimed classification, while variables encoded with noise are eliminated; building of mathematical model for the training dataset; and model validation using independent test dataset to evaluate the reliability and accuracy of the achieved classification. Different types of pattern recognition techniques have found application in food. However, they differ in the way in which the classification is achieved (Qi et al., 2021). The two methods differ in the first approach: firstly, those that focused on classes discrimination such as KNN, ANN, classification and regression tree (CART), LDA and PLS discriminant analysis; and secondly, those that focused on orientation towards classes modelling, such as unequal dispersed classes and soft independent modelling of class analogy.

9.9 Food Adulteration

Adulteration is a growing safety concern in the food industry around the globe. In adulteration, food quality is incidentally or intentionally degraded through the addition of extraneous matter or chemicals, etc. Figure 9.1 shows the major types of adulteration. Natural adulteration occurs when certain chemicals, radicals, or organic compounds that are injurious to health are present in the food. These types of adulterants are not intentionally added to food but occur naturally in it. Examples of unintentional adulterants include microbiological contamination and pesticide residues while ripening agents and food additives are typical examples of adulterants intentionally added to food.

In ensuring food safety, there is a need to automate the system to be able to make predictions or detect which adulterants are most likely to appear or present in food products. ML algorithms are commonly classified as reinforcement, unsupervised, and supervised learning. It is a model-based process that has been applied in the detection of various food adulterants over the years.

In a study by Hansen & Holroyd (2019), the combined use of un-target and target models when applied to the FT-IR spectrum was reported to be efficient in the detection of milk adulteration. A multivariate linear regression model was used in their experimental protocol. ML algorithms on the spatial data of milk were introduced by Neto et al. (2019). This method was able to identify the most prevalent adulteration methods in the dairy industry. Their proposed regression and classification technique gave better results than other traditional methods of detecting adulteration in milk and its products. A proposed regression model can quantify formalin in cows' milk, according to a study by Mabood et al. (2016). The model

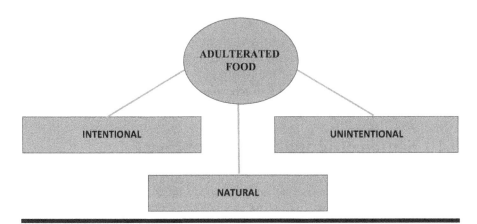

Figure 9.1   Types of food adulterant

uses F-score, recall, entropy, and precision as the performance measures indicator. The method uses the combined effect of the multivariate linear regression procedure coupled with infrared-based spectroscopy.

Milk fat adulteration at levels above 10% can be detected using a regression model. The ability of this model to achieve this was validated in a prior study by Rebechi et al. (2016). The model was appraised in terms of its sensitivity, entropy, and specificity in comparison with other techniques. Fungus identification in milk using an ML technique was reported by Jayanthi & Florence (2019). Real-time cameras were used in capturing the features of the milk species and extracted by the gradients algorithm. These were then fed to the algorithm of the SVM classification and implemented using an ARM processor. An earlier work of Rebechi et al. (2016) built a database of adulteration from relevant articles on the web. A collaborative filtering classifier was applied to determine the suitability of an ingredient and food product. Identification of adulteration in milk powder was achieved using an integrated mechanism that uses the nuclear magnetic resonance technique coupled with the least-square SVMs. Precision, recall, and F-score were used as the performance metrics (Jiang et al., 2020).

ML coupled with hyperspectral imaging has been used in the detection as well as quantification of the adulterant level in chicken added to minced beef (Kamruzzaman et al., 2016). In this study, adulteration levels of the spectral profiles were related to PLS regression models.

Certain studies demonstrated ML and laser-induced breakdown spectroscopy effectiveness for the classification of olive oils (Gazeli et al., 2020). Also, when Raman spectroscopy was used with ML algorithms, a new approach for the authentication of edible oil was developed in a study by Berghian-Grosan & Magdas (2020). This technique has the advantage of not needing to undergo the tedious task and cost of sample preparation.

The effectiveness of ML and hyperspectral imaging as a non-destructive method in adulterant detection, classification, and quantification in minced beef and pork was demonstrated in a study by Rady (2020). Although in the past, several techniques have been used in the detection of adulterants or foreign materials in beef products, this method proved to be very useful in achieving this purpose.

9.10 Sensometric and Consumer Science

Although adequate quality food can be guaranteed, it is the assessment by the final consumer that guarantees the marketability of the product. The concern of consumers over food preference, choice, and acceptability is one of the key factors influencing product decisions in food industries (Granitto et al., 2007). The assessment of food quality by the consumer is done through a process called sensory evaluation. Conducting consumer research or sensory evaluation can be a costly, tedious, and time-consuming operation, hence the ability to predict the overall acceptability of the product will play a significant role in market research. In most consumer research, a simple correlation test or chemometrics methods such as PCA, hierarchical cluster analysis, or PLS regression is used to establish a relationship between consumer preference and sensory data in the prediction of consumer acceptability of a newly developed product (Olawoye & Gbadamosi, 2020). This, however, relies on statistical and mathematical modelling, which may be inappropriate for complex data such as consumer acceptability studies. ML, on the other hand, assumes that the sensory data was obtained from an unknown and complex process, hence an independent variable uses an algorithm to predict responses and learn patterns (Chen et al., 2021). Although researchers in sensory and consumer science still use a traditional method of data analysis such as statistical analysis, information, and pattern extraction, several ML algorithms and data processing methods such as SVM, neural network, PLSR, RF, and gradient boosting have been used for relationship establishment between food sensory attributes and hedonic rating. In their studies, Rocha et al. (2020) use gradient boosted tree, extreme learning machine, and RF to predict sensory drivers that are likely to affect consumer acceptance of cheese produced from milk that has undergone ohmic heat treatment. The dataset used for the ML consists of four cheese samples and 16 sensory attributes. Their findings revealed that the ML algorithms accurately predict the sensory drivers. Granitto et al. (2007), in their research, used DTs, extreme methods such as neural networks, LDA, and RF as modern analysis tools in the descriptive analysis of sensory attributes. Although ML has found various applications in food processing and preservations, it has the potential to be used as a modern tool in sensory and consumer science over traditional data and statistical analysis tools.

9.11 Production and Prediction of Bioactive Compounds in Plants

9.11.1 Bioactive Compounds in Tomatoes

Among the vegetable crops grown worldwide, tomato fruit is the second crop having significant value, which is either consumed fresh or as processed products. The tomato has antioxidant characteristics that make it beneficial to health because of the major bioactive compounds (lycopene and phenolic compounds) that are predominant in it (Canene-Adams et al., 2005). Lately, the differentiation of fruits in the market requires a precise evaluation of these compounds. The phenolic compounds and lycopene of tomatoes were measured with multispectral imaging in addition to chemometrics methods (Liu, Liu, Chen et al., 2015). Quantitative models were developed using a backpropagation neural network, least-square SVM and PLS. Favourable results were recorded in the analysis of fruits and vegetables using PLS.

In comparison with the least-squares SVM and PLS, the performance in the content of lycopene was improved with a backpropagation neural network.

9.11.2 Bioactive Compounds of Grape Skins

Chemometric tools were combined with near-infrared spectroscopy to evaluate the concentration of polyphenols in grapes and grape skins during maturation (Ferrer-Gallego et al., 2011). Quantitative models were also developed for total phenolic compounds, anthocyanins, flavanols, and phenolic acids of grape skins using modified PLS regression. A precise and effective result could be obtained for making decisions if this method is developed and applied during harvest time.

Table 9.1   Decision Trees Applications in Hyperspectral Image Analysis of Food Products

	Characteristics of the decision tree			
Research	Decision tree model	Parameters values	Training set: Validation set	Cross-validation
Aflatoxin identification in contaminated corn kernels	CART*	-	50:50	5-Fold
Decay classification in mandarins	CART	-	80:20	5-Fold
Wheat kernels classification of infected and healthy grains	LMT*	-	80:20	10-Fold
Ropelewska et al. (2018)				
Marssonina detection in apples	CART	Split attribute criteria: Gini index; No. of splits: 100	80:20	10-Fold
Microbial spoilage detection in mushrooms	CART	-	57:43	5-Fold

Note: * CART: Classification and Regression Trees; LMT: Logistic Model Tree

9.11.3 Artificial Neural Network for Prediction of Bioactive Constituents in Plants

Rates and yields of extraction were obtained using a feedforward multilayer back-propagation ANN from three plants (leaves of Cynara scolymus and Stevia rebaudiana Bert. and roots of Arctium lappa) having medicinal properties (Ani Alupului Toboc, 2012). Input variables (power, bioactive constituents' nature, and extraction time) were considered, and the accuracy was efficient in the prediction of the bioactive constituents.

Wavelength range	Spectral preprocessing	Image processing	Classification accuracy	Decision tree computational software	Reference
400-1000	-	Image thresholding	90%	MATLAB; WEKA	Zhu et al. (2015)
400-1000	-	Image thresholding	93%	-	Gomez Sanchis et al. (2013)
400-1000	-	Image thresholding	97%	WEKA 3.9	
400-1000	Savitzky-Golay method (second derivative)	Image thresholding	80%	MATLAB R2014a	Shuaibu et al. (2018)
400-1000	-	Image thresholding	95%	MATLAB 7.0	Gaston et al. (2011)

9.12 Food Contamination and Spoilage

The formation of metabolites occasioned by food decomposition as a result of the activity of microorganisms presents not just a health hazard to consumers but an economic burden to the producer. DL, an ML procedure, is a relatively new technique in hyperspectral imaging for food. It has been successfully used in the identification of varieties and detection of foodborne diseases. In a study by Ravikanth et al. (2015), NB was successfully used in the detection of contaminants in wheat. In a related study by Cen et al. (2016), hyperspectral data using NB was deployed in detecting chilling injuries in cucumbers. Accurate classification using hyperspectral imaging was reported within the range of 85–98%. ANNs found several applications in firmness prediction in kiwi fruit, honey adulteration, cold injury in peaches, and mechanical damage detection in mushrooms (Rojas-Moraleda et al., 2017; Erkinbaev et al., 2019). It also found application as a single algorithm ML tool in the study of hyperspectral image analysis. SVM is an ML method that aims at optimizing hyperplanes. This technique has been majorly applied in food product classification, disease detection, seed viability, adulteration, and chemical constituent quantification in agricultural materials

The similarity of the human thinking process with the DT algorithm has led to the latter's application in several fields of study, such as in agricultural products classification, detection and identification of diseases in food products, and food quality evaluation (Table 9.1). Most studies have reported a classification accuracy above 90%, which shows the effectiveness of the DT as a classifier. An RF is a programming language that can be viewed as a conglomerate of DTs. There has been increased research interest in the past decade in this field as an application in ML due to their performance in their ease of usage, scalability and classification. This programming language has been applied successfully in the analysis and detection of bruises in vegetables and fruits, fungi, infection, processed fish product quality, and plant diseases (Table 9.2). Tan et al. (2018), in their study, developed a model for the identification of bruises in apples using RF. A better identification model was achieved through the supervised training of spectra for a non-bruised and bruised zone of the apple using this model. A study by Vu et al. (2016) emphasised the need to use spectral data at each pixel rather than the average spectrum of the hypercube while investigating the chemical characteristics of food products. The accuracy level was also observed to increase by over 13.5% when the RF model was built from a combination of spectral and spatial features.

LDA is a supervised learning algorithm that reduces dimensions numbers in a dataset. It is mostly used for the extraction of features, and it also improves computational efficiency and reduction in the degree of over-fitting. Based on hyperspectral data, this model had gained wide attention for food and agricultural classification (Qin et al., 2020; Liu et al., 2010; Mahesh et al., 2008).

Table 9.2 Application of Random Forest in Hyperspectral Image Analysis of Some Selected Food Product

Research	Characteristics of the random forest		Spectral preprocessing	Image processing	Wavelength range	Random forest computational software	Classification accuracy	Reference
	Number of decision trees	*Training set: Validation set*						
Fungal infection identification in strawberries	10	75:25	Baseline correction; Savitzky-Golay second derivate	Image thresholding	400-1000	WEKA	89%	Siedliska et al. (2018)
Bruises detection in apples	130	75:25	-	Otsu algorithms	400-1000	PYTHON	100%	Che et al. (2018)
Scab disease detection on potatoes	500	75:25	-	Otsu algorithm; Gaussian blurring cluster; Greedy Stepwise; Image thresholding	900-1700	WEKA	97%	Daka Neito et al. (2011)
Rice seed cultivar identification	-	75:25	-	Image thresholding	900-1700	MATLAB R200b	100%	Kong et al. (2013)

9.13 Conclusion

In this chapter, the application and analysis of ML in food processing and preservation in recent times was conducted. In comparison with the traditional methods of food processing and food data analysis, the development of ML has expanded the scope of the application of intelligent systems in food processing, leading to efficiency in food production. However, there remain challenges in the use of ML technology in food processing and preservation, such as data complexity and missing data, poor image quality, as well as high cost of implementation. Also, other conditions such as climate and environmental conditions, crop species, and geographical origin limit the application of ML in food processing and preservation. Despite this, ML techniques provide an efficient method for data processing, real-time monitoring, and extraction of information in food processing operations. Owing to this, ML technology had become an emerging field in food processing that would widely be accepted.

References

Aghbashlo, M., Kianmehr, M. H., Nazghelichi, T., & Rafiee, S. (2011). Optimization of an artificial neural network topology for predicting drying kinetics of carrot cubes using combined response surface and genetic algorithm. *Drying Technology, 29*(7), 770–779.

Akinsola, J. E. T., Awodele, O., Kuyoro, S. O., & Kasali, F. A. (2019). Performance evaluation of supervised machine learning algorithms using multi-criteria decision making techniques. *International Conference on Information Technology in Education and Development (ITED)*, 17–34.

Akinsola, J. E. T., Akinseinde, S., Kalesanwo, O., Adeagbo, M., Oladapo, K., Awoseyi, A., & Kasali, F. (2021). Application of artificial intelligence in user interfaces design for cyber security threat modeling. In *Intelligence User Interface* (p. 128). IntechOpen.

Ali, A., Qadir, J., Rasool, R. ur, Sathiaseelan, A., Zwitter, A., & Crowcroft, J. (2016). Big data for development: Applications and techniques. *Big Data Analytics*, 1(1). https://doi.org/10.1186/s41044-016-0002-4

Ali, S., & Smith, K. A. (2006). On learning algorithm selection for classification. *Applied Soft Computing Journal*, 6(2), 119–138. https://doi.org/10.1016/j.asoc.2004.12.002

Ani Alupului Toboc, V. L. (2012). Artificial neural network modelling of ultrasound and microwave extraction of bioactive constituents from medicinal plants. *REV. CHIM. (Bucharest) 63*(7). Retrieved from www.revistadechimie.ro/

Arjenaki, O. O., Moghaddam, P. A., & Motlagh, A. M. (2013). Online tomato sorting based on shape, maturity, size, and surface defects using machine vision. *Turkish Journal of Agriculture and Forestry, 37*(1), 62–68.

Awate, A., Deshmankar, D., Amrutkar, G., Bagul, U., & Sonavane, S. (2015). *Fruit disease detection using color, texture analysis and ANN*. Paper presented at the 2015 International Conference on Green Computing and Internet of Things (ICGCIoT).

Ayodele, T. O. (2010). Types of machine learning algorithms. In Y. Zhang (Ed.), *New Advances in Machine Learning* (pp. 19–48). IntechOpen. https://doi.org/DOI: 10.5772/9385

Behera, S. K., Rath, A. K., & Sethy, P. K. (2020). Maturity status classification of papaya fruits based on machine learning and transfer learning approach. *Information Processing in Agriculture.*

Bensaeed, O., Shariff, A., Mahmud, A., Shafri, H., & Alfatni, M. (2014). *Oil palm fruit grading using a hyperspectral device and machine learning algorithm.* Paper presented at the IOP conference series: Earth and environmental science.

Berghian-Grosan, C., & Magdas, D. A. (2020). Raman spectroscopy and machine-learning for edible oils evaluation. *Talanta, 218,* 121176.

Bharati, S., Podder, P., Mondal, M., & Prasath, V. B. (2021). Medical imaging with deep learning for COVID-19 diagnosis: A comprehensive review. arXiv:2107.09602.

Bhargava, A., & Bansal, A. (2020). Automatic detection and grading of multiple fruits by machine learning. *Food Analytical Methods, 13*(3), 751–761.

Brownlee, J. (2019). 14 different types of learning in machine learning. *Machine Learning Mastery.* https://machinelearningmastery.com/types-of-learning-in-machine-learning/

Brownlee, J. (2020). Supervised and unsupervised machine learning algorithms. *Machine Learning Mastery.* https://machinelearningmastery.com/supervised-and-unsupervised-machine-learning-algorithms/

Çakmak, G., & Yıldız, C. (2011). The prediction of seedy grape drying rate using a neural network method. *Computers and Electronics in Agriculture, 75*(1), 132–138.

Canene-Adams, K., Campbell, J. K., Zaripheh, S., Jeffery, E. H., & Erdman Jr, J. W. (2005). The tomato as a functional food. *The Journal of nutrition, 135*(5), 1226–1230.

Cen, H., Lu, R., Zhu, Q., & Mendoza, F., (2016). Nondestructive detection of chilling injury in cucumber fruit using hyperspectral imaging with feature selection and supervised classification. *Postharvest Biology and Technology.* 111, 352–361.

Che, W., Sun, L., Zhang, Q., Tan, W., Ye, D., Zhang, D., & Liu, Y., (2018). Pixel based bruise region extraction of apple using Vis-NIR hyperspectral imaging. *Computer and Electronics in Agriculture.* 146, 12–21.

Chen, Z., Chen, K., Lou, Y., Zhu, J., Mao, W., & Song, Z. (2021). Machine learning applied to near-infrared spectra for clinical pleural effusion classification. *Sci Rep, 11*(1), 9411. https://doi.org/10.1038/s41598-021-87736-4

Collins, J. W., Marcus, H. J., Ghazi, A., Sridhar, A., Hashimoto, D., Hager, G., Arezzo, A., Jannin, P., Maier-Hein, L., Marz, K., Valdastri, P., Mori, K., Elson, D., Giannarou, S., Slack, M., Hares, L., Beaulieu, Y., Levy, J., Laplante, G., Ramadorai, A., Jarc, A., Andrews, B., Garcia, P., Neemuchwala, H., Andrusaite, A., Kimpe, T., Hawkes, D., Kelly, J. D., & Stoyanov, D. (2021). Ethical implications of AI in robotic surgical training: A Delphi consensus statement. *Eur Urol Focus.* https://doi.org/10.1016/j.euf.2021.04.006

Daka-Nieto, A., Formella, A., Carrion, P., Vazquez-Fernandez, E., & Fern andez-Delgado, M., (2011, September). Common scab detection on potatoes using an infrared hyperspectral imaging system. In: *International Conference on Image Analysis and Processing.* Springer, Berlin, Heidelberg, pp. 303–312.

Deng, X., Cao, S., & Horn, A. L. (2021). Emerging applications of machine learning in food safety. *Annu Rev Food Sci Technol, 12,* 513–538. https://doi.org/10.1146/annurev-food-071720-024112

Deng, X., Cao, S., & Horn, A. L. (2021). Emerging applications of machine learning in food safety. *Annual Review of Food Science and Technology,* 12(March), 513–538. https://doi.org/10.1146/annurev-food-071720-024112

Di Vaio, A., Boccia, F., Landriani, L., & Palladino, R. (2020). Artificial intelligence in the agri-food system: Rethinking sustainable business models in the COVID-19 scenario. *Sustainability (Switzerland)*, 12(12). https://doi.org/10.3390/SU12124851

do Nascimento, C. F., Dos Santos, H. G., de Moraes Batista, A. F., Roman Lay, A. A., Duarte, Y. A. O., & Chiavegatto Filho, A. D. P. (2021). Cause-specific mortality prediction in older residents of Sao Paulo, Brazil: A machine learning approach. *Age Ageing*. https://doi.org/10.1093/ageing/afab067

Ekpezu, A. O., Wiafe, I., Katsriku, F., & Yaokumah, W. (2021). Using deep learning for acoustic event classification: The case of natural disasters. *Journal of the Acoustical Society of America*, *149*(4), 2926. https://doi.org/10.1121/10.0004771

Erkinbaev, C., Derksen, K., & Paliwal, J., (2019). Single kernel wheat hardness estimation using near infrared hyperspectral imaging. *Infrared Physic Technology*. 98, 250–255.

Fadel, M. (2007). Date fruits classification using probabilistic neural networks. *Agricultural Engineering International: CIGR Journal*.

Ferrer-Gallego, R., Hernández-Hierro, J. M., Rivas-Gonzalo, J. C., & Escribano-Bailón, M. T. (2011). Determination of phenolic compounds of grape skins during ripening by NIR spectroscopy. *LWT-Food Science and Technology*, *44*(4), 847–853.

Fu, L., Sun, S., Li, R., & Wang, S. (2016). Classification of kiwifruit grades based on fruit shape using a single camera. *Sensors, 16*(7), 1012.

Fuentes, M. S., Zelaya, N. A. L., & Avila, J. L. O. (2020). Coffee fruit recognition using artificial vision and neural NETWORKS. Paper presented at the *2020 5th International Conference on Control and Robotics Engineering (ICCRE)*.

Gaston, E., Frias, J. M., Cullen, P., Gaston, E., & Cullen, J. (2011). Hyperspectral imaging for the detection of microbial spoilage of mushrooms. In: *Oral Presentation at the Meeting of 11th International Conference of Engineering and Food*, Athens, Greece.

Gazeli, O., Bellou, E., Stefas, D., & Couris, S. (2020). Laser-based classification of olive oils assisted by machine learning. *Food chemistry*, 302, 125329.

Girshick, R., Donahue, J., Darrell, T., & Malik, J. (2014). Rich feature hierarchies for accurate object detection and semantic segmentation. Paper presented at the *Proceedings of the IEEE conference on computer vision and pattern recognition*.

Gomez-Sanchis, J., Blasco, J., Soria-Olivas, E., Lorente, D., Escandell-Montero, P., Martínez-Martínez, J. M., Martínez-Sober, M., & Aleixos, N. (2013). Hyperspectral LCTFbased system for classification of decay in mandarins caused by Penicillium digitatum and Penicillium italicum using the most relevant bands and non-linear classifiers. *Postharvest Biol. Technol.* 82, 76–86.

Granitto, P. M., Gasperi, F., Biasioli, F., Trainotti, E., & Furlanello, C. (2007). Modern data mining tools in descriptive sensory analysis: A case study with a Random forest approach. *Food Quality and Preference*, *18*(4), 681–689. https://doi.org/https://doi.org/10.1016/j.foodqual.2006.11.001

Guardado Yordi, E., Koelig, R., Matos, M. J., Perez Martinez, A., Caballero, Y., Santana, L., Perez Quintana, M., Molina, E., & Uriarte, E. (2019). Artificial intelligence applied to flavonoid data in food matrices. *Foods*, *8*(11). https://doi.org/10.3390/foods8110573

Hansen, P. W., & Holroyd, S. E. (2019). Development and application of Fourier transform infrared spectroscopy for detection of milk adulteration in practice. *International Journal of Dairy Technology*, *72*(3), 321–331.

Hernandez-Perez, J. A., Garcia-Alvarado, M. A., Trystram, G., & Heyd, B. (2004). Neural networks for the heat and mass transfer prediction during drying of cassava and mango. *Innovative Food Science & Emerging Technologies*, 5(1), 57–64.

Hinmikaiye, J. O., Awodele, O., & Akinsola, J. E. T. (2021). Disruptive Technology and Regulatory Response: The Nigerian Perspective. *Computer Engineering and Intelligent Systems*, 12(1), 42–47. https://doi.org/10.7176/ceis/12-1-06

Hou, X., Wang, G., Wang, X., Ge, X., Fan, Y., Jiang, R., & Nie, S. (2020). Rapid screening for hazelnut oil and high-oleic sunflower oil in extra virgin olive oil using low-field nuclear magnetic resonance relaxometry and machine learning. *Journal of the Science of Food and Agriculture*.

Islam, M. R., Sablani, S. S., & Mujumdar, A. S. (2003). An artificial neural network model for prediction of drying rates. *Drying Technology*, 21(9), 1867–1884.

Jana, S., & Parekh, R. (2016). Intra-class recognition of fruits using color and texture features with neural classifiers. *International Journal of Computer Applications*, 148(11), 1–6.

Jayanthi, R., & Florence, L. (2019). Software defect prediction techniques using metrics based on neural network classifier. *Cluster Computing*, 22(1), 77–88.

Jiang, L., Pan, L., Gao, H., & Zheng, H. (2020). Rapid identification and quantification of adulteration in Dendrobium officinale using nuclear magnetic resonance spectroscopy combined with least-squares support vector machine. *Journal of Food Measurement and Characterization*, 1–6. https://doi.org/10.1007/s11694-020-00392-6

Jumah, R., & Mujumdar, A. S. (2005). Modeling intermittent drying using an adaptive neuro-fuzzy inference system. *Drying Technology*, 23(5), 1075–1092.

Junkwon, P., Takigawa, T., Okamoto, H., Hasegawa, H., Koike, M., Sakai, K., Siruntawineti, J., Chaeychomsri, W., Sanevas, N., Tittinuchanon, P., Bahalayodhin, B. (2009). Potential application of color and hyperspectral images for estimation of weight and ripeness of oil palm (Elaeis guineensis Jacq. var. tenera). *Agricultural Information Research*, 18(2), 72–81.

Kamruzzaman, M., Makino, Y., & Oshita, S. (2016). Rapid and non-destructive detection of chicken adulteration in minced beef using visible near-infrared hyperspectral imaging and machine learning. *Journal of Food Engineering*, 170, 8–15.

Kecman, V. (2005). Support vector machines – An introduction 1 Basics of learning from data. *StudFuzz*, 177, 1–47. http://mplbci.ekb.eg/MuseProxyID=1104/MuseSessionID=08102g99u/MuseProtocol=https/MuseHost=link.springer.com/MusePath/content/pdf/10.1007%2F10984697_1.pdf

Khan, M. A., Lali, M. I. U., Sharif, M., Javed, K., Aurangzeb, K., Haider, S. I., Altamrah, A. S., Akram, T. (2019). An optimized method for segmentation and classification of apple diseases based on strong correlation and genetic algorithm based feature selection. *IEEE Access*, 7, 46261–46277.

Ko, M., Tiwari, A., & Mehnen, J. (2010). A review of soft computing applications in supply chain management. *Applied Soft Computing Journal*, 10(3), 661–674. https://doi.org/10.1016/j.asoc.2009.09.004

Kong, W., Zhang, C., Liu, F., Nie, P., & He, Y., (2013). Rice seed cultivar identification using near-infrared hyperspectral imaging and multivariate data analysis. *Sensors* 13, 8916–88927.

Korting, T. S. (n.d.). C4.5 algorithm and multivariate decision trees. *National Institute for Space Research, Section* 2, 2–6.

Kovalenko, O. (2020). Machine Learning and AI in Food Industry Solutions and Potential. SPD-Group. https://spd.group/machine-learning/machine-learning-and-ai-in-food-industry/

Li, H., & Chen, S. (2019). A neural-network-based model predictive control scheme for grain dryers. *Drying Technology*, 38, 1079–1091. DOI: 10.1080/ 07373937.2019.1611598.

Li, S., Chen, S., Liang, Q., Ma, Z., Han, F., Xu, Y., Jin, Y. & Wu, W. (2019). Low temperature plasma pretreatment enhances hot-air drying kinetics of corn kernels. *Journal of Food Process Engineering*, 42(6), e13195.

Lim, K., Pan, K., Yu, Z., & Xiao, R. H. (2020). Pattern recognition based on machine learning identifies oil adulteration and edible oil mixtures. *Nature communications, 11*(1), 1–10.

Liming, X., & Yanchao, Z. (2010). Automated strawberry grading system based on image processing. *Computers and electronics in agriculture, 71*, S32-S39.

Liu, C., Liu, W., Chen, W., Yang, J., & Zheng, L. (2015). Feasibility in multispectral imaging for predicting the content of bioactive compounds in intact tomato fruit. *Food Chemistry, 173*, 482–488.

Liu, C., Liu, W., Lu, X., Ma, F., Chen, W., Yang, J., & Zheng, L. (2014). Application of multispectral imaging to determine quality attributes and ripeness stage in strawberry fruit. *PloS one, 9*(2), e87818.

Liu, L., Ngadi, M. O., Prasher, S.O., Gariepy, C., (2010). Categorization of pork quality using Gabor filter-based hyperspectral imaging technology. *Journal of Food Engineering*. 99, 284–293.

Lorente, D., Aleixos, N., Gómez-Sanchis, J., Cubero, S., García-Navarrete, O. L., & Blasco, J. (2012). Recent advances and applications of hyperspectral imaging for fruit and vegetable quality assessment. *Food and Bioprocess Technology, 5*(4), 1121–1142.

Mabood, F., Hussain, J., Moo, A., Gilani, S., Farooq, S., Naureen, Z., Jabeen, F., Ahmad, M., Hussain, Z., & Al-Harrasi, A. (2016). Detection and quantification of formalin adulteration in cow milk using near infrared spectroscopy combined with multivariate analysis. *Advances in Dairy Research*. 05. 10.4172/2329-888X.1000167.

Mahesh, S., Manickavasagan, A., Jayas, D. S., Paliwal, J., White, N.D.G., (2008). Feasibility of near-infrared hyperspectral imaging to differentiate Canadian wheat classes. *Biosystem. Engineering*. 101, 50–57.

Makrogiannis, S., Caturegli, G., Davatzikos, C., & Ferrucci, L. (2013). Computer-aided assessment of regional abdominal fat with food residue removal in CT. *Academic Radiology, 20*(11), 1413–1421. https://doi.org/10.1016/j.acra.2013.08.007

Manikandan, R., & Sivakumar, R. (2018). Machine learning algorithms for classification. In Unknown (Issue 2018).

Martinez-Garcia, P. M., Lopez-Solanilla, E., Ramos, C., & Rodriguez-Palenzuela, P. (2016). Prediction of bacterial associations with plants using a supervised machine-learning approach. *Environmental Microbiology, 18*(12), 4847–4861. https://doi.org/10.1111/ 1462-2920.13389

Marvin, H. J. P., Janssen, E. M., Bouzembrak, Y., Hendriksen, P. J. M., & Staats, M. (2017). Big data in food safety: An overview. *Critical Reviews in Food Science and Nutrition*, 57(11), 2286–2295. https://doi.org/10.1080/10408398.2016.1257481

Meenu, M., Cai, Q., & Xu, B. (2019). A critical review on analytical techniques to detect adulteration of extra virgin olive oil. *Trends in Food Science & Technology, 91*, 391–408.

Merino, A., Alves, R., Acebes, L. F., & Prada, C. (2017). Modeling and simulation of a beet pulp dryer for a training simulator. *Drying Technology, 35*(14), 1765–1780.

Mildner-Szkudlarz, S., & Jeleń, H. H. (2008). The potential of different techniques for volatile compounds analysis coupled with PCA for the detection of the adulteration of olive oil with hazelnut oil. *Food Chemistry, 110*(3), 751–761.

Miriti, E. (2016). *Classification of selected apple fruit varieties using Naive Bayes.* University of Nairobi.

Moallem, P., Serajoddin, A., & Pourghassem, H. (2017). Computer vision-based apple grading for golden delicious apples based on surface features. *Information Processing in Agriculture, 4*(1), 33–40.

Nadali, A., Kakhky, E. N., & Nosratabadi, H. E. (2011). Evaluating the success level of data mining projects based on CRISP-DM methodology by a fuzzy expert system. *ICECT 2011–2011 3rd International Conference on Electronics Computer Technology,* 6(April 2011), 161–165. https://doi.org/10.1109/ICECTECH.2011.5942073

Naik, S., & Patel, B. (2017). Machine vision based fruit classification and grading-A review. *International Journal of Computer Applications 975,* 8887.

Nayak, J., Vakula, K., Dinesh, P., Naik, B., & Pelusi, D. (2020). Intelligent food processing: Journey from artificial neural network to deep learning. *Computer Science Review, 38,* 100297.

Neto, H. A., Tavares, W. L., Ribeiro, D. C., Alves, R. C., Fonseca, L. M., & Campos, S. V. (2019). On the utilization of deep and ensemble learning to detect milk adulteration. *BioData mining, 12*(1), 1–13.

Olawoye, B., Gbadamosi, S. O., Otemuyiwa, I. O., & Akanbi, C. T. (2020a). Gluten-free cookies with low glycemic index and glycemic load: optimization of the process variables via response surface methodology and artificial neural network. *Heliyon, 6*(10), e05117. https://doi.org/10.1016/j.heliyon.2020.e05117

Olawoye, B., Fagbohun, O. F., Gbadamosi, S. O., & Akanbi, C. T. (2020b). Succinylation improves the slowly digestible starch fraction of cardaba banana. A process parameter optimization study. *Artificial Intelligence in Agriculture.* https://doi.org/10.1016/j.aiia.2020.09.004

Olawoye, B., Gbadamosi, S. O., Otemuyiwa, I. O., & Akanbi, C. T. (2020c). Improving the resistant starch in succinate anhydride-modified cardaba banana starch: A chemometrics approach. *Journal of Food Processing and Preservation, 44*(9), e14686. doi:10.1111/jfpp.14686

Olawoye, B., & Gbadamosi, S. O. (2020). Sensory profiling and mapping of gluten-free cookies made from blends Cardaba banana flour and starch. *Journal of Food Processing and Preservation, 44*(9), e14643. doi:10.1111/jfpp.14643

Omid, M., Baharlooei, A., & Ahmadi, H. (2009). Modeling drying kinetics of pistachio nuts with multilayer feed-forward neural network. *Drying Technology, 27*(10), 1069–1077.

Ordukaya, E., & Karlik, B. (2017). Quality control of olive oils using machine learning and electronic nose. *Journal of Food Quality, 2017,* 9272404. doi:10.1155/2017/9272404

Otchere, D. A., Arbi Ganat, T. O., Gholami, R., & Ridha, S. (2021). Application of supervised machine learning paradigms in the prediction of petroleum reservoir properties: Comparative analysis of ANN and SVM models. *Journal of Petroleum Science and Engineering, 200,* 108182. https://doi.org/https://doi.org/10.1016/j.petrol.2020.108182

Ozulku, G., Yildirim, R. M., Toker, O. S., Karasu, S., & Durak, M. Z. (2017). Rapid detection of adulteration of cold pressed sesame oil adultered with hazelnut, canola, and sunflower oils using ATR-FTIR spectroscopy combined with chemometric. *Food Control, 82*, 212–216.

Pereira, L. F. S., Barbon Jr, S., Valous, N. A., & Barbin, D. F. (2018). Predicting the ripening of papaya fruit with digital imaging and random forests. *Computers and electronics in agriculture, 145*, 76–82.

Pérez, D. S., Bromberg, F., & Diaz, C. A. (2017). Image classification for detection of winter grapevine buds in natural conditions using scale-invariant features transform, bag of features and support vector machines. *Computers and electronics in agriculture, 135*, 81–95.

Prasanth, S., Roshni Thanka, M., Bijolin Edwin, E., & Nagaraj, V. (2021). Speech emotion recognition based on machine learning tactics and algorithms. *Materials Today: Proceedings.* https://doi.org/https://doi.org/10.1016/j.matpr.2020.12.207

Qi, J., Li, Y., Zhang, C., Wang, C., Wang, J., Guo, W., & Wang, S. (2021). Geographic origin discrimination of pork from different Chinese regions using mineral elements analysis assisted by machine learning techniques. *Food Chemistry, 337*, 127779. https://doi.org/10.1016/j.foodchem.2020.127779

Qin, J., Vasefi, F., Hellberg, R. S., Akhbardeh, A., Isaacs, R. B., Yilmaz, A. G., Hwanga, C. , Baeka, I. , Schmidta, W. F., Kima, M. S. (2020). Detection of fish fillet substitution and mislabeling using multimode hyperspectral imaging techniques. *Food Control.* https://doi.org/10.1016/j.foodcont.2020.107234

Rady, A., & Adedeji, A. A. (2020). Application of hyperspectral imaging and machine learning methods to detect and quantify adulterants in minced meats. *Food Analytical Methods*, 13(4), 970–981.

Rahman, M. M., Joardder, M. U., Khan, M. I. H., Pham, N. D., & Karim, M. A. (2018). Multi-scale model of food drying: Current status and challenges. *Critical reviews in food science and nutrition, 58*(5), 858–876.

Ravikanth, L., Singh, C. B., Jayas, D. S., White, N. D. G., (2015). Classification of contaminants from wheat using near-infrared hyperspectral imaging. *Biosystem Engineering.* 135, 73–86.

Rebechi, S. R., Vélez, M. A., Vaira, S., & Perotti, M. C. (2016). Adulteration of Argentinean milk fats with animal fats: Detection by fatty acids analysis and multivariate regression techniques. *Food chemistry, 192*, 1025–1032.

Rocha, R. S., Calvalcanti, R. N., Silva, R., Guimarães, J. T., Balthazar, C. F., Pimentel, T. C., Esmerino, E. A., Freitas, M. Q., Granato, D., Costa, R. G. B., Silva, M. C., & Cruz, A. G. (2020). Consumer acceptance and sensory drivers of liking of Minas Frescal Minas cheese manufactured using milk subjected to ohmic heating: Performance of machine learning methods. *LWT, 126*, 109342. https://doi.org/https://doi.org/10.1016/j.lwt.2020.109342

Rojas-Moraleda, R., Valous, N. A., Gowen, A., Esquerre, C., H€artel, S., Salinas, L., & O'donnell, C., (2017). A frame-based ANN for classification of hyperspectral images: assessment of mechanical damage in mushrooms. *Neural Computing and Application.* 28, 969–981.

Ropelewska, E., Zapotoczny, P., 2018. Classification of Fusarium-infected and healthy wheat kernels based on features from hyperspectral images and flatbed scanner images: a comparative analysis. *European Food Research and Technology.* 244, 1453–1462.

Sa'ad, F. S. A., Ibrahim, M. F., Shakaff, A. M., Zakaria, A., & Abdullah, M. (2015). Shape and weight grading of mangoes using visible imaging. *Computers and electronics in agriculture, 115*, 51–56.

Saha, D., & Manickavasagan, A. (2021). Machine learning techniques for analysis of hyperspectral images to determine quality of food products: A review. *Curr Res Food Sci, 4*, 28–44. https://doi.org/10.1016/j.crfs.2021.01.002

Samuel, A. L. (1959). Some studies in machine learning using the game of checkers. *IBM Journal of Research and Development*, 3(3), 210–229. https://doi.org/10.1147/rd.441.0206

Schulze, K., Nagle, M., Spreer, W., Mahayothee, B., & Müller, J. (2015). Development and assessment of different modeling approaches for size-mass estimation of mango fruits (Mangifera indica L., cv.'Nam Dokmai'). *Computers and electronics in agriculture, 114*, 269–276.

SDP, G. (2021). Machine learning and AI in food industry: Solutions and potential. Retrieved from https://spd.group/machine-learning/machine-learning-and-ai-in-food-industry/

Semary, N. A., Tharwat, A., Elhariri, E., & Hassanien, A. E. (2015). Fruit-based tomato grading system using features fusion and support vector machine. In *Intelligent Systems' 2014* (pp. 401–410): Springer.

Seng, W. C., & Mirisaee, S. H. (2009). *A new method for fruits recognition system*. Paper presented at the *2009 International conference on electrical engineering and informatics*.

Shaarani, S. M., Cardenas-Blanco, A., Amin, M. G., Soon, N., & Hall, L. D. (2010). Monitoring development and ripeness of oil palm fruit (Elaeis guneensis) by MRI and bulk NMR. *International Journal of Agriculture and Biology, 12*(1), 101–105.

Shuaibu, M., Lee, W. S., Schueller, J., Gader, P., Hong, Y. K., Kim, S., 2018. Unsupervised hyperspectral band selection for apple Marssonina blotch detection. *Computer and Electronics in Agriculture*. 148, 45–53. https://doi.org/10.1016/j.compag.2017.09.038

Siedliska, A., Baranowski, P., Zubik, M., Mazurek, W., Sosnowska, B., 2018. Detection of fungal infections in strawberry fruit by VNIR/SWIR hyperspectral imaging. *Postharvest Biol. Technol*. 139, 115–126.

Smola, A., & Vishwanathan, S. V. N. (2008). Introduction to machine learning (First). Cambridge University Press. https://alex.smola.org/drafts/thebook.pdf

Soltani Firouz, M., Rashvand, M., & Omid, M. (2021). Rapid identification and quantification of sesame oils adulteration using low frequency dielectric spectroscopy combined with chemometrics.

Stigler, S. M. (1986). The History of Statistics. The Measurement of Uncertainty before 1900. The Belknap Press of Harvard University, 16, 410.

Strawn, L. K., Fortes, E. D., Bihn, E. A., Nightingale, K. K., Gröhn, Y. T., Worobo, R. W., Wiedmann, M., & Bergholz, P. W. (2013). Landscape and meteorological factors affecting prevalence of three food-borne pathogens in fruit and vegetable farms. *Applied and Environmental Microbiology*, 79(2), 588–600. https://doi.org/10.1128/AEM.02491-12

Tan, W., Sun, L., Yang, F., Che, W., Ye, D., Zhang, D., & Zou, B. (2018). Study on bruising degree classification of apples using hyperspectral imaging and GS-SVM. *Optik* 154, 581–592.

Taurino, A., Capone, S., Distante, C., Epifani, M., Rella, R., & Siciliano, P. (2002). Recognition of olive oils by means of an integrated sol–gel SnO2 Electronic Nose. *Thin solid films, 418*(1), 59–65.

Vikhar, P. A. (2016). Evolutionary algorithms: A critical review and its future prospects. *IEEE 2016 International Conference on Global Trends in Signal Processing, Information Computing and Communication (ICGTSPICC)*, 261–265.

Vu, H., Tachtatzis, C., Murray, P., Harle, D., Dao, T. K., Le, T. L., Andonovic, I., Marshall, S. (2016). Spatial and spectral features utilization on a Hyperspectral imaging system for rice seed varietal purity inspection. In: *2016 IEEE RIVF International Conference on Computing & Communication Technologies, Research, Innovation, and Vision for the Future (RIVF)*. IEEE, pp. 169–174.

Walker, J. (2021). AI in Food Processing – Use Cases and Applications That Matter. Emerj Artificial Intelligence Research. https://emerj.com/ai-sector-overviews/ai-in-food-processing/

Welsh, Z., Simpson, M. J., Khan, M. I. H., & Karim, M. A. (2018). Multiscale Modeling for food drying: State of the art. Comprehensive reviews in food science and food *safety*, *17*(5), 1293–1308.

Wong, S. T., Tan, M. C., & Geow, C. H. (2019). Optimization of ultrasound-assisted ethanol extraction of hazelnut oil. *Journal of Food Processing and Preservation, 43*(10), e14138.

Yiannas, F. (2015). How Walmart's SPARK keeps your food fresh. *Walmart Inc.* https://corporate.walmart.com/newsroom/sustainability/20150112/how-walmarts-spark-keeps-your-food-fresh

Zhang, Q., Saleh, A. S. M., & Shen, Q. (2013). Discrimination of edible vegetable oil adulteration with used frying oil by low field nuclear magnetic resonance. *Food and Bioprocess Technology, 6*(9), 2562–2570.

Zhang, X., Qi, X., Zou, M., & Liu, F. (2011). Rapid authentication of olive oil by Raman spectroscopy using principal component analysis. *Analytical letters, 44*(12), 2209–2220.

Zhang, Y., Phillips, P., Wang, S., Ji, G., Yang, J., & Wu, J. (2016). Fruit classification by biogeography-based optimization and feedforward neural network. *Expert Systems, 33*(3), 239–253.

Zhao, F., Liu, J., Wang, X., Li, P., Zhang, W., & Zhang, Q. (2013). Detection of adulteration of sesame and peanut oils via volatiles by GC× GC–TOF/MS coupled with principal components analysis and cluster analysis. *European Journal of Lipid Science and Technology, 115*(3), 337–347.

Zhao, S., Zhang, S., Liu, J., Wang, H., Zhu, J., Li, D., & Zhao, R. (2021). Application of machine learning in intelligent fish aquaculture: A review. *Aquaculture, 540*, 736724. https://doi.org/https://doi.org/10.1016/j.aquaculture.2021.736724

Zheng, H., & Lu, H. (2012). A least-squares support vector machine (LS-SVM) based on fractal analysis and CIELab parameters for the detection of browning degree on mango (Mangifera indica L.). *Computers and electronics in agriculture, 83*, 47–51.

Zhu, F., Yao, H., Hruska, Z., Kincaid, R., Brown, R. L., Bhatnagar, D., & Cleveland, T. E. (2015). Visible near-infrared (VNIR) reflectance hyperspectral imagery for identifying aflatoxin-contaminated corn kernels. In: *2015 ASABE Annual International Meeting*. American Society of Agricultural and Biological Engineers, p. 1.

Zhu, X., & Goldberg, A. B. (2009). Introduction to semi-supervised learning. In *Synthesis Lectures on Artificial Intelligence and Machine Learning* (Vol. 6). https://doi.org/10.2200/S00196ED1V01Y200906AIM006

Chapter 10

Study of Disruptive Technologies for Sustainable Agriculture

Tapalina Bhattasali
St. Xavier's College (Autonomous), Kolkata, India

Xavier Savarimuthu
St. Xavier's College (Autonomous), Kolkata, India

10.1 Introduction

The demand for food is increasing day by day with a fast-growing global population. Traditional agriculture involves the rigorous use of traditional tools, natural resources, organic fertilizers, primitive knowledge, and cultural beliefs (Walker, 2021). These methods are not sufficient to meet this growing demand. The agriculture sector faces many challenges for issues such as crop disease, water management, pest control, weed management, and lack of irrigation. Traditional methods can cause the depletion of nutrients from the soil. Enhanced use of harmful pesticides can cause a lot of damage. The concept of shifting cultivation leads to deforestation. Consequently, the soil gets directly exposed to rain, wind, and storms that cause a loss of fertility. The current need is to focus on issues such as pollution control, irrigation, the use of pesticides, and environmental sustainability. Shortage of labour is another critical challenge in the agriculture sector. Therefore, it is necessary to integrate advanced technologies into agricultural practices to minimize adverse impacts

DOI: 10.1201/9781003299059-10

(Bhattasali et al., 2021). The aim of agricultural technology (agritech) is to make the production process in the agriculture sector as efficient as possible so that business becomes smart, cost-effective, and sustainable. Some of the benefits include reduced chemical run-off into local groundwater and rivers and reduced consumption of fertilizer, water, and nutrients. Technical improvements in the agriculture sector can optimize quality and production efficiency and minimize environmental impact and production-associated risks. Analyzing relevant data can provide accurate information for better decision-making to gain high-quality output. Table 10.1 represents relevant terms in the context of sustainable agriculture.

Agriculture 4.0 (De Clercq, 2018) refers to the fourth stage of revolution in the agriculture sector, where disruptive technologies such as computational intelligence, artificial intelligence (AI), machine learning (ML), the Internet of Things (IoT), the cloud, sensors, drones, robotics, the blockchain, and big data are used. This fourth revolution in agriculture (Rose, 2018) can be considered as a possible solution for the growth of high-quality agricultural products that can meet the growing demand of the global population in a sustainable way. Traditional farming equipment and farmers play key roles in this revolution. Table 10.2 presents a comparison between traditional agriculture and Agriculture 4.0.

Table 10.1   Relevant Terms in Sustainable Agriculture

Sustainable agriculture	Sustainable agriculture is high-quality product produced in a manner that protects the economic and social status of farmers and safeguards the health and welfare of all farmed species. In this way, the sustainability of the natural environment can be maintained.
Smart farming	Smart farming refers to the Third Green Revolution and the introduction of information and communication technologies into agriculture.
Precision agriculture	Precision agriculture is the application of information technology to process and analyze multi-source data. Crop yields are improved. Cost-effectiveness of crop management strategies is increased.
Agriculture 4.0	Agriculture 4.0 is a system that uses disruptive technologies such as robotics, AI, the IoT, and drones. By integrating these technologies into agriculture, companies can experience less crop damage, increased yields, minimized water and fertilizer usage, and reduced costs.
Agriculture technology	Agriculture technology implies improving yields, efficiency, and profitability by using technology in agriculture.
Vertical farming	Vertical farming is the practice of food production on vertically inclined surfaces. Instead of farming at a single level, foods can be produced at vertically stacked layers.

Table 10.2   Comparison Between Traditional Agriculture and Agriculture 4.0

Traditional agriculture	Agriculture 4.0
Analogical and mechanical technology	Disruptive technologies
Unavailability of sensing concept	Availability of sensing concept
No digital data or records	Big data
Manual labour	Robotics
Hand or animal power as tools	Automated tools
Farmer experience	Satellite image and positioning

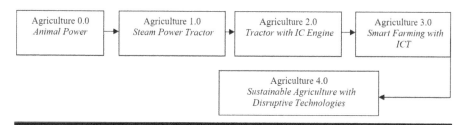

Figure 10.1   Evolution of Agriculture 4.0

Technological innovation is important for developing sustainable agricultural solutions (Bhattasali, 2021). Recent trends in disruptive technologies have interrupted the traditional workflow in agriculture and shifted the concept of smart farming (revolution 3) (Trendov et al., 2019) towards the Agriculture 4.0 era (Kovács, 2018). Figure 10.1 represents the evolution of Agriculture 4.0.

Disruptive technologies consider factors such as knowledge, law, and infrastructure, along with agronomics. Sustainable agriculture also includes issues such as geolocation, privacy, ownership of data, encrypted data, and insurance of unmanned vehicles. The Agriculture 4.0 (Liu, 2020) paradigm highlights the farmer–technology interaction for running a farm.

The rest of the chapter is organized as follows.

■ Section 10.2 briefly discusses various disruptive technologies and the impact of these technologies in sustainable agriculture.
■ Section 10.3 gives an overview of the Agriculture 4.0 framework.
■ Section 10.4 briefly presents the major applications of sustainable agriculture.
■ Section 10.5 discusses various challenges that may arise in this context.
■ Section 10.6 gives an overview of a cloud-based layered IoT framework for better agricultural management.
■ Section 10.7 concludes the chapter.

10.2 Disruptive Technologies in Sustainable Agriculture

10.2.1 Artificial Intelligence and Machine Learning

AI and ML can improve crop yields, reduce food production costs, and increase agricultural efficiencies (Banerjee, 2018).

■ AI and ML-based surveillance systems can monitor real-time video of every crop field to identify human or animal breaches and quickly generate alerts.

■ AI and ML can improve predictions of crop yields (Thongboonnak, 2011) using visual data analytics from drones and real-time sensor data.

■ Supervised ML algorithms can be used for yield mapping, which is very much required for crop planning.

■ Pest management can be improved using drone data combined with in-ground sensors. AI can predict and identify a pest occurrence.

■ The problem of shortage of workers can be solved by the use of AI-based agrobots and smart tractors.

■ Agricultural AI applications can detect most infected areas in a planting area. Using supervised ML algorithms, an optimal mix of pesticides can be determined to reduce the threat of spreading pests further and infecting healthy crops.

■ AI can measure the frequency of crop irrigation to improve yield rate, determine leakage in irrigation, and optimize the irrigation system to improve farming efficiencies.

■ AI can forecast price based on yield rates, which in turn can define pricing strategy for a given crop.

In agriculture, what seems to be a good solution during planning may change with time. AI needs to train with a lot of data for accurate predictions. However, temporal data is very difficult to get during the training of a model. Most of the data can only be obtained when the plants grow. To build a robust classifier model, a significant amount of time is required. Because data infrastructure takes time to mature, the AI (Jha et al., 2020) is used more for agronomic products such as fertilizer, pesticides, and seeds, compared to precision solutions. The concept of AI and ML is capable of changing the definition of traditional farming.

10.2.2 Big Data Analytics

The interconnection of heterogeneous objects gives rise to the concept of large amounts of real-time data. In addition to this, images, videos, and social media data are also generated. Consequently, decisions are generated by processing large amounts of data. That is why analytics is very significant nowadays. Big data analytics extends the scope far beyond farming. It addresses issues like sustainability, climate change, and predictive insights in farming operations, managing risks, making real-time decisions, improving efficiency, and securing food. Big data analytics provides farmers with various data such as water cycles, fertilizer requirements, and rainfall patterns at a granular level. Consequently, farmers can take effective decisions such as what types of crops to plant for better profitability and when crops need to harvest. This type of correct decision can improve farm yields. Distributors can easily identify inefficiencies in their supply chains and respond as necessary so that agricultural products can reach their destination faster and more cost-effectively. Consequently, farmers can apply the right products at the right rates at the right time, manufacturers can improve their production, and distributors can take maximum advantage in the market. Without analytics, no decision can be taken accurately.

10.2.3 Geographic Information System

A geographic information system (GIS) is very useful as fields are location-based. Using GIS software, farmers can track current and future changes of various factors such as temperature, plant health, and crop yields. GPS-based applications can be enabled to optimize fertilizer and pesticide application. As farmers can only deal with certain areas instead of the whole area, effort, time, and money can be saved. As satellites and drones collect valuable data on weather, soil conditions, and GIS-based agriculture, decision-making accuracy can be improved. GIS helps farmers a lot in their day-to-day activities.

10.2.4 Robotics

Robotics has the potential to bring real revolution in the agriculture sector. Weed spots can be determined and removed instead of spraying entire fields with pesticides. Therefore, robotics automation can be used to increase the sustainability of agriculture and issues such as shortage of manpower can be addressed.

An agrobot is an agricultural robot (Shamshiri, 2018) that can perform a variety of tasks. Slow, repetitive, and dull tasks for farmers can be automated using agricultural robots, which save time and reduce workload for farmers, who can focus more on improving overall production yields. Agrobots can carry out various repetitive tasks on the farm without human intervention. They can take decisions on crop production tasks such as preparing soil, seeding, transplanting, weeding, pest control, and harvesting. They can perform a variety of agricultural tasks. Agrobots can perform three main tasks: weed elimination, pests and diseases monitoring, and specialized crop harvesting. They provide a cost-effective solution as they limit the use of pesticides and reduce labour requirements in weeding and harvesting. Real-time AI and sensors, along with robotics, are used to determine the ripeness of fruits and relevant information. Robotics (Wu, 2020) can be used to perform field tasks either in automated or semi-automated modes to improve soil health, yield quality, production rate, and resource management. Robotics can reduce the load from labour and do work efficiently.

10.2.5 Drone Technology

Drones can capture different agricultural parameters and alert farmers about the progress of crops and the development of weeds in real time. Drones are used for imaging, mapping, and surveying farms. Ground drones can survey fields on wheels. Aerial drones act like flying robots, called unmanned aerial vehicles (UAVs). Drones can be controlled remotely or can fly automatically in coordination with sensors and GPS. Insights can be drawn from data captured by drones regarding yield prediction, irrigation, spraying, planting, and crop health. Drones as a service is a concept where drones can be scheduled for farm surveys. After the survey, the collected data is analysed. Field surveys are easier with the help of drone technology.

10.2.6 Remote Sensing

Sensors are utilized in remote sensing for gathering data (Kumar, 2014). The collected data is transmitted to analytical tools for analysis. Sensors monitor crops and generate notifications for any changes. An analytical dashboard helps farmers monitor the crops and take actions based on insights. Remote sensing can help to keep an eye on crop growth and prevent the spread of diseases. To cultivate suitable crops, it is very important to determine the weather pattern. Sensors sense data such as temperature and humidity for this purpose. To get the most beneficial type of cultivation, analysis of soil quality is needed for determining nutrient value, soil drainage capacity, or acidity, so that the water requirement for irrigation can be adjusted. Remote sensing is very effective in measuring soil parameters and generating warnings if something unusual happens.

10.2.7 Digital Image Processing

Digital image processing views and compares images obtained over a period to detect anomalies. Limiting factors are analysed for managing farms efficiently. To control crop quality, growth needs to be determined. A harvesting decision can be taken by mapping irrigated lands. Satellite-image data can predict yields and conduct real-time field monitoring to detect a variety of threats. Sensors can provide imagery to detect vegetation content and overall plant health.

Crop monitoring and detailed field analysis can be done using drone-based images. These can be combined with computer vision and the IoT to generate real-time alerts. Digital image processing makes it easier to discover anomalies in farming.

10.2.7.1 Image-Based Insight Generation

- **Detecting diseases**: Segmented images can be used to identify not diseased parts and diseased parts in a preprocessing step. The diseased parts are considered for further analysis. It also helps in detecting deficiency in nutrients.
- **Crop harvest identification**: Different crop images are captured so that farmers can put crops/fruits into separate stacks based on category.
- **Field management**: High-quality images from drones or helicopters can identify areas where crops need pesticides, water, and fertilizer, so that use of resources can be optimized.

10.2.8 Cloud Computing

Cloud computing offers on-demand availability of services. Shifting the storage and processing of large amounts of agriculture data to distributed storage environments improves processing time and expands the capacity of providing specialized services. Incorporating cloud computing enables sustainable agriculture as it removes costly computing resources used for decision-making. Distributed storage can provide cost-effective solutions.

10.2.9 Internet of Things

Agricultural IoT (IoT) provides a framework through which various agricultural data can be processed so that heterogeneous services can be seamlessly integrated. An agricultural IoT framework can collect, process, and integrate data in real time. IoT in the agriculture sector uses other disruptive technologies such as robots, drones, remote sensors, and image processing, along with analytical tools for monitoring crops and surveying to save both time and money.

The IoT (Muangprathub, 2019) can help mobile software become interoperable as different apps can share and use the same datasets. It reduces the need to enter the same datasets multiple times into different systems. Consequently, time and cost overhead, along with human error, can be significantly reduced. Therefore, all useful information is automatically and seamlessly unified in the farm. Profitable and sustainable farming and food production is possible (Farooq, 2020) as data can be used intelligently across the supply chain in agriculture. The IoT makes the agricultural sector smarter, which could not be imagined before.

10.2.10 Blockchain Technology

Blockchain agriculture means the use of the blockchain in the agricultural sector to improve operating processes and get profitable results. Application of the blockchain in the agricultural sector ranges from having a sustainable business and reduction of waste, to informed consumer purchasing decisions, to having smooth future transactions with fraud elimination.

10.2.10.1 Blockchain in Agriculture

Data Generation

Data is generated from crop and soil monitoring, warehousing and distribution, and retail and marketing.

Data Collection

- From crop and soil monitoring: temperature, pH, and other soil data.
- From warehousing and distribution: quality control data, transportation data, and food safety data.
- From retail and marketing: bill data, taxes, and compliances.

Data Processing

A smart contract processes incoming data. The data is then hashed and saved in the blockchain.

Blockchain Data Consumption

- Land usage: improved soil quality.
- Crop efficiency: ensuring food is safe or not.
- Flood mitigation: preventive measures can be taken quickly.
- Financial audit: automated information about annual or monthly sales through smart contracts.

Blockchain improves operational efficiency in the agriculture sector.

10.2.10.2 Decision Support System

A decision support system (DSS) helps end-users take decisions efficiently from complex datasets. Knowledge is constructed and presented through an interpretable user interface. As agricultural processes are complex and require large amounts of data, a DSS is indispensable for generating effective decisions from poorly defined and complex data at a semi-autonomous level.

In summary, it can be said that the IoT provides digital interconnection to gather and transmit data; sensor data is used for monitoring and controlling; automation can be provided by robotics, especially for primary production; the cloud environment provides computational capacity and system resource; data analytics involves

AI-based approaches and statistical methods for data analysis; and a DSS provides tools (Singh et al., 2020) to support users in agricultural management. An ecosystem for sustainable agriculture is created by the advent of new disruptive technologies. The fusion of all these technologies allows farmers to achieve better price control and yield production. A DSS helps to take complex decisions from huge datasets.

10.3 Framework of Agriculture 4.0

Advanced sensor technology provides facilities to monitor in real time, whereas robotics supports the automation of processes. Big data (Wolfert, 2017) supports historical as well as real-time data in high volumes and the data is transformed into actionable knowledge using AI-based methods. Figure 10.2 presents a six-layer framework of Agriculture 4.0, which considers core disruptive technologies required for sustainable agriculture.

At layer one, data is collected from the agriculture field using IoT devices (sensors, robotics). The data is transferred through the network at layer two. It is then forwarded to the cloud server for further storage, processing and analysis at layer three. The collected data is transformed into knowledge with big data analytics

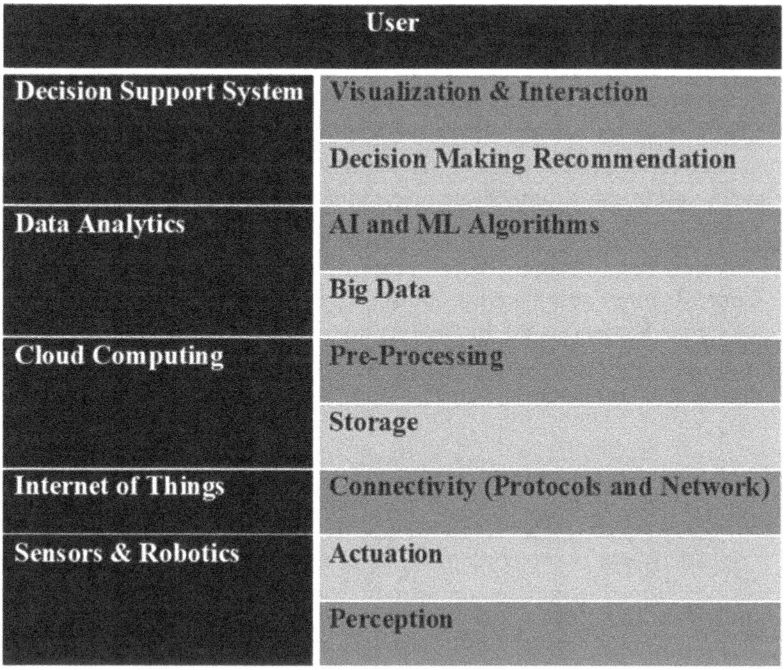

User	
Decision Support System	Visualization & Interaction
	Decision Making Recommendation
Data Analytics	AI and ML Algorithms
	Big Data
Cloud Computing	Pre-Processing
	Storage
Internet of Things	Connectivity (Protocols and Network)
Sensors & Robotics	Actuation
	Perception

Figure 10.2 Six-layer framework

at layer four. At layer five, a DSS provides the resources at layer six for optimized decision-making.

10.4 Applications of Sustainable Agriculture

Figure 10.3 represents major types of application of Agriculture 4.0 to provide sustainable solutions.

■ **Monitoring**: Smart monitoring can be a game-changer in the agriculture sector as it collects data in real time and analyze it using analytics. Consequently, farmers can take quick and intelligent decisions to increase productivity without incurring cost and time overhead and maintain a sustainable environment. Weather conditions and greenhouse gas emissions can be easily monitored. Environmental parameters such as humidity, atmospheric temperature, rainfall (Yadav, 2019), wind direction, and atmospheric pressure are collected and can be forwarded to the cloud server. Wireless sensor networks (WSNs) can provide real-time data that can be used for gas emission monitoring and meteorological analysis. Smart agricultural solutions can accurately recognize crop pests and weeds and prevent agricultural losses. The monitoring of soil parameters can be done using IoT sensors for measurement, AI for analysis, and a DSS for decision-making. A smart monitoring system is used to monitor water quality.

■ **Prediction**: Predictive models are very important for providing optimized solutions in agriculture. These models can monitor crop development and predict ideal harvest times. It is possible to minimize costs and maximize yields and profits by effectively forecasting weather conditions (Khaki, 2020). AI-based techniques can increase productivity, optimize processing, reduce costs, increase customer satisfaction, and boost supply chain performance.

■ **Control**: In an automated monitoring system, IoT sensors collect data and forward it for processing. In a fully autonomous irrigation system, sensors are

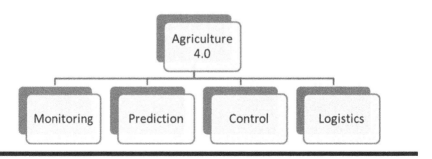

Figure 10.3   Major types of applications

used to measure agricultural parameters. The data collected from sensors is analyzed. Actuators (water pumps) can be automatically controlled depending on the values. Ideally, fertilization requires the ability to find the location where it is most needed. Disruptive technologies such as the IoT, sensors, robotics, AI, and data analytics can improve fertilization techniques. Disruptive technologies (Partel, 2019) can reduce time and manual labour and its associated costs. If target weeds can be identified, they can be eradicated directly without damaging crops, and an accurate dosage of herbicides can be sprayed at the target location.

■ **Logistics:** Disruptive technologies can provide automated and up-to-date information so that managers can take decisions to avoid losses. Transport operators can use sensor technology to monitor parameters in real time. If a predefined safety limit is exceeded, a warning is generated. It can predict delays in product delivery and recommend faster routes. By analyzing transportation data, retailers can accept or reject the product.

10.5 Challenges

The key challenges of Agriculture 4.0 can be classified into the following categories: device, network, data, application, and system.

At the device level, it is a challenge to place devices in a harsh environment such as heavy rain. As devices are exposed to wildlife, electric circuits or normal functionalities may be disrupted. Wireless devices placed in the field may become inaccessible as these have mostly limited battery life.

At the network level, connectivity, transmission rate, and size of the network are considered core challenges.

At the data level, quality, availability, privacy, integrity, and interpretability of agricultural data are the key challenges.

At the application level, the core challenges are processing varying volumes of data in real time, context-awareness, security threats, and reliability.

At the system level, scalability, flexibility, complexity, and continuous improvements are the key challenges.

10.6 Cloud-Based IoT Architecture

There is no unified architecture of the IoT for the agriculture sector. A three-layer architecture of the IoT is considered as the basic one, where a perception or sensing layer collects relevant data from the fields. Appropriate actions can be taken by actuators. A network layer transfers sensed data to the application layer through gateways and communication protocols. An application layer along with cloud servers

Layer 4	Application Layer (End-User)
Layer 3	Service Layer (Cloud and Digital Service)
Layer 2	Communication Layer (Data Transmission and Internet)
	Edge / Fog Computing Layer (Optional)
Layer 1	Physical Layer (Sensors/Actuators)

Figure 10.4 Four-layer cloud-IoT architecture

and data analytics tools is used for storage, processing, and analysis. Considering the generic applicability and requirements of Agriculture 4.0, the following four-layer architecture fits well for sustainable agriculture. Figure 10.4 represents a four-layer cloud-IoT architecture for Agriculture 4.0.

■ **Physical layer**: Physical objects are included in this layer. These are capable of sensing (sensors at the perception layer) and controlling (actuators at the control layer) in the agricultural field using a network connection. The perception layer acquires the relevant parameters from the plant, soil, and animal environment through the deployment of field sensors or robotics. Sensor nodes can collect data and transmit it to the next layer. The control layer receives commands to activate actuators or controllers in the field.

■ **Edge/fog computing layer**: The edge/fog computing layer is considered optional. The edge can perform limited data processing before transmitting to the cloud. The fog computing layer can assist edge computing and provide the fusion or aggregation of data from multiple sources. This type of layer can help reduce the load and optimize performance.

■ **Communication layer**: The communication layer transfers data between layers one and three using either wired or wireless technology and communication protocols. Gateways act as intermediaries. For a generic monitoring system, the communication layer works in one direction: from the perception layer to the service layer. For control systems, the communication layer works in two directions.

■ **Service layer**: Collected data from the perception layer, along with forecasting data and historical data, are uploaded to cloud storage. Cloud services use analytics and decision-making tools to store, process, analyze, and visualize data.

■ **Application layer**: The application layer is responsible for providing end-user access and visualization of agricultural information. Users can do agricultural management through smart applications on computers or portable devices.

10.7 Conclusion

Disruptive technology-based sustainable solutions have been a game-changer for the agricultural sector (Zambon, 2019) in terms of improving the quality of product and yield. Usage of the latest technologies not only optimizes agricultural activities using fewer resources but also automates activities by reducing human involvement. In this chapter, various sustainable solutions applied to the agricultural domain have been presented.

Disruptive technologies under Agriculture 4.0 have been considered to promote sustainable solutions that increase the income of farmers and reduce the dependence on soil and climatic conditions. Digital image processing can be combined with ML classifier models and integrated with mobile IoT and sensor networks so that farmers receive alerts on their mobile phones and control farming activities remotely.

Due to the COVID outbreak, there is an acute shortage of farmworkers. The usage of drones and robotics reduces manpower requirements in farming activities and minimizes the health hazards experienced by farmers during the spray of pesticides.

References

Bannerjee, G., Sarkar, U., Das, S., & Ghosh, I. (2018). Artificial intelligence in agriculture: A literature survey. *International Journal of Scientific Research in Computer Science Applications and Management Studies*, 7(3), 1–6.

Bhattasali, T., & Xavier, S. (2021). Technological innovations in environmental sustainability. In: *Go Green for Environmental Sustainability*, CRC Press.

De Clercq, M. Vats, A., & Biel, A (2018). Agriculture 4.0: The future of farming technology. In *Proceedings of the World Government Summit*, Dubai, United Arab Emirates, pp. 11–13.

Farooq, M. S., Riaz, S., Abid, A., Umer, T., Zikria, Y. B (2020). Role of IoT technology in agriculture: A systematic literature review. *Electronics*, 9, 319.

Jha, S., Kaechele, H., Lana, M., Amjath-Babu, T. S., & Sieber, S. (2020). Exploring farmers' perceptions of agricultural technologies: a case study from Tanzania. *Sustainability*, 12(3), 998.

Khaki, S., Wang, L., & Archontoulis, S. V. (2020). A CNN-RNN framework for crop yield prediction. *Frontiers in Plant Science*, 10, 1750.

Kovács, I., & Husti, I. (2018). The role of digitalization in the agricultural 4.0: How to connect the industry 4.0 to agriculture? *Hung. Agric. Eng.*

Kumar, G. (2014). Research paper on water irrigation by using wireless sensor network. *International Journal of Scientific Research Engineering & Technology (IJSRET)*, 3–4.

Liu, Y., Ma, X., Shu, L., Hancke, G. P., & Abu-Mahfouz, A. M. (2020). From Industry 4.0 to Agriculture 4.0: Current status, enabling technologies, and research challenges. *IEEE Trans. Ind. Inform.*

Muangprathub, J., Boonnam, N., Kajornkasirat, S., Lekbangpong, N., Wanichsombat, A., & Nillaor, P. (2019). IoT and agriculture data analysis for smart farm. *Comput. Electron. Agric.* 156, 467–474

Partel, V., Kim, J., Costa, L., Pardalos, P., & Ampatzidis, Y. (2019). Smart Sprayer for Precision Weed Control Using Artificial Intelligence: Comparison of Deep Learning Frameworks. *ISAIM*.

Rose, D. C., Chilvers, J. (2018). Agriculture 4.0: Broadening responsible innovation in an era of smart farming. *Front. Sustain. Food Syst.* 2, 87.

Shamshiri, R. R, Weltzien, C., Hameed, I. A., Yule, J. I., Grift, E. T., Balasundram, S. K., Pitonakova, L., Ahmad, D., & Chowdhary, G (2018). Research and development in agricultural robotics: A perspective of digital farming. *Int. J. Agric. Biol.*

Singh, N., & Gupta, N. (2020). Bayesian network for development of expert system in pest management. In *Internet of Things and Analytics for Agriculture*, Volume 2 (pp. 45–65). Springer, Singapore.

Thongboonnak, K., & Sarapirome, S. (2011). Integration of artificial neural network and geographic information system for agricultural yield prediction. *Suranaree Journal of Science & Technology*, 18(1).

Trendov, N. M., Varas, S., Zeng, M. (2019). Digital Technologies in Agriculture and Rural Areas: Status Report; Licence: cc by-nc-sa 3.0 igo: Rome, Italy.

Wolfert, S., Ge, L., Verdouw, C., & Bogaardt, M. J (2017). Big data in smart farming-a review. *Agric. Syst.*, 153, 69–80.

Wu, X., Aravecchia, S., Lottes, P., Stachniss, C., & Pradalier, C. (2020). Robotic weed control using automated weed and crop classification. *Journal of Field Robotics*, 37(2), 322–340.

Yadav, P., & Sagar, A. (2019). Rainfall prediction using artificial neural network (ANN) for Tarai region of Uttarakhand. *Current Journal of Applied Science and Technology*, 1–7.

Zambon, I., Cecchini, M., Egidi, G., Saporito, M. G., & Colantoni, A. (2019). Revolution 4.0: Industry vs. agriculture in a future development for SMEs. *Processes*, 7, 36.

Chapter 11

Role of Dimensionality Reduction Techniques for Plant Disease Prediction

Muhammad Kashif Hanif
Department of Computer Science, Government College University Faisalabad, Faisalabad, Pakistan

Shaeela Ayesha
Department of Computer Science, Government College University Faisalabad, Faisalabad, Pakistan

Ramzan Talib
Department of Computer Science, Government College University Faisalabad, Faisalabad, Pakistan

11.1 Introduction

Different diseases can damage various portions of the plant, such as leaf, stem, fruit, crop, and root. However, leaves are a vital and essential part of a plant and can be observed to detect and diagnose various types of plant leaf diseases (Nandhini & Ashokkumar, 2021; Sujatha et al., 2021). Most plant leaf diseases can be seen and detected by the naked eye as soon as they start to damage the leaves. However, this requires knowledge about the disease identification method, experience, and the perception of the agriculturist to save the plant from disease outbreak (Beck et al., 2020; Sampathkumar & Rajeswari, 2020). This conventional method of plant leaf disease detection and identification requires skill, a lot of effort, and time, and is not feasible for monitoring large farms. Hence, the automatic detection of leaf disease has become essential in the modern era as it helps to overcome the drawbacks of manual plant leaf disease detection methods (Trivedi et al., 2020; Patel and Sharaff, 2021).

Digital methods of disease detection offer a wide range of options, such as the comparison of plant leaves and visualization of different segments of leaves for deep analysis (Jothiaruna et al., 2021). Furthermore, early detection of leaf diseases also protects against huge losses (Kartikeyan & Shrivastava, 2021). Many digital image processing approaches are proposed and applied for the prediction of various plant diseases using plant leaf images (Gadekallu et al., 2020; Sampathkumar & Rajeswari, 2020; Nandhini & Ashokkumar, 2021).

In literature, various methods, approaches, and techniques have been proposed and applied for the prediction and classification of plant leaf diseases (Jothiaruna et al., 2021). The majority of techniques need the most relevant features to use for the efficient detection of plant leaf diseases (Roy et al., 2021). The selection and extraction of relevant features belonging to the colour, size, texture, surface, and shape of the leaves can play a significant role in the detection of plant leaf diseases (Sujatha et al., 2021). The processing capabilities to analyze redundant features and noisy and blurred leaf images is also difficult (Patel and Sharaff, 2021). It becomes difficult to select features from a huge number of features and aspects to analyze plant leaf images. Enormous efforts have been made to explore and extract optimal and relevant features of images to improve image analysis for the recognition of plant diseases. Due to inconsistency, variations, and the complexity of leaf images used for plant diseases, many feature extraction methods are not effective. Different methods can be applied to select the most suitable approach for feature selection for the analysis and efficient prediction of plant leaf diseases (Zhang and Wang, 2016; Patel and Sharaff, 2021).

Classification algorithms can have high computation cost and memory usage for high dimensional datasets (Yousaf et al., 2021). In this regard, dimensionality reduction techniques (DRTs) offer automatic methods for reducing the dimensionality of plant leaf images that can be used for efficient analysis to detect plant leaf diseases using machine learning (ML) models. Moreover, the application of DRTs can also enhance the visualization of data (Soni et al., 2020).

Features captured during data collection may consist of a large number of redundant features that make it difficult for ML models to make correct predictions accurately using extraneous and redundant features (Talib et al., 2016a,b; Gou et al., 2020). Several factors make DRTs significant to improving the performance of predictive models. Simply stated, DRTs will extract the most relevant and precise features from a collection of features for predictive analytics problems selected for evaluation, including big datasets, small datasets, balanced and unbalanced datasets, and high dimensional datasets to resolve simple or complex problems (Tsai and Sung, 2020; Sujatha et al., 2021).

Two commonly used methods for dimension reduction are feature selection and extraction (Ayesha et al., 2020; Hanif et al., 2020; Patel & Sharaff, 2021; Liu & Motada, 2007). Filter, wrapper, and embedded methods are commonly used for feature selection based on the feature's significance, reliability, and computation power (Huang et al., 2020, Choudhary & Hiranwal, 2021).

On the other side, feature extraction methods transform original high dimensional feature sets into lower dimensions (Hanif et al., 2020). The goal of feature extraction is to transform the input feature set into reduced representation. Principal component analysis, kernel principal component analysis, locality preserving projection, t-stochastic neighbour embedding, Isomap, locally linear embedding, multidimensional scaling, and self-organizing map are some commonly used feature extraction methods. These DRTs have been applied to reduce the dimensionality of leaf images used for the analysis and development of ML models for the prediction, detection, and classification of various plant leaf diseases (Beck et al., 2020; Bagheri & Mohamadi-Monavar, 2020; Bajait & Malarvizhi, 2020; Das et al., 2020; Gobalakrishnan et al., 2020; Li et al., 2020; Nigam et al., 2020; Hazra et al., 2021; Kartikeyan & Shrivastava, 2021; Yogeshwari & Thailambal, 2021). Commonly used ML models include support vector machine (SVM), logistic regression (LR), decision tree (DT), random forest (RF), k-nearest neighbour (KNN), naive Bayes (NB), multilayer perceptron (MLP), clustering, neural networks (NNs), convolutional neural networks (CNNs), artificial neural networks (ANNs), and deep neural networks (DNNs). Applications of DRTs and ML models in agriculture include plant disease management, soil quality identification and classification, yield prediction, classification of agricultural products, diagnosis of plant disease, and forecasting weather conditions for crop management and to save the water use, etc. (Benos et al., 2021; Dwivedi et al., 2021; Kartikeyan & Shrivastava, 2021; Roy et al., 2021).

This chapter presents the various DRTs used for dimensionality reduction and the role of DRTs in plant disease prediction. The contribution of this study is as follows:

- ■ Describes different DRTs for the extraction of precise features to analyze and improve the performance of different ML models for plant disease predictions.
- ■ Discusses the role of DRTs for plant leaf disease detection.
- ■ Explores the advantages and limitations of different DRTs.
- ■ Visualizes different DRTs using two synthetic datasets.

11.2 Dimensionality Reduction Techniques

There is a wide variety of DRTs that can perform low dimension transformations. These transformations can be performed using linear or non-linear transformation functions (Hanif et al., 2020; Qu et al., 2021). Other properties of DRTs that distinguish different DRTs include the capability of DRT to preserve local, global, and manifold structures (Chen et al., 2016, Gou et al., 2020; Huang et al., 2020). Moreover, parametric and non-parametric, graph-based methods, and kernel functions can be used to transform high dimensional images and data into lower dimensions (Gisbrecht & Hammer, 2015; Ayesha et al., 2020). Parametric techniques provide the parametric mapping of data points to low dimensional embedding. Non-parametric techniques such as multidimensional scaling offer non-parametric methods to transform high dimensional data to low dimensions (Gisbrecht & Hammer, 2015; Ghojogh et al., 2020a; Qu et al., 2021). The different DRTs are discussed in the following:

11.2.1 Principal Component Analysis

Principal component analysis (PCA) transforms high dimensions into lower dimensions using linear transformation functions (Wang a&nd Zhu, 2017; Feng et al., 2020). It reduces the dimensionality of data using projections and distances by calculating variances, covariance, and eigenvalues or vectors decompositions. Feature sets reduced using PCA are called principal components (PCs). The first few PCs hold the maximum information (Gadekallu et al., 2020; Nigam et al., 2020). However, one can use the number of components according to the requirements of the problem statement or according to the ML model. Generally, the first component moves according to the largest variance. Selection of the number of PCs needs a deep understanding of the requirements and analysis skills to represent data in lower dimensions. Some automatic methods also exist to decide the number of PCs, such as the Kaser-Guttman method, which select PCs until the Eigen value is greater than 1. The core goal of PCA is to represent high dimensional data using fewer dimensions while preserving original aspects of the data (Erichson et al., 2020). PCA saves storage space by reducing the dimensionality of data used for analysis. The reduced dimensions aim to preserve significant features (Bharati et al., 2020; Feng et al., 2020).

11.2.2 Kernel Principal Component Analysis

Kernel principal component analysis (KPCA) is a variant of traditional PCA used to transform high dimensional data into lower dimensions based on non-linear transformation functions (Liu & Lai et al., 2020). As compared to PCA, KPCA computes the eigenvectors of the kernel matrix. Kernel functionality enables KPCA to perform non-linear transformations of high dimensional data into lower dimensions. Polynomial and Gaussian kernels make KPCA suitable for non-linear transformations (Yu et al., 2021; Tummala, 2021). Imaging data reduced using KPCA offers better classification accuracy (Yu et al., 2021). KPCA follows an unsupervised learning approach to reduce the dimensionality of data. The selection of the kernel parameters affects the performance of KPCA. Many variants of KPCA have been developed to improve its efficiency for different applications (Binol, 2018).

11.2.3 Singular Value Decomposition

Singular value decomposition (SVD) is a linear approach that transforms the high dimensions of data into lower dimensions using matrix decomposition and linear transformation functions. SVD can be applied to almost all datasets that can be processed as a matrix (Wang & Zhu, 2017; Wang et al., 2021). The limitation of SVD is that it can reduce the dimensions of data based on linear projections (Zhang et al., 2018). Singular values (SVs) represent stable, rotation, and ratio invariant features of the image used for disease recognition. Although the SVs of leaf images represents algebraic features that may limit the efficiency of ML models to make precise predictions (Wang et al., 2021). SVD can preserve the essential features of the image that offers good performance for object recognition. Several extensions of SVD have been proposed to improve the efficiency of SVD (Zhang & Wang, 2016; Wang et al., 2021).

11.2.4 Locality Preserving Projection

Locality preserving projection (LPP) is a graph-based method that transforms high dimensional data into low dimensions using a linear approximation of non-linear Laplacian eigen maps. LPP is an unsupervised method (Gou et al., 2020). Linear projective maps can be used to preserve the neighbourhood structure of data. Classical LPP can preserve local structures only and is unable to preserve global and manifold projections (Zhang et al., 2017; Li et al., 2020). However, variants of LLP can preserve global and manifold structures (Gou et al., 2020).

11.2.5 Locally Linear Embedding

Locally linear embedding (LLE) uses non-linear functions to transform high dimensions into lower dimensional representations. It aims to preserve the local neighbourhood structure of data. LLE is an unsupervised learning approach. It is closely related to KNN as it reduces the dimensionality of data using data points of neighbours. Moreover, LLE uses graphs to represent data points (Gisbrecht & Hammer, 2015). Modern versions of LLE can work with manifold structures of data. Ghojogh et al. (2021) proposed a variant of LLE known as generative LLE, which can combine the functionalities of spectral and probabilistic DRTs to make LLE suitable for a wide range of applications and manifold structures of data.

11.2.6 Isomap

Isomap is an unsupervised learning method that uses non-linear functions to transform higher dimensions of data into lower dimensions (Du et al., 2009). Isomap saves the geo and pairwise distances of data points (Najafi et al., 2016). They transform high dimensions into a reduced feature set while preserving manifold structures of data (Gao et al., 2017). Isomap preserves the real aspects of data in lower dimensions and enhances the classification accuracy of the ML models (Huang et al., 2018). The classical version of Isomap cannot cope with generalization property and labelled data, however, its variants, such as the supervised discriminative Isomap, extend its functionality and make it suitable for multi-nature data (Qu et al., 2021). Another extension called a fast Isomap was introduced to improve the accuracy of graphs when embedding data to lower dimensions (Yousaf et al., 2021).

11.2.7 Multidimensional Scaling

Multidimensional scaling (MDS) is a non-linear DRT that preserves the distance of data points in lower dimensional projections (Gisbrecht & Hammer, 2015). It creates a matrix of distances between features and is used to reduce dimensions and preserve local distances. It can work with manifold structures of data. MDS is based on geo distance instead of Euclidean distances (Yousaf et al., 2021). Different extensions of MDS include Kernel MDS, Sammon mapping, and parametric and non-parametric MDS. Isomap is considered a class of parametric and kernel MDS (Ghojogh et al., 2020a).

11.2.8 t-Stochastic Neighbour Embedding

t-stochastic neighbour embedding (t-SNE) uses non-linear functions to map the high dimensions into low dimensional representation. It is an unsupervised learning approach. It is a non-parametric approach and is considered suitable for the visualization of non-linear structures of data. It follows the probabilistic method and can work with manifold structures of data. It is considered suitable for Gaussian distribution (Ghojogh et al., 2020b). Systematic SNE and t-SNE with a general degree of

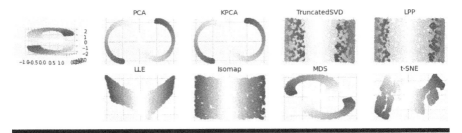

Figure 11.1   Visualization of multiple DRTs for S-Curve dataset

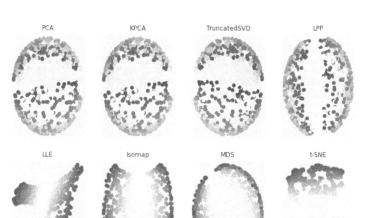

Figure 11.2   Visualization of multiple DRTs for circle dataset

freedom are considered the extensions of t-SNE. t-SNE reduces the dimensionality of data and offers a good visual representation of data (Soni et al., 2020).

The following figures show the comparison of DRTs for s-curve and circle with 2,000 data points. These figures are developed using the scikit-learn[1] Python library. [1]http://scikit-learn.org

11.3 Role of Dimensionality Reduction Techniques for Plant Disease Prediction

Many researchers have done work on leaf images to automatically and efficiently predict, detect, and classify various plant diseases using several DRTs and ML models. DRTs can be applied to reduce the dimensionality of leaf images for classification (Gokhale et al., 2020; Choudhary & Hiranwal, 2021; Dwivedi et al., 2021; Kartikeyan & Shrivastava, 2021). Gokhale et al. 2020 and Jothiaruna et al. 2021 explored the significance of different aspects of plant leaf images, such as sample size, dimensions of the image, and colour and shape of leaf images used for plant disease detection and classification. Recent applications of DRTs and ML models for plant disease prediction and detection are explored in this section.

Different kinds of rice diseases are the main danger to rice crops. Accurate identification of disease at an early stage can save rice plants and improve crop production and quality of rice. For the early detection of rice disease, Feng et al. (2020) performed three levels of fusion – data, feature, and decision fusion – for the detection of rice disease. They applied PCA and autoencoders to reduce the dimensionality. Fused and reduced feature sets were forwarded to ML models, including SVM, LR, and CNN. For the fast, automatic, speedy, and accurate detection of rice disease, Das et al. (2020) recommended a deep learning model that can automatically update and select the features for the detection of disease. The recommended approach was applied to rice leaf images for the prediction and classification of multiple diseases of rice plants. The authors developed and implemented a CNN model on the images of rice plants, and DRTs were used to extract the features of leaf images. Experimental evaluation validated the efficiency of the recommended approach.

Golhani et al. (2018) presented a brief review to explore various methods developed for the detection of plant diseases. In another study, Sandhu & Kaur (2019) reviewed and examined different dimension reduction methods used to extract precise features for the identification of various plant leaf diseases. Benos et al. (2021) provided an extensive review to examine the significance of information technology in agriculture, particularly applications of ML models. They identified the use of ML models for yield prediction, crop quality classification, and disease detection and classification to enhance the quality and production of plants and crops. Kartikeyan & Shrivastava (2021) conducted a review study to explore different ML approaches for the automatic detection of plant diseases. The author explored the main steps involved in plant disease detection and classification. Different ML models such as SVM, KNN, and ANN developed for plant disease management showed good performance levels and efficient results.

Gilbertson & Van Niekerk (2017) applied PCA and various ML models such as KNN, SVM, DT, and RF for the classification of agricultural land based on images. SVM with PCA achieved higher accuracy as compared to other classifiers. Nigam et al. (2020) implemented PCA on plant leaf image data to reduce the dimensionality and to extract valuable features for paddy leaf disease identification and classification using BFO-DNN classifier. Features were extracted via PCA to improve the accuracy of the results. In another study for plant disease detection and classification, Li et al. (2020) applied PCA, LPP, neighbourhood preserving embedding, and sparsity preserving projection. DRTs were used to reduce the dimensions of plant leaf images before applying multiple classifiers such as KNN, RF, NB, SVM, and CRC-DP were applied for the identification of disease in cucumber plant leaf images. Begue et al. (2017) applied various ML models such as SVM, RF, NB, K-NN, and MLP for the classification of medicinal plants based on leaf images.

For cucumber plant disease recognition, Zhang & Wang (2016) used SVD to reduce the dimensions of leaf images and to extract features relevant for the detection of disease in cucumber leaves. The SVM classifier was applied to predict the disease in unseen images of cucumber plants images. Moreover, to overcome the limitations of classical SVD, the author proposed the global local SVD method to extract manifold features for plant leaf images. The proposed approach achieved higher accuracy with the SVM classifier. Zhang et al. (2018) applied classical SVD and sparse SVD representations to reduce the dimensionality of leaf images. SVD was used for the

Swedish leaf and ICL dataset. The author used the reduced representation of leaf images for the recognition and classification of different plant leaves. Liu & Du et al. (2020) applied PCA to reduce the dimensionality of images used for the identification of corn disease. An SVM model was used to detect disease based on reduced features sets.

Kaur & Gautam (2021) explored the main steps involved in plant disease detection and analyzed the impact of feature extraction methods and different classifiers (e.g., SVM, AdaBoost ANN, and CNN) for plant disease management. Yogeshwari & Thailambal (2021) proposed a deep convolutional neural network (DCNN) method to classify various diseases. The author applied PCA to reduce the dimensionality of leaf images and the DCNN classifier to classify different diseases and healthy plant leaf images. PCA with DCNN achieved higher accuracy than SVM, NB, KNN, and back propagation neural networks. Hazra et al. (2021) used RF for the classification of different features such as leaf images size, shape, colour, etc.

Dixit & Nema (2018) presented a review of DRTs to reduce the dimension of plant images used for disease detection. For the early identification of fire blight disease, which damages fruit trees, Bagheri & Mohamadi-Monavar (2020) used PCA, SOM, and multilayer auto encoder to reduce the dimensionality of plant leaf images. The reduced feature set was used to classify diseased and non-diseased plants using soft independent modelling by class analogy, which achieved the highest accuracy with PCA. Sethy et al. (2020) presented a survey to explore the role of feature extraction methods and ML models to improve the detection of rice plant diseases. In another study, for the detection of rice plant diseases using leaf images, Sampathkumar & Rajeswari (2020) applied the c-mean filtering method to extract relevant features for analysis and the SVM model for the detection of disease.

KPCA-based dimensionality reduction was performed to explore various features belonging to the texture and colour of apple leaf images (Tummala, 2021). The SVM classifier was applied for the identification of disease from apple leaf images. Gou et al. (2020) applied PCA, LDA, LPP and discriminative globality and locality preserving graph embedding (DGLPGE). DGLPGE (proposed approach) achieved a higher performance score when compared with other approaches. For the timely prediction and classification of various wheat plant diseases, Huang et al. (2018) applied Isomap to reduce the dimensionality of wheat plant images. The reduced feature set was used for the classification of disease using a probabilistic neural network. Du et al. (2009) applied a supervised Isomap method to reduce dimensionality and extract precise features for the identification and classification of plants using leaf images. For the prediction, detection, and classification of various plant diseases, Reddy et al. (2019) applied the SMV model on reduced features of plant leaf images. Patki & Sable (2016) reviewed various DRTs and ML models suggested for the identification of cotton plant leaf diseases.

Gadekallu et al. (2020) introduced a new version of PCA to reduce the dimensionality and to extract relevant features for analysis. A deep neural network was applied on the reduced feature set for the classification of disease in tomato plants. In a recent study, Kianat et al. (2021) proposed a framework to employ a combination of feature selection and extraction approaches for the identification and categorization of cucumber leaf diseases. Wang et al. (2021) introduce a novel SVD to extract precise features of data for the prediction of crop diseases. In another study, for the identification of various diseased apple plant leaves, Singh et al. (2021) applied feature extraction methods and different ML models.

11.4 Opportunities and Challenges of Applying DRTs for Plant Disease Prediction

The application of computer technology in agriculture for plant disease management will certainly not automate farming but will improve the production and quality of crops and plants using few resources and data. Therefore, the application and selection of suitable DRTs and ML models offer many opportunities for the betterment of the agriculture sector. However, the selection of the right tools and techniques for the transformation of the traditional agriculture setup to digitalization poses many opportunities and challenges.

The application of digital systems for plant disease diagnosis will save lots of time and effort that is usually wasted in diagnosing plant diseases manually (Benos et al., 2021). The management of various terms and abbreviations used in the agriculture sector is a tiresome task. There is no standard format available to preserve plant and plant disease data, which raises a big challenge in digitalizing plant disease management systems. Moreover, various plants have different diseases, and variations in the terms and terminologies used by agriculturists are a big hurdle in the development of plant leaf disease diagnosis and prediction systems (Talib et al., 2016a).

The manual selection and extraction of suitable features for analysis and plant disease detection is a challenging task. DRTs provide automatic feature selection and extraction methods that improve the accuracy of results and improve the performance of ML models developed for plant disease prediction. It seems to be a suitable strategy to handle the emerging challenges of plant disease prediction systems that can bring overall enhancement in the agriculture sector (Benos et al., 2021). However, the selection of suitable DRTs and ML models for the diverse nature of plant leaf data is a challenging task and requires a deep understanding of computing technology, plants, plant diseases, and management strategies.

Automatically extracting valuable information and actionable insights from agriculture data is changing the structure of modern agriculture. The evolution of digital predictive models for the prediction of plant diseases, in particular, offers many opportunities and challenges. Opportunities can bring improvements in plant leaf disease detection systems, but some challenges represent open areas for research and development.

No doubt, the combination of DRTs and ML models seems to be a great achievement in plant leaf disease prediction, diagnosis, and management, but it requires relevant and precise features for analysis. Even the best ML model can generate the wrong results if data is not relevant and accurate. In agriculture, the digitalization of data is a new trend and needs a lot of effort to capture diverse nature and non-standardized data for the establishment of sustainable and more productive agriculture. It is anticipated that the present systematic effort will be a beneficial guide for researchers, manufacturers, engineers, ICT system developers, policymakers, and farmers and, consequently, contribute towards more systematic research on DRTs and ML models for the agriculture sector. However, for the development of an efficient plant disease prediction system, the collaboration of agriculturists and data scientists is essential for understanding plant-related data, selecting suitable methods for data analysis, and defining targets (outcomes) (Bowles, 2019).

11.5 Conclusion

This chapter explored the significance of DRTs for the detection, prediction, and classification of plant leaf diseases. The selection and extraction of some features of the plant leaf images are more important than others. For this reason, it is essential to select only precise and relevant features for analysis to attain more accurate results. For this purpose, in literature, different DRTs have been applied to reduce the dimensionality of plant leaf images and extract features for analysis. Reduced and relevant features can improve the performance of ML models for plant disease prediction. This can help plant leaf disease experts and agriculturists in predicting plant diseases and saving plants from complete loss. This chapter discussed the advantages and limitations of different DRTs and their impact on the performance of ML models used for plant disease prediction. Moreover, these techniques can be applied to other parts of plants for the prediction, detection, and categorization of different plant-related diseases.

References

Ayesha, S., Hanif, M. K., & Talib, R. (2020). Overview and comparative study of dimensionality reduction techniques for high dimensional data. *Information Fusion*, *59*, 44–58.

Bagheri, N., & Mohamadi-Monavar, H. (2020). Early detection of fire blight disease of pome fruit trees using visible-nir spectrometry and dimensionality reduction methods. *Journal of Agricultural Machinery*, 10, 37–48.

Begue, A., Kowlessur, V., Mahomoodally, F., Singh, U., & Pudaruth, S. (2017). Automatic recognition of medicinal plants using machine learning techniques. *International Journal of Advanced Computer Science and Applications*, *8*(4), 166–175.

Bajait, V., & Malarvizhi, N. (2020). Review on different approaches for crop prediction and disease monitoring techniques. In *2020 4th International Conference on Electronics, Communication and Aerospace Technology (ICECA)* (pp. 1244–1249). IEEE.

Beck, M. A., Liu, C. Y., Bidinosti, C. P., Henry, C. J., Godee, C. M., & Ajmani, M. (2020). An embedded system for the automated generation of labeled plant images to enable machine learning applications in agriculture. *Plos one*, *15*(12), e0243923.

Benos, L., Tagarakis, A. C., Dolias, G., Berruto, R., Kateris, D., & Bochtis, D. (2021). Machine learning in agriculture: A comprehensive updated review. *Sensors*, *21*(11), 3758.

Bharati, S., Podder, P., & Mondal, M. R. H. (2020, June). Diagnosis of polycystic ovary syndrome using machine learning algorithms. In *2020 IEEE Region 10 Symposium (TENSYMP)* (pp. 1486–1489). IEEE.

Binol, H. (2018). Ensemble learning based multiple kernel principal component analysis for dimensionality reduction and classification of hyperspectral imagery. *Mathematical Problems in Engineering*, *2018*.

Bowles, M. (2019). *Machine Learning with Spark and Python: Essential Techniques for Predictive Analytics*. John Wiley & Sons.

Chen, J., Wang, G., & Giannakis, G. B. (2018). Nonlinear dimensionality reduction for discriminative analytics of multiple datasets. *IEEE Transactions on Signal Processing*, *67*(3), 740–752.

Choudhary, M. K., & Hiranwal, S. (2021). Feature selection algorithms for plant leaf classification: A survey. In *Proceedings of International Conference on Communication and Computational Technologies* (pp. 657–669). Springer, Singapore.

Das, A., Mallick, C., & Dutta, S. (2020). Deep learning-based automated feature engineering for rice leaf disease prediction. *Computational Intelligence in Pattern Recognition. AISC*, *1120*, 133–141.

Dixit, A., & Nema, S. (2018). Wheat leaf disease detection using machine learning method-a review. *International Journal of Computer Science and Mobile Computing*, *7*(5), 124–129.

Du, M., Zhang, S., & Wang, H. (2009). Supervised isomap for plant leaf image classification. In *International Conference on Intelligent Computing* (pp. 627–634). Springer, Berlin, Heidelberg.

Dwivedi, P., Kumar, S., Vijh, S., & Chaturvedi, Y. (2021). Study of machine learning techniques for plant disease recognition in agriculture. In *2021 11th International Conference on Cloud Computing, Data Science & Engineering (Confluence)* (pp. 752–756). IEEE.

Erichson, N. B., Zheng, P., Manohar, K., Brunton, S. L., Kutz, J. N., & Aravkin, A. Y. (2020). Sparse principal component analysis via variable projection. *SIAM Journal on Applied Mathematics*, *80*(2), 977–1002.

Feng, L., Wu, B., Zhu, S., Wang, J., Su, Z., Liu, F., He, Y. & Zhang, C. (2020). Investigation on data fusion of multi-source spectral data for rice leaf diseases identification using machine learning methods. *Frontiers in Plant Science*, *11*, 1664.

Gadekallu, T. R., Rajput, D. S., Reddy, M. P. K., Lakshmanna, K., Bhattacharya, S., Singh, S., Jolfaei, A., & Alazab, M. (2020). A novel PCA–whale optimization-based deep neural network model for classification of tomato plant diseases using GPU. *Journal of Real-Time Image Processing*, 1–14.

Gao, L., Song, J., Liu, X., Shao, J., Liu, J., & Shao, J. (2017). Learning in high-dimensional multimedia data: the state of the art. *Multimedia Systems*, *23*(3), 303–313.

Ghojogh, B., Ghodsi, A., Karray, F., & Crowley, M. (2020a). Multidimensional scaling, Sammon mapping, and Isomap: Tutorial and survey. *arXiv preprint arXiv:2009. 08136.*

Ghojogh, B., Ghodsi, A., Karray, F., & Crowley, M. (2020b). Stochastic neighbor embedding with Gaussian and Student-t distributions: Tutorial and survey. *arXiv preprint arXiv:2009.10301.*

Ghojogh, B., Ghodsi, A., Karray, F., & Crowley, M. (2021). Generative Locally Linear Embedding. *arXiv preprint arXiv:2104.01525.*

Gilbertson, J. K., & Van Niekerk, A. (2017). Value of dimensionality reduction for crop differentiation with multi-temporal imagery and machine learning. *Computers and Electronics in Agriculture, 142*, 50–58.

Gisbrecht, A., & Hammer, B. (2015). Data visualization by nonlinear dimensionality reduction. *Wiley Interdisciplinary Reviews: Data Mining and Knowledge Discovery*, 5(2), 51–73.

Gobalakrishnan, N., Pradeep, K., Raman, C. J., Ali, L. J., & Gopinath, M. P. (2020). A systematic review on image processing and machine learning techniques for detecting plant diseases. In *2020 International Conference on Communication and Signal Processing (ICCSP)* (pp. 0465–0468). IEEE.

Gokhale, A., Babar, S., Gawade, S., & Jadhav, S. (2020). Identification of medicinal plant using image processing and machine learning. In *Applied Computer Vision and Image Processing* (pp. 272–282). Springer, Singapore.

Golhani, K., Balasundram, S. K., Vadamalai, G., & Pradhan, B. (2018). A review of neural networks in plant disease detection using hyperspectral data. *Information Processing in Agriculture, 5*(3), 354–371.

Gou, J., Yang, Y., Yi, Z., Lv, J., Mao, Q., & Zhan, Y. (2020). Discriminative globality and locality preserving graph embedding for dimensionality reduction. *Expert Systems with Applications, 144*, 113079.

Hanif, M. K., Ayesha, S., & Talib, R. (2020). Dimension reduction techniques. In *Big Data, IoT, and Machine Learning* (pp. 37–50). CRC Press.

Hazra, D., Bhattacharyya, D., & Kim, T. H. (2021). A random forest-based leaf classification using multiple features. In *Machine Intelligence and Soft Computing* (pp. 227–239). Springer, Singapore.

Huang, L., Wang, Y., Guo, W., Zhang, Q., & Yang, X. (2018). Classification of late-stage wheat powdery mildew based on Isomap and PNN analyses. *International Agricultural Engineering Journal, 27*(4), 404–410.

Huang, C. B., Abeo, T. A., Luo, X. Z., Shen, X. J., Gou, J. P., & Niu, D. J. (2020). Semi-supervised manifold alignment with multi-graph embedding. *Multimedia Tools and Applications, 79*(27), 20241–20262.

Jothiaruna, N., Sundar, K. J. A., & Ahmed, M. I. (2021). A disease spot segmentation method using comprehensive color feature with multi-resolution channel and region growing. *Multimedia Tools and Applications, 80*(3), 3327–3335.

Kartikeyan, P., & Shrivastava, G. (2021). Review on emerging trends in detection of plant diseases using image processing with machine learning. *International Journal of Computer Applications, 975*, 8887.

Kaur, P., & Gautam, V. (2021). Plant biotic disease identification and classification based on leaf image: A review. In *Proceedings of 3rd International Conference on Computing Informatics and Networks* (pp. 597–610). Springer, Singapore.

Kianat, J., Khan, M. A., Sharif, M., Akram, T., Rehman, A., & Saba, T. (2021). A joint framework of feature reduction and robust feature selection for cucumber leaf diseases recognition. *Optik*, *240*, 166566.

Li, Y., Wang, F., Sun, Y., & Wang, Y. (2020). Graph constraint and collaborative representation classifier steered discriminative projection with applications for the early identification of cucumber diseases. *Sensors*, *20*(4), 1217.

Liu, B., Lai, M., Wu, J. L., Fu, C., & Binaykia, A. (2020). Patent analysis and classification prediction of biomedicine industry: SOM-KPCA-SVM model. *Multimedia Tools and Applications*, *79*(15), 10177–10197.

Liu, H., & Motoda, H. (Eds.). (2007). Computational methods of feature selection. CRC Press.

Liu, Z., Du, Z., Peng, Y., Tong, M., Liu, X., & Chen, W. (2020, June). Study on corn disease identification based on PCA and SVM. In *2020 IEEE 4th Information Technology, Networking, Electronic and Automation Control Conference (ITNEC)* (Vol. 1, pp. 661–664). IEEE.

Najafi, A., Joudaki, A., & Fatemizadeh, E. (2015). Nonlinear dimensionality reduction via path-based isometric mapping. *IEEE transactions on pattern analysis and machine intelligence*, *38*(7), 1452–1464.

Nandhini, S., & Ashokkumar, K. (2021). Analysis on prediction of plant leaf diseases using deep learning. In *2021 International Conference on Artificial Intelligence and Smart Systems (ICAIS)* (pp. 165–169). IEEE.

Nigam, A., Tiwari, A. K., & Pandey, A. (2020). Paddy leaf diseases recognition and classification using PCA and BFO-DNN algorithm by image processing. *Materials Today: Proceedings*, *33*, 4856–4862.

Patel, B., & Sharaff, A. (2021). Rice crop disease prediction using machine learning technique. *International Journal of Agricultural and Environmental Information Systems (IJAEIS)*, *12*(4), 1–15.

Patki, S. S., & Sable, G. S. (2016). A review: Cotton leaf disease detection. *IOSR Journal of VLSI and Signal Processing*, *6*(3), 78–81.

Qu, H., Li, L., Li, Z., & Zheng, J. (2021). Supervised discriminant Isomap with maximum margin graph regularization for dimensionality reduction. *Expert Systems with Applications*, *180*, 115055.

Reddy, J. N., Vinod, K., & Ajai, A. R. (2019). Analysis of classification algorithms for plant leaf disease detection. In *2019 IEEE international conference on electrical, computer and communication technologies (ICECCT)* (pp. 1–6). IEEE.

Roy, S., Ray, R., Dash, S. R., & Giri, M. K. (2021). Plant disease detection using machine learning tools with an overview on dimensionality reduction. *Data Analytics in Bioinformatics: A Machine Learning Perspective*, 109–144.

Sampathkumar, S., & Rajeswari, R. (2020). An automated crop and plant disease identification scheme using cognitive fuzzy C-means algorithm. *IETE Journal of Research*, 1–12.

Sandhu, G. K., & Kaur, R. (2019). Plant disease detection techniques: A review. In *2019 international conference on automation, computational and technology management (ICACTM)* (pp. 34–38). IEEE.

Sethy, P. K., Barpanda, N. K., Rath, A. K., & Behera, S. K. (2020). Image processing techniques for diagnosing rice plant disease: A survey. *Procedia Computer Science*, *167*, 516–530.

Singh, S., Gupta, S., Tanta, A., & Gupta, R. (2021). Extraction of multiple diseases in apple leaf using machine learning. *International Journal of Image and Graphics*, 2140009.

Soni, J., Prabakar, N., & Upadhyay, H. (2020). Visualizing high-dimensional data using t-distributed stochastic neighbor embedding algorithm. In *Principles of Data Science* (pp. 189–206). Springer, Cham.

Sujatha, R., Chatterjee, J. M., Jhanjhi, N. Z., & Brohi, S. N. (2021). Performance of deep learning vs machine learning in plant leaf disease detection. *Microprocessors and Microsystems*, *80*, 103615.

Talib, R., Hanif, M. K., Ayesha, S., & Fatima, F. (2016a). Text mining: Techniques, applications, and issues. *International Journal of Advanced Computer Science and Applications*, *7*(11), 414–418.

Talib, R., Hanif, M. K., Fatima, F., & Ayesha, S. (2016b). A multi-agent framework for data extraction, transformation and loading in data warehouse. *International Journal of Advanced Computer Science and Applications*, *7*(11).

Tsai, C. F., & Sung, Y. T. (2020). Ensemble feature selection in high dimension, low sample size datasets: Parallel and serial combination approaches. *Knowledge-Based Systems*, *203*, 106097.

Trivedi, J., Shamnani, Y., & Gajjar, R. (2020, February). Plant leaf disease detection using machine learning. In *International conference on emerging technology trends in electronics communication and networking* (pp. 267–276). Springer, Singapore.

Tummala, S. (2021). Classification of Multi Diseases in Apple Plant Leaves.

Wang, Y., & Zhu, L. (2017). Research and implementation of SVD in machine learning. In *2017 IEEE/ACIS 16th International Conference on Computer and Information Science (ICIS)* (pp. 471–475). IEEE.

Wang, R., Cai, W., & Wang, Z. (2021). A new method of denoising crop image based on improved svd in wavelet domain. *Security and Communication Networks*, *2021*.

Yogeshwari, M., & Thailambal, G. (2021). Automatic feature extraction and detection of plant leaf disease using GLCM features and convolutional neural networks. *Materials Today: Proceedings*.

Yousaf, M., Rehman, T. U., & Jing, L. (2020). An extended isomap approach for nonlinear dimension reduction. *SN Computer Science*, *1*, 1–10.

Yu, H., Xu, Z., Wang, Y., Jiao, T., & Guo, Q. (2021). The use of KPCA over subspaces for cross-scale superpixel based hyperspectral image classification. *Remote Sensing Letters*, *12*(5), 470–477.

Zhang, S., & Wang, Z. (2016). Cucumber disease recognition based on global-local singular value decomposition. *Neurocomputing*, *205*, 341–348.

Zhang, S., Zhang, C., Wang, Z., & Kong, W. (2018). Combining sparse representation and singular value decomposition for plant recognition. *Applied Soft Computing*, *67*, 164–171.

Zhang, Z., Li, L., Li, Z., & Li, H. (2017). Visual query compression with locality preserving projection on Grassmann manifold. In *2017 IEEE International Conference on Image Processing (ICIP)* (pp. 3026–3030). IEEE.

Chapter 12

A Review of Deep Learning Approaches for Plant Disease Detection and Classification

Kusum Lata

Department of Electronics and Communication Engineering, The LNM Institute of Information Technology, Jaipur, India

Sandeep Saini

Department of Electronics and Communication Engineering, The LNM Institute of Information Technology, Jaipur, India

12.1 Introduction

Crop disease detection is an area of interest in multiple research fields. Agriculture scientists have been active in these fields for centuries and have provided robust solutions for rising issues. With the advent of computers and their application in almost every field of human life, the crop disease detection problem is also addressed with various computational techniques. Digital image processing is one of the most popular computation techniques for detecting a particular disease on crop leaves or stems (Wallen & Jackson, 1971). Artificial intelligence (AI) is a subset of digital image processing, and the subset of AI known as machine learning (ML) has revolutionised several computing study fields in recent decades.

DOI: 10.1201/9781003299059-12

The concept of ML originated in 1943 (when McCulloch and Pitts (1943) introduced a mathematical model for the neuron activity of the human brain. ML developed at a slow pace as the computational powers required for these algorithms were not available. Since 2006, the area has grown at an exponential rate, and ML has become a part of practically every solvable computer problem on the planet. It has disrupted existing techniques and provided an alternative to solve them with algorithms inspired by the human brain's processing techniques. The neocortex region of the brain processes a lot of vision, speech, and language-related neuron data. The region has a hierarchical structure with six layers (Douglas & Martin, 2004). These layers pass the inference from bottom to top in order to predict the final decision by the human brain.

Similarly, deep learning (DL) algorithms are designed to classify various classes (a disease in this case) from a set of training datasets. Thus, a large labelled dataset of affected crops is collected and trained using DL architecture to develop a model that can predict the disease for an input image.

In this work, we have focused on the crops of India. Agriculture is responsible for the livelihood of about 58% of India's population. We have focused on the major crops as this provides us with enough diversity to examine different seasons and categories of crops.

12.2 Major Crops and Their Disease Detection Using Deep Learning in India

Worldwide it is estimated that 20–40 % yield loss is due to crop pests and pathogens. India has a varied range of soil and meteorological conditions, allowing it to cultivate a diverse agricultural pattern. Plant disease causes India to lose 35% of its annual crop yield (Singh et al., 2020). In this section, we discuss the major crops of India, namely cereal crops, oilseed crops, and cash crops, and their associated diseases, which are detected using DL methods, as reported in various research articles. We consider the country's major crops in each category, namely rice, wheat, and maize in cereals, sesame, mustard, soybean, and groundnut in oilseeds, and cotton in cash crops.

12.2.1 Cereal Crop Disease Detection Using Deep Learning Methods

Losses of staple cereals, such as rice, wheat, maize, etc., directly impact food security and nutrition in a country like India. Moreover, this loss also causes substantial economic loss at various levels, from household and national to global levels. Here, we report the major diseases of cereal crops and their classifications. The primary diseases detected in cereals using DL approaches published in the literature are shown in Table 12.1.

Table 12.1   Deep Learning Methods Used to Detect and Classify Diseases in Cereal Crops

Crops	Disease name	Modality	Reference
Rice	Bacterial leaf blight, brown spot, leaf smut, blast	Leaf images	(Rahman et al., 2020), (Lu et al., 2017), (Liang et al., 2019)
	False smut, neck blast, seedling blight	Grain images	(Rahman et al., 2020), (Ahmed et al., 2020), (Lu et al., 2017)
	Sheath blight, sheath rot, bacterial sheath rot	Stem images	(Rahman et al., 2020), (Lu et al., 2017)
Maize	Common rust, grey leaf spot, northern leaf blight, zinc deficiency, round spot	Leaf images	(Lv et al., 2020), (Zhang et al., 2018)
	Southern leaf blight, Curvularia leaf spot, brown spot, dwarf mosaic, Cercospora leaf spot	Leaf images	(Zhang et al., 2018), (Agarwal & Sharma, n.d.)
Wheat	Leaf blotch, stripe rust, powdery mildew, leaf rust, smut, black chaff, Septoria, tan spot, Fusarium head blight	Leaf images	(Lu et al., 2017), (Nagaraju et al., n.d.), (Barbedo et al., 2015)

12.2.2 Oilseed Crop Disease Detection Using Deep Learning Methods

India is one of the world's top producers of oilseed crops, and they are extremely important to the Indian agricultural economy (Rai et al., 2016). India is the world's fourth-largest producer of vegetable oils. We present the major diseases of edible oilseeds crops such as groundnuts, mustard, sesame, and soybean. Table 12.2 shows how DL algorithms have been utilised in the literature to detect major illnesses in oilseeds.

12.2.3 Cash Crop Disease Detection Using Deep Learning Methods

Cotton is India's most important fibre and cash crop and a key component of the agricultural and industrial industries (Majumder et al., 2017). At the same time, the cotton crop is highly prone to diseases and pests. As a result, it is critical to research the principal diseases and their classification as the primary cause of yield loss. Table 12.3 lists the major diseases that have been detected and classified using DL approaches in the literature.

Table 12.2 Oilseed Disease Detection and Classification Using Deep Learning Methods

Crops	Disease name	Modality	Reference
Mustard	Alternaria blight, white rot, white rust, powdery mildew, downy mildew complex	Leaf images	(Rani et al., 2011), (Kumar et al., 2016)
Sesame	Phyllody, Phytophthora blight, dry root rot, charcoal rot, Alternaria blight, stem anthracnose, mildew, Cercospora	Leaf images	(El-Mashharawi & Abu-Naser, 2019), (Myint et al., 2020)
Soybean	Bacterial blight, brown spot, Septoria leaf blight, downy mildew, rust, frogeye leaf spot, target spot, powdery mildew, charcoal rot, southern blight	Leaf images	(Jadhav et al., 2020), (Wallelign et al., 2018)
Groundnut	Alternaria leaf, early leafspot, Pestalotiopsis, Tikka, bud necrosis, Phyllosticta, late leafspot, pepper spot, Choanephora, rust	Leaf images	(Vaishnnave et al., 2020), (Koshy et al., 2018)

Table 12.3 Cash Crop Disease Detection and Classification Using Deep Learning Methods

Crops	Disease name	Modality	Reference
Cotton	Cercospora leaf spot, bacterial blight, Ascochyta blight, target spot, areolate mildew, Myrothecium leaf spot, black arm, Alternaria, Alternaria leaf spot, powdery mildew, magnesium deficiency, leaf necrosis, grey mildew	Leaf images	(Jenifa et al., 2019), (Prajapati et al., 2016)

12.3 Deep Learning Architectures and Models for Crop Disease Detection

DL has emerged as universal learning that applies to almost every area of research. The method of feature extraction is the most significant distinction between ML and DL approaches. In ML, we have more human intervention in extracting features, tagging data, and eventually learning. In DL, the architecture learns the features and stores them in a hierarchical sequence. DL is more applicable under the following circumstances.

1. Where human expertise is limited in a field.
2. Where the human expertise task is time-consuming.
3. Where errors occur more with human involvement.
4. Where solutions need to adapt themselves to particular aspects over time.
5. Where the size of the problem is vast and manual processing is not possible.

Thus, for crop disease detection for many crops and their respective diseases with high accuracy, DL approaches are the best candidate.

The present state-of-the-art DL architectures and model development began with the release of AlexNet (Krizhevsky et al., 2012) in 2012. For the ImageNet Large-Scale Visual Recognition Challenge (ILSVRC), Krizhevsky et al. proposed this model and trained it on the ImageNet dataset.[1] Convolutional neural networks (CNNs) were used before AlexNet, which is itself based on a CNN. There are a total of eight layers in AlexNet. Convolutional layers make up five of these, whereas completely connected network layers make up three. Instead of using the tanh function as the activation function, the authors employed rectified linear units (ReLUs). This approach resulted in six times faster results as compared to conventional CNN models. AlexNet achieved an error rate of 16.4%, compared to the second-place result of 26.1%. CNN-based deep learning models are used not only for images but also for video applications (Wang et al., 2020; Pan et al., 2019). Figure 12.1 depicts the generic architecture of a DL-based network for crop disease detection. The stages involved are almost the same in every network, and the convolutional and pooling layers are changed for experimenting to get better results.

After AlexNet, a number of similar models and architectures were developed. The most popular ones are ZFNet (Zeiler & Fergus, 2014), OverFeat (Sermanet et al., 2013), Oxford's VGG (Simonyan & Zisserman, 2014), ResNet (He et al., 2016), GoogLeNet (Szegedy et al., 2015), and Xception (Chollet, 2017). With the availability of fast GPUs, developing highly dense networks and training them with expansive computational costs was no longer a hindrance in the process. As a result, the quality of picture classification using DL-based models has increased

---

[1] www.image-net.org/

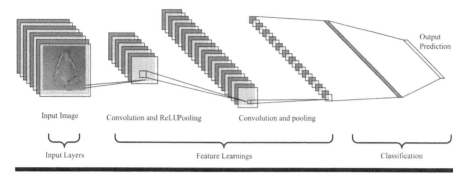

Figure 12.1 **A generic architecture for deep learning-based networks for crop disease detection**

exponentially. We organised the details of such models that had been produced over the years. Subrato et al. have reported DL-based work in this domain (Bharati et al., 2020b, 2020a, 2021b, 2021a; Khamparia et al., 2021). There has been a significant amount of development, and we have chosen the most popular and revolutionizing models for this review. Similar works is reported by Yadav, Lamba et al. (2020). Jaiswal et al. (2020), Saini & Sahula (2021), Paliwal et al. (2019), and Yadav et al. (2021) have also developed similar models for DL-based applications. Table 12.4 shows a list of these models along with their important features. These models can be used for any picture classification task, although the majority of them are used to detect crop disease. The models we used for our chosen crops are listed in the next section.

12.4 Standard Datasets Used for Crop Disease Detection

A dataset is the foremost requirement for any DL-based network. An exhaustive labelled dataset is required for proper training of the network. In this section, we have focused on datasets that are completely or partially dedicated to the crops of our context.

12.4.1 PlantVillage Dataset

PlantVillage is a not-for-profit project at Penn State University.[2] The project also aims to solve farmers' problems with crowdsourced funding. One of the major contributions of this project is the open-source availability of the PlantVillage

---

[2] https://plantvillage.psu.edu/

Table 12.4   Deep Learning-Based Model and Architectures for Image Classification

Model name	Basic architecture and functions	Features and achievements
LeNet (LeCun et al., 1998; LeCun et al., 1999)	CNN-based with 60,000 parameters	LeNet was one of the first CNN-based models designed for object classification. This was designed with a few parameters and had limited computational capabilities.
AlexNet (Krizhevsky et al., 2012)	Eight-layer CNN-based with 60 million parameters	AlexNet was the first breakthrough model to revolutionize current deep learning approaches. The model has 60 million parameters and uses ReLU instead of the conventional tanh function in the architecture.
OverFeat (Sermanet et al., 2013)	145 million parameters	The model was trained on the ILSVRC 2013 dataset, and it can be used for classification, localization, and detection. The model was the winner of the ILSVRC 2013 challenge as well.
AlexNetOWTBn (Krizhevsky, 2014)	SGD-based parallel NN	This model is a one weird trick (OWT) variation of the AlexNet in which the authors adopted batch normalization (Bn) at the end of each convolutional layer. A speedup of 6.16 times was achieved with this approach in training.
NiN (Lin et al., 2013)	CNN and MLP-based model	This model is based on the multilayer perceptron (MLP)-based generalized linear model (GLM). The CNN-based MLP layer is called MLPConv.
VGG (Simonyan & Zisserman, 2014)	140 million parameters trained on 1.3 million images	The Visual Geometry Group (VGG) at Oxford university proposed this model as their entry for the ILSVRC 2014 challenge. The team won the localization task and took second place for classification.
GoogLeNet (Szegedy et al., 2015)	22 layer deep CNN-based model with 60 million parameters	The model was the official entry from Google for ILSVRS 2014. The network consists of 22 layers. The network is based on the LeNet CNN and added a novel element called Inception. The model was the winner of the ILSVRS 2014 competition and achieved the closest error rate to the human level.

(Continued)

Table 12.4   Deep Learning-Based Model and Architectures for Image Classification   (Continued)

Model name	Basic architecture and functions	Features and achievements
R-CNN (Girshick et al., 2014)	SVM-based model	Regions with CNN (R-CNN) is designed as an object detection architecture. Initially, category-independent region proposals are generated, which defines the set of candidates for detection.
FractalNet (Larsson et al., 2016)	Up to 40 layered architectures	FractalNet is based on the idea of developing a neural network macro architecture from self-similarity. A fractal network can have different length subpaths, and these paths do not have any pass-through connections.
YOLO (Redmon et al., 2016)	The ImageNet dataset was used to train 24 layers of convolutional layers	You only look once (YOLO) is a regression issue that detects several objects in a single photograph. A single neural network is used to compute the class probabilities of the bounding boxes, which are spatially separated.
SqueezeNet (Iandola et al., 2016)	Replace large filters with smaller	This model is aimed at mobile and embedded applications. It is based on AlexNet, but with 50 times fewer parameters and a trained model that is around 0.5 MB in size. As a result, it's an excellent choice for mobile deep learning applications.
DenseNet (Huang et al., 2017)	250 layers with 25 million parameters and using the ReLU activation function	Closer layers in a deep neural network perform better than a sparse network. DenseNet exploits this feature and represents a network with highly dense layers. The overall structure is similar to ResNet. Since the input is concatenated in DenseNet, any layer in the network can access the feature maps.
Fast RCNN (Girshick, 2015)	Softmax classifier	Fast region-based convolutional neural network (Fast-RCNN) is based on deep CNN and is designed for multiple object detections in an image.

(Continued)

Table 12.4   Deep Learning-Based Model and Architectures for Image Classification   (Continued)

Model name	Basic architecture and functions	Features and achievements
MobileNet (Howard et al., 2017)	MobileNets use both batchnorm and ReLU	MobileNet is designed to focus on mobile and embedded systems-based applications. It uses a streamlined architecture that is made of depth-wise separable convolutional layers.
DeepLab (Chen et al., 2017)	SegNet-based model used ReLU	DeepLab is designed for semantic segmentation. DeepLab uses the SegNet model, which is already trained on the ImageNet dataset as its main feature extractor. Furthermore, it uses a novel residual block for multiscale learning of extracted features.
Xception (Chollet, 2017)	Trained on 350 million images and 17,000 classes with ReLU	Xception is a deep network proposed by Google for large image classifications. The model is inspired by GoogLeNet (Inception).
IRRCNN (Alom et al., 2020)	The hybrid model uses SGD and ReLU with 3.5 million parameters	Inception recurrent residual convolutional neural network (IRRCNN) is based on a hybridization of RCNN, Inception network, and ResNet. Keeping the same network parameters as the Inception network improves the training accuracy by utilizing the powers of RCNN and ResNet.
MDFC–ResNet (Hu et al., 2020)	ResNet-based network. 2 million parameters.	Multidimensional feature compensation residual neural network (MDFC-ResNet) model is based on ResNet architecture and designed for agriculture applications.

dataset for crop disease detection. The dataset was introduced in 2015, and a DL-based model tested the accuracies of the images in 2016 (Mohanty et al., 2016). The dataset contains 54,309 images. These images are compiled from 14 crops and 26 diseases. The dataset is available at GitHub. The crops included in the dataset are blueberry, corn, grape, raspberry, orange, apple, peach, cherry, bell pepper, potato, soybean, strawberry, squash, and tomato. All the images present in this dataset are prepared in a controlled lab environment. That means all the images are kept inside the lab and captured under good lighting conditions.

12.4.2 PlantDoc Dataset

The PlantDoc dataset is a real-world crop image dataset for disease detection. The dataset is prepared by the Indian Institute of Technology Gandhinagar, India. The dataset contains 2,598 images from 13 crops and 27 diseases (Singh et al., 2020). The images are captured in natural lighting conditions in the fields. This enables the training and testing to be more natural, and the dataset is used to perform disease detection using images captured on a mobile phone. The dataset is publicly available on GitHub.[3]

12.4.3 Cropped-PlantDoc Dataset

Images in the PlantDoc dataset contain multiple leaves as well in a single image. Some of those can be healthy, while a few can have a particular disease as well. The authors have cropped such images using bounding boxes and converted those bounding boxed images into multiple single leaf images. In this way, the Cropped-PlantDoc dataset was prepared. The dataset contains a total of 9,216 images for the same number of crops and diseases.

12.4.4 Plant Disease Symptoms Image Database (PDDB)

The PDDB is a freely available dataset provided by Embrapa Agricultural Informatics, Brazil. The dataset contains around 50,000 images by considering 21 crops and 112 classifications (Barbedo, 2018). The dataset contains soybean, lemon, coconut, dry bean, cassava, passion fruit, corn, coffee, cashew tree, grapevine, oil palm, wheat, sugarcane, cotton, black pepper, cabbage, melon, rice, pineapple, and papaya crop images.

12.4.5 Northern Corn Leaf Blight (NCLB) Dataset for Maize

The NCLB dataset is dedicated only to the northern corn leaf blight maize crop disease (DeChant et al., 2017). The dataset is freely available under the name nlb_annotated_public_2016 (Goff et al., 2011) from the Bisque platform of CyVerse. The dataset contains 1,796 images of maize crops. Out of these, 1,028 images are infected images, and the remaining 768 images are healthy images. This CNN-based trained model showed above 96% accuracy on this dataset for disease detection.

12.4.6 New Plant Diseases Dataset (Augmented)

Samir Bhattarai has used data augmentation techniques to create more images from samples of the PlantVillage dataset. He has created a total of 87,900 images from

---

[3] https://github.com/pratikkayal/PlantDoc-Dataset

the original dataset and shared it on Kaggle for free usage. The complete dataset is annotated and every image is downsized to 256x256 pixels for a faster training process.

12.4.7 Rice Leaf Diseases Dataset

This dataset is prepared by the Department of Information Technology, Dharmsinh Desai University, Nadiad, India (Shah et al., 2016; Prajapati et al., 2017). The dataset is focused only on the rice diseases found in the Indian state of Gujrat. The dataset contains 120 annotated images.

12.4.8 Image Set for Deep Learning

This dataset is prepared by the Plant Breeding and Genetics Section, School of Integrative Plant Science, Cornell University, Ithaca, New York (Wiesner-Hanks et al., 2018). This is the biggest dataset for a single crop, namely maize. The dataset focuses on lesions of the northern corn leaf blight (NCLB) disease of maize. This dataset contains 18,222 images with 105,705 NCLB lesions. The dataset is publically available at OSF.[4] The dataset is prepared in three different ways. In the first approach, a handheld camera is used for close-up shots of the leaves. In the second method, a 5 metre boom is used to mount the camera at height, and then the images are captured. In the third approach, drones are used to capture field images.

12.4.9 UCI Plant Dataset

The Machine Learning group of the University of California, Irvine, has developed a plant dataset with 22,632 images (Veley et al., 2017). The dataset is available on the research group's repository.[5] The dataset consists of all major US crops, including maize, soya, wheat, and apple. The dataset is not very extensive in terms of diseases but mainly exhibits the diversity in the types of crops. The dataset is more suitable to test a classification model as it contains a greater number of classes.

12.4.10 Michalski's Soybean Disease Database

This dataset is also available from the Machine Learning group of the University of California, Irvine. It is developed only for soybean-related diseases. The dataset contains only 307 images with 35 attributes (Michalski & Chilauski, 1980).

---

[4] https://osf.io/p67rz/

[5] https://archive.ics.uci.edu/ml/datasets/Plants

12.4.11 Arkansas Plant Disease Database

This extensive dataset is developed by the Division of Agriculture at the University of Arkansas System. The dataset is available on the university website. It contains images of nine fruits and 14 vegetables.

12.4.12 One-Hundred Plant Species Leaves Dataset

James et al. at Kingston University London developed this concise dataset for 100 different plants (Cope et al., 2013; Mallah et al., 2013). In this dataset, 16 images of each plant's leaves are collected. The dataset is available at the UCI Machine Learning Repository.

12.5 Performance of Different Deep Learning Algorithms Used for Crops Disease Detection

DL-based models and architecture are proposed as potential solutions for cancer detection and classification. Any such tasks must be quantified and their performance must be measured. All the approaches mentioned in the above sections fall under classification-related tasks for a DL model. This category of task can be measured with the following metrics.

12.5.1 Confusion Matrix

A confusion matrix is not a performance measuring metric but a basic concept to understand the other metrics. Let us consider a classification task for binary classification to classify leaf images in a particular image dataset. If our dataset contains a total of 2,200 images with only 200 leaf images and 2,000 non-leaf images, then a sample confusion matrix after training is shown in Table 12.5.

The model predicts 180 correct leaf images from 200 actual leaf images and incorrectly predicts 120 non-leaf images as leaf images. Thus, we can say that the true positive prediction is 180/200 = 90%, and 20 samples are predicted as false negatives. Similarly, for non-leaf images, 120 images are classified as false-positive

Table 12.5 A Sample Confusion Matrix for Binary Classification Tasks of 2200 Leaf Images

		Actual class	
		Leaf	*Non-leaf*
Predicted class	Leaf	180	120
	Non-leaf	20	1,880

and 1,880 images as true negative. These parameters help us in formulating other evaluation metrics.

12.5.2 Classification Accuracy

This is one of the simplest and most common metrics to comprehend the performance of a DL model. The ratio of the number of right forecasts to the total number of predictions made by the model defines the model's prediction accuracy. The number will always be in the range of 0 to 1, and it can be multiplied by 100 to obtain percentage accuracy. In the example given above, the classification accuracy is calculated as (180+1880)/2200 = 0.9363, or 93.63%.

12.5.3 Precision

Classification accuracy is an easy metric but not always a good way to measure the model's performance. If we have imbalanced classes in our dataset (i.e., there are more data values for one class than others), then the accuracy will be high if the system predicts more values belonging to this class. Which should not be the case for a true classifier. To overcome such issues, we use the precision metric. Precision is defined as:

$$Precision = \frac{True\_positive}{True\_positive + False\_positive} \qquad (12.1)$$

The consideration of true and false predictions makes this metric a better alternative to the accuracy metric alone. Thus, for the above example, the values of precision are calculated for the leaf and non-leaf classification.

$$Precision\_leaf = 180 / (180 + 120) = 60\%$$

$$Precision\_non\_leaf = 1880 / 1900 = 98.9\%$$

Thus we can comprehend that for this imbalanced example, the precision values are also highly varying for each class while accuracy could not provide such information.

12.5.4 Recall

Another significant parameter is recall, which is defined as the percentage of samples that the DL model accurately predicts.

$$Recall = \frac{True\_positive}{True\_positive + False\_negative} \qquad (12.2)$$

In the given example, the recall values for two classes are as follows:

$$Recall\_leaf = 180 / 200 = 90\%$$

$$Recall\_non\_leaf = 1880 / 2000 = 94\%.$$

12.5.5 F1-Score

The F1-score, or simply F-score, is a measurement metric derived from the precision and recall metrics. F-score is defined as:

$$F1\text{-}score = 2 * \frac{Recall * Precision}{Recall + Precision} \tag{12.3}$$

F1-score is also in the range of 0 to 1 and can be multiplied by 100 to obtain the percentage value.

For our given example, the values of F-scores for both the classes are:

$$F\_score\_leaf = 2 * 0.6 * 0.9(0.6 + 0.9) = 0.72$$

$$F\_score\_non\_leaf = 2 * 0.94 * 0.989 / (0.94 + 0.989) = 0.9638$$

We comprehend from the above definitions that one single performance metric cannot depict the correctness of a model. The performance of a model on a particular dataset is dependent on various parameters. The same model will perform in different ways on different datasets and under different training conditions. A particular model can perform in a different way for different feature classifications of the same dataset. It also helps us in deciding which features are better suited for a particular classification task. We've collated the results of numerous DL-based models for various sorts of illnesses on the understudied crops in Table 12.6.

12.6 Conclusion

DL is emerging as one of the best methods for fast and efficient crop disease detection and classification approaches. In this work, we have provided an extensive review of such approaches for various crops in India. We have considered eight major crops (rice, wheat, maize, mustard, sesame, soybean, groundnut, and cotton) from both the crop seasons in the country. We have also considered crops from various categories. Initially, we compiled the major diseases of these crops classified or detected by various DL-based models and architectures. After that, we provided an overview of DL architecture, as well as a timeline-based survey of all key DL-based

Table 12.6 Performance of Various Deep Learning Models to Detect and Classify Diseases on the Understudy Crops

Crop	Model used	Task	Performance of the model
Rice (Prajapati et al., 2017)	SVM	Bacterial leaf blight, brown spot, and leaf smut are the three illnesses classified.	For fivefold and tenfold validation, 83.80% and 88.57% accuracy
Maize (DeChant et al., 2017)	CNN	Northern corn leaf blight (NCLB) disease classification.	Test accuracy of 96.7%
Maize (Zhang et al., 2018)	AlexNet and GoogLeNet-based	There are eight different types of maize leaf diseases: Curvularia leaf spot, dwarf mosaic, grey leaf spot, northern leaf blight, brown spot, round spot, rust, southern leaf blight.	98.9% test accuracy using AlexNet and 98.6% using GoogLeNet
Wheat (Picon et al., 2019)	CNN and ResNet based	Septoria (Septoria triciti), tan spot (Drechslera tritici-repentis), and rust are three wheat diseases that have been identified (Puccinia striiformis and Puccinia recondita).	On a pilot test in Germany, the test accuracy was 96%
Wheat and Barley (Guth et al., 2017)	CNN	Barley: scald, Fusarium head blight, net blotch, powdery mildew, Rumalaria.	Overall accuracy of 87%
Wheat (Arnal Barbedo, 2019)	CNN	Wheat blast, leaf rust, tan spot.	Testing accuracy of 98.5%

(Continued)

Table 12.6 Performance of Various Deep Learning Models to Detect and Classify Diseases on the Understudy Crops (Continued)

Crop	Model used	Task	Performance of the model
Mustard (Cynthia et al., 2019)	CNN	Black spot of rose, Sigatoka leaf spot, grey spot of mustard.	Intersection over union of 67.34%
Soybean (Jadhav et al., 2020)	AlexNet and GoogLeNet-based	Three soybean diseases.	98.75% testing accuracy using AlexNet and 96.25% using GoogLeNet
Soybean (Wallelign et al., 2018)	CNN	Septoria leaf blight, frogeye leaf spot, and downy mildew are three soybean diseases that need to be classified.	Testing accuracy of 99.32%
Soybean (Karlekar & Seal, 2020)	CNN modified SoyNet	16 diseases classified.	Testing accuracy of 98.14%
Groundnut (Vaishnnave et al., 2020)	DCNN	Alternaria, Pestalotiopsis, bud necrosis, Tikka, Phyllosticta, rust, pepper spot, Choanephora, early and late leaf spot.	Testing accuracy of 95.28%
Cotton (Yang et al., 2019) (Yang et al., 2019)	MobileNet	Recognition for cotton spider mites' damage level.	The training set had a precision of 92.29%, while the test set had a precision of 91.88%
Cotton (Arnal Barbedo, 2019)	CNN	Areolate mildew, Myrothecium leaf spot, seedling disease complex.	Testing accuracy of 99%

(Continued)

Table 12.6 Performance of Various Deep Learning Models to Detect and Classify Diseases on the Understudy Crops (Continued)

Crop	Model used	Task	Performance of the model
14 crops in PlantDoc dataset. dCrop system (Pallagani et al., 2019)	ResNet50, AlexNet and ResNet34	Classification of 26 diseases.	The trained model has a 99.24% accuracy rate.
59 diseases of 10 crops (Hu et al., 2020)	ResNet-based model	Classification of 59 different diseases.	Training accuracy 93.96%, validation 89.92%, and test accuracy of 85.22%
58 diseases of 25 plants (Ferentinos, 2018)	CNN	Identifying the [plant, illness] combo that corresponds.	The disease was correctly identified 99.53% of the time.

architectures and models for image classification challenges. The architectures from 2012 to 2020, and all the major achievements and model configurations of these models, were compiled. The availability of a relevant dataset is the next criterion for a DL model, and we have provided details of 12 publicly available datasets relating to the crops indicated above. These datasets are made available by both private and public research groups. In the end, we provided the qualitative performance measurements for various architectures and models on different crop disease detection and classification tasks related to understudy crops. We compiled more than 25 such systems. The survey provides complete details for a researcher to gain all the relevant knowledge required for DL-based crop disease classification. The work will help the research community to choose an appropriate model for their experimental setup.

References

Agarwal, R., & Sharma, H. (n.d.). Enhanced convolutional neural network (ECNN) for maize leaf diseases identification. In *Smart Innovations in Communication and Computational Sciences* (pp. 297–307). Springer.

Ahmed, T., Rahman, C. R., Abid, M., & Mahmud, F. (2020). Rice grain disease identification using dual phase convolutional neural network-based system aimed at small dataset. *ArXiv Preprint ArXiv:2004.09870.*

Alom, M. Z., Hasan, M., Yakopcic, C., Taha, T. M., & Asari, V. K. (2020). Improved inception-residual convolutional neural network for object recognition. *Neural Computing and Applications, 32*(1), 279–293.

Arnal Barbedo, J. G. (2019). Plant disease identification from individual lesions and spots using deep learning. *Biosystems Engineering, 180,* 96–107. https://doi.org/https://doi.org/10.1016/j.biosystemseng.2019.02.002

Barbedo, J. G. A. (2018). Factors influencing the use of deep learning for plant disease recognition. *Biosystems Engineering, 172,* 84–91.

Barbedo, J. G. A., Tibola, C. S., & Fernandes, J. M. C. (2015). Detecting Fusarium head blight in wheat kernels using hyperspectral imaging. *Biosystems Engineering, 131,* 65–76. https://doi.org/https://doi.org/10.1016/j.biosystemseng.2015.01.003

Bharati, S., Podder, P., Mondal, M., & Prasath, V. B. (2021a). CO-ResNet: Optimized ResNet model for COVID-19 diagnosis from X-ray images. *International Journal of Hybrid Intelligent Systems, Preprint,* 1–15.

Bharati, S., Podder, P., & Mondal, M. R. H. (2020a). *Artificial Neural Network Based Breast Cancer Screening: A Comprehensive Review.*

Bharati, S., Podder, P., & Mondal, M. R. H. (2020b). Hybrid deep learning for detecting lung diseases from X-ray images. *Informatics in Medicine Unlocked, 20,* 100391. https://doi.org/https://doi.org/10.1016/j.imu.2020.100391

Bharati, S., Podder, P., Mondal, M. R. H., & Prasath, V. B. S. (2021b). *Medical Imaging with Deep Learning for COVID- 19 Diagnosis: A Comprehensive Review.*

Chen, L.-C., Papandreou, G., Kokkinos, I., Murphy, K., & Yuille, A. L. (2017). Deeplab: Semantic image segmentation with deep convolutional nets, atrous convolution, and fully connected crfs. *IEEE Transactions on Pattern Analysis and Machine Intelligence, 40*(4), 834–848.

Chollet, F. (2017). Xception: Deep learning with depthwise separable convolutions. *Proceedings of the IEEE Conference on Computer Vision and Pattern Recognition,* 1251–1258.

Cope, J., Beghin, T., Remagnino, P., & Barman, S. (2013). *One-hundred plant species leaves data set.*

Cynthia, S. T., Hossain, K. M. S., Hasan, M. N., Asaduzzaman, M., & Das, A. K. (2019). Automated detection of plant diseases using image processing and faster R-CNN algorithm. *2019 International Conference on Sustainable Technologies for Industry 4.0 (STI),* 1–5.

DeChant, C., Wiesner-Hanks, T., Chen, S., Stewart, E. L., Yosinski, J., Gore, M. A., Nelson, R. J., & Lipson, H. (2017). Automated identification of northern leaf blight-infected maize plants from field imagery using deep learning. *Phytopathology, 107*(11), 1426–1432.

Douglas, R. J., & Martin, K. A. C. (2004). Neuronal circuits of the neocortex. *Annual Review of Neuroscience, 27*(1), 419–451. https://doi.org/10.1146/annurev.neuro.27.070203.144152

El-Mashharawi, H. Q., & Abu-Naser, S. S. (2019). *An Expert System for Sesame Diseases Diagnosis Using CLIPS.*

Ferentinos, K. P. (2018). Deep learning models for plant disease detection and diagnosis. *Computers and Electronics in Agriculture, 145*, 311–318. https://doi.org/10.1016/j.compag.2018.01.009

Girshick, R. (2015). Fast R-CNN. *Proceedings of the IEEE International Conference on Computer Vision*, 1440–1448.

Girshick, R., Donahue, J., Darrell, T., & Malik, J. (2014). Rich feature hierarchies for accurate object detection and semantic segmentation. *Proceedings of the IEEE Conference on Computer Vision and Pattern Recognition*, 580–587.

Goff, S. A., Vaughn, M., McKay, S., Lyons, E., Stapleton, A. E., Gessler, D., Matasci, N., Wang, L., Hanlon, M., Lenards, A., & others. (2011). The iPlant collaborative: Cyberinfrastructure for plant biology. *Frontiers in Plant Science, 2*, 34.

Guth, F. A., Ward, S., & McDonnell, K. P. (2017). Autonomous disease detection in crops using deep learning. *Biosystems and Food Engineering Research Review 22*, 209.

He, K., Zhang, X., Ren, S., & Sun, J. (2016). Deep residual learning for image recognition. *Proceedings of the IEEE Conference on Computer Vision and Pattern Recognition*, 770–778.

Howard, A. G., Zhu, M., Chen, B., Kalenichenko, D., Wang, W., Weyand, T., Andreetto, M., & Adam, H. (2017). Mobilenets: Efficient convolutional neural networks for mobile vision applications. *ArXiv Preprint ArXiv:1704.04861.*

Hu, W.-J., Fan, J., Du, Y.-X., Li, B.-S., Xiong, N., & Bekkering, E. (2020). MDFC--ResNet: An agricultural IoT system to accurately recognize crop diseases. *IEEE Access, 8*, 115287–115298.

Huang, G., Liu, Z., Van Der Maaten, L., & Weinberger, K. Q. (2017). Densely connected convolutional networks. *Proceedings of the IEEE Conference on Computer Vision and Pattern Recognition*, 4700–4708.

Iandola, F. N., Han, S., Moskewicz, M. W., Ashraf, K., Dally, W. J., & Keutzer, K. (2016). SqueezeNet: AlexNet-level accuracy with 50x fewer parameters and< 0.5 MB model size. *ArXiv Preprint ArXiv:1602.07360.*

Jadhav, S. B., Udupi, V. R., & Patil, S. B. (2020). Identification of plant diseases using convolutional neural networks. *International Journal of Information Technology.* https://doi.org/10.1007/s41870-020-00437-5

Jaiswal, M., Sharma, V., Sharma, A., Saini, S., & Tomar, R. (2020). An efficient binarized neural network for recognizing two hands indian sign language gestures in real-time environment. *2020 IEEE 17th India Council International Conference (INDICON)*, 1–6.

Jenifa, A., Ramalakshmi, R., & Ramachandran, V. (2019). Cotton leaf disease classification using deep convolution neural network for sustainable cotton production. *2019 IEEE International Conference on Clean Energy and Energy Efficient Electronics Circuit for Sustainable Development (INCCES)*, 1–3.

Karlekar, A., & Seal, A. (2020). SoyNet: Soybean leaf diseases classification. *Computers and Electronics in Agriculture, 172*, 105342. https://doi.org/https://doi.org/10.1016/j.compag.2020.105342

Khamparia, A., Bharati, S., Podder, P., Gupta, D., Khanna, A., Phung, T. K., & Thanh, D. N. H. (2021). Diagnosis of breast cancer based on modern mammography using hybrid transfer learning. *Multidimensional Systems and Signal Processing, 32*(2), 747–765.

Koshy, S. S., Sunnam, V. S., Rajgarhia, P., Chinnusamy, K., Ravulapalli, D. P., & Chunduri, S. (2018). Application of the internet of things (IoT) for smart farming: a case study on groundnut and castor pest and disease forewarning. *CSI Transactions on ICT*, *6*(3–4), 311–318.

Krizhevsky, A. (2014). *One weird trick for parallelizing convolutional neural networks*. http://arxiv.org/abs/1404.5997

Krizhevsky, A., Sutskever, I., & Hinton, G. E. (2012). Imagenet classification with deep convolutional neural networks. *Advances in Neural Information Processing Systems*, 1097–1105.

Kumar, V., Lehri, S., Sharma, A. K., Meena, P. D., & Kumar, A. (2016). Image based rapeseed-mustard disease expert system: An effective extension tool. *Indian Research Journal of Extension Education*, *8*(3), 10–13.

Larsson, G., Maire, M., & Shakhnarovich, G. (2016). Fractalnet: Ultra-deep neural networks without residuals. *ArXiv Preprint ArXiv:1605.07648*.

LeCun, Y., Bottou, L., Bengio, Y., & Haffner, P. (1998). Gradient-based learning applied to document recognition. *Proceedings of the IEEE*, *86*(11), 2278–2324.

LeCun, Y., Haffner, P., Bottou, L., & Bengio, Y. (1999). Object recognition with gradient-based learning. In *Shape, contour and grouping in computer vision* (pp. 319–345). Springer.

Liang, W., Zhang, H., Zhang, G., & Cao, H. (2019). Rice blast disease recognition using a deep convolutional neural network. *Scientific Reports*, *9*(1), 2869. https://doi.org/10.1038/s41598-019-38966-0

Lin, M., Chen, Q., & Yan, S. (2013). Network in network. *ArXiv Preprint ArXiv:1312.4400*.

Lu, J., Hu, J., Zhao, G., Mei, F., & Zhang, C. (2017). An in-field automatic wheat disease diagnosis system. *Computers and Electronics in Agriculture*, *142*, 369–379. https://doi.org/https://doi.org/10.1016/j.compag.2017.09.012

Lu, Y., Yi, S., Zeng, N., Liu, Y., & Zhang, Y. (2017). Identification of rice diseases using deep convolutional neural networks. *Neurocomputing*, *267*, 378–384.

Lv, M., Zhou, G., He, M., Chen, A., Zhang, W., & Hu, Y. (2020). Maize leaf disease identification based on feature enhancement and DMS-robust alexnet. *IEEE Access*, *8*, 57952–57966.

Majumder, A., Kumar, M., Nishad, D., Das, H., & Kumar, A. (2017). Composite index for cash crop production. *RASHI*, *2*(1), 98–100.

Mallah, C., Cope, J., & Orwell, J. (2013). Plant leaf classification using probabilistic integration of shape, texture and margin features. *Signal Processing, Pattern Recognition and Applications*, *5*(1), 45–54.

Michalski, R. T., & Chilauski, R. L. (1980). An experimental comparison of the two methods of knowledge acquisition in the context of developing an expert system for soybean disease diagnosis. *International Journal of Policy Analysis and Information Systems*, *4*(2), 125–161.

Mohanty, S. P., Hughes, D. P., & Salathé, M. (2016). Using deep learning for image-based plant disease detection. *Frontiers in Plant Science*, *7*(September). https://doi.org/10.3389/fpls.2016.01419

Myint, D., Gilani, S. A., Kawase, M., & Watanabe, K. N. (2020). Sustainable sesame (Sesamum indicum L.) production through improved technology: An overview of production, challenges, and opportunities in Myanmar. *Sustainability*, *12*(9), 3515.

Nagaraju, M., & Chawla, P. (2020). Systematic review of deep learning techniques in plant disease detection. *International Journal of System Assurance Engineering and Management*, 1–14.

Paliwal, N., Vanjani, P., Liu, J. W., Saini, S., & Sharma, A. (2019). Image processing-based intelligent robotic system for assistance of agricultural crops. *International Journal of Social and Humanistic Computing*, 3(2), 191. https://doi.org/10.1504/ijshc.2019.101602

Pallagani, V., Khandelwal, V., Chandra, B., Udutalapally, V., Das, D., & Mohanty, S. P. (2019). dCrop: A deep-learning based framework for accurate prediction of diseases of crops in smart agriculture. *2019 IEEE International Symposium on Smart Electronic Systems (ISES)(Formerly INiS)*, 29–33.

Pan, X., Zhang, S., Guo, W., Zhao, X., Chuang, Y., Chen, Y., & Zhang, H. (2019). Video-Based facial expression recognition using deep temporal–spatial networks. *IETE Technical Review*, 0(0), 1–8. https://doi.org/10.1080/02564602.2019.1645620

Picon, A., Alvarez-Gila, A., Seitz, M., Ortiz-Barredo, A., Echazarra, J., & Johannes, A. (2019). Deep convolutional neural networks for mobile capture device-based crop disease classification in the wild. *Computers and Electronics in Agriculture*, 161, 280–290.

Prajapati, B. S., Dabhi, V. K., & Prajapati, H. B. (2016). A survey on detection and classification of cotton leaf diseases. *2016 International Conference on Electrical, Electronics, and Optimization Techniques (ICEEOT)*, 2499–2506.

Prajapati, H. B., Shah, J. P., & Dabhi, V. K. (2017). Detection and classification of rice plant diseases. *Intelligent Decision Technologies*, 11(3), 357–373.

Rahman, C. R., Arko, P. S., Ali, M. E., Iqbal Khan, M. A., Apon, S. H., Nowrin, F., & Wasif, A. (2020). Identification and recognition of rice diseases and pests using convolutional neural networks. *Biosystems Engineering*, 194, 112–120. https://doi.org/https://doi.org/10.1016/j.biosystemseng.2020.03.020

Rai, S. K., Charak, D., & Bharat, R. (2016). Scenario of oilseed crops across the globe. *Plant Archives*, 16(1), 125–132.

Rani, P. M. N., Rajesh, T., & Saravanan, R. (2011). Expert systems in agriculture: a review. *Journal of Computer Science and Applications*, 3(1), 59–71.

Redmon, J., Divvala, S., Girshick, R., & Farhadi, A. (2016). You only look once: Unified, real-time object detection. *Proceedings of the IEEE Conference on Computer Vision and Pattern Recognition*, 779–788.

McCulloch, W. S., & Pitts, W. (1943). A logical calculus of the ideas immanent in nervous activity. *Bulletin of Mathematical Biophysics*, 5, 115–133.

Saini, S., & Sahula, V. (2021). A novel model based on Sequential adaptive memory for English--Hindi Translation. *Cognitive Computation and Systems*, 3(2), 142–153.

Sermanet, P., Eigen, D., Zhang, X., Mathieu, M., Fergus, R., & LeCun, Y. (2013). *OverFeat: Integrated Recognition, Localization and Detection using Convolutional Networks*. http://arxiv.org/abs/1312.6229

Shah, J. P., Prajapati, H. B., & Dabhi, V. K. (2016). A survey on detection and classification of rice plant diseases. *2016 IEEE International Conference on Current Trends in Advanced Computing (ICCTAC)*, 1–8.

Simonyan, K., & Zisserman, A. (2014). Very deep convolutional networks for large-scale image recognition. *ArXiv Preprint ArXiv:1409.1556*.

Singh, D., Jain, N., Jain, P., Kayal, P., Kumawat, S., & Batra, N. (2020). PlantDoc: a dataset for visual plant disease detection. In *Proceedings of the 7th ACM IKDD CoDS and 25th COMAD* (pp. 249–253).

Szegedy, C., Liu, W., Jia, Y., Sermanet, P., Reed, S., Anguelov, D., Erhan, D., Vanhoucke, V., & Rabinovich, A. (2015). Going deeper with convolutions. *Proceedings of the IEEE Conference on Computer Vision and Pattern Recognition*, 1–9.

Vaishnnave, M. P., Devi, K. S., & Ganeshkumar, P. (2020). Automatic method for classification of groundnut diseases using deep convolutional neural network. *SOFT COMPUTING*.

Veley, K. M., Berry, J. C., Fentress, S. J., Schachtman, D. P., Baxter, I., & Bart, R. (2017). High-throughput profiling and analysis of plant responses over time to abiotic stress. *Plant Direct*, *1*(4), e00023.

Wallelign, S., Polceanu, M., & Buche, C. (2018). Soybean plant disease identification using convolutional neural network. *The Thirty-First International Flairs Conference*.

Wallen, V. R., & Jackson, H. R. (1971). Aerial photography as a survey technique for the assessment of bacterial blight of field beans. *Canadian Plant Disease Survey*, *51*(4), 163–169.

Wang, X., Niu, S., & Wang, H. (2020). Image inpainting detection based on multi-task deep learning network. *IETE Technical Review*, *0*(0), 1–9. https://doi.org/10.1080/02564602.2020.1782274

Wiesner-Hanks, T., Stewart, E. L., Kaczmar, N., DeChant, C., Wu, H., Nelson, R. J., Lipson, H., & Gore, M. A. (2018). Image set for deep learning: Field images of maize annotated with disease symptoms. *BMC Research Notes*, *11*(1), 440.

Yadav, K., Lamba, A., Gupta, D., Gupta, A., Karmakar, P., & Saini, S. (2020). Bi-LSTM and ensemble based bilingual sentiment analysis for a code-mixed Hindi-English social media text. *2020 IEEE 17th India Council International Conference (INDICON)*, 1–6. https://doi.org/10.1109/INDICON49873.2020.9342241

Yadav, K., Lamba, A., Gupta, D., Gupta, A., Karmakar, P., & Saini, S. (2020). Bilingual sentiment analysis for a code-mixed Punjabi English social media text. *2020 5th International Conference on Computing, Communication and Security (ICCCS)*, 1–5.

Yadav, K., Yadav, M., & Saini, S. (2021). Stock values predictions using deep learning based hybrid models. *CAAI Transactions on Intelligence Technology*.

Yang, L., Luo, J., Wang, Z., Chen, Y., & Wu, C. (2019). Research on recognition for cotton spider mites' damage level based on deep learning. *International Journal of Agricultural and Biological Engineering*, *12*(6), 129–134.

Zeiler, M. D., & Fergus, R. (2014). Visualizing and understanding convolutional networks. *European Conference on Computer Vision*, 818–833.

Zhang, X, Qiao, Y., Meng, F., Fan, C., & Zhang, M. (2018). Identification of maize leaf diseases using improved deep convolutional neural networks. *IEEE Access*, *6*, 30370–30377.

Zhang, X., Qiao, Y., Meng, F., Fan, C., & Zhang, M. (2018). Identification of maize leaf diseases using improved deep convolutional neural networks. *IEEE Access*, *6*, 30370–30377.

Chapter 13

Cyber Threats to Farming Automation

Muskan Gupta

*School of Computer Science and Engineering, Vellore
Institute of Technology, Vellore, India*

B. K. Tripathy

*School of Information Technology and Engineering, Vellore
Institute of Technology, Vellore, India*

13.1 Introduction

According to the United Nations, the population of the world is forecast to cross 9 billion by the end of the year 2050, which is an increase of roughly one-third of the prevailing population. Such a substantial increase will lead to heavy demand in the food production rate, and the estimated demand is almost 130% of the current demand (Roser, 2020) (Godfray et al., 2010). This issue materializes into a need to increase food production as per the requirements under the present environment. A growing population has the curse of deforestation, leading to unfavourable variations in rain and use of other resources causing soil erosion, climate change, global warming, and imbalance in biodiversity. As a result, there arises a need for a revolutionary shift in the agricultural paradigm to keep up with the ever-growing population. Consequently, there is a need to increase crop and food production to assure sustainable development. This transition can be made possible with the help of artificial intelligence (AI), the Internet of Things (IoT), and other cloud technologies (Alreshidi, 2019).

As we know, with digitization comes digital threats. A cultivated agro-terrorism attack on a huge exporting nation such as the US could affect the health of billions of users around the globe. Moreover, such attacks would make people diffident on domestic utilization and ruin the United States footing as an entrusted food exporter. The Council of Economic Advisers published a report in 2018 called "The Cost of Malicious Cyber Activity to the U.S. Economy", in which the agriculture industry was seen as one of the 16 condemnatory industries essential for taking care of both the economy and security of a nation. This shows the importance of cybersecurity in agriculture as an industry of enormous importance to any nation.

So, there is a strong need to understand more about this uprising dependence on the field of digitization. This chapter discusses the following aspects:

- Understanding what farm automation is.
- Learning the basic model of security.
- A detailed elaboration on the probable cyber threats that are seen in farm automation.
- Some use cases for actions taken against these threats to provide a clear understanding from the readers about the process for further exploration in the field.
- Finally, we discuss the future of AI applications in cybersecurity.

13.2 Farming Automation

Farming automation technologies call for an amalgamation of technology-oriented applications and data-oriented agricultural applications to expand efficiency by increasing crop production and the quality of food commodities. There are a number of smart farming use cases that comprehensively indicate the impact these recent practices can have (Vasisht et al., 2017) (Kamilaris et al., 2016) (Wolfert et al., 2017). For example, in India, data collected from farms was used to prevent and predict diseases found in a crop, which resulted in a reduction in the danger associated with the shortfall of crop production (Oerke & Dehne, 2004). Similarly, in Chile, sensors in the soil were used to measure the required irrigation needs in Chile, which as a result has decreased the amount of water consumption in farming by 70%. Smart farming (Alvino & Marino, 2017), however, is not just about primary fabrication. In fact, it also comprises the complete food supply chain (Srividya & Tripathy, 2021), which is impacted by utilizing big data analytics (Tripathy & Dutta, 2018) (Srividya & Tripathy, 2021) to gather useful derivatives regarding the farming process by fostering real-time operational decision-making and remodelling present agriculture business models (Zion & Tripathy, 2020). Smart farming improves on traditional farming methods by introducing automation devices and on-field smart sensors. Smart farming has revolutionized not only primary products but also the complete food supply industry by providing data analytics for inferring crucial information about the whole process (Walter et al., 2017). These devices and sensors work harmoniously to come up with a well-planned farming experience, as well as an enhanced crop yield. Now we have understood that farm automation is an adaptable technological change, we must understand what the security aspects involved with it are.

13.3 Security in Farm Automation

Cybercrime is one of the biggest threats to have continuously evolved over the years. If we talk about the damages caused by cybercrime, reports have suggested that it has increased from $250 billion to $400 billion in the past two years (Barreto & Amaral, 2018). This is why cybersecurity is essential to ensure the security and safety of any organization.

Agricultural cybersecurity is a swelling concern, as with technological advancement, farming is becoming more dependent on Internet access than it ever was. In the course of the past few years, the agrotechnology community has been tailored to the issue, and a momentous amount of research has been focused on it. But to understand what threats are posed, we must understand the basic pillars of security, i.e., the CIA model (Bogaardt et al., 2016).

The CIA triad model (see Figure 13.1) was drafted to usher in policies for security in any organization. The three components of CIA are confidentiality, integrity, and availability.

We discuss these three concepts in detail in the subsections to follow.

Figure 13.1 The triad model

13.3.1 Confidentiality

Confidentiality means that sensitive information should be available only to legitimate individuals and systems. A wide variety of techniques and tools are used by attackers to get access to the sensitive data of users. One of the earliest suggested approaches for preventing this is with the use of encryption techniques to preserve user data so that even if the attacker gains access to one's data, it cannot be deciphered. The Advanced Encryption Standard (AES) and Data Encryption Standard (DES) are seen as the leading encryption standards in the market (Figure 13.2).

Let's assume Ankit wants to transmit data to Ankita while maintaining confidentiality. Remember that with every encryption algorithm, a key is associated to encrypt and decipher it. So, while sending the data, it is processed using the organization's choice of encryption algorithm to produce an encrypted message " 'E", which is sent to Ankita. Now, during the transaction, if an attacker peeks into the network and accesses message "E", it will be of no use as the key used for encryption is unknown to him.

It may be noted that the efficiency of guessing a key depends on its size. For example, for 256-bit AES, there are 2^{256} different AES keys, which makes it nearly impossible to guess, thus ensuring that the data is safe.

13.3.2 Integrity

By integrity, we mean that the transmitted data should reach the destination as is, without any changes. It is a standard practice to use a hash function to inspect whether the data is altered or not. The two typical types of hash function used are Message Digest 5 (MD5) and Secure Hash Algorithm (SHA).

Let's assume Ankit wants to send data to Ankita while maintaining integrity. A hash function is applied over the data that generates a random hash value HS, which is then combined with the data and transmitted (Figure 13.3). When Ankita receives the data, she can use the identical hash function over the received data, which, let's say, gives the hash value HR. Now, if HS ≠ HR, then it can be concluded that the integrity of data has been compromised.

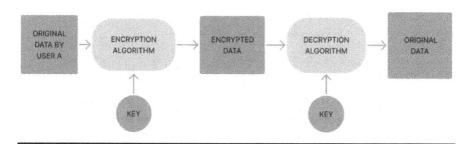

Figure 13.2 The basic cryptography system

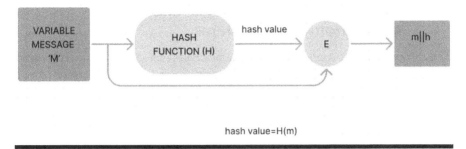

Figure 13.3 Hashing architecture

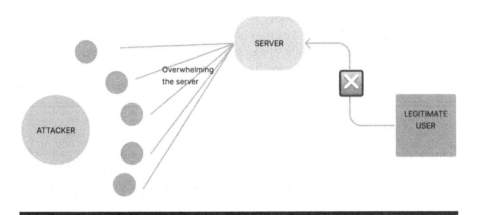

Figure 13.4 Non-availability of resource to user

RFC 1321 outlines the details of MD5. It takes messages of any length and generates a 128-bit output message called the fingerprint or message digest. It is an extension of MD4 and is slower but more conservative and complex.

13.3.3 Availability

Availability infers that the data present in the server or at the organization should be instantly accessible to legitimate users. Attacks such as denial-of-service (DoS) or distributed denial-of-service (DDoS) can make the resource available exhausted. These attacks have a severe impact on organizations and users who depend on the network as an operations tool. To furnish availability, network administrators are advised to upgrade regularly, have a plan for a flounder, maintain hardware, and prevent bottlenecks in a network (Figure 13.4).

13.4 Types of Cyber Threat in Farming Automation-Based Systems

This section elaborates on probable cyberattack types in a smart farming ecosystem. Cyber threats can be classified into two different classes, as shown in Figure 13.5.

13.4.1 Data Attacks

Data is basically any set of characters accumulated in order to retrieve information. However, data is subjective to the person who uses it. For example, if in a class, a teacher gives an assignment and we assume there are two types of students, one who referenced books to do the assignment (category A) and one (category B) who used the assignment done by category A to do their assignment. For category A, books serve as the data, while for category B, the assignment done by category A is the data. Therefore, ownership of data is a conflicted debate. However, according to the standards, ownership rights are either given to individuals or teams who have the right to access, edit, and decide on the usage of data. Therefore, possession of data by any unauthorized user or use of data with malicious intent can be termed a data attack.

The major categories of data attack include:

13.4.1.1 Ill-Intentioned Employee Data Leakage

Ill-intentioned employee data leakage is when an insider (employee) intends to deface her or his organization knowingly. This is often referred to as data exfiltration. Farmers deplore the exposure of confidential data above any other threat as it can be used against them in the produce and sale market.

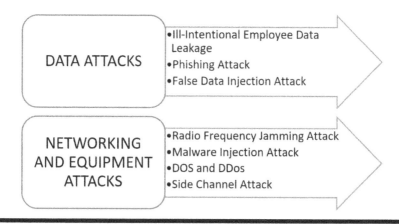

Figure 13.5   Types of cyberattack

This can be ruled out or detected in the early stages if the organization makes investments in security policies to create warning banners or the preemptive detection of such potential security breaches and threats to the organization's data.

13.4.1.2 Phishing Attack

A phishing attack involves the sending of fraudulent or fake communications to people that appear to be from an acclaimed source. For example, an attacker can send a mail with the mail ID miccrosoft.com, which is similar to microsoft.com, in order to confuse its receiver (Vignesh et al., 2013). The attack is usually made by email but can be done using other mediums such as SMS and WhatsApp. Phishing attacks can be categorized as the following:

Spear Phishing

Spear phishing involves scouting particular individuals instead of a large fraction of people. The process involves studying the targets using social media, such as Instagram, Facebook, or other platforms like bank logins, etc., so that the attack can be personalized to the victim to make it look credible and efficient. Often, this is a beginning step for initiating a targeted attack against large companies and organizations.

Deceptive Phishing

This is one of the most prevalent types of phishing attacks and involves sending a fake message or email that usually asks the recipient to click on an attachment or link present in the message.

Pharming

Pharming is a technique that involves an attacker directing a user to a bogus website. In this case, the user does not click the malevolent link on their own, but instead, the attacker blitzes the website's servers or targeted victim's computer to re-direct the user to a hoaxed site even when the accurate link is used.

Whaling

When attackers go after the high-level executives of an organization or company (such as the CEO or president of the company), this is called whaling. A lot of research is involved in this type of attack as hackers have to plan the moment of attack very meticulously. If a whaling attack is successful, it can be ruinous for the victims as high-level executives have access to a large amount of sensitive information.

Evil Twin Phishing

This attack involves attackers creating a Wi-Fi hotspot that appears legitimate and may even use a trusted SSID. When users connect to the Wi-Fi, the attacker can look into the user's network and access any account names, passwords, documents they might be viewing, etc.

Clone Phishing

This is where the hacker clones or replicates an email that has already been opened by a user. The links or attachments in the email are superseded with bogus ones and the attacker then usually lures the user in by quoting an issue with the earlier message and asks them to click on the link or download the attachment again to launch their attack.

The main goal of such attacks is to pilfer or access sensitive data such as debit cards and login details or to install malware on the end user's machine.

13.4.1.3 False Data Injection Attack

A false data injection is an attack associated with compromising data integrity where an attacker (unauthorized user) attempts to modify data that commits to important real-time arrangements. For example, if a malicious user changes the data about the soil moisture level present in the database, the analysis of the necessary watering requirement will change and, in turn, could lead to damaged crops.

13.4.2 Networking and Equipment Attacks

Networking and equipment attacks relate to connected computing appliances (e.g., laptops, smartphones, servers, and tablets) and an ever-increasing array of IoT devices (e.g., cameras, thermostats, audio/visual systems, and various sensors) that communicate with one another. The exploitation of these devices or connections is termed a networking and equipment attack.

Some examples of these attacks include:

13.4.2.1 Radio Frequency Jamming Attack

Reliance on frequency communication, such as for satellite networks, has increased drastically over the years. As far as smart farming tools are concerned, the global navigation satellite system (GNSS) is utilized to enhance the capability of products and methods such as spray rates, automatic steering, and path planning in fields. The GNSS is compassed by combining GPS with real-time kinematics technology to improve the accuracy of instantaneous locus data. This advancement has led to an increase in opportunity for attackers to block the GNSS for malevolent purposes by embedding numerous distributed low power jammers to malfunction the operation of the GNSS over broad regions and, in turn, preclude smart farming devices from operating correctly (Laajalahti & Nikander, 2017).

13.4.2.2 Malware Injection Attack

A malware injection attack cultivates through an organization's system spontaneously, which makes it an attractive target for attackers (Gruschka & Jensen, 2010; Bharati et al., 2021; Podder et al., 2021). Typically, the majority of farm arrangements wield identical software components. As a result, malware that affects a certain smart farm will most certainly affect other farms with parallel deployments. Such attacks can rapine information regarding the utilization of agricultural mediums, purchase information about livestock, vegetables and other commodities, data about agro apparatus, and so on. It can also be used in harmony with smart devices such as botnets, which can be used to perform malevolent attacks administered by a hacker. Additionally, it can be used to obstruct the operation of physical smart devices, which, in return, can have a cataclysmic impact on a certain harvest or agricultural field.

13.4.2.3 Denial-of-Service Attack

A denial-of-service (DoS) attack is an attack where the attacker aims to render a computer or other devices such as sensors unavailable to users by disturbing the normal workings of the device. Its basic intention is not to let users access the required resource. There are essentially three kinds of DoS attack: flood attacks, logic attacks, and distributed DoS (DDoS) attacks (Koliaset et al., 2017) (Antenakakis et al., 2017).

Flood Attack

A flood attack is based upon a simplified notion where the attackers dispatch an enormous amount of requests that cannot be performed by a server of an organization. This continues until the server gets hooked and surrenders to the attack because it can regain functionality only after the attack is stopped (Laajalahti & Nikander, 2017). These attacks are frequent because execution is easy. There are different types of flood attacks, which include:

- **Ping flooding**: In this type of attack, the marked servers are gushed with ICMP echo request,s which results in increased utilization of bandwidth, which gradually stops or slow the server's operations.
- **SYN flood**: In this type of attack, SYN requests are transmitted constantly by the attackers, which the marked server is ultimately bound to accept. The server generally crashes or slows down because these attacks involve the trading of acknowledgement and synchronization messages.

- **Smurf attack**: In this attack, ping messages are pinged to the broadcast IP addresses, and if there is a reply from the marked server or machine then the attack expands to a larger range of servers. This problem is less common due to improvements in modern routers.
- **UDP attack**: In this kind of attack, a large volume of UDP packets are transmitted to the marked servers, which in turn prevents authorized users from gaining access to the server.

Logic attacks

This type of intrusion method is quite distinct from flood attacks. Logic attacks involve a hacker taking advantage of unusual traffic and security holes in a system. These attacks basically prey on the weakness of the network.

DDoS Attack

In this type of attack, the intention of the attacker is to try and create disruption in the normal traffic of a targeted server, service, or network by deliberately increasing the traffic around the target through some infrastructure. This involves a combination of both logic and flood attacks. In this case, there are numerous attackers that attack the server or machine as a harmonized assault.

13.4.2.4 Side-Channel Attack

Smart farming is a use case of IoT. Thus, it is open to a few customary IoT vulnerabilities that include side-channel attacks. These attacks aim to gain details on how a system was executed rather than beguiling the vulnerability of a system. In such attacks, different channels are abused by attackers to their advantage, such as timing channels (TCs). TC exploits can be made on NoCs in accelerators or between accelerators and their caches – basically at any place where an attacker can attach itself and try to collect useful information. Another viable category of attack channel includes hardware glitching in the configuration of differences in voltage changes and system clock periods at the time of implementation of tasks. Other channels to launch an attack on include electromagnetic leakage or even sound and acoustic channels (Ukil et al., 2011).

13.5 Artificial Intelligence and Machine Learning-Based Cybersecurity Use Cases

Conventional ways of dealing with cybersecurity are gradually failing as the complexity and volume of cyberattacks increases. Attackers are now using clever and unhackneyed methods to detour controls and access firewalls to compromise supremely secure systems. One of the ways to avert such attacks is to be prepared for them in advance (Shabadi & Biradar, 2018)

AI and machine learning can help in staying ahead of posed cyber threats. The use of these technologies can help expand the purview of solutions for current cybersecurity threats. By just organizing criminal intellect without the use of thousands of research papers, AI can help drastically reduce response time. In addition, it can also enhance security in case of bogus activity or detection of a cyber-related crime (Kempenaar et al., 2016).

13.5.1 User Behaviour Modelling

Research has shown that a security attack on any business system can encourage the users in a company to have knowledge of their private authentication credentials without the user's insight. As a result, it is very difficult for anyone to prevent a cyberattack where the attacker uses a client's accreditations as the attackers have accessed the system by using legitimate resources. Therefore, AI-rooted risk management systems can be used in order to detect variations in the methodology that are not significant to the human eye, which in turn will help to sort out the password patterns of customer or user behaviour. In doing so, the system will help in detection by sending an alert to the corresponding cybersecurity team when the pattern fails, and the attacker can be stopped from causing any further damage (Bharadwa, 2019).

Darktrace, a groundbreaking AI vendor, has released cybersecurity software that utilizes machine learning to analyse network traffic to derive the standard behaviour of devices and users present in an organization (Figure 13.6). The software basically has the ability to detect any notable aberration in a user's standard behaviour, which in turn helps in alerting the company about a cybercrime.

Figure 13.6   Darktrace logo

13.5.2 Network Threat Identification

Network security is a crucial facet of security for any organization or business. The most arduous aspect of developing a noteworthy cybersecurity network process is the assimilation of various outlooks muddled in topology (network). In human terms, it would take a huge amount of time for professionals to handle all the information accumulated by the network of an organization (Shenfield et al., 2018).

Deciding whether the web application or platform under testing or development is bogus or not is one of the most crucial judgments cybersecurity professionals have to make. When extended to large-scale system networks, a lot of time is needed to determine which apps are malignant from the thousands of similar programs, given that human work is subject to error. As such, an AI-powered network security system can not only help with accuracy but also improve the time required to monitor all incoming and outgoing requests to detect any dubious patterns in network traffic.

Versive offered an AI-based cybersecurity software that utilizes dissonant identification to observe if an anomaly in data is a threat to an organization or not (Figure 13.7). The network is monitored using anomaly detection software which generates a distress signal to warn the authorities in case of a disparity in data. Discrepancies are detected based on similar cyber threat events that the organization defines.

Versive, which is now owned by eSentire, offers software called Versive Security Engine that provides enterprise-level cybersecurity that mainly focuses on studying all transactions and protects confidential data using machine learning.

13.5.3 Email Monitoring

To avoid attacks such as phishing, we must understand that monitoring emails is important because no matter how cautious a person is, even a slight error can be really detrimental to an enterprise (Dada et al., 2019). Therefore, using ML-powered monitoring software can not only help increase the speed of identification of cyber threats but also increase the accuracy of their detection (Nimodia & Asole, 2013).

Some software makes use of natural language processing (NLP) in order to understand messages, using incoming and outgoing emails to detect patterns or expressions linked with phishing efforts. In other cases, the software even uses email

Figure 13.7 **Versive logo**

Figure 13.8 Tessian logo

to see other emails, to verify if the email comprises any features that may pose any danger, such as videos of a certain size.

Tessian offers email monitoring using AI-based technology that aims to protect financial institutions such as banks from cybercrimes like phishing, data breaches, and misdirected emails. The software is based on anomaly detection and NLP at different stages to identify which emails pose threats to the affiliated system (Figure 13.8).

13.6 Future of Artificial Intelligence in Cybersecurity

The involvement of AI in cybersecurity can be seen as the start of a new era in the industry. Organizations want to be confident they will be prepared in advance with the feedback of cybersecurity specialists in order to keep the data associated with them confidential and secure, as this not only builds the reputation of the company but also helps in sustaining it (Jha et al., 2019).

The main aspect to understand is that these systems are only as effective as the data they are equipped with. Because AI-powered systems are based on "garbage in, garbage out", they require a data-oriented mechanism to handle any journey to show constant success. Once this standard behaviour is set, any AI-based algorithm can give an alert about any intrusion with the best possible accuracy rate (Munoz, 2021).

Uncertainty has become a common word in modern-day datasets. As a result, plenty of uncertainty-based models have appeared. In order to handle such situations in determining high yielding seeds for better production and more security, some technology has been obtained in Stafford (2019) and Sooraj and Tripathy (2018a). Optimization has become a technique such that one can have more profits and less cost in yielding (Shaha & Tripathy, 2018). Keeping this in mind, and following the seed to be secured in farming, some such techniques have been obtained in Gia et al. (2019), Sooraj & Tripathy (2018b) and Mohanty & Tripathy (2021).

13.7 Conclusion

The burgeoning world of smart technology equipped with communication and sensing capabilities has made many services available and also increased the efficiency and effectiveness of various tasks for mankind. Not so long ago, farming was not digitized, and digitization was required for better efficiency. However, the worldwide use of Internet-regulated gadgets and data-driven applications across different sectors have raised issues of security, making the gadgets vulnerable to cyber threats. Cyber threats are a general phenomenon in various fields. Thus, cyber threats have become an issue in farming automation along with its digitization. In this chapter, we discussed cybersecurity challenges in smart farming. We proposed some directions of research to enrich the field further. It is hoped that our efforts in this chapter will stimulate researchers to solve the envisaged problems. The research that has been done so far has not been able to satisfy the requirements of the present scenario. Therefore, further research will definitely handle data security issues in the exponentially expanding and economically crucial smart farming industry.

References

Abuan, D. D., Abad, A. C., Lazaro, J. B., & Dadios, E. P. (2014). Security systems for remote farm, *Journal of Automation and Control Engineering*, 2(2), 115–118.

Alreshidi, E. (2019). Smart sustainable agriculture (SSA) solution underpinned by internet of things (IoT) and artificial intelligence (AI). *arXiv preprint* arXiv:1906.03106

Alvino, A., & Marino, S. (2017). Remote sensing for irrigation of horticultural crops. *Horticulturae*, 3(2), 40.

Antonakakis, M., April, T., Bailey, M., Bernhard, M., Bursztein, E., Cochran, J., Durumeric, Z., Halderman, J. A., Invernizzi, L., & Kallitsis, M. (2017). Understanding the Mirai botnet, in: Proceedings of *26th USENIX security symposium (USENIX Security 17)*, pp. 1093–1110.

Barreto, L., & Amaral, A. (2018, September). Smart farming: Cyber security challenges. In: *2018 International Conference on Intelligent Systems (IS)*. IEEE, pp. 870–876.

Bharadwa, R. (2019). Artificial intelligence in cybersecurity – Current use-cases and capabilities. https://emerj.com/ai-sector-overviews/artificial-intelligence-cybersecurity/

Bharati, S., Podder, P., Mondal, M., & Paul, P. K. (2021). Applications and challenges of cloud integrated IoMT. In *Cognitive Internet of Medical Things for Smart Healthcare* (pp. 67–85). Cham: Springer.

Bogaardt, M. J., Poppe, K. J., Viool, V., & Zuidam, E. V. (2016). Cybersecurity in the Agrifood sector- Securing data as crucial asset for agriculture. *Capgemini Consulting*.

Chi, H., Welch, S., Vasserman, E., & Kalaimannan, E. (2017). A framework of cybersecurity approaches in precision agriculture. In: *Proceedings of the ICMLG2017 5th International Conference on Management Leadership and Governance*. Reading, UK: Acad. Conf. Publ. Int., pp. 90–95.

Dada, E. G., Bassi, J. S., Chiroma, H., Abdulhamid, S. M., Adetunmbi, A. O., & Ajibuwa, O. E. (2019). Machine learning for email spam filtering: review, approaches and open research problems, *Heliyon*, 5(6), e01802.

Gia, T. N., Qingqing, L., Queralta, J. P., Zou, Z., Tenhunen, H., & Westerlund, T. (2019). Edge AI in smart farming IoT: CNNs at the edge and fog computing with LoRa. In: Proceedings of *2019 IEEE AFRICON*, pp. 1–6.

Godfray, H. C. J., Beddington, J. R., Crute, I. R., Haddad, L., Lawrence, D., Muir, J. F., Pretty, J., Robinson, S., Thomas, S. M., & Toulmin, C. (2010). Food security: The challenge of feeding 9 billion people, *Science*, 327(5967), 812–818.

Gollin, D., Parente, S., & Rogerson, R. (2002). The role of agriculture in development, *American Economic Review*, 92(2), 160–164.

Gruschka, N., & Jensen, M. (2010). Attack surfaces: A taxonomy for attacks on cloud services. In: Proceedings of *IEEE 3rd international conference on cloud computing*, pp. 276–279.

Jha, K., Doshi, A., Patel, P., & Shah, M. (2019). A comprehensive review on automation in agriculture using artificial intelligence. *Artificial Intelligence in Agriculture*, 2(1), 1–12.

Kamilaris, A., Gao, F., Prenafeta-Boldu, F. X., & Ali, M. I. (2016). Agri-IoT: A semantic framework for Internet of Things-enabled smart farming applications. In: Proceedings of *IEEE 3rd World Forum Internet Things (WF-IoT)*, pp. 442–447.

Kempenaar, C., Lokhorst, C., Bleumer, E., Veerkamp, R., Been, T., Evert, F. V., Boogaardt, M., Ge, L., Wolfert, J., & Verdouw, C. (2016). *Big data analysis for smart farming: Results of TO2 project in theme food security*, Tech. Rep. (Vol. 655), Wageningen University & Research, The Netherlands.

Kolias, C., Kambourakis, G., Stavrou, A., & Voas, J. (2017). DDoS in the IoT: Mirai and other botnets, *Computer*, 50(7), 80–84.

Laajalahti, M., & Nikander, J. (2017). Alkutuotannon kyberuhat [Cybersecurity threats in agricultural primary production). Research report 30/2017, Natural Resources Institute Finland.

Mohanty, R. K., & Tripathy, B. K. (2021). Recommending turmeric variety for higher production using interval-valued fuzzy soft set model and PSO. *International Journal of Swarm Intelligence Research(IJSIR)*, IGI Global Publications, 12(2), 94–110.

Munoz, M. J. (2021). AI in agriculture: Is the grass greener?, California Review Management, Vol. 63(4).

Nimodia, C., & Asole, S. (2013). Email based LAN monitoring system, *International Journal of Scientific & Engineering Research*, 4(12), 342–346.

Oerke, E. C., & Dehne, H. W. (2004). Safeguarding production—Losses in major crops and the role of crop protection, *Crop Protection*, 23(4), 275–285.

Podder, P., Mondal, M., Bharati, S., & Paul, P. K. (2021). Review on the security threats of internet of things. arXiv:2101.05614.

Roser, M. (2020). Future population growth. *Our world in data*. Available: https://ourworldindata.org/future-population-growth

Seetha, H., Murthy, M. K., & Tripathy, B. K. (Eds.) (2017). *Modern Technologies for Big Data Classification and Clustering*, IGI Global.

Shabadi, L. S., & Biradar, H. B. (2008). Design and implementation of IOT based smart security and monitoring for connected smart farming, *International Journal of Computer Applications*, 975(8887).

Shaha, A., & Tripathy, B. K. (2018). Optimizing target oriented network intelligence collection for the social web by using k-beam search. In: *Soft Computing for Problem Solving (SocProS 2018)*. Springer, Singapore, pp. 135–144.

Shenfield, A., Day, D., & Ayesh, A.(2018). Intelligent intrusion detection systems using artificial neural networks, *ICT Express*, 4(2), 95–99.

Sooraj, T. R., & Tripathy, B. K. (2018a). An interval valued fuzzy soft set based optimization algorithm for high yielding seed selection, *International Journal of Fuzzy System Applications*, 7(2), 44–61. https://doi.org/10.4018/IJFSA.2018040102

Sooraj, T. R., & Tripathy, B. K. (2018b). Optimization of seed selection for higher product using interval valued hesitant fuzzy soft sets, *Songklanakarin Journal of Science and Technology (SJST)*, 40 (5), 1125–1135.

Srividya, V., & Tripathy, B. K. (2021). Role of Big data in supply chain management, Accepted for publication in *SCM-DA2021 Springer book-Innovative Supply Chain Management via Digitalization and Artificial Intelligence*, (Eds: Kumaresan et al.).

Stafford, J. V. (2019). Precision agriculture '19. *Wageningen*, The Netherlands: Academic Press.

Tripathy, B. K., & Dutta D. (2018). Trustworthiness in the Social internet of Things (SIoT), In: *Big Data Analytics: A social network approach*, Taylor and Francis Publisher, CRC Press, Eds: M. Panda, A. E. Hassanien and A. Abraham), Chapter- 11 pp. 231–248.

Ukil, A., Sen, J., & Koilakonda, S. (2011). Embedded security for Internet of Things. In: *2011 2nd National Conference on Emerging Trends and Applications in Computer Science*, IEEE, pp. 1–6.

United States Department of Justice. (2021). www.justice.gov/opa/pr/tennessee-man-sentenced-unauthorized-access-former-employers-networks

Vasisht, D., Kapetanovic, Z., Won, J., Jin, X., Chandra, R., Sinha, S., Kapoor, A., Sudarshan, M., & Stratman, S. (2017). Farmbeats: An IoT platform for data-driven agriculture. In: Proceedings of *14th USENIX, Symposium on Networked Systems Design and Implementation (NSDI 17)*, pp. 515–529.

Vignesh, M., Gokul Ram, T., Akhil. R., Rajesh Kumar N. S. R., & Karthikeyan. R. (2013). Analysis of phishing in networks. *International Journal of Scientific & Engineering Research*, 4(9), 196.

Walter, A., Finger, R., Huber, R., & Buchmann, N. (2017). Opinion: Smart farming is key to developing sustainable agriculture, *Proceedings of the National Academy of Sciences*, 114(24), 6148–6150.

Wolfert, S., Ge, L., Verdouw, C., & Bogaardt, M. J. (2017). Big data in smart farming-A review, *Agricultural Systems*, 153(1), 69–80.

Zion, G. D., & Tripathy, B K. (2020). Comparative analysis of tools for big data visualization and challenges. In: Anouncia S., Gohel H., Vairamuthu S. (Eds.), *Data Visualization*, Springer, Singapore, pp. 33–52.

Chapter 14

Prospects of Smart Farming as a Key to Sustainable Agricultural Development: A Case Study of India

Bhabesh Deka

North Bengal Regional Research and Development Centre,
Nagrakata, India

Chittaranjan Baruah

Postgraduate Department of Zoology, Darrang College
(affiliated to Gauhati University), Tezpur, India

14.1 Introduction

Technology has always played an important part in the development of our nation's businesses, and this is also true in the agricultural industry. The agricultural industry is reaping substantial benefits from a variety of new and developing modern technologies. In the manufacturing sector, technology is having a beneficial impact on everything from flying drones to artificial intelligence (AI). Every stage of the agricultural process, from the field to the very end (i.e., after harvesting), is now dependent on technological advances. It is becoming clearer that the world is transitioning to a

DOI: 10.1201/9781003299059-14

digital economy, and the pandemic has brought this to light. Due to the improved efficiency and transparency brought about by the move to digitization in almost every area of the economy, it was only a matter of time until the agriculture business began to experience the same benefits.

When it comes to the use of technology in agriculture, the terms precision farming and smart farming are often used interchangeably. The first phase involves developing cutting-edge production and management systems that make significant and efficient use of data about a specific area and crop. Farming 4.0, often known as smart farming, is a digitalization idea that entails using data and information technology to improve the efficiency of complex agricultural processes. Planting may be customized to a specific region via the use of a combination of smart agricultural equipment and current data integration technologies, resulting in a more efficient and transparent agricultural production process. Agricultural producers may make informed decisions based on reliable data due to the use of information technology. Individuals may get precise answers and detailed information that is instantly relevant, as opposed to a general policy overview given by the federal or state governments. Several steps in the planting process may be omitted altogether.

According to the AI evaluation conducted by the National Institution for Transforming India (NITI Aayog), agriculture must increase at a rate of 4% or higher to maintain an annual growth rate of 8–10% a year. It's difficult to emphasize the importance of digitalization in attaining this level of success and achievement. Instances of how technology is being used include automated monitoring of pasture-based free-range animals, sensor-assisted digital soil assessment, and targeted management of agricultural equipment, to name a few examples (Escriba et al., 2020). Modern agricultural practices should allow for the management of spatial and temporal variability inside as well as across land plots. Agriculture, produce and agricultural product management, logistics, mandis, and retail sellers are all making use of digitization, citing the benefits of reduced agri-waste and cost savings as justification. In the agriculture industry's digitization foundation, nanotechnology, the Internet of Things (IoT), and digital education are the three most important elements to consider.

Due to the government's and corporate sector's awareness of the industry's potential, many new initiatives are being developed. The following are some examples.

Microsoft, in cooperation with the International Crops Research Institute for the Semi-Arid Tropics (ICRISAT), created the AI Sowing App to assist farmers in the field. Farmers can use this software to identify the optimum time to plant seeds based on weather conditions. Farmers are under no obligation to install sensors or make any other investments in their crops.

The NITI Aayog has collaborated with IBM to create an AI-powered crop production forecast model that would give farmers real-time data and advice. Farming practices such as crop production, soil quality management, agricultural input management, and disease outbreak identification are all made easier by IBM's AI predictive insights model. Data will be gathered from various sources, including the Indian Space Research Organization (ISRO), the current soil health card database, the India Meteorological Department (IMD) weather prediction, and crop phenology, among others, to give farmers accurate and timely guidance. The project is being carried out in 10 "aspirational districts" in Bihar, Jharkhand, Madhya Pradesh, Uttar Pradesh, Maharashtra, Rajasthan, and Assam, as well as in other states.

The Blue River Project has developed and integrated computer vision and machine learning technologies to assist farmers in reducing fertilizer and herbicide usage by spraying only where and when necessary, thus maximizing the use of agricultural inputs, which is the primary goal of precision farming.

The government is also pushing individuals to use digital devices, which includes recent app initiatives such as Kisan Suvidha, mKisan, Farm-o-Pedia, Pusa Krishi, AgriMarket, Shetkari Masik, and Crop Insurance, etc. It is the simplicity of use, accessibility, familiarity, acceptability, and popularisation of the benefits that farmers who are fast to learn and understand the advantages would want the most. Agriculturalists are the last link in the technological chain. The government should spend time and money on spreading the benefits of digitalization. The private sector should band together, and India's best software companies can assist.

The National e-Governance Plan in Agriculture (NeGPA) intends to accelerate India's growth by utilizing information and communication technology to provide farmers with timely access to agriculture-related data. It was launched in seven pilot states in India in 2010–2011 as part of the Centrally Sponsored Scheme for Agriculture. The proposal was expanded in 2014–2015 to include the remaining states, as well as two union territories. The program has been extended to March 31, 2021, from its original expiration date of March 31, 2020 (Figure 14.1).

As part of phase 2 of the project, states were granted funds to carry out operations such as office site preparation for hardware installation and the establishment of computer training labs, as well as hardware and system software acquisition, installation, and accounting. Backup power plans are being created in every situation where feasible. Building State Project Management Units (SPMUs) and recruiting personnel, as well as connecting to hardware installation sites and digitizing data, are all priorities for the government right now. It is necessary to customize the application to satisfy the criteria of each state. In recognition of the importance of new digital and emerging technologies, the Committee on Doubling Farmers' Income (DFI) has recommended that the Indian government's digital agricultural operations be expanded and developed further in recognition of the importance of new digital and developing technologies. Remote sensing, geographic information systems, data analytics, and cloud computing are among the topics covered, as are AI and machine learning, the IoT, robotics, drones, sensors, and the blockchain.

It was decided in 2020–2021 that the NeGPA criteria would be modified, and money would be made available for approving projects for modifying and transferring online and mobile apps previously created by states to a platform that would

Figure 14.1 **Agriculture's National e-Governance Plan (NeGPA) towards a digital agriculture mission**

Source: Photo courtesy of http://breakthrough.unglobalcompact.org/disruptive-technologies/digital-agriculture/

be built utilizing digital and emerging technologies. Other states have shown an interest in putting the new legislation into effect, and some governments have authorized pilot programs to try out new technology in the meantime. These services include precision farming, crop guidance, smart cards for farmers to help with e-government, crop insurance, agricultural subsidy awards, compensation claims resolution, community/village resource centres, and other related services. The database will be made public once the data of 43 million farmers linked to land records has been verified.

Chapter highlights:

■ Use of smart farming tools in the future of agriculture.
■ Technological advancements in climate-smart agriculture (CSA) in India.
■ Evolution of cutting-edge technologies that are revolutionizing the agriculture industry in India, such as:
    ■ use of drones for agriculture;
    ■ AI and information technology;
    ■ agricultural mechanization;
    ■ agriculture financing technology (AgriFin);
    ■ technology for post-harvesting;
    ■ animal agriculture with insight;

- food and agriculture nanotechnology;
- nanotechnology-based smart pesticide formulations;
- microbe-based climate-smart agriculture;
- agriculture smart water management platform;
- using high-efficiency sun drying for smart agriculture;
- cloud-based platforms and Internet of Things (IoT) in agriculture;
- smart multi-sensor platforms in agriculture support for analysis and social decisions;
- IoT benefits in the agricultural sector; and
- smart farming's prospects and challenges.

14.2 Smart Farming Tools for Future of Agriculture

Smart farming refers to the application of modern information and communication technologies in agriculture, including robotics, the IoT, big data, precision equipment, actuators and sensors, unmanned aerial vehicles (UAVs), drones, and geo-positioning systems (Figure 14.2).

14.3 Technological Advancements

This operation makes use of sensors, communication networks, unmanned aerial systems, AI, robots, and other complex gear, as well as IoT concepts. Agricultural value is added by each of them, from data collection to management and processing, as well as counselling and guidance. Using this integrated system, people can gain

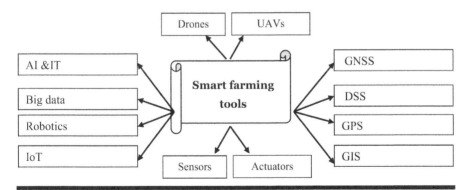

Figure 14.2 **Schematic diagram showing the prospects of applications of smart farming tools in the Indian agriculture system, unmanned aerial vehicles (UAVs), Internet of Things (IoT), decision support systems (DSS), artificial intelligence, and information technology**

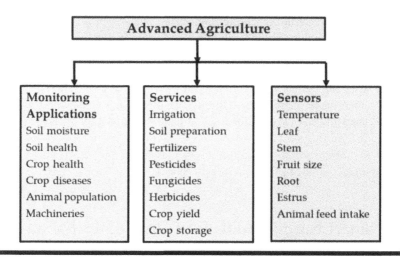

Figure 14.3   Major advanced agriculture applications, services, and sensors

Source: Adapted from Talavera et al. (2017)

fresh insights that will assist them in making better decisions and putting them into action. By enabling improved management and operations, as well as better decision-making, smart farming adds value to farmers' operations and yields. In smart farming, three different technological sectors are interlinked (Figure 14.3):

- ■ Agriculture based on crop intra- and inter-field variability that is monitored, quantified, and acted upon is known as precision agriculture. GNSS, GPS, and aerial imaging are widely used in precision agriculture to aid in total farm management, increasing farm output, and optimizing input returns. The increasing use of global navigation satellite systems (GNSS) and global positioning systems (GPS) has enabled precision agriculture.
- ■ Robotic farm equipment such as drones and farm robots are examples of how robotics, AI methods, and automated control are being used at all levels of agriculture.

A farm's activities and operations are managed via the use of management information systems, which are well-organized systems for collecting, processing, storing, and distributing data in the manner required to do so. Growing crops and monitoring their health are two of the most common IoT use cases in smart agriculture. Crop monitoring sensors collect information about the crop, including crop health, humidity, precipitation, temperature, and other parameters (Jin et al., 2020; Prestele et al., 2020). This enables us to efficiently monitor the crop's progress and any abnormalities to avoid illnesses or pests that might affect production.

The global smart farming industry is expected to reach $23.14 billion between 2017 and 2022, reflecting a 19.3% compound annual growth rate (CAGR) over the previous year, according to a BIS Research-published market intelligence report. However, according to the FAO, by 2050, the world's population will have risen to 9.6 billion people, necessitating a 70% increase in food production above present levels.

14.4 Climate-Smart Agriculture

According to the United Nations Environment Programme, climate-smart agriculture (CSA) is a strategy for directing agricultural system transformation and reorientation to successfully support development and food security in a changing environment (Clay et al., 2020). According to the National Sustainable Agriculture Coalition, the three primary goals are: increasing agricultural output and incomes in a sustainable way, adapting to climate change, and reducing or eliminating greenhouse gas emissions, wherever possible.

CSA is also an abbreviation for community-supported agriculture, which is a strategy for developing agricultural techniques that will ensure long-term food security in the face of global warming (De Pinto et al., 2020; Agrimonti et al., 2021). The agricultural cooperative of the United States offers stakeholders at all levels – from neighbourhood to national and international levels – tools to help them choose agricultural solutions that are appropriate for their specific circumstances.

According to the FAO's strategic objectives, CSA is one of their 11 corporate areas for resource mobilization, and it contributes to the organization's goal of boosting agricultural, forestry, and fisheries output and sustainability, based on the FAO's vision for Sustainable Food and Agriculture. Increasing temperature and carbon dioxide levels in the atmosphere pose a significant danger to the environment and all living things. In particular, numerous studies have found that climate change has severe consequences for crop plant health, influencing both the productivity and the quality of food-grade raw materials, with protein and essential nutrient reductions of particular concern.

The technical golden era of mankind has unquestionably begun. In the previous 150 years, we've made more development than we have in our whole existence on this planet. These are just a few examples of the many accomplishments that mankind has lately achieved, and it seems that we will not be slowing down anytime soon. There are many benefits to automating processes, including better yields and continuous production at a lower cost. Automation, especially in agriculture, is a great endeavour that, if successful, will offer us a plethora of positive outcomes.

When it comes to implementation, CSA and sustainable intensification continue to encounter major difficulties, and possible trade-offs are often neglected in the current evaluations of these ideas on a continental to global scale. Rising temperatures and shifting precipitation patterns will have a substantial impact on agriculture under changing climatic regimes. Ironically, agriculture makes a major contribution to the problem by generating yearly greenhouse gas emissions that represent roughly 11% of total anthropogenic greenhouse gas emissions.

14.5 Evolution of Cutting-Edge Technologies That Are Revolutionizing the Agriculture Industry in India

14.5.1 Drones for Agriculture

The employment of agricultural drones in the area of production is a fundamental yet valuable technological instrument, especially in terms of saving time and human resources. Drones help to minimize time waste by speeding up procedures. They are also very cost-effective, alleviating the farmer of a significant amount of financial burden. Drones for agriculture are very beneficial to farmers since they enable them to monitor crop development and take the necessary measures to improve production. There have been many advances in the field of agricultural drones, which have made them both easy to use and lucrative to operate. The production of a diverse variety of drones, each with its own unique set of capabilities, has been started by several companies (Figure 14.4).

Figure 14.4 **Drones can apply pesticides and fertilizers more accurately**
Source: BBC News

14.5.2 Artificial Intelligence and Information Technology

With the evolution of information technology and AI, the agriculture industry in India has stepped up its attempts to integrate the advantages of both. It puts both of these cutting-edge technologies into practice. Because of AI and information technology, this industry is now developing at a fast pace in areas like satellite monitoring, data analytics, and weather simulation. A significant sector that has been influenced by both technologies is precision agriculture, which is one of the most important applications. This department is responsible for the collection and analysis of data at the plant level. As a result, the Ministry of Agriculture and Farmers' Welfare is very important in this respect. Indian farmers are now able to estimate the real agricultural output and production potential of a particular region using satellite imaging and other large-scale data collection technologies, which were previously unavailable. The Indian government has ramped up its efforts, and the country's space agencies have created action plans to assist the country in realizing its full technological potential and aligning its agricultural policy with international best practices.

14.5.3 Agricultural Mechanization

To fully use India's enormous agricultural potential, increased output via timely and cost-efficient fieldwork is the most effective strategy. This is made feasible in large part due to the use of agricultural mechanization. In today's world, the majority of agricultural operations are highly automated. All farmers, particularly those on tiny and marginal farms, make use of cutting-edge technology-based equipment. As a result, the Indian government has implemented programmes, such as the Sub-Mission on Agricultural Mechanization (SMAM). Through the SMAM programme, the government ensures that every farmer in the country, particularly those in rural locations where farm electricity is restricted, can achieve agricultural mechanization. It also acts as a distribution centre for high-tech and high-value agricultural equipment and increases awareness among the target audience, which is comprised mostly of farmers, via demonstrations and technological exhibits.

14.5.4 Agriculture Financing (AgriFin) Technology

Agriculture has always been a step or two behind the times in terms of money. Debt traps and credit cycles are frequent phenomena in the financial world. The good news is that things are beginning to look better. Agriculture and finance technology synergy is gaining momentum in the agricultural sector, although at a sluggish pace. This start-up-dominated sector is beginning to affect the agricultural business, particularly in terms of shifting away from the loan system and digitizing financial records, among other things. In rural regions, a large number of companies are offering financial technology and cloud-based tools to farmers, as well as counselling and advising services.

14.5.5 Technology for Post-Harvesting

A key component of the agricultural economy is post-harvest, and low-cost technology is in great demand right now to meet this need. The post-harvest sector of the agricultural business is especially volatile as a result of its susceptibility to natural catastrophes and other external influences. It is at this point that post-harvest technology comes into play. Further, post-harvest loss reduction technology makes use of contemporary infrastructure, cutting-edge equipment, thermal processing, and low-cost preservation methods to minimize losses throughout the stages of packing, handling, shipping, and storage.

14.5.6 Animal Agriculture with Insight

Even though consumption of products from animals such as meat, milk, and eggs has decreased in industrialized countries, it is rapidly increasing in emerging ones. More agricultural production will be required to satisfy demand, enhanced door paving for automation and technological innovation, as well as intensive and sustainable farming practices and applications for precision livestock farming (PLF) (Halachmi et al., 2019). A growing number of cattle producers are relying on early medical issue indicators, which utilize sensors to alert them to particular animals in need of special attention. The market for wearable technology is booming right now. One sensor per herd/flock/school, like a camera or robot, is more frequent than one sensor per animal in systems where each animal has a lower monetary value, such as those involving sheep, goats, pigs, poultry, and fish. Data acquired by PLF sensors is useful to a wide range of actors. Current standards for exchanging sensor-generated data are lacking, which makes commercial sensors more difficult to implement. Haseeb et al. (2020) proposed an IoT-based wireless sensor network (WSN) framework that significantly enhanced the communication performance for smart agriculture. Technologies that provide reliable data may be beneficial to a well-managed farm. It is essential to develop techniques for converting data into actionable solutions to be successful.

14.5.7 Food and Agriculture Nanotechnology

As a result of the introduction of smart and active packaging, nanosensors, nanopesticides, nano fertilizers, and the fast development of nanotechnology, conventional food and agricultural companies have been able to change (He et al., 2019). Various new nanomaterials have been created to enhance food quality and safety, agricultural growth, and environmental monitoring, among other applications.

Using findings from recent research, this review highlights the most current developments in nanotechnology, as well as the toughest challenges and enticing possibilities in the food and agricultural industries, among other things. These new culinary and agricultural items include nanoparticles that are being studied for their toxicological principles as well as their potential for causing health problems in humans. Bio-inspired and bio-synthesized nanomaterials are very promising in the realm of sustainable development. In order to promote the development and application of active nanotechnology, basic challenges must nonetheless be overcome using high-performance, low-toxicity nanomaterials. Aside from laws and regulations, nanomaterial production, processing, use, and disposal all require the use of nanomaterials. Public awareness of getting new nanotechnology-enabled food and agricultural products is still lacking, making further efforts essential. As a new and sustainable alternative to conventional farming methods, we think nanotechnology has tremendous promise in the food and agricultural sectors.

14.5.8 Nanotechnology-Based Smart Pesticide Formulations

The use of nanotechnology in the development of nanopesticides is still in the early phases of investigation. The primary aim of this inclusion is to minimize the indiscriminate use of conventional pesticides, allowing them to be utilized in the environment without posing a threat to human health. Using nanoencapsulated pesticides, it is feasible to control the release kinetics of the insecticides while simultaneously improving their permeability, stability, and solubility. When used to prevent the early degradation of active ingredients in the presence of unfavourable environmental circumstances, nanoencapsulation has the potential to enhance pest-control effectiveness over extended periods. To reduce the dose of active ingredients while maintaining effectiveness and avoiding pesticide loss, intelligent pesticide delivery must be used to administer the pesticide (e.g., due to leaching and evaporation). Several researchers have looked at potential future trends in pesticide nanoformulations, such as the use of nanomaterials as antimicrobial agents and biopesticide nanoemulsions (Kumar et al., 2019). As a consequence, our assessment should be helpful in the development of regulatory frameworks for the field use of nano-based pesticides in the near future.

14.5.9 Microbe-Based Climate Smart Agriculture

Soil microorganisms play a vital role in nearly all ecosystem processes, including impacting agricultural regions' long-term production, ecosystem resilience against nutrient mining, deterioration of soil and water resources, and greenhouse gas emissions (Wagg et al., 2014). Changes in the environment have a direct influence on their capacity to operate. As a consequence, climate change is a crucial element to consider in this context since it can influence the function of bacteria in the soil, which is critical for agriculture all over the globe, particularly in developing nations. CSA is one strategy for mitigating these consequences. Under climate change scenarios, a comprehensive agricultural strategy is an integrative strategy for developing agricultural strategies that increase agricultural productivity while also adapting to and strengthening agricultural and food security systems, as well as lowering agricultural greenhouse gas emissions (Lipper et al., 2014; Paustian et al., 2016). In their findings, Das et al. (2019) tried to produce a selection of studies that highlighted new experimental concepts such as process-based omics approaches combined with advanced technological developments in agricultural science, to understand better how climate change affects eCO_2, soil microbes, and associated ecoparticles, such as an increased concentration in the atmosphere, temperature, and drought. Aside from that, researchers have looked at the function of microorganisms in agricultural management in terms of climate adaptation, greenhouse gas reduction, and soil carbon storage.

14.5.10 Agriculture Smart Water Management Platform

The use of precise irrigation in agriculture is essential for improving crop production while simultaneously lowering costs and contributing to environmental sustainability. Smart water management is essential for this to happen. Increasingly, thanks to technological advancements, the quantity of water needed by plants may be supplied with pinpoint accuracy. While the IoT is still in the very early phases of combining the various technologies required for its optimal functionality, its inherent flexibility makes it the logical solution for smart water management applications (Kamienski et al., 2019; Garcia et al., 2020). A practical method based on four pilot studies in Brazil and Europe creates a platform of intelligent water management for agricultural precision irrigation via the IoT. The architecture, platforms, and system deployments of SWAMP are described in detail in this paper, with special attention paid to the repeatability of the platform. As scalability is a key concern for IoT applications, this paper also offers a performance assessment of the FIWARE components used in the development of the platform. The results suggest that SWAMP pilots can deliver sufficient performance, but the creation of specialised configurations and reengineering of components will be necessary to allow higher scalability while using less than available computing resources at present.

14.5.11 Using High-Efficiency Sun Drying for Smart Agriculture

Because energy is one of the most demanded requirements, and because demand is increasing all the time, there is a multitude of energy research in the literature, and the number of studies continues to increase. There is a plethora of research being done on renewable energy technologies in particular, since becoming green is also a significant consideration (Sevencan et al., 2011; Zhang et al., 2016; Yilan et al., 2020). Because of this, solar energy has emerged as a major resource for achieving energy sustainability objectives. Research into a range of solar energy applications is now underway in areas such as cooking areas, heating/cooling rooms, low-temperature industrial fluid heating, drying crops, and other similar applications (Ulfat et al., 2012; Sadiq, 2018).

Uncontrolled population growth has the potential to have a major effect on the supply-demand cycle for food. The outcome of this is that any strategy to address these uncontrolled circumstances may be advantageous. Reducing food losses via experimentation with various production techniques, improving efficiency, and ensuring food security are all examples of effective solutions. It is essential to use solar drying for agricultural, marine, and animal products, among other things, to ensure food preservation and reduce food waste (Çiftçioğlu et al., 2020). Traditional sun drying, on the other hand, is a labour-intensive procedure that takes a long time. Apart from that, the product's quality may degrade under many conditions, such as microbial proliferation and growth, enzyme reactions, and insect infestations, among others. It is generally known that when it comes to using solar energy, a lot of factors must be taken into account. It is as a consequence that significant effort is being invested in improving solar energy technology for drying operations.

Çiftçioğlu et al. (2020) present a smart agricultural design for drying that makes use of a low-cost, high-efficiency solar selective absorber to achieve high drying efficiency. The device is built on a flat plate solar absorber, which warms the air that circulates through it. When comparing the prototype with fossil fuels such as natural gas, power, and liquefied petroleum gas (LPG), the prototype's levelized cost of heating (LCOH) is computed. A cost comparison for air collectors that use different selective absorbers, both unglazed and glazed, is also included in the document. The long-term cost-effectiveness of solar energy is superior to that of fossil fuels.

14.5.12 Cloud-Based Platform: Internet of Agriculture Things (IoAT)

The IoT provides a diversified platform for automating things, and intelligent farming – sometimes referred to as the Internet of Agriculture Things (IoAT) – is one of the most promising ideas emerging from the field of agriculture (Awan et al., 2020; Marcu et al., 2020). Because autonomic systems need greater processing capacity for calculations and forecasts, the idea of cloud-based smart agriculture is suggested for autonomic systems due to the necessity for higher processing capacity. In the field of urbanization growth, digital innovation and technology may aid in the improvement of the overall quality of life. Several security and privacy issues for cloud integration in smart agriculture have been shown, including the detection of hostile and hacked nodes, and the transfer of information between sensors, the cloud, and a base station. Understanding which soil sensors are hostile and which are compromised among those that communicate with the base station is a key issue in the base station to cloud connections (Yin et al., 2021). The trust management technique is one way of identifying these nodes in a straightforward and lightweight manner.

14.5.13 Smart Multi-Sensor Platform in Agriculture Support for Analysis and Social Decision

To feed the world's expanding population while reducing pollution, smart agriculture is crucial because it makes use of new kinds of sensors, data analytics, and automation to maximise yields and efficiency. A multi-sensor IoT agricultural system that comprises a soil probe, an air probe, and a smart data recorder is being developed. The integration element, as well as the innovative AI-based gas detection sensor, will be the focus points of the implementation (Balan et al., 2020). An agricultural advice system that is backed by a feedback loop from farmers, as well as the deployment of a social trust index, will enhance the system's reliability and efficiency.

14.5.14 Automation in the Agriculture Sector

Agriculture has made significant strides in terms of automation in recent years. The first fully automated farm, the Hands Free Hectare, was created by scientists and covered in an article titled "Robotic Farm Completes 1st Fully Autonomous Harvest", published by Tereza Pultarova, a renowned scientific journalist. According to the researchers, "At the moment, the machines used in agriculture are large, they operate quickly, they cover large areas of ground quickly, but with it comes inaccuracy… Small machines working with smaller working widths would provide a means to bring the resolution down." A more accurate translation would be to say that the autonomous farm represents a step toward more efficient agriculture by conserving resources.

Not to mention the fact that agricultural autonomy is rising, which shows vulnerability in the existing system, as previously mentioned. Researchers are attempting to find long-term, low-tech solutions to the problem of agricultural mechanization and automation by employing highly sophisticated robots that can perform tasks that a person may perform worse in terms of precision, consistency, and working cycle. Modern high-tech greenhouses, for example, are equipped with automated machinery and control systems that are derivatives of numerically controlled equipment. To put it another way, as the human population grows and agricultural labour shrinks, robots can help with the provision of regular and reliable food supplies. New technology, such as UAVs outfitted with powerful, lightweight cameras, is making it feasible to offer more accurate farm management advice to farmers. Consumers and farmers alike will profit from this advancement since autonomous harvesting reduces losses in the form of smart farming.

14.6 How Can One Use Technology to Create Their Ideal Farmhouse?

In contrast to normal farming, vertical farming is the technique of cultivating crops vertically rather than horizontally. Vertical agriculture is the process of growing food and medication on vertically inclined surfaces, in vertically stacked layers, or incorporated into other buildings, such as a repurposed warehouse, skyscraper, or shipping container, as opposed to horizontally inclined surfaces. Vertical farming technology allows modern farmers to grow specific high-quality, healthy, pesticide-free crops all year long with the same inputs and under strict monitoring since it allows them to use the same inputs all year.

In hydroponics farming, plants are grown in nutrient solutions suspended in water rather than in soil, eliminating the need for soil. Terrestrial plants may be grown hydroponically by submerging their roots in a solution of mineral fertilizer or by supporting the roots with an inert material such as gravel or perlite, which provides root support. The nutrients used in this kind of farming may come from several sources, including industrial fertilizer waste, duck dung, and fish waste. Industrial fertilizer wastes are one source of nutrients.

14.6.1 Obtaining Weather Information

To access satellite data and the Google Earth platform, farmers can make use of the WaPOR open-access database, which can assist them in optimizing their irrigation systems and increasing agricultural output. In agriculture, sensors are used to monitor humidity levels, light levels, temperature levels, and soil moisture levels, as well as to automate agricultural techniques.

- Using the IoT, farmers can keep tabs on the humidity, light, temperature, and soil moisture levels in this region. Agriculture is becoming more automated, with farmers being able to monitor their crops from anywhere and using methods such as automatic watering and temperature management to ensure that the plants are adequately cared for.
- Mechanization is used for tilling, planting, weeding, and harvesting. This method has been utilized by farmers all over the globe for many years. However, heavy agricultural equipment is being phased out in favour of lighter, more sophisticated technology that is much more efficient and effective, as well as simpler to operate and far more fuel-efficient.

14.6.2 The National Agriculture Market (eNAM)

The National Agricultural Market (eNAM) is an electronic trading system in India that links existing APMC mandis to create a unified national market for agricultural goods. It was introduced in December 2010 and started in 2010–2011 in seven pilot states to achieve fast growth in India via the use of information and communication technologies. The National e-Governance Plan in Agriculture (NeGPA) is a government-sponsored programme initially launched in 2010–2011 to provide farmers with quick access to farming information for fast growth in India. After being extended to cover the other states as well as two union territories in 2014–2015, the plan was finalized in 2015–2016. The programme has been extended to March 31, 2021, from its original expiration date of March 31, 2019.

According to the project's phase 2 funding, states were given funds to carry out operations such as site preparation for hardware installation and the establishment of computer training labs. They also received funds to purchase, install, and account for computer hardware and system software. Arrangements for backup power, the creation of State Project Management Units (SPMUs) and the recruitment of contract personnel, connection to hardware installation locations, and the digitization of data were all important considerations. A committee set up to advise the government of India on how to develop and enhance its digital agricultural programmes has suggested that the government's digital agriculture programmes be extended and improved further, recognizing the importance of new digital and emerging technologies. Remote sensing, geographical information systems, data analytics, cloud computing, AI and machine learning, the IoT, robotics, drones, sensors, and the blockchain are some of the topics covered by the research team.

In 2020–2021, the NeGPA criteria were determined to have changed, and money was made available to approve projects aimed at modifying and migrating online and mobile applications previously developed by the States to a platform for the construction of digital and emerging technologies. Other countries have shown an interest in adopting this new legislation, and many countries have authorised pilot projects during the development phase of the process to test new technology. As a result of initiatives such as the farmers' database and the Unified Farmer Service Platform (UFSP), access to farmer data will be transformed, allowing for the creation of tailored solutions, improved planning, and more effective monitoring of their application.

14.6.3 Unified Farmer Service Platform

The UFSP collects essential infrastructure, data, applications, and tools to ensure the uncompromising interoperability of public and commercial IT systems across the farming ecosystem of the nation. The UFSP is expected to perform the following tasks:

- Assume the key function of the agri-ecosystem agent (like UPI for online payments)
- Enable service providers (both public and private) to register.
- Allow for the registration of G2F, G2B, B2F, and B2B Farmer Services.

■ Enforce different rules and validations during the service delivery process.
■ Act as a central repository for all relevant standards, APIs, and formats.
■ Serve as a conduit for data sharing across various schemes and services, allowing for comprehensive service delivery to farmers.

14.6.4 Farmers' Database

A national farmers' database connected to land records is being created with the aim of improving planning, monitoring, policymaking, strategy formulation, and easy implementation of farmer initiatives. The goal of the database is

■ To create a national database of farmers.
■ To keep a list of one-of-a-kind farmers.
■ Utilize a unique farmer ID (FID) to identify a specific farmer.
■ To learn about the numerous plans that a farmer might take advantage of.

Moreover, a centralised farmer database will be useful for a wide range of purposes, such as the distribution of crop advice and precision agricultural production, as well as smart cards for farmers to facilitate e-governance and crop insurance, compensation claims for settlements, and the allocation of agricultural grants. The database will be made public once the data of 43 million farmers who are connected to land records has been verified and validated.

14.6.5 Benefits of the IoT in the Agricultural Sector

Smart farming enables farmers to maximize output while utilizing the least amount of resources, such as seeds, fertilizers, pesticides, and water. Smart farming is becoming more popular among farmers. Many different kinds of sensors are installed in various places, depending on the need. Farmers may use these sensors to monitor factors in their agricultural production, such as fruit or bark diameter, leaf wetness, atmospheric pressure, rainfall, wind direction and speed, solar radiation, humidity, soil and air temperature, and more. Some of the most important advantages of the IoT in agriculture today are:

■ **Data-driven decisions based on acquired data**: Farmers can obtain crop-related data via sensors. They can make better data-driven decisions based on those actionable insights, which will help them increase crop profitability.
■ **Reduce hazards**: As crop growers have access to critical information, they may forecast potential risks and obstacles at some levels. This boosts sales while lowering risk.
■ **Business automation**: By automating routine processes, crop cultivators can devote their time and attention to more important duties, resulting in increased efficiency and revenues.

■ **Increased product volume and quality**: Analyzed decisions based on real-time alerts have been shown to assist in maintaining optimal water levels, pesticide-free crops, and an overall healthy harvest.

14.7 Smart Farming's Obstacles

Smart agriculture is certainly thriving across the globe, and there is still a great deal of potential for expansion, with rapid advances happening daily. There are, however, a few problems that must be taken into account. Here are a handful of the most significant roadblocks to smart farming:

1. Concerns about security and data theft are a danger to virtually all sorts of connected systems, and smart agriculture is no different.
2. As a result of the lack of uniformity in the final analysis performed by end-users, available technologies frequently do not follow the same technical standards/platforms. In many cases, an additional gateway (or gateways) is required for data translation and transfer across standards.
3. Making sense of massive amounts of data is no easy task. It is nearly impossible to keep track of and manage every single data point and reading during the growing season on a daily/weekly basis. Although big data is increasingly being used in digital agriculture, the technology is only useful if users can really "make sense" of the data accessible to them.
4. For a great majority of present and potential precision farmers, indoor farming remains a challenge. With the global vertical farming business expected to exceed $4 billion in revenue by 2021, technical support for indoor farming is becoming more important. To establish the best growing environment for indoor plants, farmers must be able to rely on technology.

There are solutions to these issues. IoT83's Method83 is one such solution that effectively addresses and overcomes the problems and obstacles to IoT implementation and value generation on a wide scale. In the IoT, the Method83 cloud service combines machine learning, deep data analytics, and autonomous actions to assist organizations in increasing their return on investment (ROI) and decreasing their time to market. Method83 is an affordable, fast, secure, and scalable Industrial Internet of Things (IIoT) solution. Its integrated application builder tools speed up the development of sophisticated and secure applications and simplify at-scale IoT deployments as well as ongoing IoT operations, iterative development, and upgrades.

Just a few of Method83's key features include built-in scalability and reliability, simplified IoT device connectivity, a comprehensive suite of application creation tools and workflows, IoT analytics and automation, end-to-end data security, and multiple integrated services to enhance new IoT applications and services. It is a game-changing strategy for the deployment of IIoT and digital transformation. Method83 combines secure and scaleable "one-click deployment" with a suite of application development tools as well as agile and efficient software services to turn big data deployments into a cost-effective and controllable route to rapid ROI. In addition to identifying high-value IIoT use cases, the IoT83 organization is also specialized in delivering device connectivity, data transport, cloud computing, big data analytics, and connectivity to existing business systems required to fully realize the promise of IIoT and digital transformation value creation.

A constant and efficient power supply must be provided to all areas of the agricultural community as a whole, as well as to individual farmers, for digital technology to be used effectively. An electrical connection is equally as essential as digital connectivity when it comes to computer networking. Digital agriculture is the integration of new and advanced technologies into a single system that helps farmers and other stakeholders in the agricultural value chain improve food production. When it comes to making choices such as how much fertilizer to apply, the vast majority of today's farmers rely on a mix of imprecise measurements, experience, and suggestions. Following agreement on a course of action, the plan is put into effect, but the effects are not typically visible until harvest time. Unlike traditional agricultural systems that gather data less often and inaccurately, a digital agriculture system collects data more frequently and correctly and is usually connected to data from other sources (such as weather information). The information gathered is then analyzed and reviewed, allowing the farmer to make better-informed choices. Robotics and modern technology may then be used to quickly and precisely implement these choices, and farmers can get real-time feedback on the effect of their actions.

14.8 Some Examples of Smart Farming Applications

14.8.1 Aquaculture

Contamination from pollutants (which are carried into the water by rain) and sickness have distinct effects on yield. The cultivation of oysters is a fantastic illustration of this. The Yield Technology Solutions, in collaboration with Bosch, has deployed sensors, predictive analytics, and a simple user interface to help Tasmanian oyster farmers in coping with such difficulties. Thus, if growers can make more precise predictions about whether water pollutants are too high or if a disease pandemic is on the horizon, they can take preventive measures that will minimize oyster damage.

14.8.2 Potatoes and Water Conservation

Over the past 10 years, PepsiCo has successfully reduced the amount of water used to grow its potato crop by 26%. Various methods, including the identification of wastewater sources for irrigation, have been used to achieve this goal. Soil moisture is also monitored and compared against weather predictions to adjust irrigation levels as required. This can help drought-prone nations improve their sustainability and access to water by lowering their water costs.

14.8.3 Lettuces That Can Benefit People with Renal Illness

People with renal illness should avoid consuming excessive potassium in their diet, such as that found in high-potassium meals. This is becoming more of a problem in nations such as Japan, where chronic renal disease affects 10% of the population and is growing more prevalent. Fujitsu collaborated with Microsoft and others to produce lettuce that had less than 80% of the potassium content of conventionally cultivated lettuce by carefully regulating the growth parameters throughout the growing process. It was discovered that this research improved people's nutrition while also demonstrating how sensors, analytics, and data visualization may be used to develop a system that improves agricultural operations in general.

Smart agriculture methods must be addressed for the successful development of the smart village framework in other areas of development (Adesipo et al., 2020; Marcu et al., 2020). Despite the huge potential of digitization and agriculture, several issues must be addressed before they can be widely adopted and implemented successfully, namely:

- India's digital gap has been a cause for worry for a long time. According to the monthly report of the Telecom Regulatory Authority of India published in June 2020, India has over 1.16 billion cellular subscribers as of February 2020. Currently, more than 400 million individuals worldwide have no Internet connection. In India, just a tiny proportion of the population has an Internet connection.
- Unless technology is used with care, natural soil biology may be destroyed. The result of excellent technology, particularly in large agricultural areas, should never be soil erosion. This is more probable if a farmer isn't knowledgeable about technology or soil science, as is the case in India.
- Small farmers are more likely to lag behind because they lack the finances needed to invest in digital technology as well as access to new and forthcoming technologies.
- The use of digital technology necessitates a reliable and efficient power supply that reaches every corner of the farming community and farmers in particular. Electrical and digital connectivity is equally important.

14.9 Future Scopes and Challenges

14.9.1 Scopes

The future of smart farming is largely dependent on the widespread use of machine learning and image analysis tools. Chatbots, UAVs, robots, automated irrigation systems, and agricultural health monitoring will all use machine learning techniques. Smart farming will be influenced in the future by IoT and big data, differential GPS, and non-contact sensors. Smart farming, as opposed to conventional agriculture, will maximise the use of resources and inputs based on data analysis. Farmers and the environment will both benefit from the use of optimal resources.

- **Increase production**: Accurate use of agricultural inputs leads to increased crop production and quality.
- **Technical perspective**: Remote sensing can manage a larger number of resources.
- **Environmental perspective**: Smart farming minimizes waste.

14.9.2 Challenges

Smart farming is progressing slowly compared to the expected pace. A better decision-making mechanism is needed to make appropriate decisions at the right time. The growth of smart farming in India is hampered by insufficient attention to temporal change, poor focus on the whole farm, correct methods for assessing crop quality, insufficient product monitoring, and environmental auditing. The major possible challenges of smart agriculture in India are:

- Different interoperability standards for new tools and IoT platforms.
- The establishment of IoT and sensor networks is a challenge for small farms.
- Many places lack strong, reliable Internet connectivity.
- Variations in agricultural production functions with crops, various regions of agriculture, and the cycle of crop/plant growth.
- Small new businesses have entry barriers, as smart farming is dominated by large agro-IoT businesses because of the high cost of infrastructure and technology improvements.
- The use of too many gadgets may increase energy consumption.
- Indoor farming techniques are not encouraged by smart farming.
- E-waste from abandoned IoT devices and computers and outdated electrical equipment may become an enormous problem in the future.
- Many agricultural labourers may lose their jobs in the future.

14.10 Conclusion

Agriculture may become more productive, consistent, and efficient in terms of time and resources as a result of the use of digital agriculture technologies. Farmers will reap huge advantages as a result of this, as well as wider global societal benefits. Organizations may also exchange information beyond conventional industry boundaries, allowing for the development of new and disruptive opportunities. But the idea of digital agriculture is still in its early stages, with large upfront expenditures and little emphasis placed on long-term advantages. Despite this, it has the potential to revolutionize the way we produce food across the globe. Collaboration and agreement on how to overcome these barriers will be needed throughout the whole value chain to ensure broad acceptance of a solution.

References

Adesipo, A., Fadeyi, O., Kuca, K., Krejcar, O., Maresova, P., Selamat, A., & Adenola, M. (2020). Smart and climate-smart agricultural trends as core aspects of smart village functions. *Sensors (Basel, Switzerland)*, *20* (21), 5977. https://doi.org/10.3390/s20215977

Agrimonti, C., Lauro, M., & Visioli, G. (2021). Smart agriculture for food quality: facing climate change in the 21st century. *Critical reviews in food science and nutrition*, *61*(6), 971–981. https://doi.org/10.1080/10408398.2020.1749555

Awan, K. A., Ud Din, I., Almogren, A., & Almajed, H. (2020). AgriTrust-A trust management approach for smart agriculture in cloud-based Internet of Agriculture Things. *Sensors (Basel, Switzerland)*, *20* (21), 6174. https://doi.org/10.3390/s20216174

Balan, T., Dumitru, C., Dudnik, G., Alessi, E., Lesecq, S., Correvon, M., Passaniti, F., & Licciardello, A. (2020). Smart multi-sensor platform for analytics and social decision support in agriculture. *Sensors (Basel, Switzerland)*, *20* (15), 4127. https://doi.org/10.3390/s20154127

Çiftçioğlu, G. A., Kadırgan, F., Kadırgan, M., & Kaynak, G. (2020). Smart agriculture through using cost-effective and high-efficiency solar drying. *Heliyon*, *6* (2), e03357. https://doi.org/10.1016/j.heliyon.2020.e03357

Clay, N., & Zimmerer, K. S. (2020). Who is resilient in Africa's green revolution? sustainable intensification and climate smart agriculture in Rwanda. *Land use policy*, *97*, 104558. https://doi.org/10.1016/j.landusepol.2020.104558

Das, S., Ho, A., & Kim, P. J. (2019). Editorial: Role of microbes in climate smart agriculture. *Frontiers in Microbiology*, *10*, 2756. https://doi.org/10.3389/fmicb.2019.02756

De Pinto, A., Cenacchi, N., Kwon, H. Y., Koo, J., & Dunston, S. (2020). Climate smart agriculture and global food-crop production. *PloS one*, *15* (4), e0231764. https://doi.org/10.1371/journal.pone.0231764

Escriba, C., Aviña Bravo, E. G., Roux, J., Fourniols, J. Y., Contardo, M., Acco, P., & Soto-Romero, G. (2020). Toward smart soil sensing in v4.0 Agriculture: A new single-shape sensor for capacitive moisture and salinity measurements. *Sensors (Basel, Switzerland)*, *20* (23), 6867. https://doi.org/10.3390/s20236867

García, L., Parra, L., Jimenez, J. M., Lloret, J., & Lorenz, P. (2020). IoT-based smart irrigation systems: An overview on the recent trends on sensors and IoT systems for irrigation in precision agriculture. *Sensors (Basel, Switzerland)*, *20* (4), 1042. https://doi.org/10.3390/s20041042

Halachmi, I., Guarino, M., Bewley, J., & Pastell, M. (2019). Smart animal agriculture: Application of real-time sensors to improve animal well-being and production. *Annual review of animal biosciences*, *7*, 403–425. https://doi.org/10.1146/annurev-animal-020518-114851

Haseeb, K., Ud Din, I., Almogren, A., & Islam, N. (2020). An energy efficient and secure IoT-based WSN framework: An application to smart agriculture. *Sensors (Basel, Switzerland)*, *20* (7), 2081. https://doi.org/10.3390/s20072081

He, X., Deng, H., & Hwang, H. M. (2019). The current application of nanotechnology in food and agriculture. *Journal of food and drug analysis*, *27* (1), 1–21. https://doi.org/10.1016/j.jfda.2018.12.002

Jin, X. B., Yang, N. X., Wang, X. Y., Bai, Y. T., Su, T. L., & Kong, J. L. (2020). Hybrid deep learning predictor for smart agriculture sensing based on empirical mode decomposition and gated recurrent unit group model. *Sensors (Basel, Switzerland)*, *20* (5), 1334. https://doi.org/10.3390/s20051334

Kamienski, C., Soininen, J. P., Taumberger, M., Dantas, R., Toscano, A., Salmon Cinotti, T., Filev Maia, R., & Torre Neto, A. (2019). Smart water management platform: IoT-based precision irrigation for agriculture. *Sensors (Basel, Switzerland)*, *19* (2), 276. https://doi.org/10.3390/s19020276

Kumar, S., Nehra, M., Dilbaghi, N., Marrazza, G., Hassan, A. A., & Kim, K. H. (2019). Nano-based smart pesticide formulations: Emerging opportunities for agriculture. *Journal of controlled release: official journal of the Controlled Release Society*, *294*, 131–153. https://doi.org/10.1016/j.jconrel.2018.12.012

Lipper, L., Thornton, P., Campbell, B. M., Baedeker, T., Braimoh, A., Bwalya, M., Caron, P., Cattaneo, A. , Garrity, D. , Henry, K. , Hottle, R. , Jackson, L. , Jarvis, A. , Kossam, F. , Mann, W. , McCarthy, N. , Meybeck, A. , Neufeldt, H. , Remington, T. , Sen, P. T., … Torquebiau, E. F. (2014). Climate-smart agriculture for food security. *Nat. Clim. Chang.* 4:1068 10.1038/nclimate2437

Marcu, I., Suciu, G., Bălăceanu, C., Vulpe, A., & Drăgulinescu, A. M. (2020). Arrowhead technology for digitalization and automation solution: Smart cities and smart agriculture. *Sensors (Basel, Switzerland)*, *20* (5), 1464. https://doi.org/10.3390/s20051464

Paustian, K., Lehmann, J., Ogle, S., Reay, D., Robertson, G. P., & Smith, P. (2016). Climate-smart soils. *Nature*, *532* (7597), 49–57. https://doi.org/10.1038/nature17174

Prestele, R., & Verburg, P. H. (2020). The overlooked spatial dimension of climate-smart agriculture. *Global change biology*, *26* (3), 1045–1054. https://doi.org/10.1111/gcb.14940

Sadiq M. (2018) Solar water heating system for residential consumers of Islamabad, Pakistan: A cost-benefit analysis. *J. Clean. Prod.*, 172, 2443–2453.

Sevencan, S, Altun-ciftcioglu, G, Kadirgan, N. (2011). A preliminary environmental assessment of power generation systems for a stand-alone mobile house with cradle to gate approach. *Gazi University Journal of Science*, 24 (3), 487–494.

Talavera, J. M., Tobón, L. E., Gómez, J. A., Culman, M. A., Aranda, J. M., Parra, D. T., Quiroz, L. A., Hoyos, A., Garreta, L. E. (2017) Review of IoT applications in agro-industrial and environmental fields. *Comput. Electr. Agric.* 142, 283–297.

Ulfat I., Javed F., Abbasi F., Kanwalb A.F., Usmane A., Jahangir M., & Ahmed F. (2012) Estimation of solar energy potential for Islamabad, Pakistan. *Energy Proc.* 18:1496–1500.

Wagg C., Bender S. F., Widmer F., & van der Heijden M. G. (2014). Soil biodiversity and soil community composition determine ecosystem multifunctionality. *Proc. Natl. Acad. Sci. U.S.A.* 111, 5266–5270. 10.1073/pnas.132005411

Yilan G., Kadirgan M.A.N., & Çiftçioğlu G.A. (2020) Analysis of electricity generation options for sustainable energy decision making: The case of Turkey. Renew. Energy. 146:519–529.

Yin, H., Cao, Y., Marelli, B., Zeng, X., Mason, A. J., & Cao, C. (2021). Soil sensors and plant wearables for smart and precision agriculture. *Advanced materials (Deerfield Beach, Fla.)*, *33* (20), e2007764. https://doi.org/10.1002/adma.202007764

Zhang H., Gowing T., Degrève J., Leadbeater T., & Baeyens J. (2016) Use of particle heat carriers in the stirling engine concept. *Energy Technol.* 4(3):401–408.

Index